MODERN SCOTLAND

MODERN SCOTLAND

1914–2000

RICHARD J. FINLAY

PROFILE BOOKS

For Eleanor Finlay and Eddie Crossley

First published in Great Britain in 2004 by
Profile Books Ltd
58A Hatton Garden
London EC1N 8LX
www.profilebooks.co.uk

1 3 5 7 9 10 8 6 4 2

Typeset in Garamond 3 by MacGuru Ltd
info@macguru.org.uk

Printed and bound in Great Britain by
Clays, Bungay, Suffolk

A CIP catalogue record for this book is available from the British Library.

ISBN 1 86197 299 7

CONTENTS

INTRODUCTION AND ACKNOWLEDGEMENTS

W hen I first embarked on this project, my original intention was to produce a synoptic history of Scotland since 1914. It was not long before I realised that there are many gaps in the story which could not be filled by the existing literature. This resulted in a volte-face, and I have gone back to the original sources as far as possible to produce a work which I hope will be fresher than a book which is simply a review of the work of other historians. At the outset, I acknowledge the importance of my colleagues, whose work has informed this book but not necessarily directed or conditioned the debates contained within it. Furthermore, I owe my fellow professional historians a word of apology because I have not used footnotes. As far as possible I have tried to identify sources within the text.

The book is structured chronologically, with each chapter devoted to a particular period, for the simple reason that this is how most of us conceptualise the passing of time. Within each chapter, themes are explored which sometimes stretch backwards and forwards beyond the period stipulated in the chapter heading. My purpose in doing this is to provide a sense of the passage of time in a chronological sense, but also to highlight the ways in which certain events, even though they have their origins back in time, become located within certain periods.

This is a general history, and there will no doubt be complaints that certain things have been missed out. My objective was to try to produce as rounded a picture as possible and to address some of the biases towards certain themes which tend to characterise much of the existing literature. I have also included a lot of statistical material, on the grounds that this is the basic building block of history and that many of these facts and figures are not readily found elsewhere. I have tried to eschew any political perspectives, and my hope is that this book will annoy and enrage Unionists, nationalists, left and right in equal measure. Equally, I hope they will all find things to cheer them up.

Three people in particular have borne the brunt of my meandering on this subject: Isobel Lindsay, Ted Cowan and Evan Stewart. To each of them much thanks, and the usual disclaimer that they are not responsible for any faults contained within these pages. My colleagues at Strathclyde have provided much support over the last three years during the writing of this book. In particular I would like to single out Bill Wurthmann, John Young, Conan Fischer, Simon Adams, David Brown, Andrew Noble, Murray Pittock, Ken Simpson, James Mitchell and Lizanne Henderson. Thanks also to Alastair and May Stewart, Kate Finlay, Stevie Clement and Andrea, Meaghan and Liam Carroll. My wife, Jack, has put up with my rummaging in the past with great cheerfulness. Peter Carson from Profile Books has demonstrated a saintly patience with an improvident author, and I owe him a great debt of gratitude. Finally, the book is dedicated to Eleanor Finlay and Eddie Crossley

R.J.F.

BLIZZARD,
1914–1918

All honour to the lads who have put Scotland in the front at this time, to the lads of the Isles, whose womenfolk are doing their duties, to the old soldiers who have flocked again to the colours, to the sons of our great houses whose blood has so freely been given; honour to the humblest who has sacrificed with equal valour, but she still must lead in sacrifice over our brother Britons, good sportsmen and valiant fighters as they are. We must not let the sons of the Rose, the Leek or the Shamrock get in front of the Thistle.

Dundee Advertiser, 25 October 1914

These men are the Clyde shop stewards. I can assure you that every word you say will be carefully weighed. We regard you with suspicion because the Munitions Act with which your name is associated has the taint of slavery about it, and you will find that we, as Scotsmen, resent that. If you desire to get the best out of us, you must treat us with justice and respect.

David Kirkwood, Clydeside shop steward, speaking to David Lloyd George, Minister for Munitions, Christmas Day 1915

To labour in drudgery, to remain submerged, to be dumb under hard conditions of industry and living – these are not traditions with the working class Scot. He is of a free race, he thinks deeply, he feels passionately, and he acts vigorously, even though these actions are forced into illogically by the passion that prompts them ... The Scottish labouring-class is a force that must and will assert itself in self-defence, for that is the inevitable.

G. R. Blake, Scotland of the Scots (London, 1919)

BRAVE BOYS OF THE THISTLE

When news of the war broke in Scotland, it was greeted with enthusiasm, even with a sense of relief. Few had any doubts or confusion, hardly anyone had moral qualms or second thoughts about the justification for entering the conflict, and almost all were energised by the prospect of a 'real' war, as opposed to those minor colonial ones which happened from time to time. Although many people had difficulty in locating where on the globe Britain's imperial territories were, much to the chagrin of the imperial lobbyists, everyone knew where Germany was and what danger it posed. This was a war not in some faraway place, but across the English Channel, and the enemy was just over the North Sea. In the first months of conflict the nation was gripped with fears of invasion.

With the benefit of hindsight, it is easy to see Scottish society in the summer of 1914 as one of mass innocence, as few had any conception of war as it was then, let alone what it would become in the killing fields of northern France. Ideas of war had been shaped by romantic images of imperial adventure. The young lads who volunteered in 1914 were born in the 1890s. While the Boer War of 1899–1902 may have temporarily set back notions of British military might, it did not leave a lasting impression on the public's mind, because at the end of the day our boys won. For the young men who would enlist now, the Boer War had taken place before they could remember. As children, they grew up with ideas of war. Youth organisations like the Boys' Brigade (founded in Glasgow in 1883) were organised in a quasi-military style and gave their young membership a taste of the qualities that were associated with good soldiering. The games ethic and drilling were practised in the middle-class schools, where being tough and fearless and 'knowing one's duty' were essential components of a chap's education. Working-class boys picked up the same values by avidly reading adventure stories which recounted the marvellous feats which had won the great British Empire. Cheap editions of illustrated books held young attentions with action-packed stories, jammed full of thrills and suspense. Boys collected cigarette cards with pictures of ships, generals and regiments. They played games in which they pretended to be soldiers, usually 'Scots against English'. In the towns and cities in which they grew up, the parks were full of monuments erected to military heroes. Their mums and dads took them to museums where they could gaze in wonder at the marvellous collections brought back from the Empire, and they were told that one day it would be their duty to protect it.

In the small villages and towns, volunteers (part-time soldiers) paraded and exercised at weekends in full public view, with family and friends cheering them on. Their pictures appeared regularly in the local press, and – an indication of more innocent times – a great many Scots had the unfortunate initials VD (Volunteer Decorated) after their names. Service in the Volunteers chimed with a Scottish sense of civic duty and responsibility, and was a characteristic of the liberal political tradition in which 'civilian soldiers' were part and parcel of a strong civic society and the perfect antidote to conscription, which was regarded as an unenlightened feature of despotic European nations. Almost three out of every ten men between the ages of eighteen and forty-nine belonged to the Volunteers in pre-war Scotland. Unlike in England, where the navy was the public's favourite service, soldiering was considered a noble profession north of the border, and local regiments boasted a fine martial and heroic tradition.

Like most of European society, the young men of Scotland were a generation inculcated with notions of duty which were fuelled by stories of patriotism and heroism. When war broke out in August 1914, few doubted that the flower of Scotland would step forward to do its bit, but even fewer expected the tidal wave of eager young recruits who surged forward to enlist.

For many the war was a panacea for the divisions and doubts that seemed to gnaw away at the fabric of Edwardian society. Scotland was a very parochial society on the eve of conflict with most people's loyalty bound to the locality. Newspapers, organisations such as trade unions and business clubs, societies, work and family were all bound together in a confined space which formed the intellectual horizon for most people. War and the sense of national identity that accompanied it not only helped reinforce a sense of British identity, they also helped focus a sense of Scottish identity at the expense of local identity. The euphoria of war acted as a cement to bond rich and poor, Highlander and Lowlander, employers and employees, Catholics and Protestants, men and women. This new-found sense of unity and purpose was evident in the relationship between the Liberal and the Unionist (Conservative) parties, which both turned over their offices and volunteers to the recruiting agencies. Within days, the ramshackle organisation that sustained the Scottish political system – in which all women and 40 per cent of men had no vote – soon collapsed under the pressure of a relentless sea of volunteers. Uniforms, weapons, equipment, and even administrative forms quickly ran out.

The outbreak of war was exciting. Eager young men joined up before they missed all the fun. For those brought up on a diet of militarism, the war represented a splendid opportunity to demonstrate all those qualities of heroism which were the stuff of dreams. Many fantasised that their military prowess would be enormously attractive to young women, who would swoon and flutter at stories of daring adventures on the front. Many were bored. For the Scottish lower middle class (who were especially fond of militarism) life was drudgery, especially for the young. Clerks, salesmen, shop assistants, office workers and other white-collar workers starting out on their career may have had middle-class attitudes, but did not have middle-class spending power. This entailed a life of long hours, penny-pinching and subservience to a Buggins's turn system of promotion, with the constant humiliation of not having the money to maintain your social pretensions. Marriage and having fun were put off until a solid foundation had been built, which would take many men into their forties. Not surprisingly, many jumped at the chance to break the chains of lower-middle-class serfdom, and about 40 per cent of all professional men in Britain enlisted within the first two years of war. Initially it had been thought that it would all be over by Christmas, and in the grand scheme of things what were a couple of months of freedom?

For those lower down the social scale, patriotism and doing one's bit may have had less intrinsic appeal, but there were other, pragmatic, reasons for joining up. There was a strong association in the public's mind between war and industrial depression, which for the working class meant unemployment or lower wages. Joining up held out the prospect of security, regular wages, and a chance to get out before the economic axe fell. In Dundee, the well-heeled were shoved to the back of the recruiting line, on the basis that it was only fair to let those who did not have a job enlist first. Miners and manual workers queued up to take the King's shilling, and the industrial west of Scotland had one of the highest levels of recruitment in the United Kingdom. It had also a large reservoir of semi- and unskilled labour, who were the most vulnerable to industrial depression, which may have included six or seven out of every ten Scottish men. The mining industry lost just over a quarter of its workers as a result of enlistment, leading to falling productivity as older miners dug on with less experienced and less able replacements.

Pictures from the time show a carnival atmosphere in which happy, cheering and waving crowds urged young men to go and do their bit. This is what happened to one young man, Carson Stewart:

> I enlisted in the Queen's Own Cameron Highlanders on 9 September, 1914 at the Institute in Cambuslang. I really did not go there to the Institute with the intention of joining up, because whenever a lad went in to join up, the crowd outside would give a hearty cheer. So after standing around for a while I must have got carried away. So in went another recruit – me! I was duly sworn in as a soldier of the King in the Queen's Own Cameron Highlanders.
> Quoted in Lyn Macdonald, *1914–1918: Voices and Images of the Great War*
> (London, 1988)

There is little evidence that any thought that enlistment would be a dangerous undertaking, or that there would be a one in five chance that they would not come back alive. Workmates cajoled and encouraged each other on the factory floor – war would be fun and a laugh. Friends, brothers and cousins pledged in family homes that they would march together to the front. Street corners and village crossroads became unofficial recruiting offices as gatherings of young men attempted to talk themselves into military units. 'Pals' battalions were formed, which would keep those who joined up together in the same unit. The Glasgow Corporation Tramway workers formed one such group and served under the title of the 15th Highland Light Infantry. As with all young men throughout the ages, bravado, high spirits and peer pressure sedated any doubts, boosted morale and confidence, and helped carry off any waverers. In that heady atmosphere of patriotism, it took a brave man to say he was scared.

Those who refused to join up, no matter what their reason, found themselves caught up in a torrent of spleen-filled invective. In a society that believed people should do their duty through the instillation of values such as respectability and responsibility, rather than conscription, it was the task of all upright citizens to heap moral opprobrium on the heads of shirkers. This was done with considerable relish and enthusiasm. In public places – and the more crowded the better – young women handed out white feathers as symbols of cowardice to young men not in uniform, as deliberate acts of public shaming. Employers joined in this public-spirited persecution of 'cowards' by threatening them with the sack, while at the same time stating that any shortfall in wages as a result of enlisting would be made up by their own patriotic beneficence. In the music hall, Scotland's greatest entertainer, Harry Lauder, harangued the young men in his audience to do their duty, and those who left during the show because they had had a bellyful of patriotism were labelled as cowards. Negative peer pressure was a key factor in persuading young men to join up. Not only did refusal bring a social stigma to the objector, but his friends and family were tarred with the same brush. Not surprisingly, given the reserves of conviction needed to withstand the enormous social pressures, political activists and religious pacifists were the only groups who refused in any real numbers.

There was such a huge response to Lord Kitchener's appeal for the first 100,000 volunteers that recruitment had to be suspended in several parts of the country as the agencies simply could not cope. By the end of the first week in September 1914, Glasgow was able to claim that it had already recruited more than 22,000 men. Civic pride was a feature of the recruitment drive as Scottish towns and cities, encouraged by local newspapers, vied with one another to show that they were doing their bit. The *Dundee Courier* pleaded with its readers not to let the city down, while the Edinburgh newspapers expected that the city's capital status should be reflected in both the number and the quality of its recruits. The *Inverness*

Courier made great play that the Highlands had always contributed a disproportionate number of soldiers, and the Glasgow press – with the largest audience – assumed an effortless superiority. The fact that most Scottish regiments had a local base of recruitment meant that local pride was an important impetus to mobilisation. With depots overcrowded and widespread shortages of arms and uniforms, some means had to be found to control the stem of recruits. In the second week of September the physical standards required for entry were raised, which resulted in selection of the more able-bodied and rejection of the short, fat and feeble. Caustic observations were made in other parts of the country that recruitment from Glasgow was not now as great as it once had been. The passion associated with the war soon died down, however, and the peak of recruitment lasted for only a couple of months.

As combat on the Western Front began in earnest, the demand for men became insatiable, forcing a reduction in physical entry standards in 1915. Even so, about a third of a million Scots enlisted voluntarily before conscription was introduced in January 1916. Efforts to recruit all able-bodied men foundered, especially as radical politics began to grip Scottish society and news of the carnage on the Western Front filtered back home. Becoming cannon fodder for the bosses was not such a romantic proposition. For all the virtues of volunteerism, conscription eventually had to be introduced to make up the shortages in the army while keeping workers in vital industries, but it had less impact in Scotland than in other parts of the United Kingdom because of the large number of workers who were employed in reserved occupations. That said, 690,235 Scots were to serve in the armed forces during the conflict: 585,171 in the army, 72,219 in the navy and 32,845 in the air force. Using rough-and-ready calculations from the census of 1911, these totalled about half the Scottish men aged between eighteen and forty-five.

One of the reasons that such a high proportion of this age group served in the armed forces was that emigration had pulled overseas a disproportionate number of young men, leaving Scottish society with both an age and a gender imbalance. Between 1904 and 1913, some 600,000 Scots emigrated. With 10.5 per cent of the combined British and Irish population, Scotland contributed a total of 9.8 per cent of the regular and Territorial army during the war and 22 out of the 157 battalions which

made up the British Expeditionary Force in France. It should be remembered that these forces included Canadian and Indian troops, making the
Scottish commitment a sizeable one. Also, a great many Scots served in
the Australian, New Zealand and Canadian armed forces, which had their
own Highland regiments. Yet it also should be pointed out that by the
end of the war many of the Scottish regiments were being filled with Irish
and English recruits, who sometimes made up more than half a regiment.

THE WORKSHOP OF WAR

The Clyde basin was to become the most important centre of munitions
production in the British Isles. Coal, steel, ships, engineering plant, aircraft engines, shells and munitions were turned out by the thousands of
tons as the conflict created an insatiable appetite for the raw material of
war. The Clyde was able to expand its production by about a fifth during
the war, which tells us two things. First, on the negative side, it can be
argued that the industries were overmanned and underproductive before
1914 and it took the war to shave off excess fat. Second, however, it could
be said that it was a testament to the productive capacity and ingenuity of
the Clyde industries that they were able to increase output by such a margin. A balanced assessment of the state of the Scottish economy requires a
combination of both positive and negative aspects.

With so many men away at the front, it became necessary to adopt
more intensive labour-saving techniques and devices. After all, restructuring the economy to take account of the loss of about half the male workforce was no small undertaking. Part of the answer was to change working
practices, and this would spark off furious labour unrest (see below). Yet,
for all the problems associated with strikes and industrial disputes, the
productive capacity of the Scottish economy during the First World War
was impressive. Paying tribute to the work done by thirty Clydeside yards
and marine works during the war, the *Glasgow Herald* in December 1918
claimed, 'No figures can convey anything like an accurate impression of
the activity that has prevailed or the continuity of the process of turning
out new ships, while there is no way of tabulating the immense amount of
naval repair and overhaul work which has been done.'

One lasting and lethal consequence of the war was the failure of the

Scottish economy to diversify away from its traditional specialisation in the old staple industries. Before 1914 the Scottish economy was overly dependent on supplying a narrow range of goods to a narrow range of customers. These were mainly capital investment goods (ships, heavy engineering plant, railway locomotives), whose purchase was largely dependent on the health of the international economy. In an increasingly competitive world, the Scottish economy used specialisation and relatively low wages as its main form of defence. The low-wage economy arrested the development of a domestic economy based on consumer durables, which reinforced the need to compete in international markets through exports, which drove down wages. It was a vicious circle. However, there were potential growth points in the Scottish economy before 1914 which could have led to a more balanced economy. The Albion car works, a chemicals industry and light engineering did exist before the war, but the insatiable demand for munitions and the staples of heavy industry meant that most profits were to be made in the traditional sector of the economy. New industries folded as manufacturers diverted all their resources into capitalising on the ready and easy profits that could be made from war production. A cursory survey of the statistics demonstrates the capacity of the Scottish economy to churn out the material necessary for war. The war snuffed out any chance that the Scottish economy would diversify and develop in a more balanced and healthy way: instead, the future would depend on the old industries.

The Clyde was an ideal location for war production. It was beyond the reach of the German navy, and was responsible for 90 per cent of Scottish shipbuilding in 1914. Furthermore, the Admiralty had been the shipyards' most important customer in the years immediately before the war, taking some 45 per cent of all tonnage produced. The key industries of steel, coal and engineering were in close proximity to one another and well served by a transport infrastructure. Also, being in the most populous part of Scotland, the Clyde could call upon vast labour resources, which were needed to man the munitions factories. Eventually, a quarter of a million Scots would work in war-related industries in the Clyde basin.

The first task for the shipyards was to produce destroyers for the Royal Navy. However, as the German navy stayed in port and the U-boat campaign of unrestricted warfare got under way in 1916, the replacement of destroyed merchant ships became the top priority, as these were essential to keep Britain's lifeline with the United States open. In spite of insatiable demand, however, the average annual tonnage launched during the war, at 594,000 tons, was less than the 676,000 tons which made up the annual average for the three years preceding the war. Labour shortages and disputes, a tradition of specialisation, and an absence of rationalisation kept productivity down. Indeed, government intervention was required to introduce and enforce new working practices, prefabrication techniques and greater standardisation.

Steel production rocketed as demand for shells, armour plating and engines boomed, with the number of ingots and castings produced rising from 1.23 million in 1914 to 2.24 million tons in 1918. Demand was such that German prisoners of war were used to mine inferior iron ore on the island of Raasay off the West Highland coast. The war stimulated the expansion of chemical and explosive production, with the munitions plant in Parkhead, Glasgow, increasing the value of its output from £1.9 million to £7.1 million in the same period. The giant industrial conglomerate of Beardmores produced aircraft, aero engines and armour plating for tanks, and also manufactured howitzers and other artillery pieces.

Textile companies received increased orders as a result of war demand. Carpet factories were converted to make blankets for the troops, with James Templeton & Co. producing over 4 million by the end of the war. The production of uniforms and boots to clothe the army kept textile plants in the borders and elsewhere busy. The need for canvas for tents and coverings for wagons on the Western Front was another important source of demand. Dundee's key industry of jute was kept going during the war by an insatiable demand for sandbags, which were the primary means of protection in the trenches. They were produced by the million, and after a sandbag shortage in 1915 the government was forced to redirect jute from factories in India towards Dundee.

The stationing of the navy in Scapa Flow meant that the branch lines of the Highland railway were used and supplied as never before, bringing an increased flow of traffic and goods. This more than made up for the loss of tourism during the war, although a number of patriotic grouse-moor owners decided that it was in the best interest of the nation's morale to keep their shoots open.

Before 1914 the labour force in Scotland was highly stratified. The specialities of the Scottish economy – ships, heavy engineering and locomotives – required a high degree of labour specialisation. The production of ships, for example, involved thousands of workers each doing their own specific tasks. Boilermakers, welders, riveters, carpenters, painters, plumbers, scaffolding constructors, engineers and electricians, as well as labourers, were all needed in the construction of a ship, which was usually made to high specifications and would be unique. This degree of specialisation was important in ensuring the high standards of quality which gave rise to the epithet 'Clyde built'. But in wartime, when the emphasis was on producing as much as possible and as quickly as possible, this approach was cumbersome and inefficient. In order to maximise production, it was necessary to streamline the productive process.

The Scottish workforce was dominated by rigid lines of demarcation which protected the rights of craftsmen and maintained their privileges. The apprenticeship system, which required seven years' training before a man was qualified, was an effective means of keeping semi-skilled and unskilled workers at bay. Trades and skills were protected and guarded jealously. With enlistment taking away many of these skilled workers, there was no time to go through the normal process of apprenticeships and, instead, drastic action was needed to keep up production. The Munitions Act of May 1915 stipulated that, for the duration of the war, semi-skilled and unskilled workers could now be used in tasks which had formerly been the preserve of skilled craftsmen, although pay differentials would remain.

Maximising war production was promoted as a strategic objective, and workers were reminded of their obligations to produce the necessary hardware for the troops in the front line. As part of this process, the government clamped down on excessive drinking by the workforce, real or imaginary. The *Daily Record* in February 1915 carried a photograph of a pub near the Fairfield shipyard with the bar lined up with 'halfs and halfs' (half pints of beer and a whisky chaser) waiting for the workers when they finished their shift. Nor would strikes and go-slows be tolerated, because 'Every hour lost by a workman COULD HAVE been worked, HAS been worked by a German workman, who in that time has produced an additional shell to kill the British workman's brother in arms.'

Rationalisation of work practices was an effective means to boost production. Furthermore, greater standardisation took place with the importation of American machinery which enabled greater efficiency in mass production. Power tools allowed workers to complete an increasing number of tasks in a shorter period of time. Mass production arrived in the shells industry, where unskilled, largely female, labour could operate machinery which could turn out products in record time. Largely because of a manpower shortage, the Scottish economy was modernised and rationalised to an unprecedented degree. Unfortunately, this transformation was geared towards the production of war materials, which was a market that had a limited life.

CLASS CONFLICT

The stresses and strains of the demands of the war economy were soon to tell on the workforce. Full employment and rising wages ushered an influx of workers into the Clyde basin, eager to take advantage of the new opportunities in the munitions works. Full employment and a demand for workers at a time of labour shortage meant that the working class, for once, had a major advantage over the employers. The threat of the sack could be dismissed with a shrug and the knowledge that there were other employers desperate for workers. Trade unions were able to take advantage of full wages and an expanding workforce to increase their subscriptions and membership. Emboldened by their increased bargaining power, the unions were able to thrust themselves forwards as the legitimate defenders of working-class interests.

Despite the claim that it would be 'business as usual' during the hostilities, the war did affect the economy, and in an unbalanced way. The suspension of free trade in 1915 was an indication that the old notions of laissez-faire could not be maintained for the duration of the hostilities. However, this did not stop Scottish capitalists from applying the full pressure of the market, even at the expense of patriotism. Ever sensible of how best to make a buck, the Scottish landlords in the Clyde area were the first to demonstrate that profits came before patriotism. With the workforce increasing by some 20,000 in the first few months of the war, there was an increased demand for rented accommodation in this area. Landlords demonstrated that they were aware of this by yanking up rents – by about a quarter in some places. Hard-earned overtime was eaten away by rent hikes, and eviction seemed a real possibility for those families with the principal breadwinner at the front. Army pay was not enough, according to one writer to the *Glasgow Herald* on 21 August 1914:

'It is insufficient support for our dependants. How far, for instance, would my pay and separation allowance go in my case? I am 32 years, married with one child and of good physique and have already served my country in South Africa ... Who is going to meet my factor when he calls for the rent. How are my wife and child to live?'

Many Scottish families saw the landlords' quest for increased profits at a time of national emergency as morally unscrupulous. They therefore decided to take matters into their own hands. Organisational assistance came from the trade unions, the co-operative movement and the Independent Labour Party (ILP), but by far the most significant element in the rent strikes of 1915 was the collective action of ordinary people fuelled by a strong sense of moral indignation. Mass protests brought the message to the general public, with placards shaming the avaricious property owners. By the end of 1915, over 25,000 tenants were refusing to pay rent. Pictures of youngsters protesting against 'faceless' profiteers who were threatening them with eviction raised moral indignation. 'My daddy is on the front fighting the Germans, while I am at home fighting the Huns' was how one caption read. The protesters were very adept at using patriotism to bolster their cause.

The second incident of profit being put before patriotism led to the breaking of the story of the 'shell scandal', when it was leaked that munitions manufacturers were deliberately holding back production in order to inflate prices, which the government had no option but to pay. At a time of stalemate on the Western Front in 1915 and when the generals were calling for more men and munitions, the activities of the arms manufacturers were repugnant to most workers, especially those who had brothers and friends at the front. Again, the scandal was a moral body blow to the powers of capital, and helped reinforce the ethical high ground of labour and socialist activists. Indeed, the Ulster-Scot Canadian leader of the Tory Party, the Scottish businessman Andrew Bonar Law, narrowly missed being implicated in a scandal involving the export of iron ore to Germany. Jute producers in Dundee also took advantage of the situation by increasing prices in line with wartime demand, even though they were using material bought at pre-war prices. Profits rose by over 50 per cent, until government intervention regulated supply and demand.

The impact of rising prices due to wartime inflation led to increasing industrial militancy, a course of action that seemed justified because the bosses were making handsome profits and certainly did not have a monopoly of patriotism. Popular at the grass-roots level, wildcat strikes led by the Clyde Workers Committee began to break out on the Clyde in 1915, and the shop stewards used their position as leaders on the ground to agitate for pay rises of an extra 2d. per hour that the moderate leadership did not readily endorse. Dundee jute workers also went on strike, but the employers refused to give in.

Further unrest was fuelled by changes to working practices. Skilled workers enjoyed a privileged position within the working-class employment hierarchy, and entry to a trade was carefully regulated by the apprenticeship scheme, and was also often based on family connections. In an uncertain world, the ability to defend and maintain these craft privileges was one of the few compensations available to skilled workers. Acutely conscious of their status, such workers wore suits and bowler hats on Sundays and regarded themselves as a cut above the rest of the working class. The exigencies of wartime, with manpower shortages and increased demand for production, led management to seek new ways to improve productivity (see above). Workers regarded new working practices as an invasion of their traditional rights. Still more ominous was the use of semi-skilled and unapprenticed labour in areas which had been served by time-served tradesmen. The workers believed that this so-called dilution was the thin edge of the wedge. Although the newcomers were paid less than time-served men, there were suspicions that promises that their use was simply a wartime emergency measure would not be honoured and that the new practices would become permanent.

The attitude of the employers did not help matters. Lord Weir, who was put in charge of munitions production in Scotland, was renowned for his hostility to trade unions, and his attempt to attract foreign workers with higher wages than the going rate did little to endear him to the workers. Claims that inflation was eating away at increases in pay were flatly rejected, and the workers were told that they should be glad that there were unlimited overtime and bonus schemes. The Amalgamated Engineers Union responded with a ban on overtime in January 1915.

In the male-dominated working environment of the Clyde, where working traditions had been jealously and rigorously defended, the sight of young American women employed as riveters without an apprenticeship was too much to bear. Together with mounting inflation (which had raised the cost of living by about 50 per cent), deteriorating relations with the employers, and the stresses and strains of working in a society at war, it led tempers to snap. Claims by David Lloyd George, the Minister of Munitions, that war production was being hampered by excessive drunkenness among the workers did little to improve industrial relations. Crude propaganda efforts by the government to appeal to the patriotism of the workers fell on deaf ears. The use of a poem purportedly by a ordinary 'Tommy Atkins' fighting at the front, wondering why his fellow countrymen were deserting him and not supplying him with ammunition, thus putting him and his comrades at risk, was a crass piece of insensitivity – especially at a time when the patriotic credentials of capitalism were being questioned by all and sundry. Also, the poem was a piece of doggerel written in cockney rhyming slang which, in the days before *Eastenders,* few Scots could understand.

As industrial protest gathered pace, so too did the social protest. Eviction notices issued after citizens refused to pay the exorbitant rises demanded by the landlords were torn up, and neighbours and friends thwarted factors' attempts to make removals. Popular songs were an effective way of communicating the message:

> *To hell with the sheriff*
> *To hell with his crew*
> *To hell with Lloyd George*
> *And Henderson too*
>
> *I don't like the factor*
> *His rent I won't pay*

Three cheers for John Wheatley
I'm striking today

To hell with the landlord
I'm not one to grouse
But to hell with both him
And his bloody old house

In spite of shortages, rent collectors were pelted with flour and eggs by irate housewives, and on 17 November 1915 the protesters marched on George Square in Glasgow to make public their grievances and protest at the trial of debt defaulters, who faced eviction or arrestment of wages. Many husbands downed tools in sympathy, and government pressure was brought to bear on the landlords in the hope that a dismissal of the cases would stop further industrial action. The landlords backed down after negotiating a safe passage through the thousands of angry protesters. The result was a victory for 'people power'.

The agitation had quickly developed an organisational apparatus as members of the Independent Labour Party, the co-operative movement and trade-union activists stepped in to provide leadership and direction. In the close-knit communities of Govan and Partick, neighbours aired common grievances and discussed what action to take. News spread fast, and moral indignation and a deep sense of injustice seized a community which increasingly saw its world as under threat from those people above them who had controlled their lives, whether as landlord or as employer. Government intervention in the form of support to the employers and the subsequent arrest and deportation of the strike leaders to Edinburgh in January 1916 confirmed the widespread suspicion that those with money and power were against them. In such an environment, the message of socialist agitators found a ready audience.

The extent to which Clydeside became 'red' is a source of much debate among historians, with opinions ranging from those who see the agitation as a revolutionary movement threatening to bring the pillars of capitalism crashing down to those who argue that it was simply an expression of narrow social and economic grievances with little coherent political underpinning. That said, there is enough common ground to build up a fairly incontestable picture of what went on. First, there was a sharpening of working-class consciousness. Although sectional differences between skilled and unskilled workers had been ingrained in the Scottish working-class before 1914, the effects of rent rises, inflation and changes in working practices were of sufficient magnitude to create a sense of solidarity. And the fact that grievances spread out from the workplace into the community heightened the feeling of 'us and them'. Second, the fact that the best way to protect communal interests was to act as a community helped to develop increased solidarity based on class. That workers were then able to see the power of solidarity in action reinforced belief in this tactic. With an insatiable demand for labour, workers were not as intimidated by the threat of the sack as before. The pulling together of different crafts and tradesmen and the demonstration of serried ranks of workers sprouting their grievances on the shop floor gave a sense of empowerment. The frantic reaction of the bosses and their desperate attempts to threaten, bribe and cajole the workers helped to create the impression that the employers were on the run. The arrest of the strike leaders roused moral indignation and anger which steeled resolve. Workers now had enough evidence to know that they had real power.

Lloyd George, the Minister for Munitions, came to Glasgow and on Christmas Day 1915 he appealed to the workers to call off industrial action. The Minister, who had wooed large audiences before in Scotland on issues such as land reform and temperance, found to his amazement that his Welsh eloquence cut little ice with the disgruntled men of the Clyde. Booing and heckling drowned him out, and the hostility was such that he was ignominiously ushered out the back door to escape in a waiting car. To the workers, it seemed that they even had the government on the run.

With stalemate on the Western Front and mounting criticism of the handling of the war, agitation on the Clyde was a problem too many for the government. Through a mixture of compromise, which saw the use of commissioners to draft local agreements about the use of unskilled labour that by and large increased wages and conditions, and coercion, which saw further periodic arrest and imprisonment of strike leaders, high levels of munitions production were maintained. Also, in December 1915, the Rent Restrictions Act had had the momentous effect of freezing rents for the duration of the war.

The events on the Clyde taught the working class a number of valuable lessons. First, they demonstrated to the workers themselves and to others that the workers had power and could bring about social change. Second, they showed that it was as an organised and united group that it was possible to achieve things. Finally, they proved the claims of socialists that the workers should look to themselves and not to the middle class to achieve improved standards of living. With improvements in wages and rents frozen, the Clyde would remain quiet for the duration of the war. Indeed, David Kirkwood, leader of the Parkhead shop stewards, went on to win the prize of the best hat in Glasgow from his employer, Sir William Beardmore, for setting the record for shell output in Great Britain.

THE OTHER SCOTLAND

The events on the Clyde tend to overshadow the dramatic changes that were happening in other parts of Scotland during the war, but it should be remembered that strikes also broke out in Edinburgh, Dundee, Paisley, Aberdeen and elsewhere.

On the eve of war, half the Scottish population of about 4.8 million lived in settlements of more than 20,000 people. Although Scotland is represented as a predominantly urban and industrial society, the majority of the population lived in small to medium-sized towns which were located in the countryside. Towns such as Stirling, Perth, Dumfries and Inverness were important market towns and servers for the rural economy. Agriculture, fishing and forestry were the largest single occupation, accounting for about 11 per cent of the total workforce, and it should be borne in mind that married women were not counted in the census returns as workers, even though they were a vital part of the rural economy.

About a quarter of a million Scots lived in settlements of between 5,000 to 10,000 people in which, although officially classified as an urban environment, it was possible after half an hour's walk to be in the countryside. Small-town trade had a rural feel to it, with local shops taking provisions direct from the farmers. The horse was a vital means of transport, and farriers, blacksmiths and drivers were a vital part of Scotland's communication network. Railway stations were peppered throughout the rural environment, bringing much employment to the countryside. Also, much of Scottish industry was located in small towns – particularly brick-making, ironworking, and paper, leather and textiles manufacture – and was usually set in a rural environment. Most Scottish factories were fairly small and were usually family owned. In spite of the tendency to see Scotland in terms of big industrial conurbations, it did not develop the massive industrial cartels in steel and engineering which were characteristic of the American and German economies. Rather, production was small-scale, with few economies of scale and only limited capital investment. Mining was also largely set in towns within a rural environment, and in addition there were a significant number of small towns which had specialised industries, such as linoleum in Kirkcaldy or brewing and textiles in Alloa. Some towns had most of their business with the rural economy, and some were small ports or fishing villages.

Fishing was an important industry, and employed up to 40,000 men and some 50,000 seasonal women workers. Most of the catch went overseas as exports, particularly to Russia and Germany. The war disrupted the export trade, but the immediate effects of this were not readily noticed as the demand for feeding the home front would take all that could be caught. The navy employed 25,000 fishermen in the naval reserve, and over 1,200 fishing boats were used as transport, minesweepers and patrol boats. Some fishermen did well, and some 800 boats were fitted out with engines courtesy of HM government. The north-east coast was affected by security concerns, and only local boats with permits were allowed to fish. Many strategic areas and approaches were strictly off limits, which meant that fishing gravitated to the safer waters of the west.

Perhaps the most significant factor affecting rural and small-town Scotland was the number of men who went off to war. The Volunteers were most popular in rural Scotland, and arguably stronger ties of paternalism with local gentry helped to boost recruitment. In agriculture one in three men aged between eighteen and forty-five eventually joined up. The same forces of community which boosted recruitment in the cities were also at work in the countryside in the small towns and villages. Also, it might be argued that there was a greater desire on the part of young men to escape from the rural environment. The Scottish countryside had already been experiencing population loss as younger and more adventurous souls went to seek their fortunes in the big cities. The main causes of this had been boredom with the repetitive and unrelenting nature of rural labour and the fact that social mobility was almost non-existent in the countryside. Most people could predict on a daily basis what they would be doing for the rest of their lives. Service in the army was an honourable escape route from family pressure to stay on the land.

The war produced an increased demand for all kinds of goods, and in particular for foodstuffs. Fears of a naval blockade highlighted the concern that Britain was not self-sufficient in agriculture, and there was a greater demand to produce more at home, especially after the start of the U-boat campaign in 1916. That prices were going up helped to increase production as well. Unfortunately the rise in demand coincided with a shortage of manpower as a result of recruitment. Things got worse in 1916 when a poor harvest produced half the grain yields of 1914. Farming was designated a reserved occupation in 1917, and farmers and rural labourers were exempt from conscription. As part of an attempt to promote agricultural self-sufficiency, a massive extension of sowing was undertaken in the spring of 1917. The labour shortage was filled by the use of the old and the young, and the minimum school-leaving age of fourteen was suspended as part of the emergency, which meant that the whole family could be used in production, as family labour had been used in similar ways in the past.

The Women's Land Army was created to provide extra labour, although there were mixed opinions about the effectiveness of this. While some recruits took to the cause with gusto, there were grumblings about 'bloody useless women' who failed to fit into the routine of the countryside: life on the farm was a far cry from the rural idyll that they had read about in the Kailyard novel (see Chapter 3). This was especially the case where there was a well-established tradition in the countryside of using unmarried girls for the most menial and arduous tasks. The Corn Production Act of 1917, which guaranteed wages and prices was particularly useful in helping to keep women on the land who had previously been attracted to the towns and cities by the prospect of higher-paid work in the munitions factories.

Forestry and timber production also increased with the demand for wood. The fact that many forests were cut down encouraged a more scientific and pragmatic approach to the development of timber forests, especially in the Highlands.

Scottish women experienced great changes during the war. With so many men at the front, it was necessary to suspend traditional notions about a woman's place being in the home. Although labour-saving technology and new working practices could increase productivity, they could not wholly offset the shortage of labour needed to churn out the materials of war, especially while voluntary recruitment was taking men away from vital industries in the months before conscription was introduced. The war was important in demonstrating the capabilities of women. With husbands at the front, mothers were forced to lead the family in their menfolk's absence, although in reality they often did this before the war. For many the war brought hardship and loneliness. A soldier's pay was inadequate to keep up with spiralling inflation, and many had no alternative but to seek work to augment the family income. The extended social family network was important, in that childminding could be shared with neighbours, aunts and uncles, and grandparents. Just as the strikes and rent increases reinforced communal solidarity, so too the exigencies of war made hard-pressed mothers band together to share in work and childminding and, perhaps most importantly, to provide a shoulder to cry on for those who had lost someone at the front.

Work gave women a sense of comradeship and, more importantly, a degree of financial independence. For working-class girls, industrial work had been looked down upon in pre-war society, as it was believed to lead to loose morality and corruption. The most suitable occupation, it was believed, was domestic service, where the safe environment of the middle-class home was supposed to protect innocent girls from moral infection from the wicked world outside and the manners and ways of their social superiors might rub off and improve their character. The reality was quite different. Domestic service was stultifying, with many girls treated as virtual prisoners, shut off from the world outside. Many were sexually and emotionally abused, and others often had to conform to degrading forms of behaviour. In one house, servants were not even allowed to look at their master and had to face the wall whenever he appeared. Not surprisingly, the prospect of greater freedom and more money lured many women to the factories, and there they also had the moral satisfaction of knowing that their work was for the benefit of the war effort.

With increasing wages and plenty of overtime, women enjoyed a greater degree of independence than their sisters had hitherto experienced. With increasing independence came greater confidence. Work provided many women with a new experience and a greater sense of responsibility. Also, the comradeship and the work environment opened up a new world to them, which many enjoyed. Before 1914, men and women did not spend much time together in Scotland. Men tended to spend most of their time in work and at the pub in the company of other men, with the home reserved for sleep and dinner. The war increased the amount of social, if not sexual, intercourse between the sexes. Women became highly visible. They issued tickets on the trams on the way to work, and filled the shoes of men in many public and administrative duties. Furthermore, they were working alongside men in the factories, most of which had to have separate toilets built to accommodate the needs of the new workforce. Women were seen to have a fag in public, stroll down the road home in dungarees, and laugh and banter with friends in a raucous manner that would have shocked Edwardian observers.

With the loss of so many men at the front, society became more concerned with the role of mothers and children, if for no other reason than to maintain population levels, which were deemed to be a test of the nation's virility. Many of the conventions associated with courtship, marriage and premarital sex were temporarily forgotten in the more socially relaxed atmosphere of a society at war. Young lovers could be forgiven their passions if they might never see one another again, unmarried mothers found that their children were regarded as a source of national regeneration, and children in general had to be looked after to nurture a generation to replace one which was lost. Casualties at the front meant that there were already a large number of fatherless children. Increased medical provision for mothers and babies emerged as a wartime social priority. Because death was no respecter of social class at the front, it was believed that children of all backgrounds were a vital national asset.

This concern for the well-being of children also found expression in the Royal Commission on the Housing of the Industrial Population of Scotland, Rural and Urban, which took evidence in 1917. In 1914 it was estimated that half the Scottish population lived in one- or two-roomed houses, while in Glasgow it was two-thirds (see Chapter 2). According to the Revd David Watson, quoted in the Royal Commission's report:

Children are forced out of doors to give the housewife room to work. That is the saddest result of wretched housing. In my evening visitations I find children everywhere – sitting in the closes and on the stairs, trying to play, often asleep, on bitter winter nights. Sometimes they play in dark evil smelling courts, sometimes in the dimly lit streets. They learn no good, they see sights which demoralise and hear language which corrupts. Any good they learn in the school is neutralised at night.

As had happened during the Boer War, the need to keep the nation strong and competitive propelled the health and education of children back on to the political agenda.

With such changes in circumstances and attitudes, it should come as no surprise to find that women were particularly active in the rent strike and in the political agitation surrounding the Clyde. Given the pressures of inflation and the expectation that women were responsible for the household, many felt that direct action was necessary. Women were foremost in the campaign to create a £1 weekly allowance for soldiers' dependants and widows. On 15 November 1915 the *Glasgow Herald* reported one leading light, Helen Crawfurd, as telling a gathering of women that: 'This fight was essentially a women's fight. All who were taking part in the demonstration were showing their solidarity. They were asking not for money, nor for charity; they were asking for justice. She respected all laws that were just and fair, but she did not ask them to respect the law which allowed increases in rents to be enforced at the present juncture.' Women were active in the ranks of the co-operative movement and the ILP. They were responsible for organising communities to fight the threat of eviction. In the closes and wynds of the local streets and on the factory floor, politics and social and economic grievances became part of everyday conversation, as did the appeal for socialism. Although the appeal for the vote was abandoned in a burst of patriotic fervour by the suffragette movement in 1914, it would be wrong to think that politics left the agenda of women. The effect of the Rent Restrictions Act and the campaigns for higher wages and the defence of standards of living arguably made politics more important to women, especially as they were the ones left at home to fight for these causes.

Politics were important for middle-class women too. The threat of socialism and revolution brought them together to defend their own class interests, and organisations such as the Women's Institute increasingly took on a political air. The establishment of new organisations such as the Women's League Against Bolshevism, designed to fend off the dangers of socialism and promote 'traditional' family values, was ample testament to the increasingly important role of women in political life. However, the effect of the war was to take women off the agenda as a separate political issue. Instead, women became more active in politics on the basis of class interests.

POLITICS

The expectation that war could be conducted on the basis of 'business as usual' proved short-lived. Scotland had been emphatically Liberal in the Edwardian era, with the party winning fifty-eight out of seventy-five parliamentary seats in 1910. Labour and the Tories found that they could make few inroads against the Liberal hegemony. Liberal success in Scotland was based on the party's commitment to free trade, which kept industrialists happy with access to the international market, and the working class happy because it kept down the price of food. Also, the Liberals had been in the forefront of proposing social policies on education, housing and temperance, which found a ready ear among the working class. Nevertheless, cracks were beginning to appear in the Liberal Party's command of Scottish politics.

First, Labour was making headway in local elections – which should come as no surprise, because most of the direct legislation which would improve the condition of the working class came from municipal rather than central government. Legislation such as the Feeding of Necessitous Children Act, though passed by Westminster, left it up to the local authorities to decide whether they would make use of the provisions or not. So this was an area in which Labour had direct practical appeal. Second, the Liberal Party in Scotland was divided between those who regarded themselves as advanced and progressive and those who were more conservative and inclined towards the leadership. The advanced wing was increasingly discontented with the failure to implement Scottish home rule and more progressive social policies, which were perpetually being watered down by the Conservative-dominated House of Lords. Such tensions were exacerbated by the war, and would result in a gradual defection of many progressive Liberals to the Labour Party.

The Liberal Party did not have problems to seek. Its ageing Prime Minister, Herbert Asquith, who was the MP for East Fife, was not a natural war leader. Shell scandals and stalemate on the Western Front raised questions about the government's handling of the war. The decision to go to war had itself resulted in the defection of a small number of pacifists, but it was the problems associated with shortages, rising prices and industrial conflict which raised most questions in the Scottish public's mind. The working class felt themselves the victims of an oppressive government which seemed to side with the bosses, while the middle class wanted a more vigorous war policy and a tougher stance against the spectre of socialism, which was rearing its head on Clydeside and elsewhere.

The pre-war Liberal Party had based itself on the notion of class conciliation and had championed itself as the worker's friend. In an atmosphere of heightened class tensions, the party lost ground on both sides of the class divide. The events during the war further continued the party's gradual detachment from its Scottish constituency. The formation of a coalition government with the Conservatives in 1916, with Lloyd George as Prime Minister, helped to confirm the widespread suspicion that the Liberals were really a party of the bosses and dented their claims to be a party which supported the working class. The Conservatives in government would only be expected to shore up what was already seen to be a biased regime against ordinary people. The nationalist Easter Rising of 1916 in Dublin and its tragic aftermath alienated the Irish Catholic community in Scotland, which had been the Liberals' most faithful ally because of the party's support for Irish home rule. The insensitive execution for treason of the leaders of the rising caused outrage among Scotland's Irish community and effectively ended its trust in the party. The disaster of the Lloyd George coalition and a split with Asquith meant a divided Liberal Party. Although the followers of Asquith were stronger in Scotland, the sorry spectacle of the once mighty party squabbling and bickering in public at a time of national emergency confirmed the belief that the Liberals were unfit for government. Lloyd George had been a popular radical Liberal in Scotland in the pre-war era, and his rousing speeches against the landlords and the House of Lords had drawn thousands of listeners. Yet he was now being propped up in government by Conservative Party support – hardly the best credential for a supposed man of the people.

The war effectively ended normal political organisation. Both the Liberal and the Conservative parties had turned their organisations over to the recruiting drive. Furthermore, both organisations had a considerable number of staff who were already in the military, and those who were not were expected to join. The Labour Party, on the other hand, found that its organisational strength increased during the conflict. The war helped speed up a process of politicisation which had already been affecting the trade unions. It seemed to demonstrate conclusively that reliance on the Liberal Party to protect working-class interests was futile, and that effective legislation was best found by supporting Labour. That the government was forced to concede demands on wages, conditions and rents showed that working-class muscle could achieve things on its own. The trade unions were in an improved position: membership was going through the roof because of full employment, and the process of radicalisation was making ordinary members take a greater interest in politics. The unions had funds, meeting places, organisation and – most importantly – direct access to the great body of the working class themselves. The pre-war ILP had largely been confined to the lower middle class, and its biggest obstacle in realising its political ambitions was that it could not make the working class listen to its message. The trade unions would now make them listen, and the workers had a ready ear. Political activists were invited to address packed union meetings of workers who were already in a confrontational mood over wages and conditions. The message that the interests of capital and labour were different and that the capitalists were exploiting the workers by not paying a decent wage hit the right note. That Labour would defend the workers' interests and would campaign for the redress of their grievances had great appeal.

This appeal was heightened by Labour's having a number of popular and talented speakers who knew how to work an audience. David Kirkwood, William Gallacher and Harry McShane were shop stewards who had been imprisoned for their part in leading the strikes on the Clyde, and this gave them an enhanced status in the eyes of their fellow workers. They were joined by others such as James Maxton, Thomas Johnston (the editor of the socialist weekly, *Forward*, which was banned by the government in 1916) and John Wheatley, all of whom became folk heroes. Unbowed by imprisonment, employer harassment and state surveillance, they made passionate speeches in favour of socialism.

Labour was also boosted by the defection of a number of former radical Liberals, such as James Barr, J. L. Kinloch, Rosslyn Mitchell and Roland Muirhead. Although not household names, these middle-ranking Liberals brought experience and organisational ability to the Labour Party. Also, they were a good indication of the way that the political pendulum was swinging. Theatricality was an essential part of their appeal, and humour was used to good effect. Although now proponents of socialism, there was a lot in their speeches which was recognisable to their audiences from pre-war times. Many of the same themes which had formed part of the Liberal platform were still there, and as popular as ever. Home rule, temperance, land reform and denunciations of the landlords could have come straight from the pre-war mouth of Lloyd George. The Labour orators spoke with working-class Scottish accents, knew their audience's passions and fears, and played them like a musical instrument. Other orators to the far left, such as the Communist William Gallacher and the Marxist revolutionary John Maclean, were equally well known and, although they went much further in their demands than most of the Labour movement, they did at least help push audiences in the right direction.

REACTION ON THE RIGHT

The emergence of socialist Scotland, dramatic though it was, has meant that not as much historical attention has focused on the realignment on the right of Scottish politics. In 1912 the Scottish Liberal Unionists and the Scottish Conservatives united in opposition to Irish home rule to form the Scottish Unionist Party. (For convenience, however, these will hereafter be referred to as Conservatives or Tories, in line with their UK parent party.) Before the war the party had found that its appeal was confined to the western central belt, and it could win only fourteen out of the seventy-five Scottish parliamentary seats (three of which were university seats, with MPs elected by graduates). The Conservatives appeared doomed to permanent opposition north of the border. Yet they were arguably the real political winners of the war. Just as the social and economic tensions were pushing the working class towards Labour, the same tensions and the result of the rise of socialism pulled the middle class towards the Conservative Party.

The conduct of the government during the early phases of the war, together with the shenanigans of Lloyd George and the formation of his coalition, had done little to endear the Liberal Party to the Scottish middle class. The outbreak of revolution in Russia had raised fears that the same thing might happen here. Indeed, John Maclean was appointed head of a Soviet consul in Glasgow in 1917. Although some historians have dismissed the Red Clyde as a myth, it was no myth in the middle-class imagination. The *Glasgow Herald* estimated that the potential revolutionaries could call on the support of over 100,000 people. To the middle class the threat seemed real. After all, there were militant workers who were going on strike, and a mass movement had forced the government to intervene in the payment of rent, something the middle classes regarded as sacrosanct to the market. And the workers appeared to be led by committed socialists. The middle class took the leaders of the workers at their word and believed that they were about to abolish the market and take over private property. The more inflammatory a socialist speech, the more likely it was to be reported, and no one thought to question the extent to which ordinary workers shared their leaders' convictions. Faced with such alarming prospects, the middle class found the wimpish Liberals unconvincing in their claims about class conciliation. If the leaders of the workers talked about class war, then it was necessary to have the support of their own class warriors, and here the Conservatives seemed the much tougher of the two main parties.

It should be remembered that the Scottish middle class were in close proximity to the red spectre. Industrial unrest was not far away from the leafy suburbs of Glasgow's west end. In Edinburgh class tensions were rising. Although the city had a more middle-class profile, the underlings of the service economy – shopkeepers, clerks and salesmen – were joining trade unions in greater numbers than ever before, and socialist speeches were to be heard on the Mound. In Aberdeen, which had an active socialist contingent before the war, and Dundee, which already had one Labour MP, the labour movement was flexing its muscles with increased membership, and highly visible activists were doing the rounds in the city centre. One reason why the Scottish middle class felt ill at ease was that they only constituted about a fifth of the population – a smaller proportion than the quarter which their equivalents accounted for in England. Scotland's professionals were also experiencing the burden of increased income tax, which, coupled with inflation, meant that many household budgets were being squeezed.

In villages and rural Scotland, deference may have survived longer in the smaller workshops and factories, and the class tensions of the Clyde seemed quite alien. The fear that property could be confiscated, together with residual fears about the Glasgow underbelly, raised hackles in many quarters. In Scottish industries far removed from the conflict of the Clyde, the prospect of war with paternalistic factory owners was anathema. Also, while many in these industries had similar grievances, they were not as pronounced as on the Clyde. Rents did not go up as much; tenant farmers and their labourers did well because of government regulation, and some became farm owners; munitions workers out in the sticks did well on overtime. Workers might have had reason to grumble, but not to the same extent. Socialism did catch on in the mining industry, however. There was already a pronounced tradition of militancy in some parts of the country, and the war took away many workers, who were replaced by conscripts. Also, mining communities were fairly close-knit, and it was possible for grievances to coalesce into a common front in a way that was not possible in other communities which had different types of industry and workers.

Many in small-town Scotland received only information which was subject to government censorship, and were influenced by right-leaning newspaper editorials which painted the agitation on the Clyde in a lurid light. Also, patriotism maintained its tight grip. Following anti-German propaganda after the sinking of the liner *Lusitania*, German immigrants were the victims of riots in Greenock, Annan, Dumfries, Perth, Alloa and Leith. Throughout the war, military authorities received constant reports from local people purporting to have seen spies or strange signals around military bases. Also, it should be remembered that on the Red Clyde in May 1915, at a time of mounting industrial conflict, the workers at one of the largest shipyards, Fairfields, presented the King with a resolution expressing their loyalty and their determination to press forward as efficiently and rapidly as possible in their work. The King was pleased with this 'expression of patriotic resolve on the part of the men of one of the most important shipyards in this renowned industrial centre'.

The Scottish Churches, which still maintained a powerful grip on society, urged their members to be wary of the godless spectre of socialism. It is estimated that 90 per cent of sons of ministers enlisted in the war, which helped to enhance the fathers' authority in society. For others, the worry of family at the front, maintaining a home and working were enough to preoccupy the mind. While the war released pent-up passions and brought about sweeping social and economic change and turbulence, many people reacted to this by gripping more tightly to previously held notions, beliefs and values. Traditional Scotland was shocked by many of the changes brought about by war. With so many women working, church authorities noticed that sexual immorality was increasing, that the fairer sex was also drinking and swearing more, and that child abuse was on the increase. For many, traditional values appeared to be declining, and this only made them resolve to uphold them even more.

THE SOLDIERS

The soldiers tend to be forgotten in history books. Yet to write about the First World War and not take account of the soldiers and servicemen is to leave half of all Scottish men aged between eighteen and forty-five out of the picture. Arguably, in terms of the numbers it affected, the war was the single most traumatic event experienced by Scottish men in the twentieth century. Even before the fighting, it entailed a mass mobilisation and movement of men, most of whom had been confined for most of their lives to a narrow geographic locality. As mentioned before, it meant that society for the first time experienced an absence of adult males.

Even before the bulk of the volunteers had made their way to France, tragedy struck on 22 May 1915 when over 200 young men of the 7th Battalion of the Royal Scots en route to the Gallipoli campaign died in a high-speed rail crash at Gretna. Most of the soldiers had been recruited locally in Leith, and the town went into immediate mourning. It was an ominous portent of what was to come through keeping local recruits together. Statistically, the Scottish soldier would die alongside friends, family and workmates. Statistically, friends, family and workmates were likely to die with him, and news of the death of a loved one was likely to be accompanied by the news that relatives, friends and neighbours all had lost someone too. Mourning was rarely confined to one family. The experience of Leith and the Gretna railway disaster was repeated thousands of times during the war throughout the villages, towns and cities of Scotland as the battles of Loos, the Somme and Ypres took their bloody toll.

For the men at the front, the romance of war wore off quickly. Soldiers from the Royal Scots landing in Gallipoli recounted the smell of dead bodies on the beaches that greeted them when they first arrived. The Scottish regiments had a reputation for a tenacity which was at times suicidal. After the Scots' fifth attempt at a push against enemy lines in the Battle of Loos, the German machine gunners refused to fire at retreating men because the slaughter had been so great. Scottish tenacity also caught the attention of an Austrian corporal, Adolf Hitler, fighting in a Bavarian regiment: 'I can vividly recall to mind the astonished looks of my comrades when they themselves found themselves face to face for the first time with the Tommies in Flanders. After a few days of fighting the consciousness slowly dawned on our soldiers that those Scotsmen were not like the ones we had seen described and caricatured in the comic papers and mentioned in the communiqués.' (*Mein Kampf* (Munich, 1925))

Robert Service, a Canadian Scot working as a medical orderly, brought home some of the grim realities of fighting at the front in his reports for the press and in his poetry. For many of the soldiers the experience was an unimaginable horror. Our generation has grown up with graphic images of war on television news and a barrage of special effects in horror movies that have made us almost unshockable, but nothing had prepared young innocent eyes for the terrors that they witnessed in the killing fields of France. As pals were recruited together, they had to endure the spectacle of seeing lifelong friends and relations being butchered, wounded and dying. The new-found horrors of war included being cooped up in muddy trenches in the cold, damp and wet while subject to bombardment from artillery and snipers. Poison gas was a crude weapon that depended on the direction of the wind, and there was just as much likelihood that your own side would get you as the enemy. Going over the top meant the statistical likelihood of death or injury as men charged at dug-in infantry armed with rifles and machine guns which simply had to pick off their targets one by one.

The brutalising impact of war on young men is only now being addressed by historians. Supposedly, a stiff upper lip was all that was required to get through it. Scottish men were brought up to be the strong, silent type, and did not cry or express emotions. To do so was unmanly, and this lesson was beaten into them as children. Soldiers who witnessed unspeakable horrors went through their life mostly in silence, trying to forget what had happened. There was no treatment for post-traumatic stress, and Scottish society, like the rest of European society, had thousands of men who were emotionally damaged with scars that could leave a deeper impression on the mind than the body. Those who cracked up under the strain were deemed to be cowards and were shot. And, based on statistical probability, there were a number of Scottish men who were so brutalised that they came to enjoy killing.

The war changed men's outlook on life, much to the alarm of many in the social and ecclesiastical Establishment. Soldiers returned home with venereal disease picked up in the rough French brothels, and passed it on to unsuspecting wives and future brides. It was a phenomenon that no one spoke about. Attitudes to religion and morality underwent a transformation, with many men stating that they could no longer believe in a merciful God after what they had seen at the front. For some the petty conformity of Scottish society lost its meaning after what they had been through. Scotland's leading twentieth-century poet, Hugh MacDiarmid, had been a medical orderly in Greece and in France. His description fitted many when, in his 1943 book *Lucky Poet: A Self-Study in Literature and Political Ideas*, he said of a returning soldier, 'He brought back to civilisation an ardour of revolt, a sharp bitterness, made up partly of hatred and partly of pity. He saw with eyes different from those of other men – clearer or more blurred, anyhow not the same. His state of mind was grievous.'

The novelist Lewis Grassic Gibbon caught the brutalising impact of war in his novel *Sunset Song* when Chris's husband, Ewan, returns from a stint in the army. He is transformed from a sensitive man into a drunken brute with little or no feeling. Service in the army has changed him into someone who has no time for his child, he has become an adulterer, and he abuses his wife both emotionally and physically. However, so absurd was the contrast between the reality of life at the front and popular perceptions of it that Ian Campbell Hay's *The First One Hundred Thousand,* with its portrayal of the glories of war, still remained a best-seller even though it ran contrary to the experiences of hundreds of thousands of men. That few talked about their experiences at the front was reflected in Scottish literature. There was no great war poetry or novels: perhaps the Scots thought paper was not a lasting enough memorial and preferred their testaments in stone, which were erected in almost every village, town and city in Scotland.

The war ended almost as suddenly as it had begun, and a month later, in December 1918, there was a snap election in which Lloyd George's coalition government was given a massive vote of approval. The Labour Party made a tentative breakthrough, and the Conservatives did well. The divided Liberals survived, but in a haphazard manner. The Representation of the People Act of 1918 had given the vote to all men over twenty-one and women over thirty, and the electorate tripled in size. However, the election came too quickly for all the changes wrought by war to become apparent. Not everyone had been registered to vote, and there were still hundreds of thousands of soldiers overseas.

Many soldiers would continue to die of their wounds after the armistice, so the casualty list kept mounting even though these soldiers would not be counted as war dead. A lethal bout of influenza swept the country along with the rest of Europe, and took its toll of infants and the elderly. Many of the government wartime regulations were still in place, and society remained very much on a war footing. There was a last vigorous burst of patriotism in which the premier promised to hang the Kaiser and create homes for heroes. Yet, for all that, there was still unfinished business, and the changes wrought by war had still to run their course. The war had divided Scottish society between an invigorated, urban working class hungry for power and social change and a traditional rural and suburban Scotland which wanted to hold back the clock. The battle lines between them had been drawn. The big question was who would win and who would lose.

RECKONING,
1918–1927

They were back to back houses, for the most part a single room; and the outside privies were peculiarly offensive, even for Lanarkshire ... In a group of houses in the Bellshill district, we noted a dirty combined ashpit and privy; the premises being grossly exposed and looking, at the time of our visit, as if they were never cleaned. The streets were seas of liquid mud, the gutters broken in places; and there seemed to be no idea of draining off the surface water either from the general area or from the floors of the latrines ... The condition of the older houses is appalling. They are without rhones or down-pipes to carry off roof water; it simply runs down the roof and walls. There are no coal-cellars and coals are kept below the beds. There are no damp-courses at the ground level of the outside walls. There are no wash houses. The floors are of rough brick or of wood without ventilation underneath. The bare earth is exposed under the beds. The water is obtained from standpipes outside ... In certain small rows we were informed that sanitary accommodation is non existent.

Reports of the Coal Industry Commission (London, 1919)

No human being on the face of the earth, no government, is going to take from me my right to speak, my right to protest against

wrong, my right to do everything that is for the benefit of mankind.
I am not here as the accused; I am here as the accuser of capitalism
dripping with blood from head to foot.

John Maclean, head of the Soviet consul in Glasgow,

speaking at his trial for sedition, 9 May 1918

Mr Gillespie Maclean lives in a heavy square mansion of dark
dressed stone. Outside the gate stands an ornate lamp-post sur-
mounted with the town's arms, proclaiming to the world the civic
importance of him who dwells within ... Inside, all is glitter and
gleam and large purplish landscapes in gilt frames. Whatever house
Mr Gillespie Maclean may visit he will not feel any the less at
home. He will find the same massive, highly polished, much carved
furniture, the same carpets and wall papers, the same gramophone
and wireless set. For he knows that those things are what a man
should have in his house and he has taken care to have them ... The
mere sight of those foot long paragraphs interspersed here and there
by the name of Mr Baldwin set in small capitals, cheers him, during that breakfast hour when faith in mankind is at its lowest ebb,
with the knowledge that God is in heaven and the Conservatives are
in office. Not that Mr Maclean is a Conservative. Sane progress; a
reasonable measure of democracy and its freely elected representatives: believing in such things he can describe himself as a Liberal
in the truest sense. Yet, the deplorable consequences of the war, the
spread of subversive doctrines, the return to parliament of men who
are a disgrace to their country, convinced him that practical men of
all parties must unite against a menace threatening God, King, and
income alike.

George Malcolm Thomson, *The Rediscovery of Scotland* (London, 1928)

THE DEAD

The official tally for Scottish war dead was 74,000. This figure was produced by the simple device of dividing the British total by ten, in accordance with Scotland's share of the British population – applying to the
carnage something like the Barnett formula used to calculate Scotland's

share of UK public expenditure. The National War Memorial White Paper of 1921 put the figure higher, at 100,000 and some historians have argued that the total should be even higher, possibly 135,000. Indeed, one recent claim has it that Scotland had a higher death rate than any other combatant nation with the exceptions of Serbia and Turkey, whose losses were due more to disease than to fighting.

However, such figures have to be treated with caution. For example, those who died of wounds after the armistice were not counted as war dead, but could be used to inflate the figure. The tally would further increase if seamen lost offshore through accident, rather than combat, were included. Yet there are a number of reasons to discount the figures at the higher end of the spectrum. First, the Scots contributed slightly less than their proportion of population to the armed forces during the conflict, so it cannot be said that the Scots suffered more casualties on account of there having been a disproportionately high number of them fighting. Second, there is some confusion as to what officially constitutes Scottish 'war dead'. As was mentioned in Chapter 1 not all those who fought in the Scottish regiments were Scots born – these units contained a significant number of English, Irish and Welsh – so those who were killed in Scottish regiments cannot all be claimed as Scots. Third, in keeping with Scottish morbid acquisitiveness, war dead who came from a Scottish émigré family or who were emigrants themselves would often be counted as Scots: a visit to any Scottish First World War memorial will show a significant number of Scots who died in Australian, New Zealand and Canadian forces. No doubt this debate would be arcane and academic to the families of loved ones who emigrated to the Dominions, but died in France or Turkey. Scotland was a point of mourning for her émigré sons, and naturally counted them among her dead.

That said, the evidence does suggest that Scots did die in greater numbers relative to the rest of the United Kingdom. Glasgow had a death tally of 18,000 or 1 in 57 of the population, which is higher than the British average of 1 in 62 (based on the 1921 census). Dundee's death rate was higher still, with 4,213 dead out of a population of 180,000, or 1 in 43, while Edinburgh suffered less, with 4,279 out of a population of 330,000, or 1 in 77. If Glasgow, falling between the highest and lowest death rates of the Scottish cities, was representative of Scotland as a whole, with just over a fifth of the Scottish population this would produce a figure of just over 90,000.

In some places the casualty rate was enormous. In Larbert in Stirlingshire, with a population of about 5,000, the death toll was 300, or 1 in 16 of the population, although this can be explained by the inclusion of many men who served in the nearby training camp. Also, when it is remembered that recruitment tended to be higher in the countryside and in small-town Scotland, then a total figure of 100,000 deaths seems not unreasonable. The fact that Scotland had a higher proportion of the population in the Volunteers (nearly three out of ten men aged between eighteen and forty-nine) and contributed a higher proportion of enlistments before conscription than the rest of the United Kingdom may help explain the higher death rate, in that the really savage losses were sustained in the first three years of war, when Scottish participation was highest. At the end of the day, 100,000 was the number that most Scots settled for.

Scotland was determined to grieve long and hard for her lost sons. Whereas the Cenotaph in London was simple in construction and erected with almost indecent haste, the Scottish War Memorial in Edinburgh Castle was completed only in 1927 after much painstaking and elaborate work. Designed by Sir Robert Lorimer and using stained glass by Douglas Strachan and other sculptors working in both stone and brass, the memorial was striking in that the only individual honoured was the Scottish commander of the British forces, Douglas Haig. The representations, in which war is neither glorified nor condemned, are of ordinary men and women. All aspects of the conflict are depicted, from the soldiers in the field to the workers in the factory. Even the pack animals are given their place. In the main Hall of Honour, each service and regiment has its own bay, and the overall impression is of the sacrifice of a society at war. Although historically a Protestant nation, Scotland was nevertheless keen on its martyrs, and throughout the nineteenth century statues went up to the Covenanters of the seventeenth century who sacrificed their lives in pursuit of religious liberty. In many ways the war memorial continued this trend, with fairly brutal and realistic representations of conflict and suffering.

Throughout Scotland monuments were erected in nearly every town and village, gardens were renamed in memory of the fallen, factory workshops, schools and universities put up plaques to the lost generation.

About 72 per cent of those who died were under thirty years old. Further-more, the majority were ordinary soldiers, with officers accounting for one in every thirteen. Yet it should not be assumed that fatalities dispropor-tionately hit the working class. Many of the keen young bucks who joined up in the early recruitment drive were from the middle class and chose to serve in the ranks before it was all over. Also, graduates were more likely to die than non-graduates, with the universities of Edinburgh and Glas-gow having a casualty rate 50 per cent higher than the average. The impact on rural Scotland was devastating, with scores of young men wiped out in many small towns and villages. With a quarter of the population living in settlements of less than a thousand people, the loss of so many young men was more keenly felt than in the more densely populated areas, where the loss could be hidden by greater numbers of people.

Many of those who returned were wounded. It is probable that some 150,000 to 200,000 Scots suffered some form of physical wound during the conflict. Some recovered, but many did not and were forced to fend for themselves for whatever reason. In the inter-war period there were a num-ber of reports in the Scottish press and 'letters to the editor' about the 'shameful' habit of displaying wounds and missing limbs while begging in the street. Many of the most seriously injured were packed off to 'homes' which specialized in care for the blind, infirm and shell-shocked, run by a variety of charities, the British Legion and voluntary agencies. Many of the worst casualties were thus hidden away. Those with a perma-nent injury which meant they could no longer work had to rely on the Poor Board to supplement a meagre pension: most of them were sent home and left to get on with it.

While there was much popular revulsion at war and the sacrifice of so many young lives, it has to be remembered that most who served in the forces were not wounded and survived to tell their tales. Statistically, although most Scots in the armed services did serve on the front line, the proportion of the army engaged at the front at any one time had dropped from 84 per cent in 1914 to 65 per cent by 1918, increasing the chances of survival. Also, those in the naval reserve and the flying corps (apart from the pilots) were mainly confined to a support role. That said, for most sol-diers a spell at the front would be the most traumatic experience of their lives. Nevertheless, Scottish men, no matter what they had seen or what ordeal they had survived, were expected to get on with things. Many enjoyed the comradeship, which continued after the war in the British Legion. Most were proud to have done their bit for King and Country, and this was reflected in the huge turnout at Armistice Day services through-out the country. In spite of protests from pacifists, humanists and Chris-tians, the cinemas continued to show a great many movies that glorified war, which still had considerable popular appeal. It would be the late twenties and the thirties before popular revulsion at war took a grip.

REVOLUTION

As stated in Chapter 1, the war unleashed expectations of a better future among many in the Scottish working class, especially in the industrial central belt. The sudden end of the war pushed unfinished business to the top of the agenda. For those who had staffed the war industries, issues of pay, conditions, rents and standards of living were the prime concerns. With socialism as a voice to articulate their demands, hopes were raised that more change was to come, and yet fears persisted that the gains of the war would be lost in the return to normality. It was a period of confusion. The coalition premier, Lloyd George, had raised expectations with his call for 'homes for heroes'. The news of revolution in Russia and elsewhere seemed to confirm to some socialist activists that the tide of history was moving in their direction. For others, of a different political persuasion, it was a tide which had to be stopped at all costs. As with all events in his-tory, most people would be swept along no matter what. The second phase of the Red Clyde can be broken down into two parts. First, there were the planning and activities of the socialist leaders. Second, there were the aspi-rations of the workers themselves. Sometimes these two parts married up; sometimes they remained distinct entities.

The war had transformed the productive capacity of the Scottish economy. New working techniques, new technology and productive streamlining had changed the way that things were done. The question now was, would things go back to the way they were before? Conflicting messages emerged from the workers. For some the preservation of craft guilds and distinctive ranking in the labour hierarchy remained the goal, with a demand to end the wartime practice of allowing unskilled workers to undertake certain jobs because of a skills shortage. Others, fearing the onset of unemployment as soldiers returned from the front, wanted to ensure that practices were changed to ensure that there was enough work to go round. Some believed that the craft differentials were a bar to working-class solidarity and that a combined push against the employers and the capitalist system would result in benefits for all. Some workers were protesting at local grievances which were restricted to particular issues such as the ending of overtime. Baser racial self-interest motivated those who rioted against 'coloured' labour being used in the Glasgow ports. All in all, it was a cacophony of protest to which the political leaders of the working class tried to give meaning.

For a government uneasy with events in Europe and facing a nationalist revolt in Ireland, it was too easy to take the self-appointed leaders of the working class at face value. That there was much discontent no one doubted. But to what extent it was driven by agitators and how far it would go were the big questions of the day. The Scottish Secretary, Robert Munro, a coalition Liberal who had dallied with the progressive wing of the party before the war, had no doubts that there was a Bolshevist rising in the offing. In this he was indicative of the degree of political realignment which many had experienced during the war. His suspicions were confirmed by the head of Special Branch, Sir Basil Thomson, who likewise detected a revolutionary conspiracy – although it should be pointed out that Sir Basil was prone to believe in conspiracies, being convinced that the Germans were involved in the industrial disputes of earlier years. The evidence for such fears centred around John Maclean and a number of confirmed radical socialists who were only too willing to demonstrate their revolutionary credentials. Maclean was imprisoned six times under the Defence of the Realm Act for his denunciation of the war and attempts to stir up protest.

Maclean stands out as a figure of mythic dimensions in Scottish history. He has emerged as a hero both of the left and of nationalists, with both factions claiming his mantle throughout the twentieth century. Austere, Calvinist and dour, he had that much admired virtue or vice so beloved of Scottish society, a conviction in his beliefs which defied the world. A self-taught and rigorous Marxist, Maclean had come to many of the same conclusions as Lenin, believing that the bourgeois phase in history could be overturned at an opportune moment and the proletariat could seize control. He was inspired by events in Ireland, seeing them as evidence that Britain – one of the world's two dominant capitalist states, the other being the United States – was undergoing defeat from within, and argued that the Irish nationalists should be supported. If Britain and its empire could be undermined from within, he believed, then a future global war with the United States could be avoided. Otherwise, he believed, under the capitalist system the two largest powers would inevitably be drawn into conflict in competition for a dwindling number of markets. Maclean's reading of the political situation in Scotland was complex, and it can rightly be doubted that many people understood his prognosis, let alone agreed with it. But his programme was simple: a united working class would use its industrial muscle to bring the state to a halt with industrial and social protest, and the workers would take over. Yet, timing would be crucial to the endeavour.

Although Maclean had little contact with or knowledge of the thoughts of his fellow European revolutionaries, he was remarkably prescient in his prognosis. He rejected a reformist or parliamentary road to socialism, on the grounds that the capitalist system had the power to quickly and effectively regenerate itself. Like Lenin and Karl Liebknecht, he realised that timing and opportunity would be vital to the success of a revolution. Maclean believed that in 1919, with mounting industrial chaos, there was a golden opportunity to overthrow the system. Industrial, social and economic grievances had to be harnessed to a programme of political action, and Maclean was pragmatic in supporting wider causes as part of an overall strategy of socialist revolution. Unlike many fellow-travellers on the left, Maclean did not believe that the resolution of individual grievances would amount to much on its own: it had to be part of a concerted programme.

While Maclean certainly had the intellectual apparatus to diagnose the revolutionary potential in Scotland at the end of the war, he lacked leadership skills. An obdurate and dogmatic man, he believed his skills of Marxist analysis outweighed all other considerations. He was keen to make alliances with Scottish and Irish nationalists in order to help prevent what he saw as the looming clash with the United States in the global competition for markets. Likewise, he was prepared to support those strikers who were keen to preserve their craft rights at the expense of creating a unified working class with a common political agenda. For Maclean, pragmatism was the order of the day, and anything which would undermine the authority of the capitalist system had to be supported. He spoke out in favour of the land-raiding crofters, who were dismissed by fellow Marxists as wanting to turn the clock back to a peasant society in the Western Highlands. Maclean believed this would undermine the authority of the state, which would need naval bases in the Western Isles for the forthcoming war with America. Although it may seem crazy to us today, his belief that the United States and Britain would become enemies was not that eccentric at the time: it was a view held by the Admiralty during the twenties. Maclean's accommodation and pragmatism, however, did not extend to his dealings with fellow-travellers, whom he denounced for their misreading of the political situation.

After the defeat of the 'forty hours' strike (see below), Maclean believed that the opportune time for revolution had been missed and that a broad-left alliance was needed to galvanise working-class interests and keep the revolutionary pot on the boil. Education, according to Maclean, was central to the project, in order to explain to the workers how their grievances fitted into an international plan of revolution. If poor wages and bad social conditions were shown to be the result of a global capitalist system which affected all workers, then the sectional and national differences which had hampered the emergence of the working class as a mass united political movement would be removed, paving the way for unity. The blinkers, he argued, would fall from the workers' eyes. Fellow-travellers on the left, led by William Gallacher, taking their orders from Moscow, believed that a separate revolutionary party (which was to become the Communist Party of Great Britain) adhering to the International Comintern should lead the working class. Maclean profoundly rejected this approach on the grounds that Lenin was misinformed about the revolutionary potential in Scotland and the rest of Great Britain and that the strategy did not take sufficient account of the specific and peculiar local circumstances at the time. As far as Maclean was concerned, it was a strategy doomed to failure, and his constant harping on this quickly led to his isolation.

The Communist Party insisted on strict discipline and conformity and could not accommodate Maclean, whose principles were not for compromise. Relations between the two were made worse by Maclean's belief that the party was infiltrated by British intelligence. His isolation was further compounded by some basic weaknesses in his strategy. He had little time for organisation, and his campaigns usually consisted of himself and a few trusted colleagues pounding themselves into the ground touring the factory gates and street corners. He was brutally honest and, although standing as a revolutionary candidate at local and general elections, after it became clear that a groundswell of support was not forthcoming for his Scottish Workers Republican Party he would tell the electors that if they could not vote for him then they should vote for the official Labour candidate. His lack of moderation – and some might say a martyr complex – meant that he would spend half of his time after the war in jail for inflammatory speeches. His inability to compromise meant that he could find no real allies on the mainstream left, and his forthright views that the hungry and unemployed should just take food, on the grounds that it would be a legitimate revolutionary act, embarrassed moderate Labour leaders. His isolation was demonstrated by the fact that, although he was in jail for inflammatory speeches, Labour leaders were prepared to appeal for leniency on the grounds that he was more of an eccentric than a real revolutionary threat. They were right.

Years of constant nervous exhaustion, exacerbated by continuous spells in prison and a fanatic self-imposed working schedule, took their toll. On 30 November 1923 Maclean, aged forty-four, died of pneumonia after a punishing life dedicated to the cause of the working class. Some 10,000 attended his funeral, and in death his fellow-travellers could now safely place laurels on this man of principle whom they were sure history would forget.

Maclean was not forgotten, however, though his place in Scottish history remains ambiguous and has been determined largely by swings of the Scottish political pendulum. By the far left, desperate to recover a credible figure from an otherwise stagnant history of socialism in Scotland, he has been portrayed as the lost leader of the lost revolution, while some nationalists have sought to portray him as a far-sighted founder of an independent Scottish republic. For most, however, he has been a peripheral figure who did not fit in with either Scottish nationalism or the moderatism of moderate Labour. His legacy may be disputed, but it has largely been disputed by the fringe. With the collapse of Communism, it may now be an opportune time to reassess Maclean's legacy and secure his place among the mainstream.

Maclean was first and foremost a humanitarian whose sense of social justice fuelled his passion for political change. He believed with utter conviction that in Marxism he had both a prognosis of and a solution to the many social ills which faced not just Scottish society, but the world as a whole. First and foremost Maclean was an internationalist, and it is only in this context that his ideas can be understood. He was one of many European socialists who in the aftermath of the carnage of the First World War believed that the time was right to create a new social order. An obsession with the technicalities of his political thought tends to obscure the basic fact that Maclean believed in a better and more just society. Given his outlook, there is no doubt that the excesses of the Soviet Union would have appalled him had he lived. Also, in spite of his Marxist convictions, he was a pragmatist who believed that his ideology had to be flexible enough to fit in with the exigencies of the time. He believed that a Marxist analysis held the solution to society's problems, but that that solution was by no means self-evident and had to be worked at. His was a complex Marxism. Above all, Maclean was an idealist and a man of principle. He displayed many of the characteristics so beloved by the Scots in their heroes. As dogmatic and unbending as William Wallace, Mary Queen of Scots, John Knox or any of the persecuted seventeenth-century Covenanters, Maclean ensured his immortality by martyrdom.

ANGER AND A WORLD TO WIN

If John Maclean and some of his revolutionary fellow-travellers had only an occasional and somewhat fleeting relationship with the working class, it is perhaps worth remembering their motivation. Political ideas do not exist in a vacuum and, although they may have an ambiguous relationship with society, it is instructive to examine the context in which they were created and used. Compared with its progress in the pre-war era, socialism, however defined, spread like a virus through wartime Scotland. The reasons for this are not hard to find. As was mentioned in Chapter 1, the war created increased expectations among Scottish workers, who were now learning that they could achieve material and political improvements through their own efforts. And many improvements were needed. Frustrations over generations spent in inadequate housing and grinding poverty, and lives subject to chance in which unemployment, death and disease could suddenly strike, made for many potential converts. A war which showed the leaders to be incompetent and selfish added fuel to a sense of outrage and injustice. The dam of accepting one's lot in life had burst. Socialism seemed to offer a way out of the grinding poverty and bad social conditions which had been the fate of most Scots for generations.

During the war, housing emerged as the key social problem in the political arena. The Royal Commission on the Housing of the Industrial Population of Scotland reported in 1917 that it would take a quarter of a million new homes to rectify the problem. Half the population lived in one- or two-roomed housing with all the difficulties associated with poor sanitation and overcrowding. Housing conditions in the countryside were little better, in spite of the common perception of a healthier lifestyle there. The roots of the problem can be traced back to a number of features associated with urban development in the nineteenth century.

First, there were the peculiarities of Scottish building laws, which meant that houses were constructed in an expensive way – of high-quality stone and bricks to a certain thickness – and were subject to the anachronistic legal mechanism of feuing. Feus – perpetual leases of land at a fixed rate – mean that, to avoid loss of earnings through inflation, the seller would charge as much as possible. Furthermore, land for building was subject to speculative purchase, pushing up its price. This meant that Scottish housing was expensive to construct and the land purchase was costly due to feus. Housebuilding was usually done by firms who would borrow money from banks and investment trusts, and the most effective way to maximize the return on building was to build as close together as possible – thus cutting down on wasted land, which was expensive – and to divide the building into as many rentable units as possible, to maximize the revenue return, which could be used to pay off the loan as quickly as possible and so cut down interest payments.

Second, added to the peculiarities of Scottish land-purchase and building laws was the nature of Scottish society and of the economy itself.

In real terms, standards of living in Scotland lagged by 10 per cent behind those in the rest of the United Kingdom, so there was a shortage of people willing to pay for adequate housing. Also, the Scottish economy was highly dependent on exports, which were subject to periodic upturns and downswings. This meant that short interludes of unemployment were a reality for many workers. In such circumstances it was necessary to reduce the weekly family outgoings to a minimum, so that lean times could be accommodated, and rent was the single largest item of expenditure.

Third, and especially in the industrial towns, much housing was owned by the employers, who used the threat of eviction as a means of maintaining control over workers. The quest to maximize profits meant that conditions were bad, and improvements few.

Finally, bad Scottish housing was a profitable source of investment which secured a good return even for those who lived in only marginally less appalling conditions. The various friendly societies and building societies in which all canny working-class Scots saved for a rainy day invested in housing to provide a secure return. Evidence of this can be seen in the fact that, in 1914, three-quarters of all new housing built in Glasgow was one- or two-roomed accommodation.

When housing emerged as a major political problem during the war, it had deep roots which went back into the nineteenth century. And although it emerged as a key issue during the rent strike on the Clyde in 1915, it was a problem which affected the whole of Scotland. Some random statistics illustrate the extent of the problem. In the industrial towns of Kilsyth, Coatbridge and Wishaw between a quarter and a third of the population lived more than four people per room; in Clydebank, Motherwell, Cowdenbeath, Hamilton, Airdrie and Barrhead four out of ten people lived more three per room; in Glasgow almost six out of ten lived more than two people per room; in Dundee it was almost half the population; in Aberdeen it was just over a third, while in Edinburgh it was just under a third. Even Inverness in the Highlands had a quarter of its population living at more than two per room. According to the census of 1911 just over 2 million Scots lived more than two per room, just over a million lived more than three per room, and nearly 400,000 lived more than four per room. In short, three-quarters of the population were living in overcrowded conditions. Furthermore, it should be remembered that, in the official counting of such figures, two children were counted as one person. So in reality 'three people' living in two rooms was more than likely to be one man, one woman and two children.

The Rent Restrictions Act of 1915, although pegging rents for the duration of the war, meant that landlords skipped improvements and repairs to cover lost profits and, given the financially unfavourable climate during the war, housebuilding virtually ceased. The housing stock at the end of the war was in worse repair than at the start. The gradual extension of municipal powers in the field of health, housing and sanitation during the war did little to help the situation, mainly because health inspectors were reluctant to use their full powers to condemn and close poor housing, believing that it would only create homelessness and lead to further over-crowding. The extent of the problem can be illustrated by a comparison with England. Overcrowding in Glasgow was three times more dense than in London, five times worse than in Leeds, and seven times greater than in Liverpool. Even by the late twenties the figures had failed to improve. It was reported that Glasgow had 27 per cent of the population living more than three per room, Edinburgh 12 per cent, Liverpool 2 per cent and Birmingham and Manchester 1 per cent. Edinburgh, which was Scotland's least overcrowded urban conurbation, was only slightly better than England's most overcrowded city, Sunderland.

From medical reports, official investigations, autobiographies and photographs it is possible to reconstruct what living conditions were like, although it is probably difficult for today's generation to comprehend the degree of wretchedness associated with such bad housing. Rooms in city tenements were about fourteen feet long and from six to twelve feet wide. They were badly lit, with no more than one window, which may have had sunlight blocked out by neighbouring buildings. Often the walls were roughcast, with no wallpaper. Space was at a premium, and pots, pans and other kitchen utensils would be hung up on the wall. There was little ventilation, and the first thing that would have struck the modern visitor was the smell. In the days before perfumed soap and deodorants, the smell of body odour was pervasive, cooking in such small spaces meant that smells from the stove lingered constantly; the air would often be damp, as washing was hung up to dry indoors; and, depending on the sanitation habits of your neighbours, some of whom might be infirm or drunk, the smell of urine and worse could float through the tenement. Some neighbours could be dreadful:

> There was a dirty woman in a nearby close, quiet and self-effacing, who stank to high heaven and we took the smell with the personality, but I gave her a wide berth just the same. I was sternly forbidden to borrow a comb from any of her children in case I borrowed a few beasts at the same time. My mother had vowed that when she had been speaking to her she'd been horrified to see the beasts running around the wools which tied the woman's specs to her ears! I made an excuse to go to her door, and staring fixedly at the wool holding the specs, noted without as much as a shudder that my mother was right. It was no exaggeration.
>
> Molly Weir, *Shoes Were for Sunday* (London, 1970)

Noise was another feature of cramped conditions. The screams and shouts of children were a constant; the rows and altercations of neighbours could alternately be a source of entertainment or of disturbance. Privacy was an unknown concept. In such cramped conditions an escape to the WC might have been a possible opportunity for private contemplation, but most families had to share their WC with others, and stories from the time tell of queues and a constant stream of traffic. Bathing was another problem, with less than half of the population having access to a fixed bath. The habit in many Scottish homes was for the men to go out on a Friday so that the women and girls in the house could have a bath in privacy. Given such conditions, it should come as no surprise to find that, when the opportunity arose, most left the home to pursue pastimes outside. Men would meet and talk in pubs and clubs, women would gather to chat in the entrance to closes or on the drying greens, and children would play outside. That the population of the Scottish working class gathered together in these areas was obviously a factor in helping the spread of socialism.

Disease and bad health were other major problems associated with Scottish living conditions. Respiratory disease was the biggest killer, especially tuberculosis. Poor sanitation, particularly the widespread use of chamber pots and outside earth closets, encouraged disease. The close con-

fined nature of the tenements and the back-to-back houses in the industrial towns meant that infections which passed by contagion spread like
wildfire. Many diseases and illnesses were work-associated, especially in
the mining, metal, chemical and engineering industries, where poor ventilation and close proximity to gas, dust and industrial pollutants took
their toll particularly in later life. Diseases such as scarlet fever, whooping
cough, diphtheria and measles contributed to a high infant mortality rate.
The influenza epidemic of 1918 contributed to a high death toll among
both young and old. Infant mortality rates were about one in ten in the
decade of the Great War, and there was a strong correlation between survival and social conditions. The poorer the housing and the greater the
poverty, the less chance an infant had of making it to the first birthday. In
1926 the medical officer of Edinburgh reported that the death rate from
tuberculosis was 30 per 10,000 for one-roomed housing, 19 per 10,000
for two-roomed housing, and 9 per 10,000 for three-roomed housing.
Most children growing up in Scotland in the twenties could expect to
experience the death of a sibling or have friends who had a brother or sister who died.

In response to such conditions, many areas developed a strong sense
of community, which was a practical way to overcome these pressing difficulties of everyday life. Childcare was practically run on a communal
basis, with mothers and grandmothers sharing in the burden of looking
after youngsters, especially during illness or at times when it was difficult
to cope. Families were by their nature extended, with most members living near to each other. This meant that they could be called upon in an
emergency. Grandparents (mainly women, as men had a tendency to die
young) were a feature of everyday life, helping around the house and looking after children. With meagre pensions, if any, those too old to work
became dependent on children. Poverty was overcome by the helping
hands of neighbours and family. Social problems associated with childcare,
drunkenness or crime were just as like to be resolved by communal action
as by the authorities.

While it is easy to develop a rosy view of the past, in which community spirit meant that doors were never locked, the harsh reality was that
such a way of life was first and foremost a practical necessity for survival.
In the days before the Welfare State, such methods of self-help were the

only option open to most people. They bred a fierce sense of independence in which interference by the local authorities would be associated with the badge of shame: being unable to cope was something that most families would not contemplate. The feeding of children by local authorities, or being taken in the 'fever van', or having your house inspected by a health visitor, was seen as a major encroachment on personal freedom. Hence the extended family was more than willing to help out in order to deflect the knowing glances of neighbours who would gossip about an inability to manage.

Although people were poor, they were proud. This is an important point to stress, because, while our conventional understanding of social-ism has much to do with notions of state intervention, for many ordinary Scots at that time it had more to do with social justice. The idea that the state should give handouts to the poor was anathema. It went against tra-ditional notions of independence and standing on one's own two feet. Handouts were for beggars and ne'er do wells, not for respectable working folk. Rather, a sense of injustice was fuelled by a belief that workers' labour received insufficient reward. The idea that a man should be able to make a 'living wage' which would support him and his family in a reason-able degree of comfort was the driving force behind most industrial agita-tion. In the campaign for better housing, the predominant idea was that workers were being exploited by rapacious landlords, who overcharged for shoddy living conditions. Traditional notions of hard work and independ-ence were a further factor in the campaign against landlords, who were demonised to a greater extent than the bosses. The reason why landlords were castigated and why socialism chimed with the traditional notions of social justice was that, unlike the workers, who had to labour for a living, landlords made their money out of interest. This seemed very unfair, in that those with capital were destined to keep getting capital by no other virtue than of having it in the first place. Also, it was apparent that those who had no capital were at a distinct disadvantage and could be exploited by those who had. As the workers' only asset was labour, it had to be pro-moted and valued to compete with the capitalists' money on a level play-ing field.

The same idea was used to bolster support for the co-operative move-ment. Providing shops which operated on the basis of selling goods at a reasonable price for the benefit of the community, rather than for private profit, chimed with traditional notions of self-help. Such shops also provided a concrete demonstration of the inequities of capitalism, for a factor in stoking up working-class resentment at the end of the war was the unfair allocation of rations to co-operative stores. Adverts for the co-op featured a 'capitalist' holding bags of money being pressed down with a large thumb and bore the slogan 'Stop the profiteer, shop at the co-operative.' It was a simple message and a much reduced version of socialism, but one that made sense to most working people.

The 'forty hours' strike and the 'riot' in George Square in Glasgow in January 1919 were seen by many as marking the high point of revolutionary fervour in Scotland. Up to 70,000 workers, mainly in Glasgow and the west, went on strike to support the engineers' call for a maximum forty-hour week. The engineers were worried that there was insufficient work to go round, and limiting the amount of hours worked in a week was one way of maintaining full employment. Also, the working day itself was long and hard. According to Harry McShane, a socialist activist and engineer:

> Up to 1914 our week was 54 hours. All working people, including boys and girls, started at 6 a.m. and finished at 5.30 p.m., and worked until noon on Saturdays. During the war it had been extended to a 12 hour day and Saturday and Sunday working. The six o'clock start was miserable: you had to get up at five, and you couldn't go out or do anything at night because you would tire yourself out for the morning. When I worked at Dalmuir during the war I had to get out of the house before five to get the ferry to Anderston Cross and the train to Dalmuir; there were no lights on the train, nobody spoke, and the only sign of life was a spark from somebody's pipe. To get the hours reduced would be a victory for us all as well as helping unemployment.
>
> Harry McShane and Joan Smith, *No Mean Fighter* (London, 1978)

On 31 January a huge crowd of perhaps as many as 100,000 people gathered in George Square to support the strike and protest at the end of the Rent Restrictions Act. It was buoyed up by a sense of injustice over incompetent generals who had sacrificed their men in a long, futile and bloody war, rising prices, and restraints in working conditions, and the demonstrators enjoyed hearing their grievances aired by their own folk, instead of self-appointed representatives. Workers were anxious that the ending of wartime controls would mean a return to the bad old pre-war days when trade unionism was weak and employers could act with impunity. Women appalled at poor housing and social conditions, and many having lost valuable wartime employment, swelled the crowd, together with demobilised soldiers who had returned to find that their jobs no longer existed.

The authorities suspected a rising, and they should not be dismissed as panickers. Six tanks and 12,000 soldiers from south of the border were dispatched to Glasgow in case things should turn nasty. Poor police control led to a riot, with the workers' leaders and demonstrators being batoned by panicky policemen in an effort to disperse the crowd. The fighting was fierce, with violence spreading out into neighbouring streets. Some policemen who were isolated from their colleagues were stripped and sent packing, to the amusement of the crowd. They were the lucky ones, as other were given a hiding by a baying mob. Shops were wrecked, and there was sporadic looting. At a reconvened gathering at Glasgow Green later in the day, the police were repulsed by ex-servicemen.

According to a broadsheet issued by the ILP, the police intervention was further evidence of the authorities' determination to crush the working-class movement:

The outrage looks like a prearranged affair by the master class. As arranged on Wednesday, a deputation of the Joint Committee ... waited on the Lord Provost in the City Chambers, to receive the reply from the Prime Minister and the Minister of Labour, in response to his Lordship's open appeal for government intervention ... The Deputation were kept waiting for twenty minutes, and, while there, the police were ordered to draw their batons and forcibly disperse the crowd of strikers who were standing in George Square until the Deputation returned ... Those who appealed for order were also clubbed, as were other strikers, who were quietly inclined, as was shown by their defenceless condition ... The bludgeon attack on the strikers in front of the City Chambers was deliberately ordered by the officers, and was unprovoked. The attack was sheer brutality by the police to satisfy the lust of the masters for broken skulls. The masters, afraid to do their own dirty work, employ the police to do it for them.

Although there were injuries, there were no deaths, which might well have provoked an angry backlash. Where that would have led, no one can say, but similar riots in Europe which resulted in the deaths of protesters did not end peacefully. The extent to which the 'riot' was almost a revolution is impossible to say, as revolutions have their own critical point at which the momentum becomes unstoppable. That point is known only when it is reached, and how far away it was on Friday 31 January 1919, no one can say.

The following day there was no mass protest and things returned to normal with crowds at the football rather than in George Square. Just in case, however, troops were stationed in machine-gun nests at strategic points in the city, with tanks held in reserve. The authorities' unease was demonstrated by their choosing not to deploy troops from Maryhill Barracks in Glasgow, for fear that their loyalty might waiver.

The government promised to continue the statutory regulation of wages and rents for the time being, and in so doing removed one major grievance. The strike petered out after a mere sixteen days, but not before the engineers won a forty-seven-hour week. They could now start at eight in the morning, rather than six.

REFORMISM

The events of 1918 and 1919 took place at a dramatic speed, and few were able to digest the significance of what was happening. It was a confusing time. Labour had made a limited electoral breakthrough and won seven Scottish seats in the general election with almost a quarter of the vote. Most expected more to come. In the municipal elections of the following year the party did better than expected and notched up an impressive performance. What this seemed to demonstrate was that the electoral road, rather than revolution, was the best way to socialism. In any case, most of the leaders and representatives of the Labour Party were moderates. Those in favour of revolution were a minority. The failure of the 'forty hours' strike and the demonstration by the state that it would have no truck with militants helped to reinforce the message that gradualism was the best way forward. The Marxism of John Maclean failed to resonate with the Scottish working class.

Largely the reason for this was the considerable degree of continuity between pre- and post-war politics. Labour was able to present itself as the heir to the Scottish radical tradition. Indeed, an examination of Labour and Liberal manifestos reveals remarkably little difference between them. Labour advanced many of the same causes as its Liberal predecessors: land reform, temperance, home rule and social reform. Also, the movement was heavily influenced by a pre-war tradition which stressed legality, Christianity and traditional values. The editor of *Forward,* the socialist weekly newspaper, boasted that it was not read in the slums. The leaders of the labour movement such as the Revd James Barr, Neil Maclean, Thomas Johnston, James Maxton, David Kirkwood and John Wheatley were teetotallers to a man and were representative of the skilled, respectable working class. The soulless, theoretical, and abstract excesses of Marxism went against their very nature, which inclined towards an almost missionary crusade against social injustice, informed more by ethical and moral considerations than by didactic analysis.

The 'reds' were not to have it all their own way. In many ways one of the most remarkable features of post-war Scottish politics was the realignment on the right and the 'strange death of liberal Scotland'. In the post-war era, the Conservatives made an astonishing transformation from a minority in the days before 1914 (after the 1910 general elections a popular joke was that Scotland's Tory MPs could fit into two railway carriages) into a well-organised and coherent mainstream political party. Although hampered by the coalition of Lloyd George, in which they were the majority party but under the leadership of a Liberal, the Scottish Tories emerged from the general election of December 1918 with an impressive thirty-two seats and 30 per cent of the popular vote. Additionally, a further nineteen 'National' Liberals, their coalition partners, were elected with a fifth of the vote. Few doubted that the National Liberals were bound to the Tory Party and dependent on the Conservatives, so where no Tory was standing they could stand against Labour opponents with no danger of splitting the anti-socialist vote. Furthermore, the Liberal Party organisation had collapsed as a result of the split between Lloyd George and Asquith, meaning that National Liberal candidates were dependent on Conservative organisation. The once mighty Liberal Party which had dominated pre-war Scotland was trashed, winning a paltry fifteen seats with 15 per cent of the vote. Its humiliation was complete with the ejection of its leader, Herbert Asquith, from his seat in East Fife by an independent Tory candidate. One factor in explaining the former premier's defeat was his pre-war opposition to votes for women, as middle-class women – who quickly registered for the franchise – took their revenge on the 'bumbling old fool'. That said, if the combined National and independent Liberal votes and MPs were added together, the Liberals were still the largest party in terms of numbers of MPs and share of the popular vote. Although doomed to decline, this was not apparent at the time.

Politics in the post-war period had to operate in the changed circumstances of the 1918 Representation of the People Act, which extended the vote to all adult males over twenty-one and women over the age of thirty. At a stroke the electorate almost tripled, from 779,000 in 1910 to 2,205,000 in 1918. That said, there were difficulties in getting all the new voters registered. Only 60 per cent of the electorate voted in 1918, compared to 75 per cent in 1922, when Labour made its electoral breakthrough to become the largest party in Scotland.

Historians are still divided on how the class composition of the electorate was reflected in the increased numbers of voters. It is estimated that some 40 per cent of all adult males in Scotland did not have the vote before 1918, and it is easy to assume that, given the property qualifications formerly attached to the vote – requiring ownership or a certain rental value of one's residence – the bulk of the new electorate would be drawn from the working class. Yet there are a number of problems with this assumption. A great many middle-class men (particularly those at the lower end of the social spectrum, such as clerks and lower management) lived with parents and in lodgings until they had the necessary financial independence to sustain a respectable married lifestyle. Also, this group tended to be concentrated in geographical areas such as Hillhead in Glasgow, Morningside in Edinburgh or Broughty Ferry near Dundee which were quite close to working-class areas, and now that they too were entitled to vote they tended to dilute the support for Labour. Certainly one factor in explaining the difference between the 1918 and 1922 general-election results and turnout was the fact that the newly enfranchised middle class were quicker off the mark in getting themselves registered in 1918. Voting was part of a culture they were used to. The same can be said about women over thirty, as middle-class men marched their spouses off to the registration office to hold back the red menace which was considered an even greater threat than wives with independent minds.

There are a number of reasons why working-class registration was slower. First, there was the problem of demobilisation, which meant that many servicemen were not registered in time; given the class composition of the services, this worked against increasing working-class representation. Second, there was some ignorance and a distrust of officialdom which kept many potential working-class voters away. Third, there was more of the working class to register.

Hard and fast generalisations about the impact of the franchise reform are difficult because of the geographical complexity of the electorate. In the countryside, for example, reform had little impact. In the big cities and dense urban conurbations, it did make a difference. As mentioned earlier, in the towns and cities overcrowding was endemic. Given that the average age of marriage in the twenties was about twenty-six for men, this meant that a considerable proportion of young men in Scotland who were living at home were new to the franchise in these overcrowded areas. Also, there was a high proportion of labour which was casual and subject to much moving around between addresses. These men and some women who failed to qualify for the vote before 1918 would now find themselves able to vote for the first time.

It was a complex and demanding task to organise and marshal the full potential working-class vote, but by 1922 this had been done. Evidence of this is to be found in the general election in 1922, when Labour won twenty-nine seats in Scotland and supported an independent prohibitionist (who defeated the most anti-prohibitionist Winston Churchill) in Dundee and a Communist in Motherwell. The party's share of the Scottish vote went up to about a third on a larger turnout than in 1918; the Tories had about a quarter, the independent Liberals a fifth and the National Liberals 15 per cent. The political map in Scotland broadly indicated a divide between industrial, densely populated areas, which voted Labour, and largely rural areas, which voted either Liberal or Tory. In line with the increasing registration of voters, Labour did well in the cities, winning ten out of Glasgow's fifteen seats and doing well in Dundee and Aberdeen, although bourgeois Edinburgh proved resistant. Before 1918, in Dundee and Glasgow only about half of the adult males were entitled to vote, in contrast with Edinburgh, where nearly seven out of ten men could vote. This illustrates the impact both of property qualifications before the war and of the increasing working-class representation after it. Undoubtedly, Labour was the main beneficiary of electoral reform. Again, while Labour won a seat in Aberdeen, it made little impact in the rural hinterland of the north-east; nor did its impact stretch beyond the industrial heartland of Dundee into the Perth and Tayside countryside. But in the western industrial belt – in towns like Airdrie, Coatbridge, Hamilton and Motherwell – Labour did make advances, and also in the coal-mining areas of Fife.

Arguably, much of the chaos following the end of the war had died down by 1922, allowing for a more settled pursuit of politics. The campaign in 1918 had been conducted in an almost hysterical bout of patriotic fervour, with promises to hang the Kaiser, and this was probably not conducive to rational political choice among the electorate. Also, much of the fervour of the Red Clyde had faded by 1922. The 'forty hours' strike had passed, and industrial conflict and tension, though not at an end, were easing. The revolutionary tide had been stemmed, and milder rhetoric was to be heard alongside the wildmen of socialism.

Another factor in explaining the rise of Labour in 1922 was the ending of the coalition government. Although the British Conservative rank and file were keen to ditch Lloyd George, their Scottish colleagues were more hesitant, believing that the red menace was already battering at the gates and that an end to the alliance with the Liberals would split the anti-socialist vote. Such was their fear that many informal local alliances continued between Liberals and Conservatives determined to stop Labour in its tracks.

For moderates in the Labour Party, the electoral triumph of 1922 confirmed them in the belief that the parliamentary route was the best way to socialism. This did not stop many such as James Maxton from indulging in firebrand politics. Maxton declared that he wanted 'nothing more than to see aristocrat-ridden, English-ridden Scotland turned into a free socialist Commonwealth' according to the April 1924 edition of *Scottish Home Rule*. Such statements could be taken at face value, and many middle-class Scots did take them so, but it ought to be remembered that rhetoric of this kind was a great crowd-pleaser and there was a long radical tradition, stretching back before the war, of using over-the-top language. It would take getting used to, but it was very similar to classic nineteenth-century political polemic, only employing a socialist vocabulary.

THE MIDDLE CLASS STRIKE BACK

Just as remarkable as the emergence of politicised working-class consciousness was the emergence of a remarkably coherent anti-socialist front in Scotland. Anti-socialism was of such significance that it made uneasy bedfellows of Liberals and Conservatives, whose principal rivalry was based on claims as to who was best able to keep Scotland free from the red spectre. The Liberals pushed notions of class conciliation, while the Tories were more inclined to class war. It was the more bellicose attitude of the Conservatives that seems to have resonated more with Scotland's propertied classes. A miner attending Edinburgh's Royal Infirmary in November 1920 was asked by the consultant if he was on strike. When the man replied that he was, the doctor refused to treat him, saying that he was on strike too. The wartime rhetoric of 'Bayonet the Boche' was amended to 'Bayonet the Bolshevik' after 1918, and the Tories always used the word 'Bolshevik', which sounded more foreign and threatening than 'Communist' or 'socialist'.

In promoting themselves as the saviour from socialism, the Conservatives were quicker off the mark than the Liberals, who were still racked by acrimonious disputes between the Asquith and Lloyd George factions. The Tories recognised the need for effective and efficient organisation, and party membership in Scotland rose from 7,000 in 1913 to 20,000 in 1922. The party machine was overhauled, with greater emphasis placed on propaganda and on creating an effective constituency organisation which could undertake the tasks of canvassing and campaigning at elections. Ancillary organisations such as the Junior Imperial League, the

Middle Class Union and the Young Unionists were formed to add weight to the official party structure. Also, conservative (with a small 'c') organisations such as the Women's Institute, the Boys' Brigade and the Churches were called upon to shore up traditional values which were conducive to maintaining Tory support.

Whereas the Conservative Party had been associated with diehards and reactionaries before the war, its message in the post-war era was one that was modern, and it now reached out to include new target areas for support, namely women, the young, and rural communities. The Scottish Unionist Archives record that Lady Baxter toured village halls and explained to the female audiences the 'horrors of Bolshevism and that it was neither wise nor kind to protect them from such knowledge, however unpleasant'. The Conservative message of Christian family values was targeted at women, who were reminded that socialism was godless atheism. The appeal to 'mum' and her responsibility for the family's well-being was one that struck a chord among many of those Scottish women who believed in the gendered and patriarchal society. Also, it should be pointed out that the very masculine emphasis of Tory propaganda probably struck a chord with many Scottish men. War records, sporting achievements and 'having done one's duty' were frequently paraded on individual Conservative manifestos, and Tory candidates were contrasted with Liberal and Labour opponents who, if in not so many words, were denounced as shirkers and unmanly. In contrast to the rather sexless message of the Liberal and Labour parties, the Conservatives appealed to 'real' men and 'real' women.

Rural Scotland was an important target area for the Tories. The war had taken its toll on the traditional large estates. With rising income and local tax and increasing wages, many landowners found that they could not afford to maintain their traditional lifestyle. With such changes came instability as domestic staff were cut back and unemployment affected the great estates. About a fifth of all Scottish land changed hands between 1918 and 1921, establishing a pattern which would be repeated through the inter-war period as the great estates contracted. Such changes created opportunities for tenant farmers to buy their own land. Although the numbers who did so never rose above a fifth of the total, farmers' income rose by 500 per cent between 1914 and 1920 and if the money was not invested in buying land it was invested in machinery and equipment.

Whereas land reform was a great political issue before the war, it lost much of its momentum after 1918. The newly created class of farmers who, if not yet owner occupiers, had aspirations in that direction was a ready-made clientele for the Conservative Party. Labour's advocacy of land nationalisation was rejected out of hand as the mutterings of those who did not know what they were taking about, and the Liberals' pre-war association with land reform now came back to haunt them in a countryside where there were more actual and aspirant landowners than ever.

The spread of unionisation among rural labourers also brought a whiff of class tension to rural Scotland, enabling the Tories to present the spectre of socialism as something alien, urban and industrial which had no place in the countryside. And the activities of Highland land raiders who, in response to land shortages, simply set up shop on estates were regarded with terror among Lowland landowners, who were appalled at the prospect of the industrial masses turning up to take over their land. In the 1924 general election the Tories were able to capture twenty-two county seats from the Liberals, revealing that the party's rural strategy was paying dividends and that the Conservatives were now regarded as the party of the countryside.

The Tories also appealed to the young, aspirant and affluent. Birthday cards were sent to twenty-one-year-olds, and recruitment drives were made in the universities. There may have been much poverty and misery in Scotland, but there were also many young people determined to enjoy themselves without having a conscience about the have-nots, and the Conservative clubs were adept at promoting this culture of 'young bucks' and of having a good time. Social functions played on the aspirations of those lower down the social scale who wanted to 'better' themselves, and offering the chance to hobnob with a duke or an earl (usually in the presence of a hundred others) was one way to pull in the crowds.

The Conservative Party underwent a social transformation of its own during this period, with an increasing proportion of MPs being businessmen and professionals rather than from the landowning class, thus more accurately reflecting the social composition of its core support. The party also was able to call upon a new generation of politicians like Bob Boothby, Noel Skelton, Walter Elliot and John Buchan, whose values and ideas were not as far removed from those of the general population as were those of the old diehards. Indeed, it was even possible for them to advance socially progressive ideas such as those in Skelton's *Property-Owning Democracy*, which was published in 1924. By touring the various business, Rotary and other middle-class social functions, these new Scottish Tories were able to consolidate firm support.

The real loser in the post-war polarisation of Scottish politics was the Liberal Party, which was squeezed out of the middle ground. By no means inevitable, the Liberals were caught between the rock of acting as an anti-socialist bulwark and the hard place of advancing progressive social policies of their own. On both counts they were outbid by their respective competitors. While rejecting socialism as a cure for the nation's desperate social problems, the Liberals acknowledged that there was much legitimacy in working-class aspirations. Harking back to the new liberalism of the Edwardian era, they believed that socially progressive reforms would wean the working class away from socialism and stave off the threat of revolution. It was, they argued, in society's best interests to tackle the deep-seated problems of poverty. Yet much of this rhetoric had a hollow ring. After all, when the party had been in government its reforms had been minimal. Also, it had seemed to support the bosses during the war. Against the claims of Labour, which had an authentic working-class voice, the Liberals seemed jaded and worn-out. Additionally, the party had lost the support of a number of prominent radicals who now felt more at home in Labour. This was a trend which would continue throughout the inter-war period. Try as they might, the Liberals were not convincing. Paradoxically, while promoting the cause of socially advanced policies, the Liberals maintained their hold in Scottish politics largely through support for anti-socialism and a fear of Labour. The vagaries of the electoral system meant that three-way challenges could split the vote, and anti-socialist coalitions (both official and unofficial) worked to the benefit of the Liberals because they had a large residue of sitting MPs.

The Liberals reunited to fight the general election of 1923 on the basis of defence of free trade, which had been a rallying cry in Scottish politics in the pre-war era. This policy had proved cohesive in the past because it united many Scottish businessmen who worried that the imposition of tariffs would start a tit-for-tat escalation that would damage the economy, which was heavily dependent on exports. It also had working-class support because duties paid on imported food would adversely hit ordinary workers' budgets. Free trade was something like an article of faith in Scottish political circles associated with tradition. Certainly the Conservative espousal of protectionism helped galvanise the divided Liberal Party into a new-found unity in defence of a fundamental principle of belief. Because it was thought to keep food prices down, free trade also had the support of Labour, and the results of the 1923 general election clearly show that opposition to it did not pay the Tory Party any significant dividends in Scotland.

In the 1923 general election Labour continued its advance by increasing its number of seats from 29 to 34. Although reunited, the Liberals took a few casualties, dropping from 28 seats to 23, while the Tories increased their share of the vote by some five percentage points and went up from 15 seats to 16. The percentage division of the poll was Conservative 31.6, Liberal 28.4 and Labour 35.9; clearly, with each of the parties securing about a third of the votes, there was everything to play for. The Liberals were jubilant: after the split and the problems of the immediate post-war years, they seemed to have come back from the dead, and their leader, Herbert Asquith, was returned in triumph for the Paisley seat which he had first won in a spectacular by-election in 1920 in spite of a strong Labour challenge in a predominantly working-class constituency.

Such triumphalism was short-lived, however. Many Liberals, buoyed up with their own success, disastrously misread the political situation and what their electors expected. In advocating class conciliation, socially progressive policies and the virtue of free trade, they believed they were re-establishing contact with a deep-seated Scottish political mentality which enjoyed popular support. They could not have been further from the truth. It is true that there was a lot of residual Liberal sympathy, and that protectionism was unpopular, but the principal reason for Liberal success was that most of the party's MPs were in poll position as the anti-socialist candidate. The main thing the Liberals had going for them was that they could keep the reds out. So Asquith's decision to support a minority Labour government in November 1923 effectively sealed the party's fate.

Had Liberal support been firm and based on the party's policies, there would have been nothing wrong with this decision. After all, the Liberals would help to pilot socially progressive policies which were to the benefit of the working class while keeping an eye on the minority Labour administration to make sure that no excesses were carried out. It was a textbook case of class conciliation in practice, with the Liberals as the honest brokers. But that was not what their voters wanted. For Labour it was the perfect opportunity to demonstrate that the party was reasonable and responsible and thereby put an end to the myth of the red spectre. It would give it the opportunity to see what government was like and to establish its moderate credentials and administrative credibility – and if the stalwarts were disappointed at the lack of socialist policies this could always be blamed on the Liberals. The Tories were cock-a-hoop at Asquith's decision. They immediately turned their flak on the Liberals with devastating effect, denouncing their policy of class conciliation as class capitulation. How could the Liberals claim to be an anti-socialist party when they had let the reds into government? they asked. Even Asquith's own supporters in Paisley were appalled, believing that a Labour administration would be detrimental to trade and employment.

The minority Labour government coincided with a furious bout of anti-Communist fervour surrounding the Zinoviev letter, and the administration collapsed after a mere nine months, brought down by a technicality. However, this was not before some important legislation was passed – most notably John Wheatley's Housing Act, which provided local authorities with central-government subsidies for council housing. The act was hailed as an example of the kind of improvement that Labour could effect, and the party was quick to point out that more would have been forthcoming had the Liberals not brought the government down.

In the general election of 1924 the Liberals were effectively squeezed out between those committed to anti-socialism, who turned to the Tories, and those who favoured a more progressive form of politics, who turned to Labour. The fluidity in Scottish politics was at an end, and the normal two-party system was restored. The Tories did particularly well and cleaned up the majority of Liberal seats, winning thirty-eight Scottish seats with 40.8 per cent of the vote. Although Labour increased its share of the vote to 41 per cent, the first-past-the-post system helped to contain the party, which won only twenty-six seats. The Liberals were left with a rump of nine seats.

THE RETURN TO NORMALITY

Getting back to the way things were was an important priority for many Scots in the period after 1918. There was a short-lived boom which lasted until the end of 1919, largely as a result of restocking following the war. After this the economy began to experience major structural problems. The staple industries discovered that much of the international market had collapsed. Shipbuilding, which took most steel production, found that orders dried up. The moratorium on naval construction in the UK and the USA put an end to the most lucrative pre-war market for Scottish ships. International uncertainty with the post-Versailles settlement and the rise of the Soviet Union meant that there was a general lack of confidence in the international economy, and this had a knock-on effect in investment in capital goods such as ships, heavy engineering plant, and locomotives. There was a glut of ships anyway following the confiscation of German vessels, and American yards had perfected the technique of mass production. Coal was likewise affected, as the markets in eastern Europe for the output of the Fife fields dried up because of the international situation. The herring industry collapsed as a result of diplomatic and trade disagreements between Britain and the Soviet Union. Markets which had been lost during the war, such as jute and textiles in the Far East, could not be reopened as indigenous competition had stepped in to take the place of Scottish manufacturers. Germany, which had been one of the largest bulk consumers of Scottish engineering goods before the war, was in the grip of political and economic chaos. For politicians and businessmen the problem of the post-war era was to reconcile rising popular expectations with a toughening economic climate.

Wages had been the single largest cost input of the Scottish export economy (see Chapter 1), and the diagnosis was that cutting costs was the best way to remain competitive. Yet the war had witnessed rising prices and rising wages and, although there had been great progress in the use of rationalised working practices and labour-saving technology, the circle could not be squared. Fiscal orthodoxy was wedded to the idea that the world economy would soon regulate itself and things would go back to what they had been; there was a belief that when the cost of living went down and wages were restored to a competitive level then the economy would return to normal. This view was central to the issue of industrial relations, which would haunt the inter-war economy and would come to a head in the General Strike of 1926.

The agenda of fiscal orthodoxy was determined by a wider British agenda which would have major implications for Scotland. There were three key factors involved. First, and central to orthodox dogma, was the idea that the market could not be bucked and that governments were largely powerless to change or influence global economic forces. The world economy would come right in its own good time. Second, it was argued that governments could not spend more than they earned, and that the public purse would have to function within the resources provided by the state. Also, given the first premiss, it was believed that the state should not take on too much of a burden, as this would interfere with market forces. Third, it was believed that Britain should return to the gold standard (a fixed rate of convertibility) as quickly as possible, as this was necessary to stabilise international financial credibility for sterling and would lead to a resumption of normal trading patterns.

Such policies put the squeeze on public expenditure. The 1917 Royal Commission on housing stated that at least a quarter of a million new homes would need to be built to remedy the appalling conditions in Scotland. The 1919 Addison Act stipulated that local government could receive subsidies for building programmes, but these were quickly slashed by the Geddes Axe in 1921, which dried up such funds. The 1924 Housing Act, passed by the minority Labour administration, likewise made provision for subsidised state housing, only to be watered down by subsequent administrations.

A central problem with housing was that the free market could not provide homes of a decent standard at an affordable rent. Subsidies would enable local councils to let at a lower rent, yet such policies inevitably encountered hostility from those who believed in the power of market forces. Further problems emerged in the early twenties when inflation meant that building costs often spiralled out of control. The fact that councils had to use private construction firms, who faced no penalties for increased cost, added to the difficulties. For example, to build a three-apartment house in a two-storey block containing four such units of accommodation cost £300 in 1914 and £723 in 1919, but by 1920 this had risen to £900. Again, the price of land needed to build in areas suffering the worst from congestion was often high – especially in Glasgow, where the cost was more than twice that in Dundee. This high cost was reflected in the building programme, which failed in the twenties to keep pace with demand. The 1917 Royal Commission reported that there was an immediate shortage of over 130,000 houses, and that a programme of construction of 20,000 houses per year was needed for the next fifteen years. By 1928 there was no year in which this requirement was met, and in 1926 and 1927 construction failed to keep pace with growth in population. Ten years after the recommendation only 82,000 new homes had been built which was a shortfall of over 100,000.

Given that many buildings were falling into a state of disrepair and that health inspectors were reluctant to implement the full force of law with regard to sanitation and slum dwellings because this would create more homelessness, it is safe to say that in the decade of 'homes for heroes' the housing situation in Scotland had not substantially altered from the pre-war era. Glasgow's director of housing, Peter Fyfe, described an example of the problem in December 1926:

> I give you a sample in the West-end, near the river. This is a single-apartment house occupied by an ex-soldier, whom I found lying in the enclosed bed very unwell. Five adults have to dwell in this room, the flooring badly worn and uneven, several holes being on the under-side of the skirting boards, through which mice come into the apartment. Bugs infest the bed space, bottom of his coal bunker all broken and coals have to be dumped on the flooring and the woodwork on the right hand side all broken and destroyed. The factors would do no repairs – rent 21/3 [21 shillings and 3 old pence – about £1.06] per month. As one of the ex-servicemen said to me when I was leaving his humble dwelling: 'Sir it takes a hero to live in a place like this.'
>
> Quoted in *Glasgow Herald*, 18 December 1926

The government pension for this old soldier was four shillings (20p) per week. Home for heroes, indeed.

The belief that the economy would be regulated by keeping costs down led to a furious backlash by employers against wage rates and trade unions. As far as the employers were concerned, the root of all economic and social problems was the high cost of living, which had been sparked by wage rises. The 'forty hours' strike was only the first in the series of confrontations which lasted throughout the first half of the twenties. Miners went on strike in April 1921 after the government failed to endorse the Sankey Commission's report which recommended the nationalisation of the mines. Mineowners went back to their traditional method of maintaining profits by squeezing wages. The proposal to call a strike of the 'Triple Alliance' (railway workers, transport workers and miners) came to nothing, demonstrating that sectional interest was alive and well in the trade-union movement. Engineers in the shipyards went on strike in early 1922 in response to plans to cut wages, and union members were locked out for thirteen weeks. When the engineers returned, their pay had been cut from £4. 8s. a week to £2. 13s.

A strike and a lockout of jute workers in Dundee in 1923 followed the city's humiliating defeat of Winston Churchill in the general election of the previous year. The Jute and Flax Workers' Union had seen its membership rise to about 20,000 during the war and had screwed concession after concession from reluctant employers, who finally decided enough was enough. A particular target for the employers' wrath was the union's ebullient leader, John Sime. It was a clash of wills, with no concessions on either side. A four-week lockout ensued which caught out non-striking workers and caused tensions between the workers, many of whom believed they were caught up in an unnecessary dispute. A short period of arbitration was followed in June by a second lockout that drove home the employers' point and the strike was defeated, leaving the way open for the employers to pursue a policy of modernisation and rationalisation which would eventually cut the workforce by a third.

Workers' rights and the rights of the unemployed were a further source of contention in the period following the war. The advent of full employment during the conflict meant that most workers had paid enough contributions from earnings to qualify for National Insurance and hence were entitled to unemployment benefit. The pre-war workings of the 1911 National Insurance Act were designed to accommodate a minority of mainly skilled workers, and, with the arrival of unemployment and demobilisation following the war, the system was now close to collapse, especially as in 1920 the government granted an extension of relief beyond the pre-war limit in the hope that employment levels would return to the normal pre-war level. By 1921 it was apparent that this would not happen, and most of the unemployed had exhausted their insurance benefits.

Poor relief was administered by municipal authorities which were already reeling under the financial strain of improved social legislation enacted during the war. The terms of unemployment benefit and poor relief were clouded in ambiguity. Should those on strike be entitled to relief? The old notion that poor relief was the preserve of those who could not fend for themselves was subject to a variety of interpretations, with some authorities refusing to grant relief to those deemed able-bodied. Furthermore, the Scottish poor law had no tradition of providing for the unemployed, and there were no national guidelines as such. Poor relief largely depended on the wealth of local authorities and their willingness to pay out, until the Poor Law Board established guidelines in the autumn of 1921; many local authorities then ignored these. Poor relief was means-tested and set standards which were rock-bottom minimum. Single women, unmarried mothers and widows would find themselves the subject of an insidious moral inquiry by local council officials. Progressive authorities such as Falkirk and Larbert, which granted aid to the unemployed above the guide levels, found themselves subject to legal challenges from government.

The guidelines had been issued in response to serious problems of law and order. Demonstrations by the unemployed had broken out all over Scotland. During the miners' strike in 1921, riots spread throughout Fife, with much looting. In September over 2,000 protesters marched along Princes Street in Edinburgh in protest at miserly poor-relief rates. In Aberdeen a demonstration of 5,000 ended in a riot, and in Glasgow there were continual demonstrations. Even after the introduction of guidelines, the unemployed in Greenock and Port Glasgow ransacked the local municipal buildings in early 1922.

The economic situation in Scotland was made worse in April 1925 when, after a period of financial retrenchment which had already taken a social toll, the Chancellor of the Exchequer, Winston Churchill, announced Britain's return to the gold standard with sterling set at its pre-war rate of $4.86. While this decision has its defenders and detractors among British economic historians, all are agreed that the exchange rate was set too high. It did not take account of the changed economic situation of the post-war world, in which central Europe was affected by the problems associated with German reparations and global economic influence was migrating away from London to New York. The return to gold did help keep interest rates low and helped to create a more stable financial market, but on the negative side it made exports more expensive. This was a particularly serious problem for the Scottish economy, given that its traditional industries were export-led. Dundee jute, borders' textiles, Clydeside ships and engineering, and the ancillary industries of coal, steel and iron which depended on them were dealt another blow while trying to compete in a global market which was already depressed. Sticking to their belief that costs were the key factor in determining competitiveness, employers responded to the situation by attempting to reduce wages in order to increase productivity. On the other hand, the return to gold did help the service sector, particularly in Edinburgh, as banking, insurance and investments increased their hold over the city. By 1924 the service sector already accounted for just over a fifth of Scottish economic output and it was to become the fastest-growing sector of the Scottish economy.

THE GENERAL STRIKE

The catalyst for the eventual showdown between workers and employers was the mining industry. Disappointed yet again by the failure of government to nationalise the industry, and subject to obdurate masters intent on squeezing wages, the miners were in the vanguard of those advocating use of the ultimate workers' weapon which would bring the government to its knees and impose the will of the working class on the nation. The idea of a general strike did not command universal support among Scottish trade-union leaders. There were those who doubted the legality of such a strike and believed that political change had to come via the ballot box. Also, there were those who, while not objecting to the tactic, did not believe that the time was opportune. The result was that when the strike began, on 4 May 1926, the Scottish Trades Union Congress (STUC) was inadequately prepared, with most members believing that the action would be called off. Tactically and strategically, the policy was not thought out carefully, and the plan to have a first wave of strikes resulted in some confusion, with engineers involved in maintenance downing tools, but those engaged in construction carrying on with their work. The initial phase of cutting coal supplies and transport secured much support, with miners, railway workers and dockers responding enthusiastically. Those in the Scottish Horse and Motormen's Association were less enthusiastic, however.

Unlike the unions, the government was well prepared and had in place an elaborate and well-organised chain of administration which would coordinate the volunteer Organisation for the Maintenance of Supplies (OMS), the police, the military, the civil service, municipal government and the Post Office. Troops were dispatched north, and a number of Royal Navy vessels headed for Scottish ports. The Earl of Glasgow offered the use of his fascist volunteers to keep things going, but was informed by a cagey Sir John Gilmour, the Scottish Secretary, that they could enlist only as individuals, not as a group – though they were welcome none the less. At the end of the day, the government had more volunteers than it could use. Students at the universities were told that if they took on volunteering duties it would not affect their academic interests and exams would be postponed, and there was an enthusiastic rush to 'help beat the reds'. Support from St Andrews was near universal, and more than half the students at Edinburgh volunteered, and more than a third joined from Aberdeen. Only in Glasgow, where exam concessions were not as generous, was the turnout disappointing. Patriotic citizens offered their services as special constables, and many firms directed their employees into government service to tackle a threat which was classed as undemocratic and un-British. All in all, the government could rely on some 25,000 volunteers to keep Scotland going.

Notions that the General Strike was conducted and settled in a very British way north of the border should be dispelled at once. It was a time of intense class conflict and even class hatred. Students relished the prospect of driving tanks through mining villages. Those who drove buses were likely to find themselves subject to a barrage of stones, missiles and verbal abuse. Attempts to keep transport running led to clashes between police and pickets. In Aberdeen on 6 May police baton-charged a crowd which was stoning tramcars. Rioting in Glasgow between 5 and 8 May resulted in hundreds of arrests, while in Edinburgh a crowd at the Tron, near the university, was charged by foot and mounted policemen. The use of gung-ho special constables – usually students or older public school-boys – added to class tensions, as they were not disciplined, sometimes subject to panic, and sometimes eager for a fight. Flying squads of police and specials were deployed to keep the main lines of communication open by travelling along the roads to areas where pickets were gathered. Soldiers and sailors were employed to guard strategic centres such as docks, railways, explosive plants, oil refineries and power stations. Although the police never lost control of the situation and were able to maintain law and order after a fashion, the fact that troops were in position to be deployed at a moment's notice illustrates the gravity of the situation.

Arrests took place all over the country, with over 400 people imprisoned without the option of a fine for strike offences by the middle of June. Given that many others were fined, some had charges dismissed, and some were still to go to court when the strike ended, it has been estimated that perhaps some 700 people were arrested in Scotland during the strike. This was a much higher proportion of arrests and imprisonment than was the case in England and Wales, which suggests that class conflict north of the border was more pronounced. The sentences which were handed out were not lenient, and stone-throwers could find themselves with a three-week stretch on the flimsiest of evidence. James Clunie, a socialist activist in Dunfermline, was put on trial and faced at least a two-month sentence if found guilty of inciting riot *after* the strike had been called off. He escaped prison, but many did not.

The strikers failed to paralyse the country. Supply routes were kept open, there were no food shortages, and much of life continued as normal. Indeed, one of the main hazards was the reckless driving of inexperienced volunteers, which resulted in an increase in the number of passenger accidents. The decision to call off the strike on 12 May was greeted with universal relief, with both sides believing they had won. For many strikers the announcement that the strike was over led them to assume that the government had given way and that the miners had been granted concessions. When the news gradually filtered down that the strike had failed to achieve its goals, there was widespread disillusionment, anger and despair. The miners refused to give in, and would fight a lonely and futile campaign until hunger and desperation drove them back to work in November.

For those who had opposed the strike it was a time of celebration. The failure of the strike had a number of significant consequences. First, it confirmed the moderate majority in the labour movement in their belief that the parliamentary route to socialism was the best way. Second, it reinforced the growing rift between the moderate and radical left, with the latter accusing the former of selling out. Third, it heralded a period of greater integration of Scottish trade unions into larger British ones: after all, it was argued, there was greater safety in numbers among colleagues in England and Wales than in standing alone and having small size unions vulnerable to attack from the employers. Finally, it ushered in a period of demoralisation for the labour movement, which had emerged from the end of the war in confident and buoyant mood. With the defeat of the strike, the employers did not let up their assault on organised labour. The Economic League was an employer-sponsored organisation dedicated to combating socialism. In addition to its propaganda work, the league targeted known socialists and trade-union activists, passing on information to employers who would effectively blacklist such people. Worker victimisation would continue for the rest of the inter-war period. Workers returning after the strike found that wages could be cut and conditions changed.

The strike had demonstrated just how divided Scotland was, and such divisions would take a long time to heal. It had also indicated fault lines in the working class themselves. Changes in the economy, such as the increasing use of electricity, gas and oil, had diminished the absolute necessity for coal. Also, the social structure of the nation was changing. Whereas the traditional staple industries were responsible for more than 53 per cent of Scottish output before the war (and this percentage actually increased during the war), this had shrunk by over five percentage points to under half by the time of the General Strike. It was in the shrinking traditional sectors of the economy that the strike was most heavily supported, whereas support was lukewarm in the newer and growing service sector.

With the miners now back at work, as the nation entered into 1927 it seemed as if capital had shattered the threat of labour. Yet there were already signs in the wider world that capitalism was about to receive a blow which would send it to its knees more effectively than the rise of socialism. That threat came from within the capitalist system itself.

-THREE-

CRASH,

1927–1935

But she knew that she could never tell Will of that, he'd never understand, and they spoke of other things, Will of the Argentine and the life out there, and the smell of the sun and the warm weather and the fruit and flowers and flame of life below the Southern Cross. Chris said *But you'll come back, you and Mollie, to Bide in Scotland again?* And Will laughed, he still seemed a mere lad in spite of his foreign French uniform, *Havers, who'd want to come back to this country? It's dead or dying – and a damned good job!*

Lewis Grassic Gibbon, *Sunset Song* (London, 1932)

Something must be done; and done soon, if Scotland is not to lose its historic individuality. All is not well with our country. Our population is declining, we are losing some of the best of our race stock by migration and their place is being taken by those, who, whatever their merits, are not Scottish. I understand that every fifth child born now in Scotland is an Irish Roman Catholic ... Our rural population is shrinking and our industries are decaying. Our ancient system of law and justice is not what it was. Our churches, perhaps, no longer have the same hold on the heart of our people. In language, literature and art we are losing our idiom, and, it seems to many, we are in danger of very soon reaching the point where Scotland will have nothing distinctive to show the world.

John Buchan, speech in the House of Commons, 22 November 1932

This is the heart of Scotland, but Scotland is, like all countries, a confusing conglomeration, containing such strange anachronisms as Edinburgh, a great expanse of cultivated and a greater of fallow land, and a number of different races. In the course of my journeyings I came in contact with these various Scotlands, passing from one into another without rhyme or reason, as it seemed to me; but what Scotland is I am still unable to say. It is Edinburgh, certainly, and Airdrie, and Glasgow, and Kirriemuir, and the Kailyard, and the rich agricultural areas of the south, and the depopulated glens of Sutherland, and the prosperous islanded county of Orkney. It has a human north and south, east and west, as well as a geographical; but though they have been clamped within a small space for a long time, one feels they have never met ... But I should like to put here my main impression, and it is that Scotland is gradually being emptied of its population, its spirit, its wealth, industry, art, intellect and its innate character. This is a sad conclusion ... By now its large towns are composed of astute capitalists and angry proletarians with nothing that matters much in between. Edinburgh is a partial exception to this; but Edinburgh is a handsome, empty capital of the past. And as no civilisation that is composed merely of exploiters and exploited can endure for long, Glasgow, Dundee, Aberdeen and Greenock are now following Edinburgh. They are monuments of Scotland's industrial past, historical landmarks in a country which is becoming lost to history.

Edwin Muir, *Scottish Journey* (London, 1935)

THE FIRST CRACKS APPEAR

There were a number of indicators that all was not well with the Scottish economy before the Great Crash of 1929, when frantic selling of stocks on Wall Street plunged the international economy into chaos. Hopes that there would be a return to the normality of the pre-war era remained a forlorn dream. In many ways it would not be far off the mark to describe the Scottish economy in the twenties as tottering on the edge, until it was finally pushed over the precipice in 1929. Agricultural prices had been falling from their wartime high; the market for capital-investment goods had remained sluggish, with demand for heavy engineering plant, ships and locomotives in short supply. Perhaps most serious of all, there was a jitteriness in global economic circles which meant a reluctance to engage in long-term planning and investment.

With the benefit of hindsight it is easy to list all the 'should have dones' in Scottish economic history, especially during this period of structural dislocation in the inter-war era. Economically, Scotland had always been on the front line of global capitalism, subject to the particular rewards and punishments of its changing temperament, but most businessmen believed that this system had more than amply rewarded the Scottish economy in the period before the war. This was significant, because in assessing their situation in the inter-war period Scottish businessmen were used to an uncertain climate and the vagaries associated with the international economy. Furthermore, it should be remembered that the Scottish business class had done particularly well during the war, with most able to rest on fat profits made from armaments production. The purchase of art and other luxury items following the end of the war indicates that this was not a group who were strapped for cash. The only certainty in which Scottish entrepreneurs believed was that things would always pick up. This had always been true in the period before the Great War, and helps explain why some shipbuilders built ships at a loss during this time. They had faith in the international market and its ability to regulate itself, and were sure that things would improve in the next few years. In spite of the changes wrought by the war, most Scottish businessmen believed that it would only be a matter of time before things returned to normal, and throughout the inter-war period they held fast to this principle of 'wait and see'.

Nevertheless, there were a number of indications that things had fundamentally changed and that the situation after the war was very different from that before it. First, there was the problem of structural unemployment. It was estimated in 1930 that there were a permanent 100,000 men who were surplus to economic requirements. Whereas unemployment in

the pre-war era had been short-term and was usually associated with waiting for new orders to come in, the situation after 1918 was wholly different in that there was no employment of any kind for a significant element
of the workforce. Even though emigration and migration to England were
responsible for the loss of about 500,000 people between 1918 and 1931,
it was apparent to most observers that the Scottish economy did not have
the productive capacity to absorb all its labour, although the full extent of
this problem did not become apparent until the census returns of 1931.
Most of those who left were young and skilled. Between 1921 and 1926,
for example, 23,193 skilled metal workers and engineers emigrated from
Scotland, which was only 284 less than the figure for England and Wales.
Second, there was a gradual drift of business decision-making and headquarters away from Scotland, together with amalgamations which witnessed the transfer of resources south of the border. Third, and related to
the second factor, was the relatively unfavourable market position of Scotland. High rates, high unemployment and depressed incomes meant that
there was little to attract new industry, which gravitated towards prosperous markets rather than those that were struggling. Finally, diversification
failed to take place. The economy remained stubbornly reliant on the old
staples. Chemicals, light engineering, car manufacture and other con-
sumer-goods industries failed to develop.

A rough-and-ready comparison of the Scottish pre-war economy with
that of 1928, before the Great Crash, demonstrates just how far the situation had failed to get back to normal. Based on returns to the Inland Revenue for income tax, the amount of money generated by Scotland as a share
of the total UK income in 1914–15 was roughly in line with the proportion of the total population. In other words, the Scots contributed 10 per
cent of the total. By 1925 this had dropped to 9 per cent, and by 1929 it
was only 8.7 per cent, demonstrating that Scotland was getting relatively
poorer in comparison to the rest of the United Kingdom. Presented
another way, from 1914 to 1929 Scotland had dropped from a position of
equality to being only four-fifths as wealthy as England and Wales. Similar problems emerge when Scottish industrial production is examined over
the same period. Although the figures are difficult to use with any cast-
iron sense of reliability, it can safely be said that production in Scotland
failed to keep pace with that in the rest of the United Kingdom. Depend-

ing on how the figures are computed, Scottish production in terms of value in 1929 was either only marginally greater than in 1907 (the best-case scenario) or 6 per cent lower (the worse-case scenario). Either way, this is clear evidence of a largely stagnant economy. Certainly industrial output, which accounted for the lion's share of the Scottish economy, was lower in 1931 than in 1913.

Further evidence of this decline comes from an examination of those industries which were growing in the United Kingdom. The manufacture of aircraft was one of the key growth areas in the British economy and employed 11,735 people in 1924, this nearly doubled to 21,322 in 1930. Scotland produced no aircraft. In motors and cycles the workforce in England increased from 185,576 in 1924 to 233,176 in 1930. The figures for Scotland were 6,105 rising to 7,077. For Scotland to acquire the same industrial profile as England would have entailed a tripling of the workforce in this sector of the economy. Other industries which failed to arrive in Scotland were silk and artificial fibres, and consumer durables such as radios, washing machines, vacuum cleaners and refrigerators. In electrical engineering, employment in England rose by 40,000 between 1924 and 1930, to 189,000, while in Scotland in the same period it fell from 3,000 to 2,300.

One particular problem identified with attracting new business to Scotland was the high cost of rates. Between 1914 and 1927 rates in Scotland rose by 130 per cent, against a rise of 102 per cent for England. Allowing for the relatively higher increase in population south of the border, this means that, per head of population, rates were a third higher in Scotland. And those local authorities which experienced the greatest problems of poverty and unemployment were punished the most. In Lanarkshire, for example, the county-council assessments nearly tripled from £269,319 in 1914 to £803,074 by 1927.

Not only was Scotland failing to attract new industries, the old ones were undergoing a slow but steady period of contraction. For example, in the autumn of 1927 one of Greenock's two sugar refineries, John Walker & Co., closed, the tobacco firm of F. & J. Smith was shut down following its merger with Imperial Tobacco, the shipbuilder Murdoch & Murray ceased operations, and the Mossend steel plant, which at its peak had employed some 2,000 men, closed down. Fishing declined by almost a third, with the numbers employed dropping from 34,500 in 1923 to 24,400 in 1929. Over the same period of time the tonnage of boats used dropped from 118,020 to 87,100. The numbers employed in agriculture likewise experienced a decline, as did the acreage farmed. The output of coal remained almost unchanged, but that of shipping and engineering declined.

The formal control of the economy was also slipping away from Scotland. The amalgamation of the railways on a vertical north-to-south basis precluded the survival of a separate Scottish line, and the new companies had their headquarters in London. Following on from the amalgamations, repair work and construction favoured Derby and Crewe, rather than the Scottish centres at Inverness, St Rollox in Glasgow and Kilmarnock. Four of Scotland's main banks were subject to English takeover in the twenties.

All of this indicated that times were changing. Even conservative institutions such as the Glasgow Chamber of Commerce began to take note of the new economic circumstances, in particular the growing gulf between the prosperity found north and south of the border. In September 1933 its *Journal* declared:

> We must do our own thinking and win the battle on our own ground. The most nationalist of people are also the most cosmopolitan, and Scotland's complete recovery of her old spirit of economic self-help will be marked by an increasing interest in world movements affecting trade … A Scotland functioning as a real controlling centre of industry, trade, agriculture, shipping and finance is a bigger asset to the British Empire, a more profitable customer to England, France, Germany and so forth than a Scotland written all over with the words 'branch establishment'.

Further evidence that the Scottish economy was in state of decline can be seen from the records of trade from ports. The Scottish share of total UK exports and imports dropped from 7.6 per cent in 1914 to 6.7 per cent in 1926. Even more dramatic was the decline in Scottish customs revenue, which declined from 8.1 per cent of the British total in 1913 to 5.9 per cent in 1926. There is a multiplicity of explanations for this state of affairs. First, the Scots were not exporting as much as before. Second, they were not importing as much. Third, more of their trade was going through English ports. Finally, and most likely, it was a combination of all three. All of which, taken individually or together, indicates that the money earned from exports or available to pay for imports was in decline. So, even before the impact of the Great Crash in 1929, the key sectors of the Scottish economy were experiencing major difficulties.

COLLAPSE

The period after the General Strike witnessed some degree of normality in Scottish political life. The failure of the strike concentrated minds on the parliamentary arena for political combat. The Baldwin administration of 1924 to 1929 was the longest stretch of continuous government since the end of the war. In 1924 the Conservatives had been returned with a thumping 38 seats in Scotland, with 40 per cent of the vote. Reform of local government in 1929, continuously higher levels of unemployment and industrial closure, together with a perception that things were not going back to normal, conspired to shave off five percentage points of their Scottish vote in 1929, and with the vagaries of the first-past-the-post system this reduced their Scottish MPs by more than a third, to 22. Labour, whose share of the vote went up by just over one percentage point, found its tally of MPs increased from 26 to 36. The Liberals made a partial if incomplete recovery, rising from 9 to 14 seats with 18 per cent of the vote. A minority Labour administration was formed just in time to coincide with the Great Depression.

While Tories were united in what they did not want, Labour was ideologically more ambiguous. The party was united around a concept of socialism, but this had different meanings to different people, ranging from a vague commitment to social justice to nationalisation of the means of production. Labour's faith in the inevitability of socialism was almost mystical. All Labour members agreed that it was destined to come about, being a more sensible and logical system than capitalism with all its inequities. Most agreed that its arrival would be an evolutionary process as opposed to a revolutionary imposition, because all classes, including the middle class, would come to see socialism as serving their best interests. Also, it was believed that socialism would emerge as a global system, in that the whole world would unite in socialist fraternity. But such ideology represented only one strand of the Labour Party's political thought. Central to the party's success and its electoral popularity was its ability to portray itself as a promoter and defender of working-class interests. Maintaining this almost mystical commitment to the evolution of socialism while preserving working-class interests within the capitalist system until socialism happened was a difficult circle to square.

Labour was undoubtedly helped in its 1929 electoral campaign by the worsening economic climate. Yet there were a number of ideological contradictions within Labour's thinking on the problem. First, there was a certain sense of satisfaction that capitalism was seen to be in such difficulties, and many in the party felt that they could justifiably claim that the problems were not of their making but inherent in the system, and that recent experience of industrial closure and unemployment was a vindication for socialism. Yet governments are elected to make things better and preserve the interests of those who have elected them. For Labour the problem was that, until socialism arrived, the workers who were being most adversely hit by the Depression would have to be catered to within the existing system. In other words, until there was socialism, the party which professed socialism would be unable to do anything substantially different from the capitalist parties. Indeed, Labour's Chancellor of the Exchequer, Philip Snowden, was the epitome of Victorian fiscal rectitude, believing that the finances of the nation were similar to the working-class household budget: if the money was not there, then it could not be spent.

Needless to say, the experience of forming a government during a period of profound industrial depression was bound to lead to considerable strain between the various sections of thought within the labour movement. Those who were concerned with Labour as first and foremost a defender of working-class interests were motivated by the practical day-to-day concerns of life on the dole. Maintaining insurance payments to the unemployed was the most effective way to deal with the poverty wrought by lack of work, and these payments would have to be preserved whatever the cost. This was a view favoured most strongly by the trade unionists and by those representing traditional labour strongholds. Those of a more radical bent were more inclined to favour tougher socialist action such as the nationalisation of the banks. Most were somewhere between the two.

Acutely conscious of the need to defend working-class interests, yet having to operate within the restraints of both a minority administration and
a capitalist system that had not quite turned over and died, the Labour
government vainly tried to battle with the forces of industrial closure. A
final difficulty facing the Labour administration was that few had any idea
of the depths to which the Depression would sink and the utter industrial
and social chaos that would follow in its wake.

Labour was torn between two contradictory forces: a desire to maintain and defend a benefits system which would protect the party's working-class supporters and a desire to maintain the appearance of being a
credible government which operated according to the laws of fiscal
responsibility. As the situation worsened and the gap between state
income and expenditure widened, it was recognised that only an international loan would bail Britain out. One of the strings attached to the loan
set by the international bankers was that Britain would have to cut its
public expenditure, which meant benefit cuts. This immediately sparked
a rebellion in the Parliamentary Labour Party, which recognised that such
cuts would hardest affect the unemployed, who were located mainly in
Labour constituencies and as such were among the party's core supporters.
Trade unionists, who sponsored a large number of MPs and who had close
political and emotional links with many MPs, likewise resisted any
attempt to cut benefits. They were opposed by a coterie in the Cabinet led
by the Prime Minister, Ramsay MacDonald, and his Chancellor, Philip
Snowden, who accepted the internationally agreed dictates of financial law
and argued that to do otherwise and risk losing the loan would lead only
to further chaos. As far as they were concerned they had no other option,
and to resign would be irresponsible.

It was in this atmosphere of impending national crisis and the
prospect of a Labour rebellion that the idea of forming a 'Government of
National Emergency' emerged. Part of the impetus behind this was the
belief that the crisis was such that conventional party politics was unable
to meet the challenge. Also, it was recognised that the emergency was
such that whoever was in charge would have to make tough and unpopular choices and that presenting a united front would mean that no political party would shoulder the blame or suffer the potential backlash.
MacDonald, believing that it was essential for Labour's credibility as a

responsible party to be part of this development and determined to prove his credentials as Prime Minister, took the decision to see the King and form a National Government.

Although it secured his position as national leader and Prime Minister, it cost him his party's support, with the majority of Labour MPs voting not to push through the emergency cuts. At the general election of 1931, Labour was forced to contest elections against 'National' candidates drawn from 'National' Labour (which supported MacDonald), Conservatives or Liberals. The candidates for the National Government were selected on the basis of the winnability of seats. Had the contest been tight, this would have procured a more balanced mix of the parties, but as the result was a landslide for the National Government this meant that the Conservatives made up a large majority of the new administration. Scotland reflected the mood of national emergency in Britain, with most of the press urging voters to come out in favour of the National Government. Labour was in disarray, with splits emerging between left and right and lacking a coherent leadership. Organisation was also affected by the split with MacDonald, and the party was unprepared for the campaign. Furthermore, the vagaries of the electoral system worked against Labour, with most constituencies seeing a two-horse race with the National candidate. Although losing ten percentage points from its share of the popular vote in Scotland compared to the election in 1929, Labour managed to poll a respectable 32 per cent of the popular vote, which in the near-hysterical atmosphere of the campaign showed that much of its core support remained firm. Yet its number of Scottish MPs was slashed from thirty-six to seven. Further problems emerged when James Maxton decided to make the Independent Labour Party an independent left-wing organisation in 1932. The party would spend the rest of the thirties rebuilding itself.

CLOSURE

By 1931 Scotland had suffered a rash of industrial closures which would recur with varying degrees of ferocity right through to 1937. An examination of the statistics reveals the extent of the problem. At the height of the Depression in 1932 there were about 400,000 Scots officially out of work, or 27.7 per cent of the insured workforce. This percentage dropped only slightly to 26.1 in 1933, decreasing to 23.1 in 1934 and reaching 21.3 in 1935. The figure reached a low of 15.9 in 1937, only to rise slightly in 1938 to 16.3. Only the onset of massive rearmament in 1939 solved the Scottish unemployment problem. Throughout the thirties, right up to the eve of the Second World War, Scottish unemployment only once dropped below a quarter of a million, and then only marginally, in August 1937.

One of the features which marks out Scottish unemployment in this period is that it was not only much higher, but much more persistent than the average for the United Kingdom. The average percentage rate of unemployment for the United Kingdom in this period was 21.1 in 1931, 21.9 in 1932, 19.8 in 1933, 16.6 in 1934, 15.3 in 1935, and 13.0 in 1936, dropping to 10.6 in 1937. If the figures for Scotland are factored out of the United Kingdom average then it can be said that unemployment in Scotland was 26 per cent worse than in England and Wales in 1932, 36 per cent worse in 1933, 40 per cent worse in 1934, 48 per cent worse in 1935, 68 per cent worse in 1936 and double in 1937. Finally, the extent of the problem can be understood by comparison with other European countries. In 1931 the combined unemployment of Belgium, Denmark, Norway, Sweden, Finland and Switzerland was 451,000, compared to 343,000 for Scotland alone – or, in other words, Scotland had three-quarters of the unemployment of a total population which was six times greater than its own.

It was the traditional heavy industries which were hit hardest by the Depression. In 1931, unemployment was 26.7 per cent in coal mining, 58 per cent in shipbuilding and repair, 30.2 per cent in metal processing, 26.6 per cent in engineering, 30.9 per cent in flax and jute, 26 per cent in cutlery and small tools, and 22.4 per cent in building. And the figures for insured unemployment do not give the full extent of the problem. Not all workers were insured. Many self-employed artisans, shop-keepers and others in the lower middle class had no defence against unemployment, but were likely to see their livelihoods disappear as communities succumbed to the Depression. Also, those who had used up their benefits through previous long-term unemployment failed to register as unemployed, and some in casual labour would not be insured. One contemporary estimated that, at its worse, the Depression affected one Scot in three. A more accurate indicator of the problem is to be found by looking at the rates of poor relief, as unemployment benefit was subject to a time period whereas poor relief was not. Those in receipt of poor relief numbered 206,776 in 1931, 244,690 in 1932, 317,406 in 1933, and 342,040 in 1934, rising to a height of 437,379 in 1935, after which the number dropped to 377,400 in 1936, 369,337 in 1937 and was still over a quarter of a million before the advent of war in 1939. These figures show that poor relief in Scotland was a greater and more enduring problem than was the case in England and Wales. They also reveal that long-term structural unemployment resulted in a steady rise in the number of people having to resort to poor relief as their benefit ran out.

There are a number of reasons why poverty in Scotland continued to grow long after the worst of the Depression had passed. First, the Depression had a longer-term impact on the Scottish economy (see below). Second, it should also be remembered that among the skilled working class, and to a lesser extent the semi-skilled, there was a tradition of saving which could hold off the worse effects of unemployment for a time, so poor relief figures have a built-in time lag as an indicator of the effects of unemployment. Third, poor relief was a last resort, after savings, selling off possessions and reliance on family and friends had been exhausted. Fourth, there was an increase in temporary and casual working which could flit people on and off the unemployment register. Though not on poor relief, many found that their income was dramatically reduced as employers cut hours and wages and instituted half-time working for many in the lower middle class. Finally, the activities of progressive councils, a more liberal and humanitarian attitude among officials, and government intervention all increased the numbers of those who could claim poor relief, which helped to keep the figures high, but was also an indication of the depth of poverty which existed in Scotland.

Statistics and averages can convey only a limited picture of the reality of mass unemployment. The truth of the matter was that there were few places in Scotland which had an average rate of unemployment. The nature of the Depression and industrial closure meant that if you were unemployed the chances were that your entire community would be devastated by unemployment and all your friends and family would likewise be on the dole. Unlike with short-term unemployment, which had been a feature of Scottish society in pre-war times, the long-term impact of the

Depression meant that the traditional tactics of drawing on savings and relying on friends and family could not cope. As unemployment was by its nature communal in the Depression, everyone was in the same boat. Friends, families and neighbours who worked together were unemployed together, and traditional communal means of self-help were inadequate to the task. Hoping to borrow from a neighbour was now futile. Hushed up and kept out of the press for fear of losing advertising revenue from insurance companies, although brought up in the House of Commons, was the phenomenon of a spate of small insurance policies being cancelled or cashed in. Traditionally such policies were intended to ensure an adequate burial, or to provide a sum for a widow on the death of a husband, yet, of the some 10 million policies which were issued in the United Kingdom in 1929, just under half were forfeited within the year. Given the social necessity of having an adequate burial in Scottish working-class communities, the fact that such policies were being cancelled or cashed in indicates the desperation felt by many people.

The depth of poverty experienced by the unemployed was traumatic. Reports exist of children surviving on margarine, bread and milk. Also, it should be remembered that the introduction in 1931 of the 'means test' whereby a family's income was subject to scrutiny in which children's part-time income, other benefits and savings would be deducted from the maximum relief available, meant that those on poor relief were at rock bottom. Irrespective of how a family tried to cope with the situation, the means test ensured that their income would remain at a minimum. Between 32 and 33 shillings was the maximum a man supporting a wife and three children could be paid with the initial benefit, which, when the benefit was exhausted, would drop to between 25 and 29 shillings depending on the local authority. Until the schemes collapsed from lack of funds, the unemployed could find themselves sent to work either on 'indoor' relief schemes or on 'outdoor' schemes such as road building. Unemployment was made still more traumatic as members of the skilled working class found themselves placed in camps away from their families among the refuse of society. For many, poor relief or the dole was insufficient to pay the rent, which swallowed up a huge part of family income, and arrears would build up leading to eviction. Among others, miners in Fife found that their furniture was flung out on the street by the police and

sheriff officers for non-payment. A report from Edinburgh's medical officer of health stated that the minimum benefits were 30 per cent less than
what was needed for 'physical efficiency'. Adults who had left their own
home in order to try to claim benefit as staying with their parents would
be disqualified. The figures also reveal that poor relief in Scotland was on
average some 90 per cent higher per capita than in England and Wales in
the period from 1930 to 1937.

Unemployment had a profound cultural impact, and was blamed by
many critics for the collapse of traditional values, which it was claimed
would lead to the disintegration of society. Respectable society was scan-
dalized that formerly hard-working men who were upright citizens could
be placed on schemes besides those who were incorrigible indigents. Horror stories circulated of decent folk being placed in camps where male
rape, bullying and other unedifying practices took place. The extent of
poverty imposed a vicious strain on family life. Children suffered the
effects of malnutrition and the strain of living in homes where adults were
stretched to breaking point (see Chapter 4). Charity was normal for many
families, and the only means by which they could celebrate Christmas. An
eloquent appeal by the Christian Socialist James Clunie on behalf of the
children of the unemployed in Fife, published in the *Dunfermline Press* in
December 1930, demonstrates the difficulties faced in trying to maintain
some semblance of family life:

> We shall endeavour to carry out our object in order to ensure that a
> large number of children will on Christmas Eve be able to let loose
> their imagination beyond the grim conditions that bring tears in
> place of joy. The child cannot have the least notion about party poli-
> tics. Why then should it suffer from the behaviour of party politi-
> cians? Of course they should not suffer. But the children of the
> unemployed do suffer; they suffer from want of nourishment and
> insufficiency of the essentials of life. We dare not blame anybody, for
> who would wish to be placed in the dock to be tried on a charge of
> starving the young before they had known the greatness and poten-
> tial beauties of life? Who would care to face the charge that the same
> ill nourished child had not enough clothes to keep its body warm and
> comfortable, or that its footwear were not enough to keep out the

water that flows so freely in a storm. There is not a father who would face the charge! Not a mother who would suffer the agony! Those who blame the parents are unkindly and unaware of the society in which we live ... Meanwhile my appeal is for the children of the unemployed at Christmastide, to bring a little brightness into the hearts of, say, 2,000 children whose homes are not lined with all the grandeur of that season but who nevertheless have been stirred with the fairy tales and happy thoughts and the imaginary stories of fairy godmothers and supernatural legend told by their mothers.

Quoted in James Clunie, *Labour is My Faith* (Dunfermline, 1954)

Most experts claimed that it was mothers who suffered the most, because in keeping to traditional notions of being the homemaker, they often went hungry in order to feed husbands and children. Anecdotal evidence exists of women inducing miscarriage by a variety of means from the traditional bottle of whisky and hot bath to quasi-legal purgatives as the prospect of an extra mouth to feed was too much to contemplate.

The traditional family structures which had held sway in working-class communities collapsed, although the values which underpinned them did not. Men had been brought up to equate work and providing for the family with manhood, and unemployment was a psychological form of emasculation. Proud and believing in self-reliance, they found themselves thrown on the scrapheap. Unemployment challenged their notions of masculinity. Street corners were littered with groups of listless men suffering from boredom and depression. Women were left with the burden of coping with men whose lives had lost much of its traditional meaning. They would do little or no housework, believing that to be women's work, and more often than not it was women who had to take on part-time work which men believed to be beneath their dignity.

The National Government has often been characterised as non-interventionist, its standard riposte to the problem of unemployment being that the market could not be bucked and that government could not spend what it did not have. This is only partially true, as the National Government did intervene in many areas of economic policy. One of its first actions was to set up tariff duties on a range of consumer goods, to protect native industry. This was done to the amazement of former Labour government ministers, whose commitment to the idea of an international free market had led them to believe such action was not possible. It immediately threw a lifeline to the struggling makers of cars, radios, washing machines and other consumer durables. The government also encouraged a policy of cheap lending, which facilitated a credit boom through hire purchase. This was vital in shoring up the prosperity of the new 'sunrise' industries, and also helped in a massive housebuilding programme, as mortgages came within reach of more people, providing much needed employment in the construction industry. Falling prices of raw materials meant that food and other basic items became cheaper, leading to a real rise in spending power. Indeed, on average, incomes rose in Britain at an unprecedented rate. Assistance was given to the struggling farming industry by paying a bounty on the production of wheat and sugar beet.

While such policies helped to alleviate the worst of the impact of the Depression for most of the population of the United Kingdom, they had little impact north of the border. Scotland had few consumer industries, as most of these were located near to prosperous markets to take advantage of lower transportation costs. The imposition of tariffs made exports by Scotland's traditional industries more expensive, as other nations retaliated by imposing their own trade barriers. The policy of cheap money made little impact, as most could not afford it. Whereas over 3 million new homes were built in the thirties in the United Kingdom as a result of cheap mortgages, Scotland's total for the inter-war years was 317,000, with only a third of these in the private sector. New industries were put off coming north by the burden of high local rates, which were needed to pay for unemployment relief. Further evidence that Scotland was not fully participating in the new consumer revolution can be seen from car and motor-engine registrations (including agricultural machinery), which were 1,813,958 for England in 1930, but only 160,104 for Scotland. Three million wireless licences were issued for the United Kingdom, but only 195,000 for Scotland. In terms of these symbols of the new prosperity, Scotland was lagging by a third behind the rest of the country. Even the Scottish farming industry got little help from the bounties on wheat and sugar beet, as neither was grown to any great extent in Scotland, and indeed Scottish farmers were able to claim only some 5 per cent of the total available for the United Kingdom as a whole.

Whereas recovery was happening in the south of England, no such thing was possible in Scotland. Indeed, the pace of recovery in the northeast of England – which had suffered greatly in the first stages of the Depression – was faster than in Scotland by the mid-thirties. The creation of new companies and the opening of new factories is one way to gauge the relative economic health of the two nations in this period. In 1928, 8,009 new companies were floated in England and 458 in Scotland. In 1932, the English figure had increased by 2,197 to 10,206, while the Scottish one had dropped by 29 to 429. In 1932, 20 new factories opened in Scotland but 36 closed – a net loss of 16 compared to a net gain of 496 for England. In 1933, 14 opened and 29 closed, leaving a net loss of 15 compared with a net gain for England of 565. In the period 1934–5, the Scots gained 38 new factories but lost 58.

The traditional industries suffered worst in the Depression. Between 1929 and 1931 coal production dropped by about a quarter, iron by three-quarters and steel by over a half. Railway locomotive building, which had been declining in comparison to England during the twenties, stopped altogether in 1930. Shipbuilding faced collapse, with the symbolically important order for the *Queen Mary* being cancelled in 1931. In 1913 the Clyde had launched about three-quarters of a million tons; in 1933 the figure was 56,368 tons. In the period from 1921 to 1930 the Clyde launched 4,587,562 tons. By the end of 1933 the number of yards which had been closed down had contributed 857,297 tons of that total, or some 19 per cent.

The Royal Commission appointed under Sir Arthur Rose to examine the impact of the Depression had few solutions to offer the Scots. Instead, the Rose Report, as its conclusions were christened, merely confirmed the extent of the problem. According to one Tory Member of Parliament, C. Milne, speaking in the House of Commons on 22 November 1932:

Relatively speaking, as compared with England, Scotland is a distressed area. I have always held the view that there are really two commissioners in Scotland. There is Sir Arthur Rose, the Commissioner appointed under the 1934 Act for the Special Areas, but there is another Commissioner who has no statuary title. His jurisdiction is far more extensive, and in some respects his powers are far

greater. He owes his position as Commissioner to the fact that he
holds the office of Secretary of State for Scotland. He is Commissioner for that distressed area, North Britain.

By 1935 it was apparent that the Depression was taking a greater toll on Scotland than on most parts of the United Kingdom and was refusing to budge.

THE END OF SCOTLAND?

The dire economic consequences of the Depression had a profound effect
on the nation's sense of itself. Pre-war notions of Scottish identity were
heavily laden with ideas about Scotland's contribution to Britain's imperial mission. Whether as soldiers, administrators, businessmen or mission-
aries, the Scots believed that they had always punched above their weight.
The fact that the workshop of the Empire was flat broke and that the once
mighty Scottish economy was on its knees seemed to reinforce the notion
that Scotland was in a state of terminal decline. This idea was not just confined to politicians and intellectuals, but had a wide currency throughout
Scottish society and was a frequent topic in newspapers and at after-dinner
speeches. The statistics whose assiduous compilation was a feature of the
thirties were now put to use to paint an incredibly gloomy picture of the
nation's well-being. In output, health, housing and a whole range of socio-
economic statistics relating to standards of living, Scotland was lagging
behind the rest of the United Kingdom. It was thought that Scotland
would soon cease to exist as an identifiable nation. The figures which we
have already presented on unemployment and closures were used to compare the situation with England, and as it became apparent that Scotland
was not recovering to the same extent a mood of pessimism gripped the
nation. A host of books, articles and pamphlets bemoaning the state of
Scotland was published in the first half of the thirties. The political language of Scotland became suffused with terse phrases such as 'the south-
ward drift of industry', 'the slum problem', 'provincialisation' and 'the
Irish invasion', all of which were associated with national decline.

This mood of pessimism was not confined to any particular political
outlook and was shared by many of Scotland's middle class, who were certainly its most vocal proponents – the working class presumably had the

more pressing problem of unemployment to deal with. In reviewing the events of 1929, an editorial in the *Daily Record* stated that 'In certain respects the year which closes today will remain memorable to Scotland as a nation. Certainly no year within memory of any living Scot has witnessed so much soul searching. Never before has there been so much airing of the question: what is wrong with Scotland?' The economic developments of the twenties were seemingly coalescing into a frightening pattern of terminal decline and absorption into England.

In November 1932 the president of the Edinburgh Chamber of Commerce claimed in the organisation's journal that 'business after business was being bought up by English money and factories one after another closed down ... If the process of English absorption is not stopped, Scotland will drop to a position of industrial insignificance.' Similar fears were echoed by the Chambers of Commerce of Glasgow, Aberdeen and Dundee. Something close to panic was beginning to grip the middle class in Scotland, and the businessman Sir John Samuel was remarkably candid in his view as to why Glasgow faced decline:

> The changes which have been taking place in the spheres of shipping, railways, banks, steel, manufacturing, leaching, and calico printing, the drapery and soft trade goods trade, chemical manufacture, and even philanthropy, with the extinction and absorption of many Glasgow firms and the falling of others under English control. There has been an insidious campaign of suppression of Scottish affairs for a long time.
>
> *Daily Record*, 23 October 1931

The policy of rationalisation was likewise condemned by the Establishment in Scotland, because it pulled headquarters and firms south to more prosperous markets. According to an editorial in the *Scotsman* on 25 November 1932, 'Continuance of the fundamentally false policy of centralising everything on London will, sooner or later, finish Scotland as a nation and reduce her to a mere province of England.' Faith in the market and confidence that conditions would return to normal in their own good time were now being put to the test, and the Scottish business class was beginning to doubt.

The impact of the Great Depression changed the way the Scottish middle class looked at the world. It shattered many of their assumptions regarding the virtue of free trade, and few could come to terms with the changed realities of the new economic order. Evidence of the difficulty that the Scottish business class had in coming to terms with the decline of industry in favour of the service sector can be seen in the pages of the *Glasgow Chamber of Commerce Journal* in September 1933:

> It may be that a new economic age had dawned in which it will be profitable to take in one another's washing, produce luxuries for home consumption, spend what we can, and put what we can't into the bank, turn our farms into bijou residences, and our crofting areas into sporting reserves and leave it to the 'lesser breeds' to hew coal, make steel, build and repair ships, raise cattle, and grow corn and potatoes and vegetables and fruit.

Much Scottish business resentment of the south of England was fuelled by the simple belief that an economy could exist and make a living only by exporting goods to pay its way in the world. The 'invisible' economy of finance and services not only made no sense to Scottish businessmen, but was regarded with disdain, especially by the industrialists in the west. For many it looked as if the nation was spiralling ever more downwards, with no prospect of economic salvation.

As if the economic problems were not bad enough in themselves, they exacerbated existing social problems which had remained intractable throughout the twenties. Improvements in housing, health and poverty were elusive, and better social indicators and more accurate statistical evidence (see Chapter 4) conclusively demonstrated that the nation was falling behind the rest of the United Kingdom. Added to such problems, there was a spate of moral panic as razor gangs in Glasgow seemed to demonstrate that youth was out of control. This was in spite of the efforts of the prominent war hero Major Malcolm Spier, who was given special dispensation to use his 'hairbrush' to spank young hooligans in Barlinnie jail to teach them a lesson they would not forget. (A pastime which would nowadays cost a senior politician good money could be passed off as a public duty in those more innocent times.) The newspapers were full of stories about badly behaved women and children who were challenging existing social conventions.

Jazz, dance halls, 'American' movies and even 'Italian' ice-cream parlours were all indicted as inducing lower moral standards. The authority of the Church was no longer what it once was, and seemed incapable of holding back a sweeping tide of immorality that was engulfing the nation. Efforts to curb the widespread practice of gambling and to halt the working class's persistent interest in drink, boxing and football proved futile. Even the cultural influence of the nation was seen to be in decline, with the best efforts of the new generation of writers either going unnoticed or being dismissed by contemporary critics as rubbish. At Burns clubs, Rotary meetings and various other functions throughout the thirties, speakers expatiated on what they believed was the decline of Scottish nationality. The formation of the Saltire Society in 1936 was designed to shore up Scottish identity at a time when contemporaries feared for its survival.

There were two further phenomena which were deemed to be particularly responsible for this state of affairs. First there was the fear of widespread Irish immigration, which had take place over generations and was now deemed by many to be threatening the extinction of the Scottish race. Coupled with the 'Irish invasion' there was widespread emigration, which was believed to be taking away the best and most able of the Scottish population, leaving only the young, weak and infirm to face the Irish onslaught. According to the writer George Malcolm Thomson:

> The first fact about the Scot is that he is a man eclipsed. The Scots are a dying people. They are being replaced in their own country by a people alien in race, temperament, and religion, at a speed which is without parallel in history outside the era of the barbarian invasions ... The present generation of Scots youth – the last, perhaps, to be predominantly Scottish in race – exhibits the symptoms one would expect to find in young people reared in such an environment, with such an education and inspiration. Among the working-classes the old pride of craftsmanship is dead; lazy shiftless and physically degenerate, they make no strenuous attempt to find a footing for themselves in a country they believe to be doomed, while at the same time they do not emigrate until they are compelled to do so.
>
> *Caledonia; or, the Future of the Scots* (London, 1927)

Thomson argued that by 2027 Scotland would be an Irish colony, with the Scots a minority in their own land. As in most European societies during the Depression, many sought shelter from the economic tidal wave by turning to an ethnic or racial nationalism.

INVASION

The so-called 'Irish Question' or 'Irish Menace' of the thirties was largely a figment of the imagination. Official government figures released in 1930 showed that Irish immigration into Scotland had virtually ceased. Between 1924 and 1928 there were 103,461 passengers to Scotland from the Irish Free State compared with 95,982 people going the other way. Further figures released after the census of 1931 showed that 124,296 of the population of Scotland were born in Ireland, of which 67,905 were born in the north and 55,487 in the Free State. This was 34,724 fewer than in the census of 1921, and hardly evidence of a Hibernian influx. In fact, the English population of Scotland, at 164,299, was larger than the Irish. Yet this did not stop a host of politicians and commentators describing an imaginary horde of Irish immigrants who not only came to Scotland to steal the natives' jobs but also were attracted by the higher rates of poor relief.

Anti-Irish sentiment had long existed in Scotland and drew on two main fonts of inspiration. First there was the Orange tradition, which had been imported from Ireland but had largely gone native by the twentieth century as Orangism was able to draw on much of the shared historical and cultural traditions of Scotland and Ulster. Confined to the working class in the western central belt, the Orange movement failed to mobilise itself into an effective political organisation. Even Scottish Conservatives were wary of it: its unthinking hostility to Catholicism was such that the Tories believed there could never be any effective control over the movement. Also, given that Orangism was largely a raucous working-class movement with a penchant for drunkenness and street brawling, too close an association with it would alienate respectable middle-class supporters.

The other anti-Catholic tradition in Scotland was altogether more sinister. Confined mainly to the middle class and drawing its ideas from so-called 'scientific racism', its adherents attributed the supposed deficiencies of the Irish to their Celtic racial stock. The Catholicism of the Irish and their supposed laziness, dirtiness, and proclivity towards crime and squalor were explained as a form of genetic preference. Such views had filtered through Scottish society in the latter part of the nineteenth century and the early part of the twentieth, although it is important not to exaggerate their significance, especially as recent research has shown that the divide between Protestants and Catholics in the working class was not as great as was once thought. Furthermore, sectarianism was unknown in many parts of Scotland. For example, the Western Highlands of Scotland, which was a last bastion of fundamentalist Presbyterianism, was an area most sympathetic to Catholic Irish nationalism, largely because of support for the shared social goal of land reform.

The experience of war sharpened anti-Catholic sentiment, as the Irish were exempt from conscription in their own country and the Scottish press was full of lurid stories of a rush to get back to the emerald isle before being drafted. In March 1916, at the height of the Battle of Verdun, the *Glasgow Herald* claimed that 'Cross channel steamers leaving the Clyde during the past few nights have been taking hundreds of men eligible for military service from outlying districts in Scotland back to their home in Ireland.' These stories resurfaced in the thirties as examples of Irish duplicity: when conscription loomed the Irish were quick to disappear, it was said, yet when the danger was past and the prospect of jobs or poor relief beckoned they were quick to return to Scotland. Similar claims were made in 1938, at the height of the Munich crisis, when it was said that work on many road improvements in Scotland had had to be suspended as many of the foremen and labourers had hurriedly left for Eire.

The Irish war of independence and the subsequent civil war had an impact on Scotland. There was a vibrant Sinn Fein movement in Scotland after 1918, with some eighty branches in existence. Gun-running was carried out, and support for the war emanated from many quarters, convincing many in Scotland that loyalties within the Catholic community were first and foremost directed to Ireland. The flying of the Irish tricolour at Celtic FC's football ground elicited hostile responses from many in Scottish society. For traditional, conservative Scotland, in which loyalty to the Empire was taken for granted, the war of independence confirmed notions of Irish treachery. The 1918 Education Act, which provided local-authority funds to maintain separate Catholic schools, was denounced as 'Rome on the Rates' by middle-class Scots who traditionally objected to paying for anything above the minimum, let alone subsidising a religion which they believed to be foreign and alien.

It was in this semi-poisonous atmosphere that the Scottish Churches began to stir the flames of racial and religious hatred. Split by the 'Disruption' of 1843, the Established Church of Scotland and the United Free Church of Scotland were both Presbyterian, but were separated by a history of schism which now seemed to have no place in the very altered circumstances of the post-war era. Each had the idea that it was the 'national' church. Sensing a decline in their authority with the rise of socialism and the increased presence of the state in a number of areas in which the Churches had played a leading role – such as education and poor relief – many began to think about ways in which the Churches could reassert their authority and find common cause. In 1922 the Church and Nation Committee of the Church of Scotland published a document called *The Menace of the Irish Race to Our Scottish Nationality*, in which it outlined what it saw as the danger of the Irish taking over Scottish society. Clearly driven by a concerted effort by dedicated bigots, letters in the press and resolutions at the general assemblies of both Churches painted a lurid threat to the Scottish way of life. In the *Scots Magazine,* for example, there were numerous suggestions that if the Irish were sent back then unemployment would drop, and that employers should in future discriminate in favour of Scottish workers. Letters were published citing examples of how Irish foremen would only employ Irish men. Most of these had been planted. In 1929 the Churches ended their historic schism and united under the leadership of the new moderator, Dr John White, who was one of the most vociferous proponents of anti-Irish sentiment.

Scotland's Catholic community not only came under assault from the Church, but was attacked by many of Scotland's political, cultural and intellectual community. Many figures such as George Malcolm Thomson and the regius professor of law at the University of Glasgow, Andrew Dewar Gibb, engaged in what can only be described as a racist diatribe against 'the Irish'. The Irish were blamed for squalor, poverty, drunkenness and crime, which were believed to be an innate racial feature of the Irish. Such were the views of Andrew Dewar Gibb:

They form an appreciable proportion of the population of Scotland, breeding as they do not merely unchecked, but actually encouraged by their own medicinemen ... They are responsible for most of the crime committed in Scotland, which otherwise would be the most law abiding country in the world. Wheresoever knives and razors are used, wheresoever sneak thefts and mean pilfering are easy and safe, wheresoever dirty acts of sexual baseness are committed, there you will find the Irishman in Scotland with all but a monopoly of the business. Glasgow is cursed with gangs of young loafers who prowl about in the East End in Bridgeton and Calton, attacking one another and often the police and strangers. Their names as the newspaper reports show are Irish to the extent of ninety per cent.

Scotland in Eclipse (London, 1930)

Gibb's claims that 'the Irish' were responsible for most crime, and that their population was rising out of control, were accepted as fact by many. Scottish Tory MPs were able to argue against Scottish home rule on the basis that if a parliament were granted it would be controlled by the Irish. John Buchan, not normally know for outlandish statements, even recited the often made claim that one in every five children born in Scotland was now 'Irish Catholic'. The official government figures which showed that Irish immigration into Scotland had virtually ceased made no difference to the alarmists, who continued to spew out spurious statistics of an Irish takeover of Scottish society. Control of fictitious Irish immigration became a common theme of proposed remedies for what was wrong with Scotland. In an examination of Scotland's problems in the thirties, one author recommended the use of expatriation as a solution. The proposal should not be dismissed as the inconsequential ravings of a fanatic, for his pamphlet sold over 55,000 copies:

We stand in danger of being supplanted on our own soil by the unselected and uncontrolled influx of a population from Ireland. There are said to be 600,000 Irish on Clydeside; one out of every six people is of Irish extraction. (Scottish) nationalists have neither hostility nor contempt for the Irish people. But if they believe that Scotland has not received the best type of Irish immigrant, they need only look to police court reports and prison statistics to find corroboration … They ask for Scotland the elementary right of a nation to set up social standards and to exact assurances of loyalty to our Scottish outlook. And in particular they seek to make an end of the intolerable position by which Scotland under the terms of the Anglo Irish treaty cannot return to the Irish Free State those of its subjects who become a burden on the public purse of Scotland.

John Torrence, *Scotland's Dilemma: Province or Nation* (Glasgow, 1939)

'Irish Catholics' were blamed for dragging areas down into ghettos, and that they caused 'moral infection' was a normal claim. Descriptions of the Catholic community in Scotland as a 'cancer' were also common. Such ideas and spurious facts and figures were common currency in many areas of Scottish society, so demonstrating the pervasive nature of sectarianism in parts of Scotland. Clearly influenced by the ideas of the far right, most polemicists believed that there would be a race war. In *Scotland's Dilemma* John Torrence also declared that 'Unless measures are taken to arrest and control immigration and to put into the hands of the Scottish people the key to the racial destiny of their country, there will inevitably be a race conflict of the most bitter kind.' As late as 1937 the Church of Scotland was sending a delegation to the National Socialist League of Churches in Nazi Germany.

In such an atmosphere it should come as no surprise to find that the Catholic community in Scotland maintained a strong sense of its own identity, which was moulded by the hostility its members felt as outsiders – 'strangers in a strange land'. Many of the standard assumptions about the Scoto-Irish community need to be dispelled at once. Contrary to what Protestant polemicists claimed, the Catholic community never made up more than 12 per cent of the population and, although the vast majority of its members lived in the central belt and were of Irish descent, there were indigenous Scottish Catholic communities in the Highlands and the north-east. Sectarianism was largely unknown outside western central Scotland. Irish immigration in the nineteenth century and twentieth century was composed of about 25 to 30 per cent Protestants, who brought with them to Scotland their Orange traditions. Over time, these traditions came to assume a native hue, but given the Glasgow–Belfast shipbuilding nexus, with skilled labour travelling freely to and fro, they were given a regular top-up from Ulster. Many Scots outside the central belt were inclined to see religious sectarianism as an Irish import.

Other common assumptions regarding the Scoto-Irish community concern its members' social status and political affiliation. The depiction of most Scoto-Irish as unskilled or semi-skilled labourers at the bottom of the social pecking order is broadly correct, but it must be remembered that, as a social group, the unskilled and semi-skilled made up about 60 per cent of the population, which means that numerically, given that the Scottish Irish made up only 12 per cent of the population, there were more Protestants in this group than Catholics. Which relates to a further assumption: that the Catholic political affiliation was Labour. This also is true but, again, numerically Labour's support was predominantly Protestant and, given the social status of the Scoto-Irish community, its members' political affiliation was determined more by class than by religion. In other words, Scottish Catholics and Protestants voted for Labour for broadly the same reasons. Although Labour made concessions to the Catholic community regarding education and contraception (which it refused to promote as many feminists advocated), there is no real evidence to suggest that there was a specific Catholic programme issued by Labour to attract voters: at most there was tokenism. And recent evidence suggests that the Catholic Church was relatively weak in dictating its members' political affiliation: that Irish republicanism did not have the wholehearted approval of the Church did not stop the Scoto-Irish community's full-scale endorsement of it, for example.

Likewise, the description of Scotland's Catholic community as 'Irish' needs qualification. As befitted the ultramontane nature of the Church, mainland Europe was more of an influence in terms of inspiration, theology and practice than Ireland. This was especially the case in regard to social policy and the Church's stalwart commitment to anti-Communism and support for the Franco regime in Spain's civil war. Furthermore, many of the associations commonly attributed to Irish culture were largely skin-deep. Most attention has focused on football support, in particular for Glasgow Celtic and for Hibernian FC in Edinburgh, yet soccer was regularly denounced by Irish nationalists as an Anglo-Saxon game which no self-respecting Irishman should endorse. While football was a vehicle for the expression of a separate religious, and possibly national, identity, the fact remains that this identity was expressed within the parameters of Scottish society and not through the Gaelic games which were the supposed bedrock of Irish culture. Indeed, the Gaelic games never took off in Scotland to the same extent as in other Irish communities around the world. Nor was there a flourishing Irish-language movement. That the campaign for Irish independence eventually ended in civil war must have had a damping effect on the enthusiasm for Irish nationalism. Indeed, some prominent pre-war Irish home rulers, such as Patrick Dollan and John Wheatley, were profoundly anti-nationalist by the late twenties, believing nationalism to be nothing more than a bourgeois construct to divert the workers' attention away from what should be their real aspirations. For all that the Scoto-Irish community supported the Labour Party, Ireland was never held up as a socialist or nationalist paradise. Indeed, it was forgotten in Labour Party circles.

The inter-war era brought limited, but nevertheless significant, progress for the Scoto-Irish community. The 1918 Education Act brought the Catholic school system within the state system and provided funding from local authorities. This was achieved without compromising religious principles. Religious instruction and access by the priesthood, as well as scrutiny of entry to the teaching staff, were guaranteed. Some social mobility was also possible, with members of the community breaking into the teaching, legal and professional classes. As the Scoto-Irish community developed almost as a society within a society, it evolved its own middle class. Shopkeepers, landlords, journalists, teachers, lawyers and businessmen emerged to take over prominent positions within the community. Catholics began to make their presence felt in politics, with people like John Wheatley carving out a successful parliamentary career which was cut short by his untimely death in 1930, and in local government Patrick Dollan was to become Glasgow's first Labour Lord Provost in 1938. Yet sectarianism remained a marked feature of the industrial central belt. In Glasgow and other industrial towns, violence would break out among youths, although sectarianism was not the only reason for this – youthful aggression and thuggery were also important factors. There was crowd trouble at football matches. Yet Edinburgh was the area with most problems. Churches were burned down by bigots, priests were attacked, and the city had its share of rabid anti-Catholics, such as the ex-soldier John Cormack, whose Protestant Action Force made some impact in local elections. Unlike in the west, where much of the violence was episodic and spontaneous, the violence in Edinburgh was marked by an almost ideological underpinning.

In assessing the impact of sectarianism in inter-war Scotland, it should not be divorced from what was happening elsewhere in the world. At a time of global economic crisis and rising racial nationalism, Scotland reflected these trends. Immigrants and those of a different race were used as scapegoats for problems which were seemingly insurmountable. Yet, that said, a racially motivated Protestantism did not emerge as a coherent political force in Scotland, in spite of the best endeavours of some. One Protestant fundamentalist, Alexander Radcliffe, refused to embrace fascism because it came from the Catholic country of Italy. While some local councillors were elected on a religious ticket, they were few and far between. Also, while there was violence in the towns and cities, it was not of an order that threatened social stability. Although sectarianism existed in the workplace and Catholics were effectively barred from certain jobs, it should be borne in mind that entry to the skilled trades was carefully controlled and that just as many Protestants would be kept out. It could be argued that entry into the shipyards was dependent more on family connections than on religion.

EXILES

The extent of emigration from Scotland can be illustrated by recounting a few compelling facts and figures. By 1931 there were probably as many people born in Scotland living in the United States and Canada as there were in the nation's most populous city, Glasgow, which had a population of over a million. Between 1921 and 1931, Scotland lost at least 393,000 people (63,000 going to England), although recent work has revised these figures to 446,212 and 77,769 respectively. Such statistics are notoriously difficult to gauge with absolute accuracy, as immigration has to be factored into the equation, but these figures are about the same as the combined total emigration in the same period of Belgium, Holland, Norway, Sweden, Denmark, Switzerland and Finland, whose total population was

36 million. Also, it is highly likely that between a quarter and a fifth of all Scots in the world in 1931 were not living in Scotland.

Whereas in the nineteenth century emigration was celebrated as a feature of the Scot's adventurous, entrepreneurial and dynamic character, in the inter-war era everyone put it down to the poor social and economic opportunities at home. Given the weak performance of the Scottish economy and the continuing problems of poor housing, health and poverty, it should come as no surprise to find that many Scots chose to leave. As one Scot living in the United States explained:

> It would not seem that the stay at home Scot even begins to realize how low are his living standards compared with those of his kin abroad. The migrated family which once lived in a two-roomed house in Scotland now considers five or six none too many, and the house will have a bathroom, a dining-room, a living-room, an outside porch, probably a little lawn in front and one behind, a basement with private washtubs, a system of hot air, steam or water heating to every room, an individual front and an individual rear door, excellent natural light. The family possessions will often include a radio, electric vacuum cleaner, electric washing-machine, electric iron, electric toaster, a refrigerator and so on ... From the standard of living point of view Scotland is a backward country, and the Scot abroad is increasingly aware of it and ashamed that others must also see it.
>
> Arthur Donaldson, in *Scots Independent*, October 1931

Traditionally, it has been claimed that, had those Scots not left, unemployment would have been greater, poverty more endemic, and housing shortages more acute. This, however, tells only one side of the story. The loss of about a tenth of the population – and an even greater proportion of the working population, given that most emigrants were workers – had to have a significant impact on the economy. The relationship between emigration, skills shortages and capital drain is a difficult one to establish, but those who left clearly had the money to do so and the skills to sell. For example, one out of three Scottish engineers left to work in more advanced economies, either in England or in the United States. One feature of emigration is that it draws away those who have work and money. Leaving is motivated not by poverty, but by the fear of poverty, and it remains an unanswered question to what extent emigration damaged Scottish society's ability to cope with the structural problems of the inter-war economy. It might be said that the drain of capital, skills and workers did more harm than good, because it limited the ability of society to adapt to changed circumstances.

There are a number of reasons why Scots emigrated in such large numbers. First, there was a culture and tradition of emigration to which people could attach themselves. There were few families in Scotland which did not have an emigrant advanced guard somewhere in the world. This was important, because it meant that most Scots who left were not leaving for an unknown destination: they were usually going to friends or family who would provide accommodation and line up work. Usually there was more than one friend or family member there, and a steady stream of communication provided potential emigrants with detailed knowledge of what to expect. Living conditions were invariably superior, and the family back in Scotland could only listen in envy as letters from America recounted how the emigrants were paid twice as much as in Scotland, how their houses and apartments were bigger, and how they had things like inside toilets and baths. For many housewives, emigration and improved living standards would give them access to domestic technology which meant a real escape from the drudgery and back-breaking duties of a wife and mother.

Coming from an industrial society, Scottish emigrants usually had skills which were in demand in the new world. The average emigrant tended to be young, urban and from the skilled working class, although Scotland exported a significant number of engineers, doctors and clerics. In the 1920s agents from the New Zealand, Australian and Canadian governments actively recruited in Scotland, looking especially for agricultural workers. The exodus from the north-east due to emigration helps explain why the area was the one which used most tractors in the inter-war period, as a result of manpower shortage. In contrast to imperial perceptions of the Irish, the Scots had a reputation for hard work and honesty, which made them more attractive to the immigration officials in the Dominion nations of New Zealand, Canada and Australia. The notion that the Scots were well educated also stood them in good stead, and the nation's image as godly and puritan was important in securing work for many young women as domestic servants.

The idea of emigration as a form of social policy by default had a lot of currency in Scotland. Given that there was a strong imperialist senti-ment, the belief that a steady flow of loyal subjects to the Dominions would help maintain the bonds of Empire was an important one: it was believed that emigration offered a better way of life particularly to those who were most industrious and those who were willing to take a chance. To a certain extent, the possibility of emigration seemed to many to excuse the poor social and economic conditions at home. This was especially the case in the Highlands, where emigration and migration had a devastating effect on the population (see Chapter 4), which declined faster in the first half of the twentieth century than at the times of the clearances a hundred years earlier. The lack of land for crofting and also, it should be empha-sised, poor employment and social opportunities drove many young peo-ple away from the Highlands. Policy towards the Highlands and policy towards emigration were contrasted by critics. For example, in 1927 there were some 7,000 outstanding applications for enlargement of existing holdings or to settle new ones in the Highlands. The total cost to settle a family in New Zealand, Australia or Canada was quoted at several thou-sand dollars, whereas in the Highlands it was estimated as only £300. Yet the government refused to subsidise landholding, though many critics, in line with much European thinking, advocated a back-to-the-land policy as an antidote to the crash of industrial capitalism. It was pointed out that those countries which had a larger agricultural sector than Scotland suf-fered less unemployment. Delinquent children, orphans and other young-sters were parcelled out to the Dominions almost as a social policy. It was believed that the wide-open spaces of the Australian outback or the Cana-dian prairies provided a healthier climate for children who had grown up in the degenerate cities. Also, they would be among a better class of peo-ple, which would provide the best environment for moral correction. Many children were used simply as cheap labour or worse. Some found greater opportunities for the employment of their delinquent talents – much to the disgust of the immigration authorities, who had no hesitation in deporting them.

The destinations of Scottish émigrés can be gauged from the figures for the six months ending 30 November 1929. Of the 21,809 who left in this period, the largest group – 9,392 – went to Canada, although many of them would have the USA as their final destination (travel to British North America was cheaper); 7,986 went directly to the United States. Australia came a poor third, with 1,706; South Africa and New Zealand attracted about 500 each, with India taking 800.

The United States was the most popular destination, and, according to official US government figures, 129,193 Scots settled there between 1920 and 1928. This was about 20,000 more emigrants than came from England, meaning that in per-capita terms Scottish emigration to the USA was nine times higher than English. Another remarkable feature of this was that the United States imposed immigration quotas in the early twenties and imposed more stringent tests on its potential new citizens. Having family in America of good character who could vouch for emigrants was an important factor in securing entry. Also, that the Scots tended to blend into American society and were not as vocal in proclaiming their ethnic identity as were the Germans, Italians and Irish may have been a factor in securing their acceptance. This was especially the case as the United States became more isolationist and introspective in the inter-war years. Certainly Scottish-nationalist attempts during the period to whip up sympathy for the cause of the old country had little impact. Again, the reputation of being well educated helped, and many of the supposed characteristics of the Scots chimed with American values. Presbyterianism, the work ethic, thriftiness and independence, although subject to stereotypical mickey-taking in the USA, were not that different from the characteristics that Americans liked to portray as their own.

Of the 124,700 Scots who emigrated in 1927–9, 92,000 were over the age of eighteen; 48,000 of these were men and 44,000 were women. That a quarter of those who left were children indicates that a high proportion of the total was made up of families. Of those who left in this period, the vast majority were skilled. Twelve per cent were drawn from commerce and the professions, 10 per cent came from agriculture, nearly a quarter were engineers, almost 15 per cent were artisans of some kind, with the rest coming from mining, building and transport. Such figures in themselves reveal those areas of the economy which were suffering contraction.

RE-CREATING SCOTLAND

For some, the crisis of the inter-war period represented an opportunity to re-create Scotland anew. Some saw the project as entirely cultural, for others it was entirely political, and for many the two aspects were tied together.

Scottish identity had coexisted and reinforced British identity throughout the nineteenth century without any sense of contradiction. In the aftermath of the Great War, however, many of the assumptions and values which had been at the heart of Scottish identity before 1914 became subject to challenge. In this respect Scotland was no different from most modern societies which experienced political and cultural upheaval following the First World War as the influence of democracy, secularism and political ideologies more suited to the age of 'mass man' took effect. In the twenties modernism made its impact on Scottish culture, with old cultural values being torn up and replaced by ones deemed to be more appropriate. At once both international and national, the resulting phenomenon became known as the Scottish renaissance.

The Kailyard (literally meaning the cabbage patch) was the prime target for renaissance wrath. Novels of the Kailyard school had presented a cosy image of Scotland as a small-town paradise where the hero, after a narrow scrape with the evils of the big city, would come to see that decency, safety and respectable values were located in the small village after all, and that parochialism was the best option. Critics such as C. M. Grieve (aka Hugh MacDiarmid), James Leslie Mitchell (aka Lewis Grassic Gibbon), Edwin Muir and others denounced such prevalent notions of Scottish culture as phoney and fake. 'Sham Bards for a sham nation' was how Muir put it. Other targets included the excessive veneration for a couthie image of Robert Burns, who was sanitised out of his real existence, and the portrayal of all Scotland as a repository for Highland images.

The objectives of the renaissance were to shake things up and address the current political and social issues of the day, and to make contact with artists in other countries to bring Scotland into the mainstream of European and global culture. Yet the renaissance was not a unified movement in the sense that all its members were committed to the same political and cultural objectives. Rather, the renaissance is used as a broad term to cover a general flourishing of Scottish culture in the inter-war period. Some of its members, like Grieve and the novelist Neil M. Gunn, were committed nationalists who were keen to see their artistic endeavours as part of a broader political/cultural campaign which would lead to a greater degree of independence. Others, such as Mitchell and Muir, while contributing to a distinctive Scottish literary revival, were politically motivated by an international socialism which was in many ways antipathetic to the aspirations of Scottish nationalism. Not only were there divisions in terms of politics, their artistic ideas also exhibited a great deal of diversity, with on the one hand Gunn using the straightforward technique of the novel written in English and on the other MacDiarmid reinventing the Scots language and experimentating with poetic form.

While the artistic achievements of the renaissance have been recognised by subsequent generations, their reception by contemporaries was more or less universally hostile. MacDiarmid's efforts to re-create the Scots language by going back to the medieval 'makar' poets as a base encountered near universal hostility from contemporary critics. Indeed, many saw the attempt to re-create the language as evidence that Scots was already dead and that the best that could be achieved was a sort of cultural embalming. MacDiarmid's interest in medieval Scots was motivated by a desire to find as pure and uncontaminated version of the Scots language as possible – free from English corruption. Strongly influenced by Irish and other European nationalists, MacDiarmid believed that language was an essential part of the nationalist programme, and that the more distinct and separate a language the more separate and distinct the national culture. As he saw it, liberating the Scottish language would enable Scotland to shake off its English cultural influences, and this would pave the way for political independence.

MacDiarmid was also anxious to shake off the phenomenon of the Burns cult. The popularity of Robert Burns remained undiminished, but MacDiarmid and others believed that this was a baleful influence on the development of Scottish culture. According to MacDiarmid:

> It would seem that most of the people who write essays or books dealing with Burns first of all cut themselves away from all literary standards and deal with their material in a hopelessly demoded manner. Why is this? If Burns is the great world poet he is

acclaimed to be, his life and poems ought to be susceptible to re-presentation and re-interpretation in terms of current modes of biographical art and literary criticism. But some fatality seems to dog almost every writer on Burns, forcing him to write in a fashion that prevents his book taking, in and for itself, any reputable place in the class of studies to which it belongs ... What this comes to in the long run is that interest in Burns is confined to inferior minds, and the poet's reputation is not being continually renewed and readjusted to modern consciousness as it ought to be.

Scots Independent, February 1929

MacDiarmid argued that, first, the hero-worship of Burns put a brake on cultural development, in that many believed that the Scots language had reached its apogee with him and could go no further. Second, the idolatry of Burns had neutered Scottish culture: all that now happened was that people gathered once a year to recite poems and songs in a mindless fashion; thereafter it was forgotten. Third, Burns was used as a totem by the Establishment to give credence to traditional values and bolster the political status quo.

A final factor conditioning MacDiarmid's programme was a touch of intellectual snobbery, and this arguably was central to its eventual failure as a mass movement of national liberation. MacDiarmid's linguistic reconstruction put it beyond the reach of much of the population, most of whom would have a good working knowledge of a Scots which was closer to that of Burns than to that of the medieval makar Henry Dunbar. MacDiarmid's insistence on linguistic purity condemned his programme to being of interest to only a small minority.

Irish nationalism was a more important example for most Scots who were interested in pursuing a cultural road to independence. In part this model was very much a creation of the nineteenth century, when nationalist bourgeois intellectual movements had a profound effect on emergent nations, and it would have little relevance in the changed circumstances of the inter-war era, in an age of mass democracy where the majority of the population deemed social and economic conditions more important than laying claim to a separate language. This point was grasped by the political nationalists, who kept the cultural nationalists at arms length precisely because in class-riven Scotland their message would be deemed irrelevant by most people.

Like the cultural nationalists, the political nationalists were not a unified body. There were those who favoured a form of devolution, as well as those who wanted complete political separation from England. If these divisions were not significant enough, there were also those who sought to achieve their political goals by means of a new political party which would secure an electoral mandate, and those who believed their goals could be secured by working with the existing political parties.

Home rule had been part of Scottish political culture from before the First World War, and in 1913 a bill had actually been presented at Westminster, but was not enacted. Home rule continued to loiter in Scottish political circles after the war, largely because Labour had inherited this policy as part of the radical tradition. In 1922, when the Clydeside MPs left for London to take up their parliamentary seats, they assured their audiences at public meetings that there was no subject which aroused greater enthusiasm in Scotland than home rule. In 1924, when a private member's bill proposing home rule was talked out, it led to scenes of uproar from Scottish Labour MPs. Yet by 1927 this enthusiasm appeared to have died on its feet, as a similar occasion drew only a lukewarm protest from the Scottish Labour Party.

The reasons for this are not hard to find. In the first place, Scottish home rule was picked up by Labour without much thought. It was a crowd-pleaser in the early twenties, and its reductive message that Scotland's problems were all the fault of the English was used by many like James Maxton to guarantee an enthusiastic burst of applause. As an article of faith that had its origins in the pre-war radical tradition, it could be endorsed by left and right. As time wore on and the social and economic condition of post-war Scotland became more apparent, the policy was subject to a rethink, with the ideas of John Wheatley forming the dominant influence. Wheatley was one of the few thinkers to address the issue of how socialism would be achieved in an international system of capitalism. Drawing his ideas from a wide range of sources, and in particular the Soviet Union, he believed that the conversion of Britain and its empire to socialism would be the most effective way to help create an international socialist system. Wheatley placed economics at the centre of his thought, and the reality of the situation in Scotland was that to remedy the endemic social and economic problems would require greater resources than Scotland alone could supply. Indeed, the full resources of the British state would have to be used in a planned way to tackle these issues, and obviously this meant that Scottish home rule would be irrelevant to solving these problems. To further the social and economic interests of the Scottish working class, he argued, it was necessary to employ a British strategy. Scottish home rule lost its *raison d'être*.

NATIONALISM

It was in reaction to Labour's lukewarm approach to the issue of home rule that the first modern nationalist party in Scotland appeared – the National Party of Scotland. The NPS was founded in 1928, when the members of the Scottish Home Rule Association, the Scots National League, the Scots National Movement and the Glasgow University Nationalist Association decided to find common cause and create a new party dedicated to 'Scottish nationalism'. From the outset, the party was an ideological mixture. It included moderate home-rulers who wanted to form their own party in the belief that its success at the polls would inspire the mainstream parties, in particular Labour, to take up the home-rule mantle once more in earnest. Others drew their inspiration from unyielding Irish nationalism, and for them devolution or home rule failed to satisfy a lust for complete political independence. There were even those who believed that some form of greater Scottish political representation would help to cement a British identity. Not only was there confusion about the ideological objectives of Scottish nationalism, there was also disagreement about how it ought to be achieved, with some arguing for a mandate from the electorate by contesting elections and others who were in favour of pressure-group tactics. In spite of such contradictions, when the NPS announced its existence in April 1928 most were optimistic that it marked a new era in Scottish politics. Such hopes proved forlorn, however, when the party was able only to dent the electorate in a number of by-elections and when it was able to field only a handful of candidates at the general election of 1929.

The lack of progress exacerbated the latent divisions within the NPS, with moderates blaming radicals and radicals blaming moderates for the poor electoral performance. Although out of kilter with reality, the public perception of the NPS was none too helpful, with accusations made by the press that if the nationalists had their way the result would be a closing of the border with England and compulsory Gaelic and kilt-wearing. Hugh MacDiarmid as a leading literary nationalist, though insignificant within the political structure, was only too happy to oblige the media with over-the-top appearances as the stereotypical nationalist nutcase. Other nation-alists, such as Lewis Spence, gave full vent to anti-English bigotry:

> To detail the facts plainly and beyond peradventure, the land of Scotland is more surely in the grip of its hereditary enemy than ever. Its people are denied the use of two thirds of its soil, which is retained for the purpose of English sport and leisure, devoted to the recreation of Southern idlers. Its wealth is at the disposal of the English Treasury. Its commerce has become a playground of exper-iment for English interest. Its people are banished in thousands, their places taken by English, and the policy which dictates this is most assuredly the fruit of a definite English conspiracy to destroy the Scottish race.
>
> *Freedom for Scotland* (Edinburgh, 1929)

The sense of frustration at the lack of electoral progress was worsened both by the impact of the Great Depression and by the associated political crisis, in which it was believed that nationalism would emerge as the major political force as it appeared to be doing on the European mainland. A number of opinion polls showed that home rule remained popular with the electorate and that much of the social and economic discontent engen-dered by the Depression was taking on a nationalist air. To explain the fail-ure to capitalise on this, the moderates blamed the radicals for pushing a programme which went too far, while the radicals believed that it was the timidity of current policy which held back support.

The moderate imperative to rid the party of its fundamentalist image was given a further boost by the appearance in 1932 of a right-wing, mod-erate, self-government organisation called the Scottish Party, which claimed to be for greater autonomy but would not endorse the supposed excesses of the NPS. The Scottish Party was not a proper political party as such, but was rather a collection of disgruntled Tories and Liberals who believed that Scotland was not being treated adequately by the current political system. Another salient factor in qualifying support for Scottish nationalism was a belief that nationalism could be a dangerous force if it fell into the wrong hands, and the Scottish Party was driven as much by a desire to keep a lid on Scottish nationalism as by a wish to promote it. For moderates in the NPS, the appearance of an 'Establishment' home-rule movement which contained such figures as the Duke of Montrose, Sir Alexander MacEwen, the former Liberal Lord Provost of Inverness, R. D. Anderson, editor of the *Daily Record,* and Sir Daniel Stevenson, former Provost of Glasgow, presented a serious challenge. Although such figures in the Scottish Party did not belong to the premier league of Scottish politics, they had that extra Establishment cachet which the National Party lacked, and the NPS's leading moderate, John MacCormack, was determined that the best way forward for the nationalist cause was to unite the two parties.

Using the novelist Neil M. Gunn as a go-between, points of agreement were reached. One of the key factors in paving the way towards unity was the shedding of the National Party's fundamentalist or radical wing. On the pretext of their having breached party discipline, radicals including Hugh MacDiarmid were expelled from the NPS, and in April 1934 the Scottish National Party (SNP) was born out of the fusion of the NPS and the Scottish Party. However, the purges of the National Party had robbed the movement of some of its most dedicated and committed activists and by no means all those who were expelled were fundamentalists. Furthermore, the Scottish Party had no groundswell of members or supporters, but simply assumed positions of leadership within the new organisation.

The organisational and ideological disarray which had characterised the National Party was nothing compared to the shambles which was the early SNP. In keeping with much of the empty rhetoric of the National Government of the time, the SNP put forward no realistic social or economic proposals. Instead, it complained about injustice to Scotland and issued meaningless appeals for Scottish national unity. Eschewing class, the nationalists appealed to nobody, and the rhetoric of nationalism could not deal with the class-based socio-economic concerns of a society struggling with the Depression. Not surprisingly, the SNP fared little better than its predecessor in making electoral progress. A promising start in 1934 soon turned to electoral impotence as the party failed to field enough candidates in the 1935 general election, and at by-elections it struggled to pass the 10 per cent mark. Just as happened with the NPS, party discipline collapsed. Some members also belonged to other political parties; others believed in pressure-group strategies, while others were committed to contesting elections; some advocated complete independence, while others were content to push for devolution. All this happened under a lacklustre leadership which was often too concerned with its own agenda to notice that the party was organisationally and ideologically fragmenting. By 1935 the nationalists had firmly established themselves on the fringes of Scottish politics, and they would remain there for another thirty years.

Throughout the first half of the thirties Scottish politicians were wary that nationalism could take off and become a major political force. As was mentioned earlier, the events in mainland Europe, where depression coupled with political instability had conspired to pave the way for successful nationalist movements, seemed to suggest the same outcome in Scotland. In 1932 every baronet and titled individual in Scotland, together with the great and good of Scottish business, signed a declaration against Scottish nationalism warning of the dangers that separation from England would bring. It was called the Ragman's Roll, after the document which was signed in the twelfth century pledging the Scottish nobility to Edward I. If nothing else, it revealed that the Scottish Establishment took the threat of nationalism seriously. In all this panic, no one seemed to notice that the nationalists were in fact doing so badly.

The period of the Depression marked a profound change in the culture of Scottish politics, with the positive interpretation of the Union in which the Scots more than contributed their fair share being transformed into one which was inclined to emphasise Scottish reliance and dependence on England. At its heart it was a negative and defeatist ideology which was used to counteract Scottish nationalism. The former Conservative Chancellor of the Exchequer Sir Robert Horne, speaking in the House of Commons on 22 November 1932, declared:

I am not one of those who deride the Scottish home rule movement,
nor am I disposed to treat it lightly. On the contrary I am sensitive
to the same influences as most of my countrymen ... The Welsh are
showing the kind of wisdom that is generally attributed to the Scot,
because, knowing that the amount of their unemployment is so
much greater than elsewhere, probably they realise that they would
find great difficulty in providing unemployment benefits by themselves, and they are wiser to rely on the richer country than to seek
separation.

Other politicians joined in with this cacophony of national defeatism. The
Scottish people were warned that any dalliance with nationalism would
result in even greater job losses and further economic dislocation. Economics were only one part of the argument: altogether more sinister and
perplexing were the cultural aspects, which seemed to betray a psychotic
self-hatred. Before the Union of 1707, claimed the Tory MP for Aberdeenshire, Bob Boothby, writing in *The Nation* on 9 March 1929, the Scots
were a 'miserable pack of savages contributing nothing to civilisation'.

Other examples of national self-effacement appeared regularly in the
newspapers as politician after politician rose to reverse previous notions
that the Scots not only ran and controlled the Empire, but had been
responsible for its creation in the first place. The threat to Scottish
employment in England and the Empire was raised as a major objection to
the creation of a parliament in Edinburgh. 'Are they [Scottish home-
rulers] willing to shut out Scotsmen from taking the biggest positions?'
asked the Tory MP, Anne Horsburgh in the same debate that Horne had
spoken in. The Scots were informed that they depended on England for
jobs, money, culture, security and improvement. This shift from a positive
interpretation of Unionism to one which was nakedly self-defeatist and
self-interested was arguably the most profound shift in Scottish political
thinking of the twentieth century. The notion that the Union was not a
partnership of equals but one of dependency would continue to haunt
Unionism for the next seventy years. For most Scots in the inter-war years,
however, politics came second to the day-to-day business of getting on
with life.

-FOUR-

LIVING,

1935–1939

Barra has as many people as it can comfortably hold – two thousand two hundred and fifty at the last census with an extra four or five hundred in the summer months when the herring boats are at work. What do the people do? Well they cultivate their crofts – many of them would fish if the inshore fishing had not been ruined by the intensive trawling since the war. The young men go to sea. The young women go away to service or to work at the gutting of herring as far north as Lerwick or as far south as Yarmouth. But there are always plenty of young men and young women on the island, and the dances which are held all the year round except during Lent and Advent in one or other of the three parish halls are, often enough, too full. Barra is an extraordinarily happy place. Laughter is the keynote. There is always a good story going the rounds. Gaelic is a great language for wit, and with three-quarters of the population of Barra speaking both Gaelic and English, the native Gaelic wit salts the English. And it is not empty laughter. Barra passed through some fierce ordeals during the last three centuries in the way of persecution, evictions and famine, but I do not want to harrow your feelings by dragging up the old unhappy past. The point I would make is that the laughter of Barra has experience behind it. It is a mellow fruit which has ripened after a frosty spring.

Compton Mackenzie, 'Fifty Three Years Old: 1936', *My Life and Times: Octave Seven 1931–1938* (London, 1968)

Ay weel may ye wonder, sae lang keep it under,
Wi' our face to the grund-stane, our back tae the wa',
But our warst fears are ended, our fortune has mended,
We're fed and well fended since whisky's awa,
I mind our wee biggin wi' scarcely a stick in't,
Our bed was the floor on a wee oickle straw,
Sae seldom we cookit, sae hungry it lookit,
That the starved mice forsook it, but whisky's awa.

See noo, whit a change – we've a weel stockit girnel,
Abundance o' bannocks, wi' hams ane or twa;
Our fire it is cheery – sae ance and eerie –
Can shelter the weary – since whisky's awa.
Ye thoughtless, who rin on the rough road to ruin,
Come, join total abstinence! – join ane and a'!
For naething can mend ye, nae kind friend will fend ye –
Nae guid will attend ye, till whisk's awa.

'Whisky's Awa', popular temperance song

If I had not been blessed, in youth, with an athletic fleetness, if I had not known the joy of leaping and dancing, if I had not known those moments of exhilaration when one's only expression of the knowledge that it is good to be alive is to strain the body to exhaustion – then I might have been tempted now to despise the pride of mere physical fitness, to sneer at the daily adulation of the boxer, or the football player, or the tennis star. But having known the same pride of youth – the sheer muscular exuberance which forces one to run against the wind or to lay hold of a friend and bear him to the ground – having known this, I am saved from jealousy and cannot betray the body by denying that it is a fine thing to feel the life that is in flesh. Even yet I can feel it – as if a statue grown warm, not bitter, with the desire to run.

William Soutar, *Diaries of a Dying Man*, ed. Alexander Scott
(Edinburgh, 1954), entry for 5 March 1935

CHILDHOOD

In the general election of 1935, those born in 1914 would have attained their majority and been entitled to vote. Many, no doubt, would have reflected on their life to date and what the future would hold. The experience of growing up in Scotland was conditioned by social class and geography. Poverty and overcrowding were the two key determinants of whether or not you would survive your first six months. The infant mortality rate for Scotland in 1937 was 80 per 1,000 births – or, put more simply, out of every thirteen children born, one would die before their first birthday. In that same year there were 87,810 children born, of whom 7,050 failed to make it to their first birthday. If that statistic was not shocking enough, in the period from 1900 to 1937, 94,991 children died within their first year, which in all probability was almost as big a death toll as the nation had experienced during the First World War.

The infant mortality rate had been declining in the twentieth century, and there was a particular improvement in the chances of survival for those babies who lasted through their first month. What was of particular concern to the medical authorities was that Scotland's infant mortality rate was not decreasing at the same rate as that of other advanced western societies. Whereas Scotland had similar rates to England and Wales at the beginning of the century, by 1937 they were about a third higher. Had Scotland managed to keep pace with the rest of the United Kingdom, this would have meant that about a further 1,800 babies would have survived in that year. In spite of its splendid international reputation for medicine, Scotland's dismal record in infant mortality was surpassed in Europe only by Poland, Hungary and Italy. Children in Ireland, Canada, America and Germany all had better odds on reaching their first birthday, while babies in the Netherlands had twice the rate of survival of their Scottish peers.

Statistical averages can convey only part of the picture, as there were large differences between the various parts of Scotland. In the larger towns and cities, the infant mortality rate was 90 per 1,000, in the smaller towns it was 69, and in the countryside it was 66. Even within these categories there were wide variations. In the poverty-stricken west the rate was 114 for Kilmarnock, 104 for Glasgow, and 99 for Coatbridge. Prosperous Edinburgh had a rate of 70, while Dundee had 87 and Aberdeen had 72,

which demonstrated in a fairly crude way that infant mortality was linked
to overall wealth. Such a conclusion becomes more apparent when looking
at the figures for the mid twenties and early thirties, which reveal that
Glasgow was the only city which failed to improve its rate. In the ten years
after 1927, Edinburgh dropped from 80 to 70, Dundee from 138 to 87,
and Aberdeen from 105 to 72. Further evidence can also be brought to
bear to show the link between child death and poverty. Children born to
unmarried parents had a 50 per cent higher chance of death compared to
those born in wedlock, perhaps because they tended to be in the lowest
income bracket. Statistically, the larger a family was, the greater its
poverty would be, and consequently the greater the risk of child death.
The poorer a family was, the greater the overcrowding, and the greater the
risk of infant mortality. The main physiological causes of child death were
failure to develop and infectious diseases, both of which were associated
with poverty and overcrowding.

Such statistics can only partially reconstruct for us today what must
have been a horrendous experience for a great many Scottish families. Few
were unaffected by the phenomenon of child death and, although the poor
were its principal victims, its grizzly tentacles were just as capable of
striking out at the prosperous and the well-to-do. The death of a child was
something that most would experience, either through their own family
or through neighbours. Statistically, most Scottish children would have
played with at least one child who had lost a sibling. Even those who managed to reach the magic age of one were still vulnerable to a host of infectious diseases which could kill a child. Growing up in inter-war Scotland,
it would be hard to ignore the phenomenon as mothers would have to dash
off to comfort the grieving family and certain homes would suddenly
become forbidden to children. Molly Weir remembered the dread that
could spread through the community:

> The mere whisper of 'fever', that infant scourge, sent our mothers
> sick with dread. With twelve families to a close, infection could
> spread like wildfire, and the sight of the fever van struck a chill
> into our hearts. But curiosity among us children was always
> stronger than fear and we would gather on the pavement to catch
> a glimpse of a swathed figure on its way through the close to the

ambulance, and shudder with relief that it wasn't one of us on the stretcher.

Shoes Were for Sunday (London, 1970)

The full extent of private grief can never be known. Scotland was both a stoic and a reticent society in which the expression of emotion was frowned upon. Mothers and fathers were told never to mind because there was always time for another child, or that they should count their blessings because their other children were healthy. As is so often the case in Scottish history, the record is silent when it comes to emotion, but that silence does not make the pain of child death any less real, only more tragic.

It is probably true to say that most children experienced a happy time growing up, and this is reflected in countless biographies. Materialism was unknown to most youngsters, and the absence of toys and other goods was not felt. Children had to improvise and use their imagination. This is reflected in the variety of games which were played at the time. They were nearly all centred outdoors, to get away from the cramped living conditions, and involved a crowd. Gender conditioning began at an early age, with boys and girls dividing themselves into their respective camps. Parents looked upon gender confusion with horror, and woe betide a boy who preferred skipping with the girls to the rough and tumble of boyish activity. Such a child would receive the opprobrium of all males in the vicinity. Hide-and-seek, cowboys and Indians, British bulldog, and football reflected the physical attributes thought to be required for a successful transition into manhood. Skipping, hopscotch and family role-playing were the normal activities for girls.

While such rigid gender typing may strike us as odd today, it has to be remembered that it was a society which rigorously enforced notions of masculinity and femininity. A boy who did not grow up with manly attributes was unlikely to make a success of himself. Taunting, picking on, merciless teasing and social ostracisation awaited the effeminate boy or man. It was a hard society, and boys had to be tough to survive. Crying and showing too much emotion were controlled and eliminated, not only by parents but by society in general. Boys did not cry. The Scottish language of child-rearing was remarkably rich in its complexity, and reveals the society's attitude to children – especially boys. 'Sissy', 'Jessie', 'big girl' and 'big girl's blouse', 'Nancy', 'cry baby' and other such epithets which connoted weird or unusual were applied with great liberality to any boy who was not unambiguous in his display of masculine attributes. The corresponding attitudes existed towards girls, who were trained from an early age that imitation of mother was the most appropriate form of behaviour. Girls were encouraged to help around the house, to do housework, and to look after the males in the family. The acquisition of domestic skills was thought to be an absolute prerequisite for marriage, which was deemed to be every girl's goal in life.

There was an unusually wide range of words associated with physical punishment. 'Leathering', 'battering', 'tanning', 'skelping', 'bleaching', 'whipping', 'hammering', 'roasting', 'hiding' and 'thrashing' were familiar expressions for most children, as was the term 'doing' – as in 'You'll get a doing.' Perhaps the most bizarre of all was the way that almost any part of speech could denote a threat of physical punishment. Question: 'Can I go out?' Answer: 'I'll "out" you!' Question: 'Can I have a sweet?' Answer: 'I'll give you a sweet!' Skelps and clouts were usually confined to the ear or head, while leathering and tanning were directed at the behind. Children of all classes had one thing in common, which was that there was no stigma attached to the use of physical punishment. Perhaps the main difference was that the middle class (including teachers) had a preference for using instruments such as the cane or the strap, whereas the working class simply used their hands or everyday objects like a wooden spoon, a belt or a brush.

Physical punishment was not simply the prerogative of the parents, and in many working-class communities discipline was a communal activity in which misbehaviour could be arbitrarily dealt with by a clout on the ear or a kick in the arse. Punishment could take place in public, and for particularly heinous crimes children could be beaten publicly in front of neighbours against whom they had transgressed. The police, shopkeepers, teachers and other authority figures were more than happy to dispense summary justice against children, and the worst thing that children feared was that having already beaten them, an angry adult would then haul them off to their parents, where the whole process was likely to be repeated.

EDUCATION

There was an expansion in education provision following the First World War largely as a result of greater state intervention and optimism fuelled by the prevailing atmosphere of creating a land fit for heroes. The 1918 Education Act replaced the existing 947 local school boards with thirty-eight education authorities – one for each of the thirty-three counties and one each for Edinburgh, Leith, Glasgow, Aberdeen and Dundee. (The Edinburgh and Leith boards were amalgamated in 1920.) In 1929 the education committees were brought under the control of local authorities following the reform of local government. The 1918 act proposed raising the minimum school-leaving age by one year to fifteen, advocated free secondary education for all, and believed that the new education authorities would be more effective than the old school boards in ensuring that staffing, buildings and infrastructure would be efficiently maintained. The act also brought Catholic schools within the state system (see Chapter 3). Finally, it was hoped that there would be extensive reform to bring the system more up to date and meet the needs of a changing society.

Such optimism proved forlorn, as central-government funding was cut back in the twenties and local authorities found that the effects of social and economic dislocation placed increasing demands on their resources. The cost of schooling increased dramatically in the inter-war period, rising from £9,372,000 in 1919–20 to over £14 million in 1938–9, with two-thirds of expenditure going on staff salaries. By the end of the Second World War central government would come to bear the cost of two-thirds of such expenditure.

The quality of schooling depended largely on social class, although there was a powerful myth in Scottish society which stated that anyone with the necessary ability could use education as a passport to improvement. This myth of the 'lad o'pairts' – not 'lass o'pairts', notice – was greatly cherished and was held up by many as evidence of the country's natural egalitarianism and meritocratic nature. Certainly Scottish children were fed a diet of meritocratic hero stories in which great Scottish luminaries such as James Watt, David Livingstone and Thomas Carlyle were used as examples of how people could pull themselves up by their bootstraps, study, and get on in the world. The idea that Scottish education was meritocratic and enabled the best to rise in society had many powerful backers, who believed it to be an important part of national identity. James Graham Kerr, the regius professor of zoology at Glasgow University, was one such:

> Among our Scottish affairs there is hardly any that arouses a more vivid and widespread interest than the education or upbringing of our citizens. Both we ourselves and those outside Scotland rightly attribute to our system of national education much of the success attained by our countrymen during the decades of the last century. But when we come to contemporary education we find, contentious folk as we are, no longer agreement, but rather embittered controversy between those, on the one hand, who regard our education as splendid and flawless and those, on the other, who regard it as a black disgrace. Truth to tell, many of our harsher critics betray rather a lack of sense of proportion: while appreciating the obvious faults of today, they seem to forget the enormous advance during the past century ... It is a particular source of pride to us Scots that our race has produced so many winners in life's race who at the start were handicapped by poverty and entire lack of family influence.
>
> The Duke of Atholl et al., *A Scotsman's Heritage* (London, 1932)

This myth had long pervaded the thinking of the Scottish Education Department (SED). Under the leadership of Sir Henry Craik and John Struthers, from 1885 to 1922, it was thought that there were essentially two types of children: those who were good with their heads and those who were good with their hands. The former would become the leadership class of the future, while the latter would be the workforce. Intelligence was the key to one's future social position, and while this may seem on the surface to have been an egalitarian philosophy, in that everyone had an equal opportunity, the prejudice of the SED came through in repeated statements that the former would in all probability be drawn from the middle class while the latter would come from the working class. The extent of egalitarianism in the Scottish Education Department was an acknowledgement that there might be a few gifted and bright boys among the children of the working class – hardly evidence of equal educational opportunities. That a number of gifted individuals from poorer backgrounds had come through the system in the past was frequently held up as evidence that it was fair. It was smugly assumed by many that the reason there were so few lads o'pairts who rose through the ranks of educational opportunity was that the vast majority of the working class were thick. In addition to this institutional prejudice, working-class children faced all sorts of practical barriers to progress.

Given the belief that there two types of children (boys), it followed that there must be two types of school. One would train up the leadership class by preparing pupils for university, whereas the other would equip pupils for a life in industry. (Girls tended to be taught how to be good wives and mothers.) Following on from the belief that the majority of the leaders would be middle class and the majority of the led would be working class, children were given different kinds of education depending on their social background. Given that Scotland was divided on the basis of social geography, this meant that pupils in middle-class areas would go to middle-class schools, while those living in working-class areas would end up in schools which reflected the social class of their intake.

All children were given an elementary education until the age of twelve. After that they were divided into 'senior' and 'junior' secondary schools. The former offered four- and later five-year courses of an academic nature which would lead to a Leaving Certificate that was made up of subjects at 'higher' and 'lower' levels. This was essential for university entrance and for professional jobs. The latter, which had lower and poorer levels of staffing and resources, continued with basic elementary work for a further two, or possibly three, years. Local authorities, strapped for cash, streamed pupils into appropriate schools, according to the results in an examination taken at the end of primary school, and the senior secondary schools in most cities charged fees. Finding cash for travel and fees put off many working-class parents.

The curriculum reflected these basic divisions, with middle-class children being exposed to a wide range of subjects, principally English, Greek, Latin and mathematics, which were essential for going on to university, while the working class built upon the staple of the 'three Rs', reading, writing and arithmetic, with some maths, geography, history, drawing and science thrown in. Whereas the former subjects demanded a high level of input from teachers and hence smaller classes, in the latter knowledge could be dispensed in the most cost-effective way through rote

learning in large classes. Culturally, the schools reflected the supposed different aspirations of the pupils, with the middle class going in for individualism, the games ethic and a desire to build personality – usually through
beatings and tough physical punishment both on and off the sports field –
while the working class were taught to be deferential, obedient and pliant.
Perhaps the only thing that both types of school shared was the belief that
children could be moulded through physical punishment. In special retail
outlets throughout Scotland, teachers could buy the tawse, a leather strap
usually hardened in pig's blood, which was considered as vital an educational tool as the computer is today. In 1938 one anonymous adult com-
mented on the long-term effect of physical punishment:

> I myself have seen ... a teacher maddened by the stale air of the
> school, the monotony of her life and the hopelessness of keeping 40
> children in order, who raved like a lunatic, who hit children round
> the ears, banged them on the heads with slates and thrashed them
> until the more sensitive ones were in abject terror and the rest in a
> state of intense excitement. I myself, an intelligent child and will-
> ing to learn, a child for whom knowledge and imagination were
> delightful adventures, have gone to school for weeks on end, terri-
> fied of what might happen if one of our teachers, over-driven to the
> point of neurosis, were to break out that morning. That is twenty
> years ago; but I still wake up afraid, dreaming that I am in the
> infant room and that my teacher is enjoying a half hour's sarcasm
> enforced with the tawse on a class of an average age of nine.
>
> J. R. Allan, ed., *Scotland – 1938: Twenty-five Impressions*
> (Edinburgh, 1938)

The widespread beating of children at school had very few critics. It
chimed with the nation's sense of physical toughness and manliness. Having themselves previously been victims, most parents approved with the
dictum that 'a good beating' had not done them any harm. A society of
well-rounded individuals indeed!

The 'lad o'pairts' myth was kept going by some rural areas in the
north-east and the central belt where it was still possible to achieve a
degree of social mixing in the schools. It was mainly in such outposts that

the gifted lad of humble social standing could be spotted and encouraged by the teacher or 'dominie'. In such areas the social mix had to contain sufficient numbers of middle-class pupils to warrant 'senior' secondary status, but with enough room to take in children from the labouring classes. In the north-east especially there was an important tradition of bequests and bursaries which made it possible for children of humble backgrounds to get the most out of education. Certainly the figures do show that, in spite of the hard-and-fast social divisions which covered most of Scotland and determined the type of education that a child received, there was more access in the north-east. In the country as a whole the number of certificates issued increased from 1,700 before the war to 4,000 by 1939. Also, it can be said that more children were getting more schooling, as the number increased from about 40,000 in 1914 to 91,000 in 1938. Yet the almost static elitist nature of Scottish education is exposed in the figures for pupils in the fifth and sixth years, which rose from 6,576 in 1926 to 8,459 in 1938, which is exactly in proportion to the increase for the total number in secondary schools.

Most children experienced a fairly harsh form of education. In working-class areas children would be taught in classes of about fifty in which the main teaching implements were the 'three Bs': the Bible, belt and blackboard. Learning difficulties were overcome by physical punishment: if children were incapable of providing the correct answer, it could be beaten into them. Classes sounded like the ceremonies of some weird cult as children chanted the times tables, biblical passages and the alphabet in order to learn them by rote. Education was about imparting knowledge, and the concept of child-centred learning was unknown save in the experimental theories of the Scottish educationalists A. S. Neill and R. F. MacKenzie, both of whom had to leave Scotland to implement their policies. There were a number of humane and dedicated teachers who did their best to expand the educational horizons of their pupils, but in conditions which were largely unfavourable. Most working-class children had a suspicion of authority, as did their parents, and it was expected that most would leave school at fifteen to seek work to augment the family income. Their culture came under sustained attack as Scots was denounced as 'slang' and, in the Highlands, Gaelic was seen as a bar to progress. Undoubtedly many teachers believed that they were doing missionary

work. The philosophy that most children needed only the basic requirements of education meant that a two-tier system worked to the disadvantage of the majority. Vocational education such as metalwork and
woodwork was in pitifully short supply, so most youngsters were forced
into subjects which both they and their teachers thought would do them
no good.

Times were just as tough for teachers themselves. Eight hundred had
joined up in the first few months of war in 1914, and there was then a
shortage of male teachers which lasted into the mid-twenties. Most of the
profession came from upper-working-class/lower-middle-class social origins and occupied a distinctive position of authority and respectability
within their local communities. By and large the social origins of the profession were reflected back into the community, in that those from more
privileged backgrounds tended to teach in the better schools while those
of more lowly standing ended up in working-class areas. Much of this can
be explained purely with reference to economic factors, in that the better
qualified had spent more time at university and had had the financial support necessary for this, whereas those facing financial pressure acquired the
minimum qualifications needed for a job. Better schools attracted the better qualified. In 1924 a general degree was made compulsory for male candidates who applied for a teaching certificate, and between 1928 and 1939
the proportion of graduates in the profession rose from 27 per cent to 41
per cent.

One reason why Scottish education was never able to break free from
its obsession with a strictly academic curriculum was that the hierarchical
structure was reflected within the profession. According to James Scotland, the principal of Aberdeen College of Education, writing as late as
1969:

These academic aristocrats [those with first-class honours] were
often to be found in the more selective schools like Hutchesons',
George Watson's and Aberdeen Grammar, but in the thirties at
least there were many also in higher grades [advanced classes in
other schools]. A Third, on the other hand, was regarded as something very inferior, recognised on a lower salary scale, hardly counting as honours at all and certainly barring its holder from all the

more lucrative posts. These views of course were further evidence of the Scottish reverence for academic achievement. There was a well-recognised hierarchy in the profession, scrupulously observed by teachers themselves, with secondary masters more highly regarded than primary, men more highly than women, university graduates more than non-graduates, honours men more than ordinary. A first class degree was worth more than 'excellent' in practical teaching. And in the secondary world the lowest place was reserved for teachers of domestic and technical subjects.

The History of Scottish Education, vol. 2 (London, 1969)

In 1938, Scotland's 29,061 teachers taught in 3,146 schools. Slightly more than half of these schools were to be found in the big cities and towns, with the rest being dispersed evenly between the rural/industrial and the rural areas. Of the teaching total, there were about two women teachers for every man. Men tended to better qualified, with seven out of ten having a degree, compared to only three out of ten women. Women faced systematic discrimination. In 1919 the SED guaranteed a minimum salary for men of £150, which rose by £10 increments to £250. Women started at £130, rising by £5 increments to £150 and then by £10 increments to £200. Put another way, men would eventually earn a quarter more than women, and in the fourth year for a man and a woman starting at the same time the pay differential would be just under a fifth. Women also faced the marriage bar, which meant that only spinsters could become full-time teachers. Except in the small number of private all-girl schools, women never stood a chance of being promoted to head of department or headteacher. Between 1931 and 1935 teachers had their salaries reduced by public-sector cuts.

Teachers often found themselves in a somewhat ambiguous relationship with the community. Scotland was plagued by a small-town mentality in which 'I kent his faither' was used as a pretext to rubbish social mobility. There was a lot of jealousy of those who had come from similar backgrounds but had managed to 'better' themselves. Many working-class parents resented what they saw as interference from the education authorities over issues such as health, truancy and the child's behaviour. Along with the clergy, teachers were unlike other professionals in that they were subject to moral scrutiny by the local community. Teachers were not expected to go to the pub, gamble or engage in other such activities. Their political activity was monitored, especially if it was of a leftward persuasion.

Given such circumstances, it should come as no surprise that next to no 'gifted' pupils were rescued from this system. In the conditions of the average school, with endemic overcrowding, low expectations and mutual cultural hostility between pupils and teachers, it is difficult to see how a young Einstein could possibly be given a chance to demonstrate his or her talent. Even if such a figure emerged, the considerable financial outlay required to transfer to another, more appropriate, school would be beyond the means of most parents and, given that most families conceived of themselves as an economic unit, would have meant the sacrifice of valuable earning power. Not surprisingly we find that in the University of Glasgow, which traditionally had the largest number of working-class students, the social composition of the student intake remained unchanged from before the First World War. Even though male working-class students made up just under a quarter of the total, most of these were mature students and part-timers. They had not come via the secondary-school system. Paradoxically, the Scottish myth of an egalitarian and democratic education system engendered a complacency which helped to reinforce the rigidity of class-based schooling.

The failings of Scottish education did not go unnoticed by its minority of critics. The elitist nature of the system meant that a small number of students were catered for, but for the rest there was little. This was the main cause of contention, as many realised the vital link between economic development and a good education system. According to HM Inspectors of Schools report for 1928–9:

> Advantage should be taken of the change coming on through the raising of the school age to make a drastic change in our educational procedure. At present it is still too scholastic. Let us face the fact that a great proportion of our children are never going to do much good on that line and let us draft a curriculum of a largely practical nature, making for increased efficiency and fitness for the ordinary work-life of by far the greater number of pupils ... it is worth con-

sideration whether the pupil who is inclined towards practical things rather than to book learning should be delayed by failure instead of being diverted into a course where his head and hands will find congenial instruction.

As with so many good intentions, finance proved to be the stumbling block, especially in the wake of the Great Crash, when local authorities, who paid for education, found themselves under increased financial pressure with the rising cost of poor relief due to unemployment. Yet, with the economic crisis of the thirties, more attention was focused on education as a means to help the ailing economy by producing a better-trained workforce. The dogma by which education was dominated by academic standards was denounced for its failure to provide most children with the practical skills they would need in the future. The 1929 HM Inspectors report claimed that such standards meant that about half the children in primary schools were 'retarded', while an authority cited in the report declared that 60 per cent of boys and girls in day schools failed to reach a 'normal' standard in education, and that out of 350 pupils who started on a secondary course only 15 completed it or gained the Leaving Certificate. It went on:

> Time is being wasted on trivialities and minutiae which are of no practical value. Much valuable time is wasted on making pupils work out long 'sums' in arithmetic and in some schools a whole series of them is prescribed for cotter children to work out at home. No sane teacher who knew anything about the arrangements of a working-class home would be guilty of such gross stupidity or cruelty.

There was little change in the education system, and calls for more practical and technical education for the majority went unheeded, as did the calls for a new philosophy. Economists complained that technology and engineering still failed to attract the same social cachet as did the arts and bookish forms of learning. The education system was a pyramid on which there were two roads: one led to the top and a degree, the other went nowhere. Evidence of the inappropriateness of the curriculum for most children can be found in the occupational structure of the Scottish workforce. Sixty per cent of males were classified as industrial workers, 11.5 per cent as commercial, 11 per cent as rural, and only 2.75 per cent as professional. The figures for women were a third in industrial occupations, 26 per cent in general service, a quarter in commerce, and 7 per cent in the professions. Writing on the eve of the Second World War, James Bowie, the principal of Dundee's School of Economics and Commerce, summed up the failures of Scottish education:

> The primary school and the university are the starting-point and the termination respectively of the education system. For the vast majority the one is inescapable, the other unattainable. At 14 or 15 compulsory education ends and our children pour out in all directions. They represent only the green fruit of an education system. Almost universally, instead of a healthy curiosity and a keen appetite for knowledge, they have acquired a 'scunner' at the whole business. Very few are eager to continue their general education, but some few busy themselves in acquiring skills at a price on the market. The rough and tumble of industrial life, and the living conditions to which they are subjected, far from being an educative process are much too frequently in effect de-educating. The mental age of our people is reckoned to be only 12, with the result that our institutional make-up, our social habits, our manners, our political and economic and international policies, our boasted democracy reach only a meagre level. Our Scottish educational system may have been in the past one of our great achievements, but today in most directions leadership is no longer in our hands.
>
> *The Future of Scotland* (Edinburgh, 1939)

HEALTH

Inter-war Scotland was not a healthy place, although on the whole, the health of the nation had improved. The average life expectancy in 1931 was 56 for men and 59.5 for women – an increase of 10 years for both sexes since 1900. The population of Scotland in 1931 was 4,843,000, of which just over half were women. Some 1,356,000 were under the age of 14, while just under 315,000 had managed to survive to over 65. And 52.4 per cent of men were married, while the figure for women was 47.5. The average age of marriage was 28 for men and about 26 for women. Most Scots lived in Glasgow and the central west, which accounted for 2,326,000 people; 655,000 lived in the east-central area of Edinburgh and Lothian; 225,000 lived in the central area of Stirling and Clackmannan; Dundee and its environs of Perth and Fife accounted for 675,000; Aberdeen and the north-east had 444,000 people; the south-west had 141,000, the borders 110,000; and the crofting counties and the Northern Isles had 293,000.

Deaths from infectious diseases and tuberculosis had declined, but bronchitis and pneumonia remained stubbornly persistent, while cancer had increased slightly. Just before the Second World War, 38 per cent of men voluntarily enlisting for the army were rejected on health grounds. Rickets had been a plague among children before the First World War. It softened the bones, which led to deformity, and weakened the immune system against other diseases. Whereas almost 1 in 10 children contracted the disease before 1914, this statistic dropped to 1.5 per 100 children by 1938. There was a steady decline of childhood diseases such as measles, scarlatina, whooping cough, diphtheria and croup, which before 1914 had been responsible for a third of all deaths in the 1–4 age group and a quarter in the age group 5–9. One of the biggest problems identified in school medical examinations was the state of children's teeth. Of the 205,206 children seen during routine inspections during the school year 1936–7, a staggering 116,161 were found to have between one and four teeth decayed, while a further 30,519 were found to have more than five teeth decayed. Tooth decay affected all social classes and was due to the increase in sugar in the diet, especially sweets. Dentists were also in short supply, with one school dentist per 11,000 children. Class differences came out in the fact that the middle class were able to use private practitioners and get remedial fillings, whereas for many other children the damage was such that extraction was the only solution.

One problem in measuring the health of the nation in the thirties is that statistics were collated only for those workers who were insured. In examining these figures, a number of points have to be borne in mind. First, the official statistics will underestimate the extent of illness because, although there is a clear correlation between poverty and physical well-being, a large number of unhealthy unemployed would not have been insured. Second, age and health were vital qualities in securing employment, and it can safely be assumed that the older and less healthy would be found disproportionately among the long-term unemployed and hence uninsured. Third, a disproportionately high number of the unhealthy unemployed were suffering from industrial illnesses which were particularly associated with the heavy industries, and so were not typical of the nation as a whole.

In 1931 there was a total of 1,787,700 insured workers, of whom 667,000 were women. In that year respiratory troubles, including tuberculosis, which could be inflamed by influenza, accounted for nearly a third of the cost to health insurance. Rheumatism accounted for 13 per cent, digestive problems 10 per cent, circulatory problems 8 per cent, and 'nervous' diseases, including insanity, 7 per cent. A variety of other ailments, including accidents, accounted for just under one out of ten days lost at work. By 1936 1.7 per cent or 30,754 workers were continuously ill throughout the year and accounted for 40 per cent of all days lost through illness. This was a result of a steady rise during the thirties, demonstrating that preventive medicine had some way to go. Mental illness accounted for about a fifth of Scotland's chronically ill, followed by rheumatism, respiratory illness, circulatory problems and tuberculosis, which each accounted for just over 10 per cent. Those suffering chronic illness lost on average 179 weeks' work for men and 188 weeks for women, and might expect to suffer the problem on average for five and a half years in their working lives. Of those not chronically ill, slightly less than a quarter of the insured workforce was ill at least once during 1936, with influenza as the most common complaint. The average duration of the illness was 22.7 days, and the average number of times off work was 1.2.

The place of work had a direct bearing on health. Miners were the most unhealthy, due to respiratory diseases which were a result of working in damp and polluted atmospheres. Next came workers in textiles and paper-making, which, though not prone to dampness, had problems of poor ventilation and a polluted atmosphere. Those in transport, food and drink were third on the list, followed by metal and agricultural workers. The building trade was less healthy than commerce, while those men least prone to sickness were to be found as cooks, waiters and others working in domestic service. The sickest women workers were to be found in transport and domestic service, where contact with the public was probably responsible for high rates of infectious disease, though such infections were usually of short duration. Industrial and agricultural workers fared worse than those in secretarial and commercial employment, with the best health enjoyed by those working in the manufacture of food and drink. Men tended to be incapacitated by respiratory and digestive problems, whereas women tended to have a higher incidence of mental illness and of infections associated with being run-down.

Where you lived also affected your health. By and large, the more urban the settlement the more unhealthy it was. The number of days lost through illness and chronic sickness was lowest in the Highlands and Islands, followed in ascending order by the north-east, the borders and the industrial central belt, demonstrating clearly the correlation between health and the rural environment. What the statistics do not show, however, is the correlation between poverty and health, in that the survey material relates only to the working population.

Working women – it is difficult to generalise about women per se – tended to be ill more often and for longer periods of time than men. As has been noted above, stress (usually classified as insanity or neurosis) was one of the most common complaints; another was anaemia. By and large, women tended to be employed in low-paid and unskilled work. Anecdotal evidence suggests that many women worked to supplement meagre family incomes, and often would take on work which an unemployed husband found demeaning. As they were still expected to carry out their domestic role of caring for the home and children, this must have put considerable stress upon them. We know that married women were more likely to be ill than unmarried women, and that stress and anaemia are caused by fatigue and poor self-maintenance, all of which supports the argument that the health of working mothers was compromised by poor economic conditions and poverty. Maternal mortality rates offer another glimpse into the well-being of women in the thirties. The rate in Scotland between 1931 and 1935 was 61 per 1,000 births, or, put another way, the 89,306 births in this period witnessed the death of 5,451 women – an average of over 1,300 deaths per annum. The death rate declined in 1937 to 4.8 per 1,000, in part because of the Maternity Services Act, which led to an increase of services and advice during childbirth. By 1936 over a third of mothers were using antenatal services.

For many experts, diet was a source of concern. Again the statistical evidence available to us is drawn from those who were insured, so we should factor this downward to take account of the unemployed in drawing up an overall picture of consumption in Scotland. Work carried out on England by the Pilgrim Trust in 1937 demonstrated that in areas of high unemployment about a quarter of children were suffering from malnutrition. Furthermore, the reports of medical officers throughout Scotland in the inter-war period drew attention to the poor state of health of the children of the unemployed, with many pointing out that means-test provision was inadequate to provide a healthy diet. Some of these issues were picked up by a 1937 report on nutrition which had been commissioned by the Secretary of State for Scotland. It pointed out that insufficient milk was consumed, and that the average half-pint should be increased to seven-eighths of a pint per day. Not enough fruit and vegetables were eaten, and potatoes should replace some of the sugar and highly milled cereals in most diets. An official inquiry into the average expenditure of a Scottish working-class household in 1937 showed that 41 per cent of income went on food. Meats (mainly sausages and beef) accounted for about a fifth; bread, biscuits, cakes and cereals took slightly less than a fifth, as did cheese, milk and eggs; while fruit and vegetables accounted for about a tenth, as did fats. Jam and sugar, together with fish, also made up a tenth.

For most families, the fare was plain: porridge in the morning, and the ubiquitous 'piece' or sandwich for working fathers, with children making do with either cheese or jam for lunch. Home-made broth was common, as were mince, stew and potatoes. Contrary to popular assumptions, boiling was the traditional way of cooking in Scotland, with shallow-frying of sausages and eggs as a supplement. On average, Scots spent less on fish and chips than the English. Yet, for those with money, Scotland was a gastronomic treat. Will Y. Darling, the treasurer of Edinburgh Corporation and, according to his own description, a fashionable draper and the most distinguished figure in Princes Street, penned this culinary advice for would-be visitors to Scotland:

Begin the day, therefore, my dear visitor to Scotland, with a glass of hot water and proceed to a noble breakfast commencing with porridge from Scottish oats, milk or cream from Scottish cows and – if you must sweeten the dish – there are sugars made in Scotland, but let me recommend to you the golden syrup or treacle of Greenock – a Scottish production of over a hundred years. From porridge you will proceed to the finnan haddock or the grilled trout, and then to the Ayrshire bacon, Lanarkshire tomatoes and eggs from the farm over the hill ... Luncheon may consist of Scottish broth, boiled salmon, roast beef – with green peas and new potatoes in season – pastry or tart, followed by a whang of Dunlop or Scottish Cheddar cheese ... Having lunched as you have done, an alternative menu must be provided. Smoked salmon as a *hors d'œuvre* followed by hare soup: you would then have Moray Firth soles and proceed to roast mutton. You may prefer the loin, but for the grand meal the saddle is indicated, especially if you support it with that distinctive quality of claret which, imported from Leith, is a different beverage altogether from what one drinks in France. You will have the red currant jelly and baked potatoes and the appropriate sprouts, cabbage or cauliflower. Your sweet should be a substantial one and your fancy might turn to a Scottish trifle made of Scottish sponge cakes, heightened with a port or sherry, or you might prefer a couple of good Scotch apples, well baked. In any case the joys of the table are not over with that course, for a Scottish savoury awaits your further delectation. It might be a croute of herring or a cheese and bacon savoury, or you might resume again the acquaintance which you made at luncheon with the Scottish Cheddar.

J. R. Allan, ed., *Scotland – 1938: Twenty-five Impressions*
(Edinburgh, 1938)

AMUSEMENT

The inter-war period witnessed a significant growth in popular entertainment. Increasing commercialisation of sport and pastimes, such as cinema and dancing, meant there were now new opportunities for more Scots to spend their leisure time in different ways. The impact of new technology in the home, such as washing machines and vacuum cleaners, reduced the burden of housework for many women, giving them more time for relaxation. New forms of 'mass' culture supplemented traditional forms of entertainment, many of which were centred in the home. Cars and radios were new consumer durables which were now available to many families.

Traditional notions of leisure were still governed by the Victorian concept of 'rational recreation': in other words, pastimes should, it was believed, be morally uplifting and make the pursuer a better person. Such ideas had been formulated at a time when it was felt that something had to be done to wean the working class away from 'unrespectable' pursuits such as drinking, gambling, blood sports and the like. Instead, gardening, stamp collecting, playing in a band, model-building and reading (but only decent literature) were encouraged by mechanics' institutes, employers and local authorities. Further edification could be found in museums, art galleries and exhibitions, which would broaden the citizen's horizons. In spite of these best efforts, many stuck rigidly to 'unrespectable' pursuits, and would continue to do so throughout the inter-war period.

Much of Scottish entertainment centred around the extended family, whose members usually lived close to each other. Family get-togethers were common, and would feature 'turns' by individuals renowned for singing or storytelling. Music was important, and at least one family member would have an instrument such as an accordion, fiddle, ukulele or banjo. Most players were self-taught. The more well-to-do would have a piano. Old airs and favourites would be churned out, with most people knowing one another's repertoire. Chatting and gossip were another favourite way of passing the time. The oral tradition survived well into the twentieth century, and families would have makeshift local historians and genealogists. Everyone's history, and family history too, was known to a number of individuals who would recount, often over several generations, when a particular family moved into the area, what their parents and grandparents were like and what they had done, who had married whom, what their problems were, and, perhaps most significant of all, what skeletons were locked up in the family cupboard and who were the black sheep. In the cities, towns and villages of Scotland, everyone had a history. Humour was also an important fixture, with each family having its share of natural comedians and practical jokers. Trousers were sewn up, laces tied together, drunk men put on the wrong bus, dummies and hideous objects placed in bed next to a sleeping innocent, and in more rural areas donkeys and other farm animals could be tied to someone's door. Such events were recounted with great hilarity.

The Great Depression affected many forms of communal popular culture. Brass bands had been popular in a great many factories and mines, and were usually sponsored by the employers. This paternalistic patronage declined as industry closed and cutbacks and financial squeezes took their toll. Employers often provided wedding presents, and in the countryside the visit to the 'big house' was common at Christmas. The so called 'voluntary' sector of popular culture provided a bridge between more modern mass forms of popular culture and traditional Victorian notions of leisure and amusement, with the YMCA and the Boys' Brigade continuing to provide scope for youthful activity which was considered respectable and would keep youngsters away from harmful pursuits. Teetotalism still attracted many adherents – though it has to be said that they were mainly women and children, with the target audience of men remaining fairly impervious. Gardening, pigeon-fancying, modelmaking and other hobbies still remained popular.

The growth of mass commercial forms of leisure was perhaps the most significant factor affecting the way in which people amused themselves in the inter-war period. Cinema was the most popular of these new activities. Going to the 'pictures' was a cheap evening out for the family, and the reasons why it became so popular north of the border are not hard to find. In a society where there was endemic overcrowding, little privacy and a great desire for some form of escapism, the cinema met a need. Children looking for adventure and excitement, courting couples denied time alone, and men and women who lived in dreary conditions and worked at dreary jobs could all escape into a fantasy world to forget all their cares for several hours in the warmth and dark. The cinema offered a window on the world which enabled the viewer to be transported to magical and romantic places far away. Silent movies came to be replaced by the newfangled talkies in the late twenties and, although initially they had problems picking up the American accents of Hollywood, Scots soon mastered the jargon. The number of cinemas mushroomed in the inter-war period, and on the eve of the Second World War Glasgow had 104, Dundee had 28, and

Aberdeen had 19. Most medium-sized Scottish towns also boasted a picture house.

The cinema helped to reinforce many conventional values. Arguably, it helped to sharpen notions of gender roles, with men aspiring to be tough guys and women aspiring to the femininity of the star actresses. The movies may have brought about a revolution in romance for young couples. Scotland was, and arguably still is, not renowned as a nation of lovers. Romantic role models were few and far between, but the glamour of the movies helped to refine notions of how the young and in love should behave. Also, it may be that the movies helped to give the younger generation a sense of separate identity, and the growth of gang culture in the inter-war period demonstrated that some youths began to see themselves as a distinctive group. Movies helped to fashion dress sense and introduce some of the latest crazes from across the Atlantic, one notable spin off of which was the growth in dancing.

Not everyone was a fan and many critics claimed that the new medium was having a deleterious effect on the morals of the nation, especially among children. Scots law complicated the procedures for censorship, in that local authorities could intervene only if there was a threat to public safety. Most followed the official Home Office guidelines, which classified films as either A for adult or U for universal viewing. Yet there were many reports of confusion. In 1931 the Aberdeen Juvenile Organiser's Committee investigated the appropriateness of the grading of 190 films which had been shown in recent months. Twenty-five had been classified as adult, while 118 were given a universal certificate and the remaining 47 had no classification at all. The committee was horrified to learn that many of the U films should have been categorised as A and that some adult films had been shown at children's matinees. According to the critics, the showing of inappropriate films to children would lead to 'unhealthy excitement': crime, murder, suicide, gang and prison life, fighting, drunkenness, indecency, gambling, sex and general immorality. Two hundred children were surveyed to see what effect the pictures had on them. Most went at least once a week to watch war and adventure films, yet there was little evidence to show that cinema was corrupting their morals.

Glasgow in particular went 'dancing daft' between the wars, with

159 registered dance halls catering for some 30,000 people. Given that there was little opportunity for either privacy or social mixing between the sexes, the dance floor provided an ideal opportunity for younger people to meet members of the opposite sex, although chaperones were always on hand to ensure that there was at least a foot's distance between the respective bodies. Copying their favourite American movie stars, young men dressed in three-piece 'paraffin' suits and had their hair slicked back in the latest fashion with a fag dangling from the side of the mouth while gathered together and eyeing up the girls. Having plucked up enough courage, they would then approach young women in a nonchalant way and ask them to dance. Style and coolness were an essential part of image, and the ability to dance was a measure of social kudos. Dance halls were alcohol-free and provided a relatively cheap evening out, but there was often trouble as a result of gang activity. The importation of American jazz and swing helped to create a generational difference.

Chip shops and 'Italian' ice-cream parlours were another source of concern to authorities, as they acted as magnets for groups of young people, although it was not clear if it was the gathering of groups or the parlours themselves which caused problems. The appearance of slot machines was denounced both as idle entertainment and as an outlet for gambling. Even without the ice-cream parlours, youths would tend to congregate on street corners, and certain areas of towns and cities were popular meeting places.

Gang culture in the late twenties and thirties was a particular focus of attention for the authorities. Glasgow, in particular, acquired a fearsome reputation for itself, although much of this was a result of the publication in 1935 of *No Mean City* by Alexander McArthur and H. Kingsley Long, which painted a lurid picture of a degenerate youth culture where violence was a way of life. However, the portrayal of the city as riven with razor-wielding psychopaths was largely the product of a fertile imagination. For many contemporaries the rise in gang culture was symptomatic of a wider social malaise in which respect for authority, family values and other social mores were breaking down largely because of the scourge of unemployment – though under-employment, rather than unemployment, was probably the feature which was common to most youths. In fact gang culture had existed before the war.

Most gangs were based around a particular territory and, given the sectarian divisions within many cities, gangs would manifest themselves in the religious guise of their local community, which would mark them out as different from others – although it has to be stressed that there was a degree of crossover and many gangs would fight others of the same religious denomination. Boredom, the quest for excitement and the construction of a macho identity were the main propellants of the culture. Curiosity also played a part. In Glasgow, Billy Fullerton's Bridgeton 'Billy Boys' gang ran into hundreds of members (800 according to many estimates) who regularly met to have it out with their predominantly Catholic rivals 'the Norman Conks'; on occasion they would attract so many spectators at their fights that the police would find it impossible to intervene.

In most Scottish towns and cities, working-class youngsters hung around street corners, and gangs provided an alternative to mainstream culture. For many youths they represented no more than the opportunity to chat and pass away the time or play football. Hierarchies were formed, and rules and codes were established. In its most extreme form this would lead to violence. Fighting prowess was a source of pride, and reputations would lead to challenges which resulted in spectators and hangers-on. Territory was to be defended, and encroachments were to be punished. Dance halls and other public venues could be scenes of confrontation. The culture of the gang was male-dominated, and many fights were initiated by a possessive attitude to women. Girls often hung on to the gangs' coat-tails by carrying weapons into the dance hall, as they would not be searched. They were usually the young and naive, who were allured by the fantasy of romance, and they were not treated as equals. Women were frequently beaten up by jealous boyfriends, young mothers were left to fend for themselves, and families were left to go hungry as the men engaged in their macho fantasies.

Gang culture was a sordid affair, and far removed from the romantic tough-guy image. Rackets, intimidation and murder were some of its consequences. Glasgow had the biggest problem, as a result of overcrowding and other social problems, but by the mid-thirties the problem was being erased by the use of new police tactics which combined greater intelligence with speedy responses through the use of cars and radios. Violence was met with violence, and it was well known that the police were none too gentle with an offender who assaulted one of their own.

Along with cinema and dancing, football was the great love of most Scottish men's lives. The game was a focal point for regional, religious and national identity, and accounted for most Scottish men reading the newspaper backwards. Children would emulate their heroes and teams on the streets, while the older generation would analyse match results and endlessly debate the strengths and weakness of key players, future match prospects, and forecasts for the season. Punditry became a major pastime for many. The inter-war period witnessed the commercialisation of football, with teams which had the biggest support, and hence most money, coming to the foreground. The establishing of the Scottish League in 1890 helped turn the sport into a source of national pride, with Scotland winning twelve out of the twenty internationals against England between the wars in what would become known as the 'golden era' of Scottish football. The 'beautiful game' helped to provide a welcome diversion from the harsh economic realities of the Depression, and it was an inspiration to many working-class youngsters who saw it as an escape route from the dreary realities of ordinary life by offering fame and money. Football attracted huge audiences, and matches against the 'auld enemy' never failed to bring out more than 100,000 supporters: in 1937 a new world record for attendance was created at Hampden Park when 149,515 turned up to cheer on the Scottish nation. In the Scottish League, Rangers and Celtic, able to draw on the largest base of support, could expect 30,000 to 40,000 spectators for a normal match, while an old-firm game or a cup final would break the 100,000 barrier. Teams were highly localised, and inevitably this meant that a sectarian dimension was added to football, with only Aberdeen escaping this phenomenon given that there was no large Catholic community in its population.

Sectarian tensions and crowd trouble built upon their pre-war foundations to reach new heights in the inter-war years. Rather than create animosity between fans, religious differences helped to consolidate it, although there were plenty of bigots on both sides of the divide. Heightened sectarian tensions, which culminated against the backdrop of economic depression, did little to ease the situation. Riots and crowd trouble were a regular feature at games between Celtic and Rangers, Hearts and Hibernian in Edinburgh, and Dundee and Dundee United, though other combinations of these teams could prove just as bad. Flags, banners, chants and songs accompanied the fans in increasing numbers, and in the case of Celtic and Rangers had a clear sectarian dimension.

Many of the ailments which have plagued contemporary football were alive and well between the wars. Travelling fans caused problems, and a Celtic v. Greenock match in 1922 caused a bigger riot than amendments to poor-relief payments. The press regularly denounced the mindless hooligans who accompanied teams, though the players were often no better themselves, with fights regularly breaking out on the field. Pitch invasions would result in the assault of opposing teams, and threats to the safety and well-being of referees were a common occurrence. Bottles, rivets, slag from industrial waste and sundry other objects would rain down on the pitch, and it was not unknown for fans to turn on their own team if it failed to live up to expectations.

The family holiday was an increasingly common feature in this period, with factories and workplaces usually closing down for two weeks for the local fair. For city folk there was a widespread belief that it was best to get out into the countryside or to the seaside to get some fresh air. Local seaside resorts acted as holiday outposts for the cities, and were within easy reach in a couple of hours by ferry or train. On the west coast, towns such as Rothesay, Troon, Largs and Dunoon catered for Glasgow's teeming masses, while Burntisland, Portobello, Crail and other east-coast settlements acted as a magnet for Edinburgh folk. Dundoneans could escape to Arbroath, Broughty Ferry and Brechin, while Aberdonians could sample the pleasures of Stonehaven and Montrose. Farmers could also earn an extra few pounds during the summer months by renting chalets in the countryside, which were usually situated in picturesque valleys.

As ever in Scotland, wealth determined the type of experience enjoyed. In the seaside resorts, the affluent would have access to the central hotels with the best views, while the more down at heel were confined to the cheaper boarding houses on the fringes. The prosperous would sample the delights of the local restaurants, while ordinary folk would make do with the culinary offerings of the local chip shops. Dance halls, cinemas, ice-cream parlours and fairground attractions added to the atmosphere.

As a tourist destination, the Highlands were largely confined to the wealthy, on account of travelling costs, or to those who had family in the area. Oban, Morven and Ullapool on the north-west coast were out of reach for the majority, while the Braemar area in the north-east was able to cash in on the royal residence of Balmoral to entice a wealthy clientele.

The motor car was an increasingly common sight in Scotland in the late thirties, and in 1938 there were some 147,000 cars and a further 31,000 motorcycles. The car increased the number of day trips possible and opened up the opportunity of the touring holiday. One consequence of the rise in road traffic was an increase in danger to public safety. In 1938 there were 20,415 road accidents, in which 655 people were killed and 5,309 were seriously injured. In the same year there were at least 66,254 road offences, of which nearly 45,000 resulted in a conviction. The true figure is probably higher than this, because drunk driving was categorised under offences relating to drunkenness, and it had to be shown that the driver was drunk without the aid of modern medical equipment. Needless to say, the definition of drunk varied throughout the country. One reason why driving was so dangerous was that, of the 25,987 miles of public roads in Scotland, only 6,700 miles were either trunk roads or class-one roads; there were also class-two and class-three roads, but an astonishing 15,354 miles had no classification at all.

One feature of life in the inter-war period which attracted much attention was what today we might call the development of an underclass. As was described in Chapter 3, poverty remained a blight on the landscape of Scotland right up until the eve of the Second World War. For many social commentators the real problem was that many of the blighted communities were undergoing a process of self-replication over generations. In other words, the children of the unemployed would themselves become unemployed. Much of this debate has a remarkably, and chilling, modern ring to it. The listlessness, lack of hope and despair associated with life on the dole were passed on to the next generation. Breaking this cycle was a major concern for public moralists and public policy-makers, who attributed most of the blame for this state of affairs to the unemployed themselves. Attempts at improving the conditions of the very poor tended to be reported in a very negative way. One English visitor to Glasgow, Cicely Hamilton, writing in 1937 of the efforts to rehouse the poorest, claimed that:

It stands to reason that men and women who have dwelt for years, perhaps all their lives, in the squalid surroundings of a Glasgow rookery are likely to need persevering instruction in the arts of domestic cleanliness ... One little woman who we called on in her slum would I suspect, need a good deal of attention from the health visitor before she discarded the sluttish habits acquired in her years of squalor. She was a friendly little soul, with a sloping forehead and unwashed face, who, like most of her fellow-slum-dwellers, seemed quite pleased to be called upon; the mother of three grubby infants under school age – one of them in arms, one old enough to stand and stare at us, one crawling on the unmade family bed where, in the unrestrained manner of infancy, it had recently obeyed a call of nature. There were two more absent at school, the mother told us; presumably, being better clad and washed than their younger brethren – the education authority would see to that, providing at least the necessary footwear. A query with regard to the husband and father brought the all too frequent reply that he was out of work; the income that he and his family obtained from the public purse being thirty-nine shillings a week.

Modern Scotland as Seen by an Englishwoman (London, 1937)

Conventional wisdom held that family size was related to poverty: the more children one had, the poorer one would become. A frequent source of concern was 'errant fathers', men of no responsibility who kept on producing children who would be maintained by the state until there were so many children that work was no longer economically viable for the family. This so-called 'wage stop' was a result of the Unemployment Assistance Board paying two shillings per week for every dependent child, which meant that fathers of large families could not secure a wage equal to what could be obtained through public assistance. Of alarm to social commentators was the fact that these men were generally unskilled, and therefore unlikely to secure a job with good wages, and had often married while young and unemployed. They were contrasted unfavourably with 'respectable' men who worked to maintain their family even though they were financially no better off.

There was an increasing incidence of child abuse, of which 'failure to provide' was the variety most commonly reported by the Royal Scottish Society for the Prevention of Cruelty to Children. 'Feckless' parents bore the full weight of society's opprobrium, which increased with the reporting of cases of child neglect and cruelty. Stories of drunken parents dropping acid on their toddler and of children sent out to look for cigarette butts late at night and foraging in bins for food were told in courts throughout the land and relayed to the public by the press. Men bore the brunt of the guilt, as failing to provide for the family was a gender crime in patriarchal Scotland. As far as the authorities were concerned, mothers were just as likely to be victims as were children. Even in some cases where the mother was guilty of neglect, as in the case of one young woman who left her two young children alone at night to go dancing while her husband was on the night shift, the father was severely rebuked for failing to control his wife.

The ethos of respectability had a long pedigree in Scottish society, and, with greater state intervention highlighting the failure to maintain appropriate standards among certain elements of the community, this meant that there would be no let-up against two of the greatest evils or pleasures: gambling and drink. Although these two great social evils were enjoyed by a large part of the community, their impact on the lives of the poor meant that public moralists had an effective stick to wield in the renewed campaign against 'feckless self-indulgence'.

Gambling was a major source of concern for public moralists, as it violated many of the sacred tenets of respectability. First, it was not rational, as it placed one's fortune in the hands of Lady Luck. Second, it could not lead to self-improvement, because the gambler's ill-gotten gains had not been attained by hard work, which was the only acceptable way to improve one's position in society. Third, it was not thrifty, but meant that money was diverted away from savings and the household. Finally, because of all the above, it was immoral and evidence of a lack of character.

It was argued that the deleterious effect of gambling was made worse by the impact of the Depression, unemployment and increased levels of poverty. The Royal Scottish Society for the Prevention of Cruelty to Children certainly believed that gambling was having a serious impact on the lives of women and children:

There has been much ink spilled regarding the Betting Laws of the country and more especially in connection with the 'Street Bookie'; he is certainly a nuisance and a danger, especially to women betting, but compared to the 'gambling school' his responsibility for the 'failing to provide' complaint might not be as great as thought. Every weekend from Friday till Sunday night great 'gambling schools' gather at different places and play at 'pitch and toss' and it is not an infrequent occurrence for men to stand at the 'school' and gamble away all the money they have received from the Labour Exchange or in a few cases their wages. The mother in such cases is usually the complainer, but it is remarkable how often one finds she is very unwilling to take the extreme step of having her husband reported to the Procurator Fiscal.

RSSPCC Executive Committee Report (Edinburgh, 1932)

In addition to causing poverty, gambling was denounced as a source of crime. In the House of Commons the Revd James Barr, the chair of the Parliamentary Labour Party, frequently cited cases where betting had led to a life of crime to sustain the habit. On 3 April 1936 he quoted the sheriff of Banffshire, who had stated, when sentencing a man for theft, that 'the root of the trouble is the demoralising effect on the accused of indulging in an extremely silly form of amusement, betting on football pools. A great many people do, and it is the cause of a great deal of crime in the country.'

While it is no doubt the case that gambling did bring misery to many people, it is perhaps as well to remember that most of the information we have about betting in this period comes from its most vociferous critics. Betting was legally confined to private members' clubs, which only the wealthy could join, and inside registered horse- and dog-racing tracks. Of those who could not travel to one of the racetracks scattered throughout the length and breadth of Scotland, many took great delight in placing a bet either with friends or with the innumerable illegal betting establishments. Any sporting fixture, or any uncertain outcome, could be the subject of a bet. In towns and cities, small shopkeepers and street-corner touts ran underground operations, with horse racing as the preferred object of gambling. Children were employed to take slips back and forth and to keep an eye out for the forces of law and order.

Of concern to many was that gambling opportunities were believed to be on the increase. Football pools were popular because they were conducted by post and therefore legal. Fruit machines could be modified and operated illegally to pay out cash tokens. The tote (totalisator) made its appearance in the late twenties, with many official and unofficial syndicates springing up. The number of dog-racing tracks increased in the early thirties. In 1934 the authorities clamped down with the Betting and Lotteries Act, which banned all totes and lotteries outside the grounds of registered horse and dog racecourses, but in reality there was little that could be done to stop people having a flutter. Yet there were some features which the critics of gambling failed to pick up on, especially the strong connection with ideas of rational recreation. Gambling was condemned because it was feckless, in that it was believed to depend on a random act of chance. Yet much of the betting was in reality very specialised and informed. Gambling on dog and horse racing was based on form, with many punters using specialist knowledge built up from the sports pages. So, although subject to chance, the action was based on reason, skill and knowledge. The same qualities were also involved in forecasting the outcome of other sporting fixtures. Many actually boosted their self-esteem and their standing among their peers by their ability to use specialist knowledge to predict accurately the outcome of events. Even the tote was subject to the same powers of reason and rationality. The stake was usually small, but the reward for winning was high. Most played it on the basis that the rewards of winning were such that it made no economic sense not to play.

The pub remained a focus for the recreational activities of men. It was a place where friends socialised, free from nagging wives and screaming kids; it was a place where casual work could be found and, for a brief time, cares be forgotten. Alcohol consumption per head of population was on the decline from the First World War, as a result of price increases due to taxation. Scottish pubs tended to be bare and staffed only by men, and windows were boarded up or had opaque glass so that innocents passing by would not be tempted in. The pub was an exclusively male culture, and women were either barred outright or were frowned upon in an exceptionally unwelcome atmosphere. Women drinkers generally had to resort to the off-licence.

The pub was a rite of passage for young men, who would there be initiated into the mysteries of male bonding. Manliness was associated with consumption, and holding one's drink was an essential part of male self-respect. The Scottish delight in buying rounds and the equally Scottish habit of ensuring that everyone bought a round, meant that consumption was regulated by the fastest drinker. A couple of rounds in a group of five would mean ten drinks consumed per person. This would be increased if the company went in for a 'half and half', which was half a pint of beer and a shot of whisky. 'Fly halfin' it' – the technique whereby the purchaser would buy himself an extra whisky and drink it surreptitiously at the bar while ferrying the drinks to his friends – was a major breech of pub etiquette, especially if a kitty had been established. Failing to buy a round would lead to social ostracism. As with child-beating, Scots vernacular had an unusually large vocabulary for being drunk. In addition to standard English words, one could be 'guttered', 'blootered', 'gassed', 'reekin', 'canned', 'jackied', 'smashed', 'wellied', 'pished', 'steamin', 'mingin', 'stoshious' and 'fu'. Interestingly, there is no Scots word for being slightly drunk or tipsy, which in all probability was assumed to be merely a transient phase unworthy of a name.

Although the number of pubs remained fairly constant during the inter-war years, at about one for every 800 people, the amount of spirits drunk declined by about a fifth, although it was still about a third of a gallon per head of population per year. Deaths due to alcohol and crimes of drunkenness were also on the decrease. The twenties and thirties witnessed the coming of age of a section of society which had grown up with total abstinence and which continued its assault on the evils of drink. Teetotalism and prohibition were most strongly associated with the Labour Party, whose Members of Parliament were total abstainers to a man. Many of them had witnessed first hand the dire effects of alcoholism on family life, and believed that prohibition was an essential social reform. In October 1928 James Barr had summed up his position in the House of Commons:

I believe in the socialisation of the means of production, distribution and exchange. But while I stand for the socialisation of public utilities, I am opposed to the socialisation of public perils and the socialisation of public iniquities. I say this, that, no matter how perfect be the social commonwealth or the social system that you put up, if you leave this dark river of death flowing through the land, it will corrupt the best social state that ever entered into the dreams of man. It will poison its communal life at its source: it will besmirch our noblest ideals; it will turn our rising sun into darkness, and it will eclipse for us our new millennial dawn. But with the liquor traffic removed, we shall raise a new generation ready to step in and possess the promised land – children of the new day, with the light of knowledge in their eyes, a virtuous populace that will rise awhile and stand guardian over our new social commonwealth, keeping it pure and unsullied and handing it down ennobled and enhanced to those who shall come after us.

Local councils, such as Kirkintilloch, outside Glasgow, were able to implement local vetoes on the sale of alcohol, and in fact that town did not have its first pub until after the Second World War. Temperance received its most vocal support from women, who recognised that they were the section of society which suffered most from alcohol abuse. Sunday schools and organisations such as the Band of Hope targeted the young in an endeavour to hold back the tide of alcoholism. Children were shown exhibitions which demonstrated the consequences of drinking. A worm would be placed in a jar of water and then a jar of whisky to show the harmful effects of alcohol. Speakers would recount a life of sotten misery, and show how they had now cleaned up their act. Finally, the children would sign an ornate pledge, which they were allowed to keep, promising not to let a drop of liquor pass their lips.

Temperance reformers had only limited success in their endeavour to turn Scotland dry. There were a number of polls on the issue, and by the eve of the Second World War the 'wet' vote, at 1,624,006, was about a third larger than the dry vote, at just over a million. However, some thirty areas did adopt a no-licence resolution and, together with the 302 areas that had never had a licence, that meant that about a tenth of the population lived in a no-alcohol area.

RURAL LIFE

The agricultural community was hit just as hard as those working in industry during the thirties. In spite of rosy representations of a healthy life in the countryside, falling prices meant that this sector of the Scottish economy was contracting, and so experiencing problems of poverty and unemployment unique in such an environment. The difficulties of agriculture were given an extra piquancy among Scotland's intellectual community because of the widespread belief that industrial capitalism had failed the nation as a result of the Great Depression. 'Back to the land' was a fairly constant leitmotif in the novels of Neil M. Gunn and Lewis Grassic Gibbon, and though Edwin Muir and Hugh MacDiarmid managed to disagree on almost everything, even they shared the belief that the 'soul' of the nation was to be found in the days before the Reformation and the rise of an industrial capitalist society.

Many critics asserted that the health of the agricultural economy and the well-being of society went together, and were keen to contrast the Scottish experience with that of Denmark, Ireland, Holland, Norway and other small agricultural nations. Certainly the figures seem to bear them out. Only 9 per cent of Scotland's insured workforce was employed in agriculture, compared with 17 per cent in Belgium and 28 per cent in Holland, both of which enjoyed less unemployment and poverty, a higher standard of living, and lower infant mortality rates. Creating a nation of small farmers and rural industries was promoted as a way to escape mass unemployment, and rural reorganisation was almost a compulsory prescription for rectifying the nation's ills. After all, if a family could grow its own food and maintain itself in self-sufficiency, there would be no need for employment. Indeed, the 1931 census shows that agriculture, which was still the single largest employment sector of the Scottish economy, had the lowest rate of registered unemployment.

Such notions of rural regeneration were not confined to Scotland, but were symptomatic of a widespread European movement which believed that the answers to the national and moral degradation of industrial capitalism were to be found in the countryside. While many of the solutions proffered were simplistic and romantic and had little chance of addressing the fundamental problems, the fact that they engendered such widespread interest is testament to the importance that Scottish society attached to its rural community.

The raw statistical material of the census fails to convey the importance of agriculture to Scottish society. Those bracketed as working in farming and fishing do not account for all those who made their living from the rural economy. The countryside was a complex society made up of many different strata. Blacksmiths, for example, were classed along with industrial workers as metalworkers, and the many porters and managers of the rural railway network were designated as belonging to the transport industry. Officially there were 104,000 people working in agriculture on the eve of the Second World War, which was a decline of over 20,000 since the end of the First World War, but this army of agricultural workers did not exist in a vacuum, and needed a whole range of people and occupations to supply its various needs. The typical small town servicing an agricultural community would have a railway station, a court, a police station, a couple of churches, warehouses, a smithy, a school, hotels, a range of shops, and one or two mills on the outskirts. The working population ranged from the professionals such as the schoolteacher and the bank manager, to the skilled such as millers, wrights, slaters and carpenters, to the unskilled labourers and handymen. The existence of a large estate nearby would create employment in the 'big house' for domestic servants, gamekeepers, drivers and cooks.

Many towns with a population of 5,000 to 10,000 could be described as rural/industrial in that, while having their own factories, much of the local focus was on servicing the rural hinterland. The following towns with a population of over 10,000 served as significant centres for the supply, sale and distribution of agricultural produce: Alloa, Arbroath, Ayr, Dumfries, Dunfermline, Falkirk, Forfar, Fraserburgh, Galashiels, Hawick, Perth and Inverness. Beyond the small towns, one in five Scots lived in settlements of less than a thousand people. While it is difficult to arrive at an accurate figure – so much depending on what criteria are used to define an 'urban' settlement – probably about four out of ten Scots lived in an environment which was mainly rural in its setting and/or depended on the agricultural and fishing industry for much of its local trade. Scotland also contributed a disproportionate amount to the overall agricultural output of the United Kingdom. It had 75,850 landholdings, compared to

391,941 for England and Wales. The nation had a sixth of the total British cattle, and almost a third of the sheep. It was also more productive and regularly produced a better crop yield than south of the border. Hence the contemporary interest in the state of the rural communities.

The agricultural economy was fairly well defined in terms of geography. The borders were dominated by sheep farming, which supplied wool to the local textile industries. Dumfries and Galloway specialised in dairy products, which were supplied to local urban centres. Ayrshire likewise specialised in dairy products and potatoes, which fed the Glasgow conurbation. Lothian was a mixed farming area, which supplied Edinburgh and grew animal feeding crops. Dundee and its hinterland had a specialisation in market gardening, which supplied the local jam and preserve industry. The central area east of Glasgow and extending north to Stirling and Perth was a mixed farming area, and the rural north-east was renowned for its beef cattle. The Kingdom of Fife was an area of mixed farming.

The crops grown in Scotland were wide and varied. Just over 15 million acres were in use on the eve of the Second World War: 10.5 million acres were used for rough grazing, just over 1.5 million were permanent grassland, and the remaining 3 million were used for crops. Oats were the most common crop, and accounted for just over half the total production. Next came animal feeding crops such as turnips, cabbages, beans and peas, which made up just under a quarter of production. Potatoes constituted under a tenth, fruit one sixteenth, and vegetables slightly more than a fortieth. Barley made up 7 per cent of crop production, and wheat, which was given a subsidy, accounted for only about 5 per cent. This last point was a sore point for Scottish farmers, as the subsidy favoured their counterparts in the south to the tune of about £6 million a year. Likewise, sugar beet, which was not grown in Scotland, was subsidised to the tune of £4 million a year. In spite of demands from the Scottish farming community, potatoes, barley and oats received neither protection in the form of tariffs on imports nor a subsidy. The price of barley dropped by 500 per cent in the inter-war period, and howls of complaint were made that the beer industry was given a tax cut of a penny per pint to help demand whereas the distilleries received nothing.

The Highlands were dominated by small crofts which kept sheep. Throughout the land there were specialist cheese producers, from Lockerbie in the borders to Orkney in the north. Poultry and pig farms were also spread throughout the country. The fishing industry was largely concentrated on the north-east coastline around Aberdeen, but there were also smaller fishing fleets around the north-west coast.

Livestock was the most important sector of the rural economy, accounting on average for about three-quarters of the value of output in the inter-war years. In 1939 there were 100,000 horses, 8,000,000 sheep, 1,349,000 cows, 252,000 pigs and 7,711,000 poultry. The value of the agricultural output was estimated at £38,133,000, of which cattle sales accounted for almost £10 million. Milk production made up just over £9 million, sheep £4.3 million, pigs £1.6 million, and eggs £3 million. The impact of falling world prices for meat and mutton meant that the livestock industry was subject to severe competition from cheap imports from abroad. One contemporary estimate calculated that of every £100 spent on food, £63 went on meat, eggs and dairy products, yet only £29 of this total was spent on domestically produced fare. This too was a source of considerable political tension between farmers and the government, in that there were no import duties on foreign food which could afford the native producer some degree of protection. Also, the fact that Scotland was more dependent on livestock than England did little to ease matters.

In many ways, the rural economy was better than the urban one at hiding deep-seated poverty. The battery of improving legislation which followed in the wake of the First World War was drafted with the urban community in mind, yet the countryside also suffered from considerable social ills. Whereas poverty and poor housing conditions in the towns and cities were concentrated and on public display, the scattered nature of rural society meant that its problems were not under the constant gaze of the public: medical, sanitary and housing inspectors would have to actively seek them out. Although grants were available for improvements to rural workers' housing, they were seldom taken up because of the requirement of the farmer to match funding. It was estimated that one in three houses in the rural lowlands had no sanitary provision, and the 1937 Report on Rural Housing in Scotland found that three-quarters of houses inspected were unfit for human habitation. Descriptions of living conditions frequently note that dampness was a major problem, and that many residents had to walk a short distance for their water supply. Floors were

often made of clay or earth, and many pointed out that the living conditions in the byres and barns were better. Also, a large army of seasonal
workers were housed in the most basic of conditions in bothies which consisted for the most part of a roof and walls with little else. Part of the problem was that, if rural labourers reported their conditions to the
authorities, cash-strapped farmers would not make improvements, but
would rather evict the tenants and close the houses down. Both farmers
and workers agreed that this was not a solution. Evidence of the state of
the rural economy can be found in statistics which show that by 1936
there were almost 30,000 applications for new buildings and enlargement, yet only a quarter of these were completed; 12,630 were withdrawn,
and a further 9,814 were outstanding.

The problems of falling prices and rural depopulation were compounded by the growth of forestry in the inter-war period. Although the
figures vary, with some confusion between areas which were used as deer
forest and those which were used simply for tree production, a contemporary estimate by the Scottish National Development Council claimed that
as much as a fifth of the total area of Scotland was under some scheme of
forestation. Declining agricultural prices were the major cause of growth
in forestry, as landowners could claim grants for planting trees. This was a
source of complaint from the agricultural lobby, which claimed that such
policies were effectively decommissioning land which could be used for
smallholdings. Indeed the acreage under cultivation declined by about a
fifth in the inter-war period, while in the same period the Forestry Commission acquired about half a million acres.

Related to this issue was the political hot potato of land ownership.
Land reform was a trusty staple in the rhetoric of the left, and Scotland was
still a nation dominated by big landowners: it was estimated that a hundred individuals owned half of the land area. The problem had a special
resonance in the Highlands (see below).

The Scottish National Development Council produced a number of
reports which highlighted both the problems and the potential of Scottish
agriculture in the late 1930s. It was estimated that the total cost of food
imports in 1932 which could have been produced at home was £17 million. In fact, some 45 per cent of Scottish food was imported, and had government policy been geared towards protection of domestic suppliers this

would have entailed an 80 per cent increase in Scottish agricultural production, leading to an increase in employment of about 50 per cent.

The fishing industry experienced dramatic decline in the inter-war period as a result of collapsing prices and lost markets. The herring industry was the worst affected, because of the loss of markets in eastern Europe. The number employed in 1914 was 20,500, which dropped to 16,000 by the mid-thirties, and a corresponding drop took place in those employed in processing – from 16,000 to under 10,000. The Report for the Scottish Fishery Board in 1935 noted a drop in the total number employed (including those working in ancillary occupations) of 26,000, to 60,000. The north-east was the area hit hardest by the decline in the industry, although greater use of steam trawlers which concentrated on white fish helped to maintain the volume landed. The North Sea catch was 5.5 million hundredweight in 1913, but dropped to 3.75 million by the mid-thirties, giving rise to fears of overfishing and dwindling stocks. Inshore fishing had its worse year in 1935, with haddock having virtually disappeared.

Steam trawlers, which could trawl deeper and wider, effectively put the small fisherman out of business. Those fishing only a few miles from shore in small boats could not hope to compete against vessels which could fish in deep waters in voyages that could last up to three weeks. White fish was the most profitable part of trade, as most of it was destined for the domestic market and not subject to tariffs. The increasing popularity of fish and chips in the United Kingdom was an important factor in the growth of steam trawlers, although the Scots did not benefit particularly from this popularity in that they tended to catch the more expensive fish rather than the cheaper and coarser varieties. There were 320 steam trawlers in Scotland before the Second World War, and these made up slightly less than a third of the British total, most of the others being located in Hull and Grimsby. The Scottish trawlers, most of which were based in Aberdeen, were not as advanced nor as big as their English rivals, and tended to concentrate on quality rather than quantity. Another factor which disadvantaged the Aberdeen fleet was its distance from the profitable markets of the south.

In 1938 a total of 275,000 tons of fish were landed in Scotland. Half of this tonnage was made up of herring, while the other half was white fish, with haddock being the most common. The total value of fish landed was estimated at £4 million. But, although comprising half the catch, herring accounted for only about a quarter of the total value – the same proportion as haddock, even though this made up only about a third of the catch. About half the herring catch went overseas, mainly to Germany. The herring industry had been based all around the coast of Scotland, but wartime disruption had seen it shift to the west coast. Further difficulties dogged the industry – such as the cost of ice, which was higher in the Western Isles than in Aberdeen – and the cost of transport to market, together with Sabbatarianism, made it uneconomic. As with farming, many commentators believed that the fishing industry was badly managed and that one potential solution to its problems was to increase domestic consumption. On average Scots ate about three times as much meat as fish, and a rough calculation estimated that the average Scot consumed one herring per year. The Herring Board maintained a broadly pessimistic view of the future for the industry, and sought to reduce the catch and the fleet to accommodate the low domestic demand. The use of marketing boards was an idea mooted at the time to increase consumption, but it fell on deaf ears.

HIGHLANDERS

On Hogmanay 1919, a ship, HMY *Iolaire*, approached the shores of the Western Isles heading in to the port of Stornoway. On board were 283 troops returning from the war. With land in sight, most of the men believed they were the lucky ones: they had survived the carnage. The Isle of Lewis had sent 6,200 men into the services out of a total population of 30,000, and more than 1,000 had died. Buoyed up by promises of 'land for heroes', the survivors could look forward to better times. Most of the men were former naval ratings, and they would soon be home and reunited with friends and family, who had gathered at the docks to greet them. As the *Iolaire* entered the narrow channel, the looming lights of Stornoway harbour could be seen in the night sky. And then disaster struck. The ship hit rocks known as the Beasts of Holm and went down, drowning 205 men. The Great War began for Scotland with the tragic accident of the Gretna train crash and ended with the equally tragic sinking of the *Iolaire*. It was an ominous portent for the future of the Highlands.

The Highlands received increased public attention in the inter-war era, as many commentators saw the region as the spiritual heart of Scotland and increasingly used the Gaels and their land as a metaphor for the wider problems which affected the nation. Yet, paradoxically, for all this interest, nothing seemed to be able to solve the twin problems of population decline and economic retardation. The bigger the decline, the greater the interest. In an era of 'mass-man and machinery', cultural commentators sought to save the soul of the nation by returning to the simpler qualities of the Celtic spirit. Neil M. Gunn, Compton Mackenzie, Hugh MacDiarmid, William Power and others of the Scottish renaissance looked to the Highlands for a different Scottish cultural home.

The economic and social bedrock of the Highlands was crofting. In 1886 the Crofters Act enshrined in law a number of features which would preserve what was to become a fairly archaic economic and social structure. Crofters could pass on their crofts, and were protected against the arbitrary power of landowners to increase rents or evict tenants. These crofts were small farms which barely produced above subsistence level, and the income of crofters had to be augmented by part-time work in fishing, deer forests or seasonal activities. The principal complaint of crofters in the inter-war period was land shortage, in that more land was needed to augment crofts to make them more economic, or land was needed to satisfy the demand to establish new crofts to encourage an increase in population.

The Crofting Commission was the government-sponsored body which had the task of arbitrating disputes between landowners and crofters, but its effectiveness was hampered by two factors which had been firmly established before the First World War. First, there was a huge backlog of cases, which undermined confidence in the system and meant that cases could take years to resolve. Second, the commission had only limited powers of compulsory purchase, which could be used only if it was shown that a landowner was not using land in a responsible manner. This was notoriously difficult to prove, and could be settled only after a lengthy legal process. As a result of this, the commission had little land which it could dispose of, and certainly did not have enough to satisfy the demands of crofters.

Relations between landowners and crofters were never friendly, and had been conditioned by a history in which the former were blamed for clearances, evictions and famine and the latter were seen as infringing the rights of private property. The effect of the war was to harden attitudes on both sides of the divide with crofters believing that military service gave them a moral entitlement to land, while landowners, along with other property owners, were prepared to jealously guard their rights against the encroachments of state-sponsored socialism. In 1919 the Land Settlement Act was passed in the face of landowner opposition. This act augmented and partially replaced the 1911 Small Landholder Act, and provided funds for the purchase of estates, but wartime inflation meant that these funds had dried up by the early twenties. The result was that land raiding, whereby landless crofters would merely set up shop on vacant land, was an intermittent feature of Highland society in the inter-war period.

Seizures took place in Lewis in 1918, and, in spite of Scottish Office denials, they were the most effective way to acquire land. Land reform attracted considerable political sympathy in lowland Scotland, and was pursued most eagerly by the Labour Party. The Scottish Office's attitude towards land raiding was driven by political considerations. First, the Scottish Office did not want to draw attention to the problem for fear that it might encourage emulation. Second, there were concerns that it might spread out of the Highlands into the Lowlands. Finally, the seizures were usually of a limited scale, so that a resolution was possible – especially as the size of the holding granted was also usually small. About two-thirds of all landholdings were under fifteen acres, and in Harris and Lewis more than half were under five acres.

It would be unfair, however, to put the blame for the problems of the Highlands on land shortage. The biggest difficulty Highlanders faced was making a living out of a stagnant economy. Agricultural prices fell during the inter-war era and herring fishing collapsed, affecting the main sources of earnings for crofters. Alternative employment was available in forestry, tourism and sporting estates, but it failed to compensate for all the lost income. In essence, the problem was simple: crofting in itself provided an insufficient economic base to encourage an expansion in population at a reasonable or acceptable standard of living. Some of the difficulties, although much exaggerated, were outlined by the Nairne Committee, which reported in 1928:

The problem in the Highlands involves historical, racial, economic and social considerations entirely different from other parts of Great Britain. We are dealing with a community which has never been industrialised, and resists any attempt at industrialisation. Land is the basis of its existence and determines the form of social life. It has refused to acquiesce in any of the attempts to change the method of using or holding land which have been made in the last 150 years, and the legislature has been compelled to meet the claims it has made to be allowed to live life in its own way. The Highlander not only insists on living in the Highlands, but insists on living in his own strath or on his own island. What seems an obvious fact to an observer accustomed to other modes of life, is not accepted as a fact by the Highlander. He insists on being given land in his own district, and would rather have a hopeless patch of his own native heath than a fair holding in a strange glen.

Report of the Committee on Land Settlement (London, 1928)

A comparison of the 1881 census with that of 1931 shows that the Highlands and Islands had lost over 68,000 people in that period. Evidence that land shortage was not the only cause of population decline can be demonstrated by the fact that by 1931 there were some 4,000 outstanding applicants for new landholdings in Scotland. Assuming that all these were for the Highlands, they represented probably about 4 per cent of the population, which stood at 300,000. It should also be borne in mind that most of the applicants would be single or just married, with few children. Even if their applications were granted, they and their families would not make good all the lost population.

Emigration had been part of the Highland tradition since the eighteenth century, and it was in response to poor social and economic circumstances that many left in the twenties. An exclusive concern with economics was a major source of complaint for many commentators and critics of government policy. According to a former Lord Provost of Inverness, Sir Alexander MacEwen:

We are suffering today not from economy, but from economists. The people who want to rationalise and centralise everything may know something about industry, but they know little about the needs of a peasant population. Their calculations omit all consideration of social and spiritual values. When these superior people visit a Highland croft and see small oats growing on the lazy beds and the cattle and the sheep seeking their scanty nourishment, they exclaim that it is impossible for people to live under such conditions.

The Thistle and the Rose (Edinburgh, 1932)

Sir Alexander went on to give a spirited defence of Highland society and economy, and argued that Highland life was better than that of the unemployed. Yet, as with so many defenders of the Highlands, his was a rosy-glow perspective on the biting hardship endured by the crofting community. The plain fact of the matter was that economics and the standard of living were important, and Highlanders voted with their feet for better lifestyles in the Lowlands or abroad.

Along with the population decline came a still greater drop in the number of Gaelic speakers, from 183,998 in 1911 to 130,080 in 1931. Although the Gaelic language had been subject to persecution, a major factor in its decline was a widespread belief that English was a vital economic necessity. Like most parents throughout the world, Highlanders wanted to give their children the best start in life, and it was believed that an inability to speak English would confine their children and limit their opportunities.

The major problem facing Highland society in the inter-war period (and long before this) was that the geographic and topographic peculiarities of the region made it very different from the rest of Scotland, and this resulted in difficulties in integrating its society and economy into the whole. The Highlands were peripheral. Most of government policy, which in the case of the crofting community came from the Scottish Agricultural Board, was directed on a Scotland-wide basis and could do little to address the distinctiveness of Highland society. Calls for the appointment of a special areas commissioner, who would address the problems of the Highlands on a similar basis to that of the development areas for the industrial west, were rejected. The Highlands were a Scottish hinterland which was left to fend for itself. Yet, in spite of this, a great deal of ink was spilled on plans for regeneration. Calls were made for the greater use of forestry and associated timber manufacture. The creation of hydroelectric schemes was advocated, to provide rural industry with a cheap source of power. Improved transport and infrastructure would facilitate the development of tourism. Fish canning and processing, as the soap magnate Lord Leverhulme had planned for Lewis when he bought the island immediately after the First World War – before giving up in exasperation – would modernise the fishing industry. All these plans were based on one vital premiss: government intervention. It would take a world war to achieve this.

- F I V E -

WAR,

1939–1945

There was little remnant of a passive (or non) resistance left in this land when appeasement for very shame and futility could go no farther. And when war ultimately came to our world there were no Quislings in Scotland, and but few who carried pacifist surrenderism the length of making no preparations for the relief of suffering among the civilian population. A stray peace-pledger or two may have continued to cry aloud that A.R.P. and ambulance, water supplies, hospitals, food storage and transport, shelters for homeless folks, and fire precautions were only capitalist war propaganda. But these theories were never – so far as I know – carried to the length of refusing to eat food that had been carried on a ship where the crew had dared to protect themselves with life-belts and guns against submarine attacks; and the most extreme peace-pledger drank his tea and paid, therefore, a war tax like the rest of us.

Thomas Johnston, *Memories* (London, 1952)

Pride of race is a reality for the British as for other peoples. Any measure taken now, by allowances for children, to stop the promotion of the infertile as well as of the able can have no immediate effect on the quality of the breed in this generation and little in the next generation. But as in Britain today we look back with pride and gratitude to our ancestors, look back as a nation or as individuals two hundred years and more to the generations illumined by Marlborough, or Cromwell, or Drake, are we not bound also to look forward, to plan society now, so that there may be no lack of men and women of the quality of those earlier days, of the best of our breed, two hundred and three hundred years hence? In the past, many a great individual has sought to perpetuate himself in a noble family. The great free people of Britain should now make sure that they will maintain their breed at its best and will have a posterity worth of their past.

Sir William Beveridge, memorandum prepared in connection with the
Galton Lecture, Royal Medical Society, London, 16 February 1943

'And how do you think things are going to shape on earth now?' Asked the Questioner.

'Obviously, as I have suggested.'

'No more war?'

'Certainly. There may, of course, be barbaric skirmishes here and there, but never again total war. We have taught the future leaders too much for that. No leader of any great area or nation will ever again turn to war. He will not try to gratify motive in that old-fashioned way. Out of violence comes violence. Reptiles crunch each other up. What distinguishes man from the reptile is his mind or brain. To be truly and scientifically effective, you must work on that. In short, the method will be psychological, with just enough force behind it to make it completely persuasive. Not a force you parade. A hidden, invisible force, appearing every now and then mysteriously – to apprehend a doubter, to withdraw him temporarily from society, and to show him the error of his ways. When your method is perfect he will realise that however much what he had wanted to do might gratify his own desires, it would have been destructive to society. The parallel is the father dealing with a recalcitrant child. The wise father convinces the child. The unwise merely thrashes him.'

'But what about those nations who cry Freedom' asked the Questioner.

'Freedom!' echoed the Newcomer. 'Merely a meaningless sound carried over from the reptile age.'

Neil M. Gunn, *The Green Isle of the Great Deep* (London, 1943)

THE GUILTY MEN

The Second World War initiated a fundamental change in attitudes to the role of government and the use of state power. The 'can't do' mentality of the inter-war era was replaced by a bold new vision which stressed not only the ability of state power to transform society and economy, but also its moral obligation to do so for the benefit of all. Such a revolution in ideology was underpinned by the sense of failure which seemed to characterise the decade of the thirties. In retrospect it was perceived as a selfish era in which 'guilty men' not only presided over mass unemployment and social inequality, but had crossed the moral rubicon of appeasing the fascist dictatorships. Society now faced fighting a war against fascism while coming to terms with a sense that injustices had been committed by government against its own people. For all practical purposes, it was soon accepted that the war would not command the universal support of the people unless government could atone for the wrongs which had been committed against those who were now needed to fight for freedom.

There was an added piquancy in that the areas which had suffered most during the Depression were also the areas which were most important for the production of the raw materials needed for war. The collapsed heavy industries of Wales, the north-east of England and central Scotland were reflated to keep the light of civilisation burning, but the men and women who staffed them would not easily forget the years of misery they had endured when society did not need them. There was a determination that, when the war was over, things would never be the same again. There would be no return to the empty promises of 'homes for heroes'. The war against social injustice was a price which would have to be paid for a successful war against Hitler. Somebody had to take the blame for appeasement and social inequality, and Neville Chamberlain and his old fogeys fitted the bill. The legacy of the 'guilty men' was particularly strong in

Scotland, as was the attachment to the idealistic hope for a fairer society which accompanied it. In the glare of the spotlight of post-war reconstruction, the thirties looked a particularly awful period, and there was neither sympathy nor forgiveness for those who had presided over this shameful era.

The period from 1935 to the outbreak of the Second World War in Scottish politics was characterised by a sense of aimless drift, as the solution to the nation's endemic social and economic problems proved elusive. In the popular imagination, the period tends to be dominated by images of unemployment, hunger marches and poverty. The reality was that for most of the British population (including the Scots) it was a time of rising living standards. Most people had growing incomes, which could purchase a wider range of consumer goods which were designed to make life more pleasant and enjoyable. The travails of the unemployed were a minority concern which the majority regarded with uninterest and, in some cases, even hostility. Yet, for all that, it was clear that the gap between Scotland and the rest of the United Kingdom was failing to close. It was a frustrating period for politicians of all hues. Conservatives who made up the National Government were well aware that they were failing to deliver. Brave words and cheery assessments of the economic prognosis failed to dispel the pessimism. Staged events such as royal visits, plans to hold an Empire exhibition in Glasgow in 1938, and the opening of show-case industrial estates at Hillington on the outskirts of the city could only scratch at the surface of the nation's problems. The Secretary of State for Scotland, Walter Elliot, summed up this sense of impotence in 1937. Writing about the use of gesture politics to cover up the fundamental unease which permeated Scottish society, he declared that these

> will not in themselves dispose of the problems upon whose solution a general improvement in Scottish social and economic conditions depends. It is the consciousness of their existence which is reflected, not in the small and unimportant Nationalist Party, but in the dissatisfaction and unease amongst moderate and reasonable people of every rank – a dissatisfaction expressed in every book written about Scotland now for several years.
>
> Scottish Office Memorandum, 'The State of Scotland', 18 December 1937

The mounting complaints about the condition of Scotland forced a rethink about the nature of government. At a simple level, the debate was about greater autonomy and recognition of Scotland's national status while maintaining the existing political structure. With evidence that Scotland had failed to weather the economic storm and that social and economic discontent could erupt into a nationalist backlash, the National Government appointed a commission under Sir John Gilmour to examine the issues.

Nationalism was not the only factor to be borne in mind. First, there was the issue of the growth of government. Existing departments had expanded; others were newly created, and their remits kept growing. The government was also taking on greater responsibilities, and it was believed that the existing structure was too inflexible and required streamlining and clearer organisation. In 1926 the Scottish Secretary was upgraded to Secretary of State and had a permanent seat in the Cabinet. In 1929 local government was reorganised and the local burghs were abolished – which many nationalists pointed out was a violation of the Treaty of Union. Piecemeal social legislation, much of it enacted during the First World War and relating to sanitation, housing and health, was delegated to local authorities, who found it difficult to shoulder new responsibilities. There was a quest for greater uniformity in payment of unemployment benefit and in educational and health provision, but the old structure was incapable of delivering the required new standards. Second, strategic factors were also a consideration. With rearmament beginning to take shape and international tensions on the rise, it was believed that there was too much concentration of government in London, which was vulnerable to air attack. Dispersal of government departments would reduce the risk of successful enemy strikes. Third, there had to be some appeasement of those clamouring for change in the structure of government who advocated some form of home rule on the grounds that the decision-making process was too removed and remote from the people of Scotland. It was claimed that a Scottish parliament would more accurately reflect the democratic aspirations of the Scottish people. But this might let the nationalist genie out of the bottle.

Much of this debate was dominated by issues of symbolism and was motivated by a desire to satisfy the demand for greater recognition of Scotland as a distinctive national entity within the United Kingdom. It was in response to this that the Gilmour Commission recommended that the Scottish Office be moved from its then location in London to Edinburgh. It was argued that administrative devolution functioning from a distinctive Scottish outpost would be a powerful symbol of Scotland's distinctive identity. News that the competition to build this outpost, St Andrews House, had been won by an English architectural firm, however, immediately brought howls of protest from the nationalist community.

If symbolism was an important part of appeasing Scottish national sentiment, nevertheless there was also a desire to reform government. It was argued that the process of governing Scotland from Scotland would be more effective and efficient. Propagandists for the proposals claimed that decisions about Scotland would now be taken in Scotland by Scotsmen. The Scottish Office would be staffed by civil servants who were experts in their respective departments – roads, agriculture, prisons, education and the like – and who would now be living close to their areas of responsibility. So the spin ran. In effect, administrative devolution provided the appearance of greater autonomy without compromising the existing political structure's ability to set the agenda and dictate policy. Far from appeasing critics, the new structure of Scottish government was denounced by nationalists and Liberal and Labour home-rulers as increasing centralisation and making government less accountable. It was argued that the streamlining of government departments in the Scottish Office under the leadership of the Secretary of State for Scotland actually made government less subject to public accountability and scrutiny. For Labour in particular, the reforms of government in Scotland were just another way to freeze the party out of the structures of power.

Oligarchy would be a good way to characterise the government of Scotland in the thirties. The new status of the Secretary of State consolidated the authority of the Scottish Office and considerably increased his power. Complaints rang out that the Secretary of State was more like a colonial governor-general, rather than a democratically elected politician. The abolition of local education boards and parish councils and the placing of the increasing power of central-government authority into the hands of one man was denounced as an attack on the democratic ethos of the nation.

Yet the political structure of Scotland tells only half the story about power in Scotland on the eve of the Second World War. The politicians of the National Government were fairly well connected to a business infra-structure which commanded a huge part of the Scottish economy. While Scottish business leaders were, in public at any rate, keen to extol the virtues of the market economy and the principle of limited government intervention, their actions betrayed a greater concern for survival which contradicted those two fundamental tenets of their creed. They displayed a tendency to inter-mix their business interests with others in conglomer-ations that afforded them protection from the chill winds of competition. There was a remarkably degree of homogeneity in the ownership structure of the Scottish economy, and many contemporaries thought they detected what looked suspiciously like a consolidated ownership class that acted principally to protect its own interests. And this class was not averse to some forms of government intervention, especially in the form of subsidies for industry, while at the same time denouncing the 'extravagance' of expenditure on social policy. The members of this oligarchy were described by the socialist campaigner Thomas Burns as 'the Real Rulers of Scotland', in his 1939 book of that name, and the picture he painted was one in which the National Government and its business allies combined to exert an iron grip on the political, social and economic life of the nation. In spite of Labour having made a good showing in the general election of 1935 and winning almost the same share of the Scottish vote as the Con-servatives, the first-past-the-post system conspired to limit the number of Scottish Labour MPs to twenty, compared to thirty-seven Tories. Burns, like a growing number of Labour activists, believed that home rule was a necessary means of counteracting the overbearing political and economic power of this narrow clique who were not subject to any democratic checks and balances.

Central to Burns's critique was a belief that political power was of no consequence without economic power. In order to change society, he argued, control had to be wrested from the hands of those who com-manded the heights of the economy. This argument had a lot of support within Labour ranks, and was crucial in determining the party's stand on Scottish home rule. James Maxton and members of the ILP concurred with this view, and it had been used in the early thirties to distance the labour movement from supporting a parliament in Edinburgh. Yet, as Labour failed to make an electoral breakthrough and the party and its trade-union allies were confined to the periphery of decision-making in an increasingly corporatist economy in which new government powers and agencies were believed to be playing an ever more important role in economic life, Scottish home rule was seen as a way of letting Labour back into the decision-making fold. A Scottish parliament, it was argued, would be able to subject business leaders to more checks and controls. In the future, the balance between economic and political control would play an important part in determining the party's stance on Scottish self-government, and by the late thirties economic power was believed to be the more crucial. But whether this control could best be achieved by Edinburgh or by Westminster remained, for the time being, undetermined.

A small number of individuals exerted a remarkable degree of control over the Scottish economy through their interests in coal, iron and raw materials, shipbuilding, steel and engineering, and finance. They were linked by an intricate spider's web of connections, most of which were centred on the directors of the steelmakers Colvilles Ltd. Given that traditional heavy industry still accounted for a disproportionate part of the Scottish economy, these industrialists wielded great power. Sir James Lithgow, John Craig and Sir Steven Bisland were the three key players whose reach extended throughout the Scottish economy. They were followed in importance by Sir Adam Nimmo, Alexander Wallace, R. T. Moore and J. A. Hood, who, though not as powerful, still held substantial overlapping interests.

The career of Sir James Lithgow provides an interesting insight into the interconnectedness of the ownership of the economy. Lithgow and his brother, Henry, were the directors of Lithgows Ltd, one of the largest shipbuilding companies in the United Kingdom. Sir James was also the chairman of the Federation of British Industry (the forerunner of the Confederation of British Industry (CBI)) and had extensive connections with the Conservative Party. In shipbuilding, he was also chairman of the Ayrshire Docks Company, David Rowan Ltd and Armstrong Whitworth Shipbuilders Ltd. He was also on the board of directors of William Lithgow Ltd, National Shipbuilders Security Corporation Ltd, Fairfield Shipbuilding and Engineering Ltd and New Palace Steamers Ltd. In short, he was on the boards of eight out of the twenty-eight major shipbuilding companies. One of his fellow directors in Colvilles Ltd, John Craig, was on six different boards, and a fellow director in the Ardrossan Harbour Co. Ltd, Sir Alfred Read, was on a further six. Only seven of the main shipbuilding companies were unconnected to a nexus that involved Lithgow, Craig or Read.

Sir James was also active in the iron, coal and raw-materials sector of the economy. He was on the board of James Dunlop & Co Ltd and Nimmo & Dunlop Ltd, as also were his brother, Henry, John Craig and Sir Adam Nimmo, the last of whom was on the board of a further four companies. Through his membership of James Dunlop & Co., Lithgow was connected to R. T. Moore, who held positions in a further eight companies which were involved mainly in coal and electricity. Lithgow was active in the steel and engineering industry through Beardmores Ltd, Richard Thomas & Co., Glasgow Railway Engineering Co. Ltd and the Steel Company of Scotland Ltd. In the financial sector, Sir James was on the board of Credit for Industry Ltd, along with his fellow Colvilles director Sir Steven Bisland, who was also active in the following: Scottish Industrial Estates Ltd, Special Areas Reconstruction Ltd, Scottish National Trust Co. Ltd, Second Scottish National Trust Co. Ltd, Third Scottish National Trust Co. Ltd, Glasgow Stockholder Trust Ltd, Scottish Amicable Insurance Company and the Union Bank of Scotland Ltd. Based on the known figures, Sir James was active in industrial concerns which had a combined capital value of in excess of £11 million.

In total, the eight directors of Colvilles sat on the boards of over fifty companies in Scotland. Yet their grip reached far beyond the confines of the industrial sector. Industrialists also had a remarkable degree of control over the Scottish financial sector. Alexander Wallace of the Fife Coal Company was a co-director of the First, Second and Third Edinburgh Investment Trust Ltd companies, which had assets of over £3 million, and a director of Standard Life Assurance, which had assets of £26 million. He was also on the board of the Bank of Scotland, with fellow industrialist John Craig, to oversee the deposits of £39 million. William Thompson of Shotts Iron Company was on the board of the Commercial Bank of Scotland Ltd, which had deposits of £42 million, and was a director of the Life Association of Scotland, which had funds of £8 million. R. L. Angus of

Bairds was on the board of Clydesdale Bank, which had £34 million in deposits. Although the post-war nationalisation of industry was condemned by many for taking power away from Scotland and placing it in London, the reality of the Scottish economy in the thirties was that it was in the hands of a narrow oligarchy. There is a case to be made that nationalisation helped to democratise and liberalise the economy by removing it from the hands of a self-perpetuating industrial clique.

In explaining the failures of the inter-war economy, a number of factors have already been highlighted. The failure to diversify, skills and capital shortages, and government policy all added to the woes of Scottish economic development. And the fact that the heights of the economy were commanded by such a narrow range of individuals adds a further dimension to this catalogue of failure. In spite of the rhetoric which was regularly spouted concerning the virtues of the marketplace, it is hard to see how the economy could be competitive when such unofficial, quasi-monopolistic practices went on. The Scottish economy was a cartel in all but name. It has been noted by many commentators, then and since, that business in Scotland was conservative and slow to adapt to change. Yet such an incestuous system of ownership and mutual self-support would not lead to increased competitiveness, but would tend towards stasis.

A charitable interpretation of the industrialists' actions is to see them as a forerunner of the corporatist tendencies which emerged after the war. As will be discussed below, the business community in Scotland was not backward at coming forward with demands for greater government intervention. A less charitable interpretation of their actions, however, is that they were motivated by naked self-interest. The existence of multiple directorships within so many companies which, on paper at least, should have been competitors is hardly indicative of free-market economics. Accusations of price-fixing abounded.

While many businessmen had lost faith in the free market, they had not lost their belief in the desirability of private profit and were fairly unabashed in their claims that it was in the nation's best interests that the state should help shore up the interests of private industry. According to Sir James Lithgow, such intervention was more important than social welfare, which, he believed, was damaging to the economic structure:

It ought to be clear that no nation can stand a sudden sprouting even of social amelioration without demoralising influences setting in to destroy the healthy growth which has taken place ... Are we getting value for money for the vast sums provided from the fruits of industry for universal education of our people? Some considera- tion should be given to the question whether industry can provide suitable jobs for the great majority of those to whom higher [i.e. secondary] education is given at great cost ... The true solution is to return to something nearer the standard which we set ourselves, on which we were a contented people in 1901 ... We must wait for the time when the real productive capacity of our people may by gradual growth catch up with social standards which have for the present outstripped the international value of those who enjoy them ... Who can truly assert that the various forms of payment of allowances during unemployment have had the effect of bringing back into employment many of the recipients so much fitter and happier than was customary when such allowances were not so gen- eral and uncontrolled.

Address to the International Engineering Congress of 1938, Glasgow

Like many of the other leaders of the Scottish economy, Sir James looked not forward, but backwards to a time when wages were low and poor social conditions made for a desperate workforce. His preference was not for cor- poratism in the sense of government, business and the workers cooperat- ing for mutual benefit: rather, government intervention was supposed to be for the exclusive benefit of industry, and to our eyes this is more like the economics of the Third World.

Again, the close relationship between the financial sector and the heavy industrial sector does not seem to have been a healthy one, and may account for the failure to diversify into new areas. Another tendency was for companies to own subsidiary companies, often working in the same area, which gave the appearance of being separate though in actual fact they were highly connected. This structure of interlocking connections and multiple directorships, at worst, could be held responsible for produc- ing a complacent and lazy attitude. It was effective as a means of stifling competition, but its cost in terms of the modernisation of the Scottish economy was great. Scotland was left with an dying economic structure which would be kept going only by rearmament, and even then, with the advances in technology, not even war could advance it much beyond its traditional parameters.

The way in which this informal cartelisation worked in practice can be gleaned from a few examples. Colvilles (chairman John Craig; members of the board Sir James Lithgow and F. E. Rebbeck) supplied Lithgows (chairman Sir James Lithgow) and Harland & Wolff shipbuilders (chairman F. E. Rebbeck; member of the board John Craig) with steel. John Craig also used his position as a director of the Ardrossan Harbour Co. Ltd (a subsidiary of Coastlines Ltd, which part-owned David McBraynes Ltd, the largest Scottish coastal shipping operator) as a means to secure further orders. Yarrow & Co. of Scotstoun and Alexander Stephen & Sons Ltd were two shipbuilders which on the surface seemed to have no connection with Colvilles; however, their chairmen, Sir Harold Yarrow and A. M. Stephen, respectively, were both directors of the Steel Company of Scotland, which was owned by Colvilles. Similar patterns of interlocking directorships and companies owning other companies were to be found in the steel, coal and engineering industries. In coal, James Nimmo & Co. Ltd was owned by Nimmo & Dunlop Ltd, which in turn was owned by Colvilles Ltd. Such structures could cross different industries, and Beardmores Ltd owned nine subsidiary companies and also a half share in the Glasgow and Iron Steel Company, the other half being owned by the shipbuilding company Swan Hunter Wigham Richardson, which also owned Barclay Curle & Co., shipbuilders, and John C. Kincaid & Co., marine engineers. The chairman of Beardmores was also chairman of the Triumph Motor Company and the Motherwell Brick Co. Ltd.

These business links were reinforced by a variety of social networks, which included clubs and societies. Business had extensive links with the Conservative Party, and most Tory MPs in the thirties came from this sector. The Secretary of State for Scotland in 1939, Colonel John Colville, was a former director of the family firm and was married to the sister of Scotland's leading banker, Sir Steven Bisland, who in turn was married to a Colville. The giant pipe-manufacturing firm of Stewart & Lloyds Ltd had close business connections with Tube Investments Ltd, whose chairman, Arthur Chamberlain, was the Prime Minister's cousin. Further evidence of the degree of complacency within the business elite can be gleaned by their heavy reliance on government subsidy, especially for the shipbuilding industry. Rearmament was essential to the survival of heavy industry in the late thirties. In 1939 an annual subsidy of £500,000 was made available to shipbuilding in a package which over five years would mean a total of £2.5 million in grants and a further £10 million in loans to assist the industry.

Many historians have pointed to work which was carried out in the thirties as paving the way for the post-war corporatist economy in which government, trade unions and business would work together on the basis of planning and demand management in order to stimulate orders and ensure full employment, with all the social benefits that that would entail. Organisations such as the Scottish National Development Council, the Clydesdale Bank's annual Scottish economic surveys and the work of individual commentators such as Charles Oakley and J. A. Bowie all identified the structural imbalance of the economy and its heavy reliance on the staple industries as being at the heart of the social and economic difficulties of the nation. Also, their proposed remedy of greater diversification, greater government involvement with planning, and more sustained use of regulation seemed to point towards future developments.

Yet, for all this, some qualifications have to be made. The Scottish industrial lobby was hostile to government intervention, with the exception of direct grants to industry, and it was Sir Steven Bisland and Sir James Lithgow who headed the Scottish Economic Committee (SEC), which was charged with finding solutions to the problems of the economy. In 1936 the Secretary of State for Scotland, Walter Elliot, officially recognised the SEC as the authoritative organisation in respect of economic forecasting. For all the recommendations, Scottish industrialists were reluctant to diversify, and Sir James's only venture into a 'new' industry was Scottish Aircraft Components Ltd, which acted as a contract developer for steel and engineering components which would feed business into existing industries. The SEC's main attempt to branch out into new industries was the development of the Hillington Industrial Estate, which by 1939, employed only 2,000 people – mainly unskilled women workers, who did not have trade-union rights. The failure to employ more people and attract more business was compounded when, in 1939, the government had to shell out £5 million to build a factory for Rolls-Royce on the remaining half of the estate, for the construction of aircraft engines. This had the effect of further making Scottish economic recovery dependent on rearmament, which, as most pointed out, was only a transient solution. The rather lame efforts of the SEC, whose other showcase was the Glasgow Empire Exhibition in 1938, were contrasted unfavourably with the activities of the Scottish Co-operative Wholesale Society, which employed a total of 14,500 workers who produced furniture, clothes and other domestic products to the tune of some £7 million a year, without any government subsidy whatsoever.

For whatever reasons, Scottish industrialists remained tied to outdated notions, set in their ways and determined at all costs to preserve their dominance in the economic structure. Underlying all their actions was a suspicion that any programme of economic diversification might undo their monopolistic grip of heavy industry on the Scottish economy. The war would take away that control.

TOTAL WAR

Few doubted that the prosecution of the war would mean the full mobilisation of the nation's resources. Fear of war in the thirties was driven by a belief that the next conflict would be still more calamitous than the last and might even bring about the end of civilisation. There was a widespread fear that the bomber would always get through and spew poisonous gases on to defenceless civilians below. Protecting the innocent and keeping the vital industries going would require a Herculean task of organisation. The cities of Glasgow, Edinburgh and Dundee and the naval base at Rosyth were deemed to be likely targets for bombers, and so required the evacuation of children. The total number evacuated came to 175,812, of whom 62,059 were unaccompanied children, while mothers with pre-school children, teachers and helpers made up the rest. This represented about 37 per cent of the school population of Scotland. Special departure points had been prepared in advance, and the evacuation took place over a period of several days. Children from Edinburgh were sent to Banff, Berwick, Clackmannan, Inverness, Midlothian, Nairn, Peebles, Roxburgh, Selkirk and West Lothian. Those from Rosyth were dispatched into the nearby countryside. Glaswegians departed for Aberdeen, Argyle, Ayr, Bute, Dumfries, Kinross, Kirkcudbright, Lanark, Perth, Renfrew, Stirling and Wigton. The children from Clydebank and Dundee were sent out into the nearby countryside.

Evacuation was extremely stressful, both for parents and for children. To begin with it may have seemed like a great adventure, although the long journeys were often uncomfortable and few children had any real understanding of what was going on. They did not know why they were leaving or what would happen to them. They were carefully labelled and ticketed, with their names and addresses pinned on to them, and looked a pitiful sight as they carried their gas masks and luggage. On arrival, children were often put on display, with the locals being invited to choose their own evacuee. Those who were last to be chosen felt unwanted. Some Catholic children ended up in Protestant homes. Brothers and sisters struggled to be kept together, and most of the city children found themselves in an environment which was totally alien. Many had a hard time: the pain of separation and alienation was simply too great to be overcome. Some were billeted with unscrupulous families who only wanted extra ration cards and/or extra labour to help out on the farm. But many families did their bit and volunteered to take in evacuees, and after a period of readjustment many children settled down to a life of relative peace and tranquillity. Indeed, through evacuation, the war was responsible for Scotland becoming reacquainted with itself, and many of the evacuees maintained connections with their billeted locality long after the conflict was over.

However, the system of billeting often failed to rouse patriotic duty in the countryside, and there were increasing complaints that the middle class were shunning the evacuees and that it was left to the poorer rural labourers to take the strain. The Duke of Argyle, for example, refused to let his castle at Inveraray be used for billeting, and when forced to by government legislation he kept the evacuees in the basement. Local accents and dialects were often a real stumbling block, with the Glaswegians who were evacuated to Aberdeen believing that they had been sent to a foreign country, while their hosts struggled with similar problems of comprehension. Few evacuees had seen farm animals, and life in the country was a revelation. The 'vaccies' could often face a rough time both at school, where they were the object of fun among local kids, and in the home, where they were regarded as intruders who vied for the affection of mum and dad.

The evacuation helped to highlight some of the real class and cultural differences which existed in Scotland. As many as a third of children from the inner cities failed the medical test, which revealed large numbers of cases of malnutrition and underdevelopment. Nits, lice and skin disease were another widespread problem. Working-class children struggled to cope with the realities of middle-class life – few had experienced the luxury of an indoor toilet, for example – and there were many complaints from outraged citizens that these children were not house-trained. Meal times could prove problematic, with awkward moments regarding dinner-table etiquette and a reluctance to eat anything that was not their usual fare. Many complained about the dirty and unhygienic manners of the evacuees, who had to be trained in hand-washing and cleanliness. The strain of separation and the strangeness of their new homes meant that bed-wetting reached epidemic proportions. Medical officers' reports to the Scottish Office record that the town clerk of Rothesay complained to the Department of Health for Scotland that 650 out of the 1,494 children sent were of 'a very undesirable class, very dirty and very unruly'.

The alien environment, hostility among the host community and, above all, the failure of the war to break out in earnest meant that many of the children and their mothers drifted back to the cities during 1940. Many families took the decision that, in spite of the danger and hardship of spending nights in an air-raid shelter, it was better for the family to stay together. By the end of the 'phoney war', government had come to accept that the policy of evacuation had been a failure and efforts were made to improve its record. Higher allowances were paid, and greater use was made of propaganda in the cinema to show the effect of aerial bombardment. Also, it was stressed that the system was voluntary and that there was no question of families being broken up against their will. Instead, the emphasis was on the safety of the child. It took the effect of bombing in the Clyde area in March 1941 to increase the numbers being evacuated.

The government's plans for war involved dividing the United Kingdom into units which would be under the control of regional commissioners. In August 1939 the Labour politician Thomas Johnston was appointed the regional commissioner for Scotland, to be assisted by five district commissioners. Johnston was responsible for the coordination and administration of the government's war plans. The emergency services would have to be expanded to deal with the threat of bombing. Extra firemen, wardens and first-aiders were recruited, many initially full-time, but the pattern emerged of volunteers complementing a skeleton staff, and this had the advantage of ensuring that workers would not be withdrawn from industry. The town of Ayr had a system of emergency workers who were complemented by volunteers, and this became the template for the rest of Scotland. The 7,000-strong police force was augmented with 12,000 part-time auxiliaries, while those employed in government service more than tripled to 65,710. Local-authority employment also increased, although only by 10 per cent, to 52,570.

For those not evacuated, defence from the bomber meant either the Anderson shelter, which was made of corrugated steel and dug into the back garden, or a designated shelter, which was usually a basement owned by the municipal authority. One major problem for the inhabitants of Scotland's cities was that few of them had a garden in which they could install a shelter so the most common type of shelter in the cities was a strutted close in a tenement building which was reinforced with scaffolding and protected by sandbags. The tops of postboxes were painted with gas-detecting paint. Blackouts were designed to ensure that bombers would not be able to use the lights from towns or cities either as an aid to navigation or as a target: the first casualties therefore rolled in from an increase in road accidents and other domestic mishaps. Citizens were given instruction about the kinds of poison gas they might expect, which included blister gas, lung irritants, mustard gas, and even sneezing gas. Households were instructed to tape up anything that might shatter as a result of a bomb blast and were told not to keep quantities of inflammable material. One problem for the authorities was the distilleries' stockpiles of whisky, which were highly inflammable. It was the attempt to move some of these to safety in America that resulted in a shipload going aground off the island of Barra, immortalised in Compton Mackenzie's novel *Whisky Galore*.

Preparing for war was an enormous task. Industry had to be converted to war production and staffed by essential workers. Steel, coal, shipping, munitions, engines and machinery production had to be boosted to maximum. By the end of 1938 the Dundee jute industry went into overdrive to meet the insatiable demand for sandbags; beaches were dug up to fill them. Recruits for the armed forces had to be organised, mobilised and earmarked for duty. Domestic goods had to be rationed and their production safeguarded and controlled. Roads, railways and shipping had to be turned over to transporting the materials, men and women necessary for war. Hospitals, schools, cinemas, town halls and other public utilities would likewise fall within the jurisdiction of the war effort. Coastal defences had to be shored up, and anti tank-traps laid along the coast. Comprehensive chains of command had to be created, and areas of special responsibility and authority defined. Civil-defence authorities were established to oversee the implementation of government regulations. The state, which had taken a back seat in the life of citizens before the war, now become a part of everyday reality. It told people what to eat, where to work, and where they could and could not go; it issued news about their efforts; and it attended to their needs in the extraordinary circumstances of total war.

There were a number of differences between the mobilisations of the First and Second World Wars. First, the grim experience of the First World War in which friends joined up together and died together would not be repeated. The effect of sustained casualties on a particular community would not be felt again, and the mixing of men into different units would produce a more random casualty pattern. This mixing was made easier by the use of conscription from the outset, which meant that the flow of men and women into the armed forces could be controlled. The Argyll and Sutherland Highlanders became known as the Argyll and Bolton Wanderers because of the large number of English recruits within the regiment. Also, whereas the infantry had been the main focus of recruitment in the First World War, the Second would require a much larger component of specialist and service soldiers. Developments in technology meant that the army required a larger number of ancillaries such as engineers, communication experts, drivers, fitters and supply workers. The development of the air force likewise meant a need for a large number of specialist servicemen.

One of the fundamental difficulties in assessing the Scottish contribution to the British war effort is to disaggregate it from the total. The mobilisation for war was done through a central command system, which meant that separate Scottish tallies were not kept in the same way as they were for the Great War. It can, however, be said for a start that the Scottish economic contribution could not have been as great a proportion as was the case during the First World War. As has been explained in the previous chapters, the productive capacity of the Scottish economy had been falling behind the UK average. Furthermore, the technological state of the economy was not as advanced, and many of the new industries which were required to make the instruments of war, such as aircraft, tanks and motor vehicles, were lacking in Scotland. The tendency for components to be produced in Scotland but moved south for the more complex process of assembly was indicative of how the Scottish economy had been lagging behind. The population had also been diminishing, and by all accounts was in much poorer shape than that of England and Wales. Even if mobilisation for war production was evenly spread throughout the United Kingdom on the basis of population, the fact that Scotland was starting from a lower base than England and Wales means that technological and productive-capacity gaps would have remained. Evidence of this is to be found in the fact that unmarried women who were conscripted for industrial work had to be moved to factories in the Midlands because similar work was not available in Scotland.

One important facet of Scotland's contribution to the war which was not affected by economic and demographic decline was geography. Strategically, Scotland was vital for the British war effort. With the nearest coast and port to the western hemisphere, Scotland was a vital link for the supply of war material. The population of Orkney quadrupled to 80,000 as a result of the influx of soldiers and sailors to the naval base at Scapa Flow, and the Highlands became one large training base as the air force practised bombing runs and soldiers carried out military exercises. To facilitate the movement of men and materials, the number employed in the railway service in Scotland during the war doubled to 30,000.

The lack of hard statistical evidence which relates specifically to Scotland makes it difficult for the historian to assess the ways in which the war affected the economy and society and so arrive at a meaningful conclusion about the extent of the nation's contribution to the war effort. However, examination of statistics for before and during the war does highlight the main changes. Planners for post-war reconstruction estimated that work would have to be found for about a third of a million people as a result of demobilisation and the rundown of armament industries, though it was believed that most factories would be converted to peacetime production. The war effort absorbed the labour of many, such as pensioners and married women, who it was believed would afterwards go back to a life in the home. Also, as Lend-Lease kicked in and the United States entered the war, the economic priorities of the British war effort moved increasingly towards providing military manpower which would be armed by American economic muscle, to the extent that by 1943 the production of bombers was the industrial priority of the British government. By 1944 there were 4.4 million men and 450,000 women in the British armed services, and it is not unreasonable to assume that Scotland contributed about half a million to this total, based on its share of the British population. Arguments can be made to increase this number, given the productive limitations of the Scottish economy, which would have made more people available for armed service, or to decrease it, given that agriculture, mining and shipyard work were reserved occupations and accounted for a higher proportion of the workforce in Scotland than in the rest of the United Kingdom. British figures indicate that a third of working men were in the armed forces, and if the same proportion applies to Scotland then the figure still comes out at about half a million.

The exigencies of 'total war' led to the creation of the command economy, in which government directed and controlled industrial production. State intervention would become the hallmark of British economic policy after 1945, and it can be said that planning through demand management – in the sense that government stimulated growth to regulate and ensure full employment – owed much to the wartime Keynesian economic experiment. Planning for reconstruction was much in vogue in Scottish economic circles during the war (see Chapter 6); however, it is important to separate the experience of wartime, which was dictated by short-term strategic interests, and that of the post-war period, which was determined by long-term factors. In order to prosecute the war with maximum efficiency, government had to maximise the production of essential war materials and minimise the production of non-essentials. To do this, it was necessary to convert as many factories as possible from producing the latter to producing the former. This would have a significant impact on the Scottish economy. Government had to operate within the existing parameters of the UK economy, and, in spite of the claims made by the Secretary of State for Scotland, Thomas Johnston, that Scotland was getting a larger share, the distribution of war production would follow established patterns which were created in the pre-war era. The Scottish economy in the late thirties was largely reflated as a result of rearmament, which created demand for the heavy industries. This trend would continue.

As has already been noted, a limited consumer industry north of the border was a significant economic weakness, and as the war would restrict production of non-essential items it follows that a smaller Scottish sector producing these would be squeezed harder than the larger sector in the English south-east, which had the advantage of economies of scale. Even non-essential materials were subject to the criterion of maximising production. Clothes, furniture, footwear, building work and electrical goods would still be needed, even during war, and it made more sense to award orders for them to the factories and outlets which could produce the most with minimum disruption to the war effort. One effect of this was that the government imposed on 'non-essential' factory space in Scotland a ratio of 90.9 per cent for storage to 9.1 per cent for production. The comparable figures for England were 71.6 per cent for storage and 28.4 per cent for production. This meant that Scotland's capacity to produce consumer goods was more run-down by the end of the war.

Although the Ministry of Aircraft Production employed over 100,000 people in Scotland, mainly producing engines and wing components, most light engineering work centred on the south-east of England. In short, strategic considerations meant that the war reinforced the existing trends which were prevalent in the pre-war British economy. Government intervention was important, and by 1945 some 700 new industrial enterprises had been authorised in Scotland, employing a labour force of 90,000 – although this was dwarfed by the 250,000 who remained working in the traditional heavy industries. Indeed, employment in this sector increased by just over 50 per cent.

Raw materials, food, engineering and ships would form the bulk of Scottish wartime output. Scottish industrial production centred on engineering and on shipbuilding, which together more than quadrupled the value of their output in the period from 1935 to 1948. This was largely due to the demand for merchant shipping, which was being lost in huge numbers as a result of the Battle of the Atlantic, and by 1943 five ships were being launched per week, which was about 40 per cent of the British total. The number employed in the yards increased by three-quarters, to 65,000 and those working in marine engineering increased by a third, to 25,440. The production of guns, aircraft and vehicle components nearly tripled, while those employed in general engineering increased by more than half. Explosives were another important part of war production, with the number employed increasing by two and a half times, to 24,000. Coal was a vital commodity, essential not only to keep the home fires burning, but also to keep the wheels of industry turning. In spite of conscription of the 'Bevan boys', numbers in the mining industry decreased, productivity declined, and output dropped by 30 per cent. This was a result of both inexperienced miners and mine exhaustion.

The production of food was another vital task, given that most food-stuffs were imported and therefore subject to the threat of submarine war-fare. A subsidy of £2 per acre was made available to farmers to convert grassland for crop growing. As a result of this, the production of oats rose by 33 per cent, wheat by 32 per cent, barley by 72 per cent, and potatoes by 57 per cent. Farmers were guaranteed fixed prices for their produce, and their incomes doubled during the war. Farming was declared a reserved occupation, but this was insufficient to meet the demand for labour and the Women's Land Army was drafted in. Numbering about 10,000 in Scotland, these women drove tractors, planted crops, tended livestock, and maintained fences and building. They were also helped by 19,000 prisoners of war.

AN ISLAND RACE

The war on the home front was a battle for hearts and minds. It was the role of the Ministry of Information to make sure that the population was moti-vated and had its morale kept high. Plans for reconstruction and the prose-cution of a 'just' war, in which the nation was fighting not only for survival but for decency and civilisation elsewhere, were two key themes which were regularly hammered out on radio, in the cinemas and in newspapers. The need to keep everybody onside was an essential component of British wartime propaganda, and this meant blurring class and national distinctions to create an image of Britons from all walks of life pulling together and working in harmony for victory. The period therefore witnessed a state-sponsored promotion of an idealised British national identity which would obviously have ramifications for Scottish national identity.

This is significant in two respects. First, the state now had access to a much more powerful mass-media machine. Radio and cinema could reach people in a way that was not possible by print, which in any case remained largely subject to Scottish control. As a means of exerting emotional influence, cinema and radio were much more effective, and the images which could be conjured up had a more immediate, dramatic and lasting effect. People could hear for themselves Churchill's emotive pleas and see in the newsreels the grim realities of a nation at total war, with troops and civilians all pulling together to do their bit. Second, notions of Britishness were constructed to have a popular appeal which emphasised similarity and downplayed diversity. This was the era of a 'thousand years' of British history and of the 'island race'. Even Scottish politicians, such as Walter Elliot and John Buchan, bought into the idea of the long continuity of British history, and references to Elizabeth I, Francis Drake and the defeat of the Spanish Armada were used to construct a none too subtle message that the British nation could stand alone against superior forces and still win. Many Scots servicemen took courses run by the Army Education Corps in which history, politics and current affairs received an Anglocentric interpretation. Also, the left came to intellectual prominence during the war and had an in-built aversion to anything that had a whiff of nationalism about it. Too often an interest in the distinctiveness of Scottish society was dismissed as parochial and narrow-minded. Wartime films typically portrayed Jock, Taffy, Paddy, the obligatory chirpy cockney (who seems always to get shot) and others from the English regions all working together under the supervision of an essentially nice, but naive, officer from the middle class. They all come to see one another's virtues, and bond together as a team. It was a portrayal of class, regional and national harmony, buoyed up with a thorough sense of decent British values.

There is a myth that the war brought about a levelling of British society. The common experience of bombing, rationing and conscription, and the expectation that every man, women and child had to do his or her bit for the war effort, was supposed to have blurred the class barriers which were previously such a prominent feature of society. The reality is that class differences remained intact and were probably strengthened. Most statistics demonstrate that an individual's experience in wartime Britain was determined more by class than by any other factor. Rationing, although seemingly egalitarian, assumed that a manual labourer needed the same amount of food as a desk worker. Those on low incomes found that their clothing rations went on cheap items which would not last as well as expensive ones which only those on high incomes could afford. Much of the experience of war was determined by the material possessions that you had before it began. A well-stocked home survived the privations better than one which was not. There was a vibrant black-market economy, which meant that those with money could still purchase luxury goods, albeit at a price. Class was the key determinant in the likelihood of being bombed: middle-class suburbs were safely away from strategic targets. National service, likewise, was shaped by class. Those with an education or holding a professional position were natural officer material, while those in manual labour were likely to be drafted into the ranks. Even within civilian life, the natural class barriers and distinctions of rank were maintained.

That said, it would be difficult to claim that the experience of total war did not change attitudes. For most Scots, there was an increased awareness of the British state, simply because it was omnipresent in society. Rationing, conscription, emergency controls, propaganda and mass mobilisation all contributed to the feeling that the Scots were part of a larger struggle which they shared with their fellow Britons. And, should they forget, the Ministry of Information and the BBC were always on hand to remind them. The experience of war also laid to rest the major source of complaint north of the border. Scotland had experienced relative social and economic decline and had missed out on the prosperity enjoyed by the south of England as a result of the creation of new sunrise industries and a consumer boom which was buoyed up by government economic policy. This had given rise to widespread resentment that the Scots had not been fairly treated and that the lifeblood of the nation was being sucked out by the prosperity of the south, which pulled workers and industry away from

Scotland. But the belief that the United Kingdom was divided into a poor north and a wealthy south was suspended by the Blitz. The fact that the areas which attracted such jealousy for their prosperity and new industries were now subject to the attention of the Luftwaffe did much to provide a kind of atonement for the divisions which had characterised inter-war British society. Messages of sympathy and support poured out from Scottish cities and towns to the people of London, Coventry, Birmingham, Bristol, Southampton, Portsmouth and Leicester. Fifty thousand civilians died in the United Kingdom as a result of bombing (30,000 in London alone), and a further 86,000 were seriously injured. In Scotland, 2,414 civilians died as a direct result of war, which meant that the Scottish death rate was half the overall British rate. A further factor in eliciting Scots' sympathy was that over 70,000 of their fellow countrymen and -women had moved south in the inter-war period, leaving anxious relatives wondering whether family members had fallen victim to the Luftwaffe. The bombing of cities in the north of England, which had suffered just as badly during the Depression, perhaps helped to convince most of the people in Scotland that they had got off quite lightly.

The most sustained attack on Scotland was at Clydebank, which suffered the highest density of damage experienced by any British town or city. Glasgow, Greenock, Aberdeen and Edinburgh also experienced attacks, but not of the same ferocity as the two-day Clydebank Blitz, which demonstrated that a protracted air attack on Scotland would have been disastrous. There were inadequate air-raid shelters, poorly coordinated rescue services and a structure of housing in the cities which bombing would have made lethal. The Scottish system of tenements meant that the population was more tightly packed than its equivalents in England, who lived in back-to-back houses. Indeed, a sustained campaign of aerial bombardment on the Scottish cities would have produced a casualty rate comparable to that experienced by Germany in the latter stages of the war. All these failings were exposed in March 1941 during the Clydebank Blitz.

There was a degree of inevitability that the Clyde estuary would be targeted. It was an area which was important for the production of war material, it had a strategic docking facility, and it was easily identifiable from the air by its distinctive geography – the German pilots simply had to follow the river Clyde. It was expected to be targeted, and decoy lights were placed in the nearby countryside to put the bombers off the scent. Also, its having been visited by a delegation from the German navy in 1938 should have given the game away. The entire area had been converted to war production. The Singer's Sewing Machine factory had been converted to produce components for armament production, particularly parts for aircraft wings. The John Brown shipyard was engaged in the construction of destroyers and escort ships. A large part of the district was designated a Royal Ordnance factory producing medium-calibre guns. There was a large naval fuelling depot as well as storage and docking facilities. Finally, there was a population of 50,000 which lived in a very concentrated area and was all doing vital war work. On the evening of 13 March 1941, 236 German bombers set off from their bases to attack Clydebank, the Govan shipyards and the Rolls-Royce factory in Hillington.

At 9.10 p.m. the air-raid sirens went off, ten minutes before the attack began. Over the next eight hours 270 tons of high explosives and 1,700 incendiaries would be dropped on the burgh. One of the first places to be hit was the library, which acted as the control centre for civil defence. The electricity, gas and water supplies were cut, and there was extensive damage to residential areas. The local emergency services were overwhelmed, and at 4.00 a.m. units of firefighters from all over central Scotland were drafted in. One difficulty which emerged was that the different fire services used different equipment, which gave rise to incompatibility: fire crews found themselves with hoses and nozzles that did not fit together. The severing of the water supply meant that the canal had to be used, but the pumps were not of sufficient strength to get water to the parts of town which were on higher ground; these areas were left to burn themselves out. The dangers of tenements were cruelly exposed, and in one direct hit a front wall was blown off, killing eighty-eight people. There had not been a significant raid on Scotland before this, which meant that many people had become complacent. When the bombers struck, there had been little in the way of an evacuation and some 7,000 children still remained in the town.

Residents awoke to utter devastation. German attacks normally occurred over two days, so the population had a chance to evacuate before the attack the following night. Most simply headed out into the nearby countryside. When they returned the following morning, they found that the town had been utterly flattened. Only seven buildings survived unscathed, and, out of a population of 50,000, 35,000 were left homeless. Over 1,200 people were killed, and some 1,100 were seriously wounded. Fortunately for the Scots, the nation's remoteness and the fact that bombers had to travel overland to hit the key industrial targets meant that there were no further significant air strikes.

The experiences of servicemen and -women did much to enhance the sense of British identity in Scotland. The mixing of so many men and women from all over Britain had the effect of introducing Scots to a wide range of different people from south of the border. For the majority of the half-million Scottish service people, the English were no longer an abstract concept: they were chums, comrades and friends. Although hostilities were still reported, such a massive social inter-mixing could only help to break down national barriers. At the start of the war, a few Scottish service personnel would have had limited contact with the English and Welsh, but most would not have been south of the border. Conscription introduced Scots, and the English for that matter, to the rich panoply of English regional culture. Hundreds of thousands of Scots were billeted in England, where they found kindness, friendship and romance. It introduced them to different worlds, and helped to build up an image of the English more complex than the narrow stereotypical picture of the snobbish, bowler-hatted, umbrella-wielding gent of Scottish popular culture. Most travelled extensively and saw for themselves 'Britain' in its geographic sense. The barrack-room and military service were a common cultural experience for many British men and were responsible for the introduction of a range of English colloquialisms into the language of Scotland. People started to talk about having a nap or a kip, or a cup of char and some bully for tea.

Likewise, there was a flow of English personnel to the north, usually for training. And Scots not only had more English in their midst: there were also Poles and Americans. GIs caused considerable excitement, largely because of the huge influence Hollywood had had in Scotland, as the Scots preferred American movies to those produced in the United Kingdom. Yet the GIs mainly passed through Scotland on the way south to prepare for the invasion of Normandy. The brash American with nylons, chocolate and real cigarettes did not stay long enough to arouse envy, admiration, hostility or jealousy.

The stresses and strains of total war did lead to a mini social revolution. The mean age of marriage, which had been rising during the Depression, fell and there was an increase in the number of couples tying the knot. Undoubtedly, the prospect of death due to bombing or combat helped to focus the mind and dispel doubts as to whether the time was right. The chance that young couples might never see one another again relegated conventional marriage worries about career, finance and accommodation to the back of the queue. There was probably an increase in promiscuity, although no one can say this for sure, and there was a small increase in the number of illegitimate births and a soaring rise in the rates of venereal disease. According to the 1943 Medical Advisory Committee (Scotland) Report on Venereal Diseases:

> An actual increase of venereal disease has occurred, though owing to statistical difficulties the incidence could not be assessed precisely. Between 1939 and 1942, 58,000 persons were exposed to risk of acquiring infection and 29,000 contracted a major venereal disease. The increase is more marked in ports and large towns and the data suggest that it is due to the temporary influx of service personnel and seamen; although a decline will probably occur with the return of normal conditions, the situation warrants energetic action.

The Scottish Office tried, but failed, to implement a policy of compulsory notification.

This was one feature of an invigorated health policy. In anticipation of huge numbers of casualties a system of Civil Defence hospitals was established mainly in the industrial west, which was expected to take the brunt of any bombing campaign. As casualties failed to come in, it was decided that these hospitals would be used to treat the workforce, in part because they were standing idle with nothing to do, and also because the treatment of illness would help the war effort. Some 34,000 patients received free specialist medical attention, and the scheme was considered such a success that it was extended to the rest of the country. GPs were encouraged to send their difficult cases to the Civil Defence hospitals, and some 10,000 were treated. In effect, a free national health service came into existence.

THE STRONGMAN IN THE CABINET

The appointment on 9 February 1941 of Thomas Johnston as the Secretary of State for Scotland can be seen as a watershed in the development of twentieth-century Scottish politics. Few Scottish politicians have had as much influence, nor has any been held in such high regard. Johnston had been active in Labour politics from before the First World War, and in 1906 he helped to found the socialist newspaper *Forward*. He was a cool head on the Clyde during its period of unrest during the war, and remained a seminal figure in the development of the Labour Party during the twenties and thirties. Johnston was a politician who matured with age, evolving from the vitriolic radical who published *Our Scots Noble Families* – a catalogue of every misdeed perpetrated by the Scottish aristocracy – to an arch-pragmatist. (Rumour had it that he went round the second-hand book shops buying up copies of his youthful literary indiscretion.)

Johnston had a number of invaluable qualities which would shape his career. First, as a journalist, he was able to bridge the intellectual and the populist. While not the most original of Labour's thinkers, he was able to grasp the importance of planning as an economic strategy and its significance for the post-war reconstruction of Scotland. As a populist, he was able to understand the importance of propaganda and the need to get a message across in a way that made it accessible to the widest audience. Second, Johnston was an able administrator, with a firm grasp of detail and a capacity for relentless hard work. Third, and perhaps most important, he was the consummate politician. Austere, sober (he was an ardent teetotaller) and with a natural gravitas, he commanded respect and authority. He knew how to play the game, and not only had an understanding of his own party's internal political manoeuvrings, but was able to use his position as Secretary of State for Scotland to maximum advantage in the internal wrangling of Churchill's wartime Cabinet.

It was Johnston's success in combining his role of political guardian-

ship of Scottish interests with performance on the wider British stage
which marked him out as a figure of distinction. The imposition of a
planned economy which would direct state intervention opened up new
opportunities to tackle the endemic problems which had plagued inter-
war society. Under the guise of boosting wartime efficiency, Johnston was
able to argue his case for a welter of social and economic reforms which
would have long-term benefits in Scotland. Fundamentally, the fact that
the Scottish economy was overdependent on heavy industry could now be
rectified by the use of state resources to promote greater diversification by
attracting new light industries. Johnston was quick to grasp the significance of the post-war application of planning in the economic and social
field, and almost immediately set up structures which would plan for
post-war reconstruction (see Chapter 6).

The style of government changed too. Although Labour had been left
out in the cold during the thirties as the roots of corporatism began to take
hold, Johnston was careful to build up as large a consensus as possible. The
formation of the Committee of the Ex-Secretaries of State for Scotland was
a triumph of spin, if not of substance. Designed to bring together the
experience of all the former Secretaries of State with a view to offering
advice on the problems of wartime planning and the development of post-
war policies for reconstruction, the committee came up with little of
value. Hydroelectric development for the Highlands, the herring industry,
sheep farming, gas grids, water supplies, dairy farming and health services
received more discussion than industry or housing. Yet it signalled a triumph for the way in which policies would now be formulated in Scotland.
The fact that most of the Ex-Secretaries were Tories demonstrated a commitment to consensus and a determination that the best ability rather
than party allegiance would be the guiding factor in the promotion of policy – or so the spin ran. The inclusion of trade unions within wartime
planning suggests that the corporatist tendencies of the thirties were simply expanded outwards to take in the Labour movement and its allies.
What Johnston was able to do was to present this to the Scottish public as
a major departure in government. The secret coterie of business leaders
and National Government politicians which had wielded so much power
in the thirties had had little public profile, with the exception of Sir
Steven Bisland. The presentation of an alliance of business, trade unions

and politicians all working together could therefore be hyped as a completely new beginning. The inclusion of Labour and the trade unions was presented as a victory for democracy, as was the inclusion of social policy in the planning process.

In many ways it is easy to see the drift of Scottish politics into British corporatism and state planning as a foregone conclusion with the advent of war. Yet, for all that, the situation was much more ambiguous. One of the reasons for Johnston's enduring popularity was his ability to harness Scottish nationalism (with a small 'n') to his campaign. In speech, manner and culture he was clearly a Scot, in contrast to the typically Anglicised nature of his predecessors. He had been a nominal supporter of Scottish home rule throughout his career, although the strength of his commitment varied in intensity depending on the political circumstances. One consistent leitmotif in Johnston's public utterances was the complaint that Scotland was neglected and not given its due by London government. On the one hand this claim could be used to endorse home rule or devolution, but on the other hand it could equally be used to promote the development of corporatism and British state planning. Johnston was a master of stirring up Scottish grievances, which ranged widely – from the price of tomatoes to the manufacture of buttons for Scottish military uniforms in England to the conscription of young female labour for English factories. As part of his endeavour to bring about greater Scottish self-government, Johnston held revamped meetings of the Scottish Grand Committee in Edinburgh. This clearing house for uncontentious Scottish legislation took on the gloss of being a sort of parliament, even though it commanded only some 40 per cent attendance from Scottish MPs. Bob Boothby, the Tory MP for Aberdeenshire, did not give it a ringing endorsement:

> The first meeting of the 'Scottish National Parliament' was a pretty dismal fiasco.
>
> We were treated to a discourse on the distribution of whisky by Tom Johnston (I could have told him a thing or two about that), and some observations on the subject of Town Councillors by Lord Alness (who I thought was dead).
>
> To the horrified dismay of all present, and in particular of Geordie Buchanan [the MP for the Gorbals in Glasgow], a 'vote of

thanks' was then moved; and we were told that, if we were good, we could see some 'educational' films next door. 'I like my films to have a love interest', said Jock McEwen, as he hurriedly left the building, accompanied by yours truly. Not an auspicious start. But perhaps better than nothing.

Quoted in Robert Rhodes James, *Bob Boothby: A Portrait*

(London, 1991)

Although achieving little, the convening of Grand Committee meetings in Scotland did give the appearance that some form of self-government was on the agenda. In December 1941 Johnston claimed that devolution was necessary because of a lack of time in Westminster to deal adequately with Scottish affairs, and this view was endorsed by the Scottish Council of the Labour Party. Indeed, as late as the general election of 1945, Labour's commitment to a Scottish parliament ranked second in its list of priorities after the defeat of Japan.

Nationalism had a chequered career during the war. Progress in the late thirties had been dismal, and the SNP was prone to much factional infighting with little in the way of party discipline. At the 1937 annual conference it was decided to implement a policy of non-conscription unless the government agreed to a referendum on Scottish home rule. By the time of the outbreak of war in 1939 the nationalist leadership, fearing a popular backlash against such an unpatriotic policy, had reversed this decision and instead drew up plans to form a provisional government which would continue to fight a German Army of Occupation should an invasion force land. Not all its members agreed with this, however, and a small number refused to be drafted. Initially, the leadership thought that this small, but vocal, minority could be contained.

Although lacking in organisation, finance and membership, the SNP did have one tactical advantage it could use as a result of the war. A political truce had been declared between the main parties for the duration of the conflict, which meant that, should a by-election arise, the sitting party would field a candidate while the opposition parties would stand down. As the nationalists were not party to this agreement, they could make direct political interventions. The first came in April 1940 in Argyll, where they had a straight fight with the Tories. The SNP did well, winning 7,000 votes against the Conservatives, who won with 12,000 votes. It was easily the best nationalist electoral performance to date, but it did not indicate that nationalism was on the move. First, the SNP vote was high by virtue of the party's monopoly of the opposition vote. Second, it was also a time of government unpopularity, as the Chamberlain regime was in its death throes.

For the nationalist leadership, the threat of unwelcome by-election interventions was a policy they believed could be used to put pressure on the government to make appropriate noises about Scottish home rule. Johnston duly obliged, especially as the nationalists made it clear that they would intervene only in Tory seats. By late 1941, however, the nationalist policy had begun to unravel. A by-election in Edinburgh Central went uncontested because the SNP did not have adequate resources and organisation, which brought howls of protest from the rank and file.

Further problems emerged in early 1942. The trial for refusing conscription of Douglas Young, an eminent classicist who was well over six foot tall and always wore a kilt, attracted much public attention. Young was a nationalist, and argued in his defence that he was not a pacifist and that were there a Scottish government he would have no objection to conscription. He contested only the right of a British government to conscript him. Colourful, brazen and outspoken, Young raised a lot of interest in his argument, but little sympathy. He came across as the typical thron Scotsman. His activities were deeply embarrassing to the SNP leadership, which had endeavoured to portray itself as fully supportive of the government's war effort. In part, this was to bolster an endeavour by the nationalist leader John MacCormick to form a cross-party convention in favour of devolution, with Liberal and Labour allies. (Nevertheless, the SNP did break the wartime electoral pact by intervening – a policy which it justified on the grounds that the Conservatives were the only party which was officially hostile to devolution.) Worse still for MacCormick, Young clearly commanded a bedrock of support among the rank and file who were fed up with the leadership's policy of inaction. Such irresponsible and unpatriotic action, MacCormick believed would lead to a collapse of the nationalists' standing with possible home-rule allies in other parties.

The final indignity for the nationalists came at the Cathcart by-election in April 1942, when their candidate polled a mere 5 per cent of the vote and finished last. This amply demonstrated the impotence of the SNP. MacCormick blamed the poor showing on the bad press generated by the trial of Young, while radicals in the party blamed the leadership and its timid strategy. At the party's annual conference in the summer there was a very public split, with MacCormick and his followers storming off to form the Scottish National Convention, which would act as a pressure group to solicit cross-party support for home rule. The rump left in the SNP was led by Arthur Donaldson and Robert McIntyre, both of whom believed that there could be no quick-fix solution to the shortage of industry. They set about implementing a strategy which would promote the cause of Scottish political independence (not devolution) by contesting elections, to win a popular mandate. The SNP would therefore have to build up its organisation, maintain and impose party discipline, and carve out a distinctive political identity which would garner electoral support. It would be a long haul and an arduous task, but the experience of relying on pressure-group tactics and other British political parties had convinced them that there was no other option. In effect, the SNP as we now know it was born.

The new strategy paid dividends in 1944 at a by-election in Kirkcaldy, where Douglas Young secured a respectable share of the poll and was only beaten into second (and last) place by a couple of thousand votes. The campaign focused on Scottish grievances, in particular the conscription of female labour to work in factories in the Midlands. This was portrayed negatively on two fronts by the nationalist campaign. First, it added ammunition to the complaint that not enough industry was being sent north and that England was hogging the lion's share to such an extent that it did not have the labour to cope. The solution to the problem, it was claimed, was to open more factories in Scotland. Second, there were emotive appeals about the plight of young, innocent Scottish women being taken away from the security of their families and homes and cast down in a sea of immorality where goodness knows what might happen. These struck a resonant chord with the electorate.

The SNP won its first parliamentary seat at Motherwell, in April 1945. The candidate, Robert McIntyre, managed to push Labour into second place, no doubt benefiting from Tory and Liberal voters. McIntyre used his short spell in parliament to good effect, with a number of interventions regarding social and health policy – he was a well-known public-health specialist – and he was offered a safe Labour seat if he was prepared to switch sides. He refused. McIntyre also had the distinction of raising the ire of Winston Churchill after his refusal to accept sponsorship to take his seat in the Commons. Sir Harold Nicolson recorded that

> A young man of the name McIntyre has been elected as a Scottish nationalist for Motherwell. He refused to be introduced by any sponsor, since he does not recognise the Mother of Parliaments and wishes to advertise himself. He advanced to the Bar without sponsors and the Speaker told him that he could not take his oath, as that was contrary to standing orders. At which many members rose offering to sponsor the cub and put an end to the shaming incident, but he refused. He was therefore told to go away and think it over, which he did, shrugging vain shoulders. Next day he thought better of it and accepted sponsors; but even then, as he reached the box, he said, 'I do this under protest', which was not liked at all. He is going to be a sad nuisance and pose as a martyr.
>
> *Diaries and Letters*, ed. Nigel Nicolson (London, 1966)

McIntyre received a lampooning in the press and was featured in a cartoon in *Punch*. But he had made his point and had demonstrated that the SNP could get its members elected. The result seemed to vindicate the strategy of contesting elections, but it would take several years to convince other like-minded nationalists that this was the only policy to pursue. In any event, the general election in July 1945 deprived the nationalists of their only MP.

The chequered history of nationalism during the war helps partially to explain the evolution of the Labour Party's stance on home rule during this period. When nationalist interventions seemed capable of inflicting damage, as was the case in the early forties, Labour seemed to swing behind home rule. As the nationalists divided and their electoral support withered away, Labour showed less interest. A late SNP resurgence in 1944 and 1945 again brought forth favourable Labour utterings. Yet, for all that there were committed Labour and trade-union home-rulers, the events of the war had vitiated the *raison d'être* of a Scottish parliament. The

British state and its effective use by an equally effective Secretary of State for Scotland more than amply demonstrated that planning and the distribution of government resources were equal to the task of social and economic reconstruction. Bigger was better, and the greater the access to resources the more that could be achieved. Johnston had set a new Scottish political benchmark, and success would henceforth be determined by the ability of the Secretary of State to secure maximum funding from the British state. While devolution offered the prospect of greater local control, it still remained an unknown prospect and questions were raised about the possible implications for the allocation of British resources, with many civil servants arguing that it would at best muddy the waters, and at worse would diminish the returns. Devolution would add a nationalist dimension to British state planning and would highlight the fact that Scotland would demand more than its fair share, bringing the unwelcome prospect of an English backlash. In any case, the planning system had been running for the duration of the war and was tried and tested. As many politicians, planners and civil servants were only too aware, the post-war reconstruction of Scotland would require more resources than the nation could provide by itself. In the forthcoming scramble for new housing, welfare provision and economic restructuring, it was argued, it was best that the criteria used to define allocation be set at a British level. Furthermore, competition would be fierce, and Scotland had faced comparatively light war damage compared to England, where some 450,000 homes had been destroyed or rendered unusable. A parliament in Edinburgh, it was believed, might draw unwelcome attention to that fact.

SIX

RECONSTRUCTION,

1945–1954

We, the people of Scotland who subscribe this Engagement, declare our belief that reform in the constitution of our country is necessary to secure good government in accordance with our Scottish traditions and to promote the spiritual and economic welfare of our nation.

We affirm that the desire for such reform is both deep and widespread throughout the whole community, transcending all political differences and sectional interests, and we undertake to continue united in purpose for its achievement.

With that end in view we solemnly enter into this Covenant whereby we pledge ourselves, in all loyalty to the Crown, and within the framework of the United Kingdom, to do everything in our power to secure for Scotland a Parliament with adequate legislative authority in Scottish affairs.

The Scottish Covenant (Edinburgh, 1948)

The Board (Hydo-Electric) is planning the co-ordinated full development of all Highland water-power. A survey already completed estimates a potential annual output of over 6,000 million units. The Highlands and Islands, in fact all that area known as the North of Scotland, have first claim on the electricity produced within it. The Board have also to make available, at the lowest practical cost, bulk supplies of electricity suitable for the needs of large electro industries, in the hope that by this means new industrial enterprises may be attracted to commence operations in the Highlands. The electricity surplus to these needs is exported to an assured market in Central and South Scotland. The price paid for this exported electricity is the price of electricity produced by the most economical coal-powered station in Britain. At present the cost of production is more in favour of hydro-electric plant than a coal-fired steam station, and the Board can therefore earn revenue with which to finance the uneconomic distribution schemes in sparsely populated areas.

'Hydro-Electricity' in *Scotland 1947*, ed. Henry Meikle for the Scottish Council (Industry and Development) (Edinburgh, 1947)

But soon there would be arriving at Kingisbyres the builders with their thousands of feet of 'softwood', their acres of prefabricated beaverboard partitions, their endless buckets of urine-coloured distemper. From the local towns each morning the bus-loads of clerks, and in the little beaver-boarded cubby-holes, with their cups of tea and their doggy calendars stamp-papered to the partition, there would begin the long little jealous rows of bureaucracy. In the servants' bedrooms the major bureaucrats would sit with their feet upon a carpet and all their dreams would come true. And lastly there would come the men with big machines.

There had been a protest in the *Scotsman,* and a reply from a senior official. He had referred to the economic situation of the country – to the price to be paid for beating Hitler – made the point that although Kingisbyres was doubtless this, it was not the other – and implied that if the owner was sufficiently public-spirited to sell his home to supply our grim necessities, frivolous aesthetes should keep quiet. It was awfully reasonable, even a little wistful, but when you read it you knew that the author would defend, with the same cheerfulness and ability, the demolition of St Paul's to make way for a municipal laundry.

J. D. Scott, *The End of an Old Song* (Edinburgh, 1954)

PLANNING

During the war, ambitious plans were made for the post-war reconstruction of Scottish society. Planning was predicated on the assumption that there would be greater state activity: indeed, government would be the fundamental driving force behind change. It was also accepted that planning would reconstruct Scottish society and Scotland's economy in ways that would bring about greater social justice and ensure a more equitable distribution of wealth.

The war initiated a revolution in management. The need to maximise production and to control and regulate all aspects of society and the economy elevated the position of the 'expert'. Government in the thirties was tarred with the brush of amateurism, but the exigencies of war promoted the young, talented and bright. Old sloppy ways of doing things had to be replaced by scientific management. Buggins's-turn promotion had to give way to the elevation of the best and most able. Targets were set, outputs were monitored, and achievements were assessed. Problems had to be solved by whatever means, and imaginative and creative solutions were lauded. It was accepted that the best way to deal with problems was to use experts, whose greater knowledge of particular issues would best illuminate the solution. Complex problems which covered many issues required many experts who could combine their wisdom to work together to effect a successful outcome. It was an environment that favoured the ambitious and bold, who were not afraid to utilise whatever resources came to hand – and in a command economy those resources were great and often available.

There is no doubt that the experience of power and control whetted the appetite of the technocrats, experts and bureaucrats, who would not be satisfied to go back to timid strategies once the war was over. Indeed, if the revolution in management could work in wartime, why, they asked, should it cease in peacetime? After all, the problems of post-war society were arguably a bigger challenge. The experience of war had convinced them that all problems could be solved: all that was required was expertise and political will.

Events during the war had strengthened their position. The publication of the Beveridge Report in 1942 committed the state to guaranteeing the social and economic well-being of the citizen from the cradle to the grave. Ways and means would have to be found to ensure full employment; decent accommodation would have to be built; social policies to ensure a safety net for the most vulnerable would have to be constructed and paid for; and the delivery of free universal health care and education had to be established. It was, in short, a planner's heaven. The resources of the state would be turned over to experts to construct the perfect society – or so the theory went.

Expectations were high at the end of the war. The Beveridge Report caught the mood of the people, and information from Mass Observation confirmed that the public did not want to go back to the non-interventionist policies of the thirties. The war had witnessed the emergence of an informal political contract between people and government in which the efforts of the former had to be rewarded by the latter. The Welfare State was the price of total war, and, while there were minor differences of opinion between the Labour and Conservative parties, a consensus was established that the aspirations of the people would have to be met.

Not surprisingly, there was great enthusiasm north of the border for more government intervention, because there was a lot for the state to do. The thirties had left a legacy of poor opportunities for the Scottish people. There had been a craze for the collection of statistics, all of which showed that Scotland had missed out on most of the social and economic improvements which had been experienced by the rest of the United Kingdom. Unemployment rates had been higher, poverty more endemic, housing was overcrowded, and health was poorer. Full employment and a state-sponsored medical service during the war helped to reverse some of these trends. Planning and state intervention promised a way out of the intractable social and economic malaise which had plagued inter-war Scottish society. Yet the politicians had their work cut out for them in convincing the population that there would not be a return to the bad old days. A report on the war industry in Scotland, published in 1941, argued that most workers expected things to go back to the way they were in 1939. Indeed, many were saving in anticipation of the expected economic downturn which would accompany the peace. Further findings from Mass Observation confirmed that there was a large element of scepticism about post-war prospects.

Not surprisingly, politicians had to work hard to convince potential voters that the future was bright. Trade unionists, local-government officials, academics and members of the Churches added their voices to the chorus for greater government intervention. Thomas Johnston recounted his victories in the British Cabinet to the press. Scotland had forged ahead with compulsory health care, placed rent restrictions on furnished accommodation, instituted special legal devices to deal with juvenile delinquents, issued grants to local authorities for housebuilding, and set in motion ambitious plans for the reconstruction of Scottish industry. Such developments made an impact, and helped to convince many that better times lay ahead – although it should always be borne in mind that widespread scepticism was an important factor in raising the political ante. Public support could not be taken for granted. Johnston's speech of thanksgiving in Edinburgh in 1945 gives a flavour of how it was expected that the lessons and techniques of wartime could be carried on into peacetime:

It was this unity of purpose that saved us, took us from the brink of destruction and gave us the strength to achieve victory. It was this corporate all-in national effort, each for all, that enabled us to match the hour, and to withstand – at one period entirely alone in the world – the organised fury of the Fascist and Nazi powers of darkness. If we could only recapture part of that enthusiasm, *élan* and common purpose, recapture it for the much needed reconstruction and betterment of our world – if only we could lift great social crusades like better housing and health from the arena of partisan strife, what magnificent achievements might yet be ours. In unity lies strength: in concurrence, the possibility of great achievement in better housing, better health, better education, better use of leisure, greater security in income, and employment. In barking at each other's heels; in faction fighting and strife over non-essentials lie frustration and defeat for everybody.

Quoted in Thomas Johnston, *Memories* (London, 1952)

It is difficult to say with any degree of certainty what Scots expected after the war. Certainly most would have hoped that things would improve, and that the pace of interventionist policies which had been established during the war would not slacken. It is probably accurate to state that most believed that things would change, but were uncertain how far that change would go and what impact it would have. In any case, they had made it clear that the status quo was unacceptable, and most politicians – in public at least – accepted this.

It was no secret that the root cause of the nation's problems lay in its economic structure. There was an overdependence on heavy industry, which had significant knock-on effects. First, there was not enough diversity in the economy, with the consequence that should the traditional sector experience a downturn, as had happened between the wars, then the other sectors would not have the strength to take up the slack. This had previously resulted in long-term mass unemployment, with all the social evils attendant upon it. Second, the traditional heavy industries themselves were believed to have a limited shelf-life, in the sense that they were not at the cutting edge of modern industrial developments. If the economy was to advance and maintain its competitiveness, then it needed to attract lighter industries which were part and parcel of a developing consumer market. This trend had been established before the war in the global economy, and there was no reason to believe that it would not continue to grow. Third, Scottish industrial production, and too much of the same type of production, was concentrated too much in the western central belt. Industry which was more geographically dispersed would help create more balance in the economy, in the sense that it would prevent the devastating social consequences of a wholesale closure that was concentrated in one place. The obverse of this argument was that, with economic growth points dispersed around the country, the knock-on effects of prosperity would reach a wider area.

In essence, the main problem of the Scottish economy related to the concentration of heavy industry in the western central belt. According to the Nuffield College Social Reconstruction Survey, which published its assessment of the prospects for the industrial areas of Britain in 1945:

> It seems improbable that the development of new industries in the new Government works will solve more than part of the problem of surplus labour. It is impossible to make any exact estimate; but it

seems clear that, if developments in the industries which were established before the war are allowed to take the course which has been suggested above [the promotion of consumer industries], the maximum practicable amount of development in the new munitions industries would still leave many thousand workers unemployed even in a good year after the war. It is clear that it will be necessary for some time to come – probably for some decades – to continue and intensify the measures adopted before the war to accelerate the development of new industry on the Clyde. To avoid unemployment in the meantime it is necessary to find some way of maintaining employment in the older industries which otherwise might decline. In view of the nature of the industries of West Scotland there are two natural suggestions. The first is a shipbuilding programme on the lines suggested . . . [for] the North-east coast; a programme of this kind may be desirable in any case, quite apart from the problem of unemployment. The second is to take steps to ensure that the Clyde obtains as large a share in expenditure in Great Britain arising out of programmes of industrialisation and general development in backward countries which are at present under consideration. The iron and steel, locomotive engineering, constructional engineering and machine tool industries of the Clyde have long experience in supplying the type of demand which is likely to arise from these programmes.

M. P. Fogarty, *Prospects of the Industrial Areas of Great Britain*
(London, 1945)

This was the British perspective of the problem north of the border. The Scots had their own perspective, and the difference between the two lay in emphasis, with more attention in Scotland focusing on attracting new light industry, rather than propping up the old. Johnston had established the Scottish Council on Industry in 1942 with this specific remit in mind. There were also other planning committees which dealt with building and the distribution of industry. Local councils got in on the act and argued that future social provision, infrastructure and industrial development should be worked out on a regional basis with the relevant government departments. Plans were put in place for the harnessing of hydroelectric power, particularly in the Highlands. This project was a personal favourite of Johnston's, and was much influenced by the experience of the inter-war Tennessee Valley Authority, which was one of the most prestigious projects initiated by Roosevelt's 'New Deal' programme in the USA.

Each part of Scotland was expected to have its own distinctive problems to deal with after the war. Attention focused on fishing in Aberdeen, and it was stressed that the city had to do more to capitalise on its geographic position. The fishing fleet had failed to modernise to the same extent as in Hull and Grimsby. Newer, bigger and better trawlers were required. The granite and construction industry was flagged as a potential area for growth, as it was reckoned that a third of houses in the city needed to be replaced. The problems of the other north-east fishing towns were more serious. The herring industry had suffered a collapse, and most of the boats were obsolete. A committee report in 1944 recommended measures to finance and re-equip the industry on a better footing, as well as to increase domestic consumption through the better use of marketing.

The timber trade had seen the harvesting of most of the forests during the war; it was expected that it would take at least twenty years before production could get back to normal. The creation of a forestry corps of some 30,000 workers to plant new areas was announced in March 1944, and it was expected that the north-east would benefit from this. Likewise the 1943 Hydro-Electric Development Act was expected to bring benefits in the form of extensive electrification of the area. It was believed that this would help to establish a large number of small manufacturers.

The jute industry was the biggest problem for Dundee. It had been buoyed up by wartime demand, but it was recognised that it had been losing its competitive edge even before the war. Indian-produced jute was 70 per cent cheaper and it was reckoned that, even with technological upgrades, the price gap could not be closed. It was expected that peacetime would see the displacement of between 15,000 and 20,000 workers from the industry, although reorganisation and rationalisation, together with improved housing, it was argued, would see that number drop by 5,000 if a large part of the female work force could be persuaded to stay at home. The local construction industry was expected to take on new workers, as a quarter of the housing stock needed immediate replacement with a similar number expected to be built over a twenty-year period. The other industries of printing, linen, preserves and carpet-making were thought to be in sound condition and ripe for expansion. Improved transportation with bridges across the Tay and Forth would facilitate easier access to markets and open up the possibility of tourism.

The mining industry was the main focus of attention in West Lothian, Midlothian and Fife. Wartime demand for the heavy industries had offset the loss of markets in Europe. Yet, even though employment in mining actually dropped during the war, it was believed that there would not be significant change in the manpower requirements. Building was expected to do well through the high demand for new housing, and this would have a knock-on effect on the linoleum and carpet firms. The area was also blessed with textiles and paper-making industries, both of which were expected to do well. Again, the Forth and Tay bridges would improve access to markets and transport infrastructure for the area of Fife.

Farmers all over the country had seen the introduction of guaranteed prices and various marketing schemes. Efficiency and output had increased, and it was believed that demand for food would remain high.

The most important piece of planning in Scotland to emerge from the war was the Clyde Valley Regional Plan. A report was also drafted for the central and south-eastern area, but it concluded that there was not as great a need for government intervention in the east as there was in the west. Edinburgh was a magnet for prosperity, and a representative of the city's corporation told the 1940 Royal Commission on the Distribution of the Industrial Population (the Barlow Commission) that there was no need for a special industrial plan because 'In Edinburgh we think we have sufficient attractions to attract the industrialist without preferential treatment.' Edinburgh and its environs had a well-balanced industrial sector, a strong service sector, and a solid foundation of prosperity upon which post-war reconstruction could be based. The same could not be said of the Glasgow area. It was expected that the construction industry would do well, given that the area had the worst standard of housing, but, even taking into account the transfer of workers into this industry, it was expected that new employment would need to be found for some 60,000 to 80,000 workers.

The Clyde Valley Plan was evidence of the ambition which had overtaken planners during the war. It did not limit its discussion and recommendations to economic criteria, but placed these in a wider context which involved social policy as well. It represented 'total' planning. Its key argument was that the traditional engineering and shipbuilding industries had a limited future and would decline. The report was heavily influenced by the experience of the thirties, which had witnessed a slump in demand for capital investment goods, and argued that lighter industry, manufacturing goods for the consumer market, should in future form the mainstay of economic development. It argued for more out-of-town industrial estates, like Hillington, which would act as a magnet for new industry. Such estates would help in the dispersal of population, and should be shored up by improvements in social and transport infrastructure. Coal and steel would move from being ancillaries of the shipbuilding and engineering sector to become ancillaries of new industry. Crucially, the plan called for further and more specific planning which could be coordinated as part of a national strategy. It was a bold vision for the future.

One important aspect of the plan was that it took a bird's-eye view of the problems and was not hobbled by the need to accommodate specific business interests or local concerns. It cut through the sectional interests which had raised most of the objections to ideas of planning in the thirties. One criticism which could be levelled at the report, however, was its rather too bleak assessment of the traditional industries. Not enough attention was focused on transition, and questions about investment and modernisation went unanswered. This was rather odd, given that heavy industry was still the most important sector of the economy.

While targets were prepared and plans were laid down, it is important to remember that this was a difficult enterprise which was made still more complicated because no one could predict with certainty what the immediate circumstances of the post-war era would be. Furthermore, it should not be forgotten that planners did not exist in a vacuum, and, while the exigencies of wartime meant that they were largely able to get on with the business of drawing up blueprints free from interference, this was not a situation that was likely to last.

Economists and planners made their proposals largely on the basis of an objective reading of the situation. In many ways, planning was the intellectual framework which gave ideological support to Keynesian demand-management economics. If government was to intervene in economy and society, then it had to do so in a structured and organised way. Anything else would be chaotic. Yet, in the real world, far away from abstract economic theory, there were others who wanted their pound of flesh. Ironically, the same corporatist political structure which allowed the experts to project so freely would also ensure that planning would be subject to greater external pressures. Planners had no real constituency, no economic power, and no large supporting membership. On the other hand, politicians would have to appease voters, trade unionists would have to protect and promote members' rights, and businessmen would have to ensure profits. The plan which could accommodate all these vested interests was a good one indeed. But, as so often happens in history, the best laid plans o' mice and men gang aft agley.

GOVERNMENT

Given that the government was going to take more control of the nation's resources and use them for the benefit of all citizens, it followed that it would need to expand its organisational apparatus. An extension of government power called for an increase in the number of civil servants to implement and oversee policy. In the case of Scotland, this meant an expansion of the Scottish Office. It is an oddity of history that, in the period that marks the extension of British centralised government and state centralising powers, government in Scotland should take a distinctive form as an almost separate branch of the executive. While the Welfare State was intended to promote greater uniformity in British life – after all, it was based on the principle of universal provision – it apparently required a unique arm of government to oversee it north of the border. No one thought this odd at the time; indeed, it was expected.

The arrangement was formally enshrined in the report of the Balfour Committee, which was convened in 1948 and reported in 1954. It stated that, as far as possible, those administrative functions that applied to Scotland should be dealt with by the Secretary of State and the Scottish Office. Whereas previously not all areas were covered by the Scottish Office, now there was to be created a department of government which was effectively all-encompassing in the range of its responsibilities. Whereas roads in

1. Military parade in Princes Street 1946, (Scotsman). Such parades helped to reinforce British identity in Scotland by highlighting Scotland's role in the armed services.

2. The Queen Elizabeth, *Clydebank (E.N.A.). Shipyard workers often invested a great deal of emotional capital in the ships they built, as they produced one-off, never to be repeated products. The contrast with mass production could not be greater.*

3. *Fishing workers*: left *mending fishing nets*; right *packing kippers*, 1935 (*Crown Copyright*). In spite of its importance, its favourable geographic position and the numbers it employed, the Scottish fishing industry has never had the attention or government support shown to many industries which have long since died.

4. *The Singer factory (plus sheep), Clydebank* 1947 (*Valentine*). As can be seen, the idea that the landscape of central Scotland was dominated by industry is somewhat over-exaggerated.

5. *Early combine harvester, East Lothian 1937 (J. A. More). A reluctance to work the long hours and the relative isolation have meant that there was a constant exodus of labour from farming, forcing many to turn to new technology.*

6. *Dyeing wool, Harris. In the thirties if you asked to go to the toilet in Harris you would be taken to an outhouse where urine was collected as it was the only naturally available source of ammonia, necessary to bleach the wool. It was this process which gave Harris tweed (and the House of Lords) its distinctive smell for most of the twentieth century.*

7. *The Scottish Nazis: cartoon, 1933 (*Evening Times*). Poking fun at the Scottish nationalists was popular pastime for many commentators in the thirties.*

8. *'The Cinema Yields to Scottish Culture': cartoon, 1933 (*Evening Times*). Although much lauded today, the artists of the Scottish renaissance received a less than enthusiastic welcome from most cultural critics in the thirties. Note the representation of Hugh MacDairmid as Rudolf Valentino.*

9. Tossing the caber (you can't beat a touch of Kitsch) 1938 (Topical Press). While many Scots are tired of the stereotypical representation of 'tartan' Scotland, they tend to forget just how prominent it was and is.

10. Sun-ray treatment: kids getting blasted with radiation while standing to attention, 1948 (Norval). This picture captures perfectly the paternalistic authoritarianism of much of the early National Health Service in Scotland.

11. *Holiday-makers, Largs, 1935 (Scottish Travel Association). The advent of low-cost flights to sunnier climes has meant that the traditional seaside towns have experienced decline in the latter part of the twentieth century.*

12. *Gala Parade in Denny, Stirlingshire, late 1930s. The communal nature of small-town Scotland was reinforced by such events which would often have fairs, circuses and travelling shows.*

13. Jute lassies, Dundee 1929 (Dundee Courier and Advertiser). Dundee women were a force to reckoned with. The Jute lassies were not averse to 'having a go' if someone got in their way, as the local court records show.

14. Fisher lassies, Barra, 1935 (C. M. Angus). The small-scale nature of fishing in the western Highlands found it difficult to compete with the advent of trawlers in the thirties.

15. *Highland school kids, 1930 (Scholastic Souvenir Company, Blackpool). Note the lack of school uniforms which, apart from private schools, only began to be introduced to Scotland in the sixties.*

16. *Men's clothes in the thirties: well-dressed man (hat, suit and tie), two more traditional working-class (bunnet or gap, and no tie) and kids.*

17. *Dunoon Labour Ladies Society, 1940s.*

England and Wales would be subject to the Department of Transport and prisons were the responsibility of the Home Office, in Scotland they both fell within the jurisdiction of the Scottish Office. Given that much of the thrust of government legislation in the post-war era was concerned with universal provision of basic social services, it needs to be asked why this model of government was applied in Scotland. After all, social security, unemployment benefit, family allowance, free medical treatment, educational provision and access to housing were all supposed to be the same throughout the United Kingdom, and these were the great reforms which the public were most interested in. Why did it need a separate arm of government to oversee them in Scotland? There is a twofold answer to this question. First, there was the matter of Scottish law, which required separate legislation to implement policy in Scotland, and, second, government was to build on existing structures.

Scottish law is based on the Roman system, in that it is dictated by principle, rather than on precedent, as is the case in England. By and large, this has tended to produce a more philosophic approach to the understanding and application of law in Scotland. Also, the organisational structure of the legal system is different from that in England, in that it has two positions instead of the one post that is occupied by the Lord Chancellor. The Lord President of the Court of Session is the head of the judiciary, and the Lord Advocate is the chief law officer of the Crown. The Scottish legal profession was, and is, a powerful body within Scottish society, and has jealously guarded and protected its position. From the time of the Union of 1707, which guaranteed the integrity of Scots law, there has been a close relationship between law and politics, in the sense that all legislation affecting Scotland has had to be framed in such a way as to fit the technicalities of the legal system. Mostly this has meant passing the same bill as in England and Wales, but with the obligatory 'Scotland' in brackets – for example, the Education Act (Scotland) of 1945. And the legal system has also been important in reinforcing the geographic border between England and Scotland.

By and large, Scots and English law have tended to work in harmony, but on occasion the former has reared up to assert its independence. For example, in 1953, Lord Cooper, Lord President of the Court of Session, ruled that there was no basis for the principle of 'unlimited Sovereignty of

Parliament' in Scots law, because it was

> a distinctively English principle which has no counterpart in Scots
> Constitutional law. It derives its origins from Coke and Blackstone,
> and was widely popularised during the nineteenth century by
> Bagehot and Dicey, the latter having stated the doctrine in its clas-
> sic form in his *Constitutional Law*. Considering that the Union Leg-
> islation extinguished the parliaments of Scotland and England, and
> replaced them by a new Parliament, I have difficulty in seeing why
> it should have been supposed that the new Parliament of Great
> Britain must inherit all the peculiar characteristics of the English
> Parliament but none of the Scottish Parliament, as if all that hap-
> pened in 1707 was that Scottish representatives were admitted to
> the Parliament of England. That is not what was done . . . I have not
> found in the Union Legislation any provision that the Parliament of
> Great Britain should be absolutely sovereign in the sense that Par-
> liament should be free to alter the Treaty at will.
>
> *MacCormick and Another* v. *Lord Advocate* (1953)

This point has been subject to much debate ever since, and has given rise
to the widespread belief that in Scots law sovereignty lies with the people,
which was used as the basis for the Scottish Constitutional Convention's
1988 *Claim of Right* that argued the case for the establishment of a parliament in Edinburgh. In more recent times it was even ruled in Scotland
that weapons of mass destruction were illegal under international law,
although this was subsequently overturned on appeal. Given the tenacity
of the Scottish legal system, the extension of government powers in Scotland had to accommodate its special position.

Governments have to work with the material, or in this case the
administration, that they have. Obviously the war had entailed a massive
increase in state power, but it was not immediately apparent that such
power would remain during peacetime. The move towards greater state
intervention as a post-war strategy coincided with an expansion of the
powers of the Scottish Office during the war. In order to regulate and control society and the economy with immediate effect, the government had
no option but to turn to the existing departments of state. In 1939 gov-

ernment structure in Scotland was reorganised into four departments: the Department of Agriculture for Scotland, the Scottish Education Department, the Department of Health for Scotland, and the Scottish Home Department. These administrative units carried out the bulk of Scotland's wartime administration. This template was subsequently used as the basis for the expansion of government powers in the post-war period to create the modern Scottish Office. As a result of wartime legislation, the responsibilities and remits of the departments had grown to such an extent that to reverse this trend by the use of single British departments was deemed neither practical nor necessary. Furthermore, the reign of Thomas Johnston during the war had encouraged Scottish civil servants to defend, maintain and expand their role against encroachments from British counterparts. This had the effect of promoting loyalty to a distinctive Scottish Office identity. The number of civil servants in Edinburgh had more than doubled to 5,000 during the war, and by and large it was believed they had done an effective job. The maxim was, 'If it ain't broke, don't fix it.'

The administrative revolution which accompanied the war was further bedded in by the exigencies of the immediate post-war situation. Even if it had been wanted, a different system of centralised British administration was not possible because it was still necessary to maintain effective regulation and control of resources after the war. The government simply could not take its feet off the pedal of the command economy. If it should be deemed desirable, this could be done only after a period of considerable readjustment. The experience of the European mainland demonstrated only too clearly that social and economic chaos was fuelling the rise of Communism, and politicians were well aware that a tight grip would need to be maintained to effect an orderly return to normality and stability. Bureaucrats would be needed for this process, which would also provide further opportunities to show the benefits of planning and the role of state intervention in social and economic policy.

The Scottish Office made good progress during the war and was instrumental in laying down the basis of the National Health Service in Scotland. In essence, the coordination which was required during wartime was in 1945–8 extended and consolidated in consultation with the Ministry of Health in Whitehall. Five regional boards were established which had the remit of bringing into one administrative structure the city hospitals, the university medical departments, the various privately funded hospitals, the local-authority institutions, and the wartime Emergency Hospital Service which ran the Civil Defence hospitals. Pre-war local health committees were replaced by local health executives, and cover was extended to all people and not just the insured workers. The Department of Health increased its remit to cover coordination with dentists, pharmacists and opticians as part of the campaign to provide free universal health care. These developments meant that the National Health Service in Scotland evolved not only more quickly than its southern counterpart, but along distinctive administrative lines dictated by the Scottish Office.

The Department of Health established itself as the linchpin of the post-war house-building programme, having beaten off territorial encroachments from the Ministry of Works in London. Local authorities and the Scottish Special Housing Association (which had been established to beef up provision in the areas with greatest need) had to have the approval of the Department of Health before building could begin. The department's architects, surveyors and administrators checked proposals to ensure that they conformed to regulations dealing with health, social amenities and impact on the surrounding locality. They also had to assess the impact on the availability of building resources and materials, which remained in short supply and had to be rationed. Furthermore, as local authorities and the Special Housing Association received a subsidy from central government for each house built, the Department of Health, which administered those subsidies, was able to regulate the construction programme for Scotland.

Although an arm of central government, the Scottish Office would develop in a distinctive way because of a number of peculiar features. First, although delegated with the task of implementing policy, the Scottish Office would not simply become a replica of British administration. Rather, the Scottish Office developed along lines which reflected the relative importance of certain departments in relation to Scottish society. For example, education, housing and agriculture played a bigger and more important role in the administration of Scotland than was the case for England and Wales because these areas were accorded a higher priority than the average elsewhere in the United Kingdom. Power within the Scottish Office reflected this. Second, because of the nature of devolved administration, the respective boards and departments in Scotland had a smaller staff than their counterparts in England, which meant that a lot of the detail of policy planning and the depth of expertise that existed south of the border as a result of economies of scale were impossible to achieve. For example, when the Scottish Office and Whitehall discussed policy initiatives, it was invariably Whitehall which led the way, because of its ability to plan and develop strategy in a way that was not possible with only a few civil servants. As a result, many UK-wide initiatives would have only a minimal Scottish input. However, in relation to the first point, housing, education and agriculture tended to have a larger Scottish Office input on British policy, because of the relative importance of these areas to Scotland. Third, because of distance, Scottish administration was out of the London civil-service loop. There was little opportunity to take part in day-to-day discussions with other departments, so Scottish civil servants found that they missed out on the gossip, rumours, and work on impending policy objectives that characterised much of the life of the service in London. Distance, together with limited staff, meant that, unlike London departments, the Scottish Office rarely initiated policy directives. Finally, Scottish civil servants were expected to cooperate and contribute to UK-wide policies. More often than not this meant putting the case for as much of the pie as possible. In this respect the Scottish Office was similar to most other government departments, in that they all tried to screw as much money out of the Treasury as possible.

In essence, the Scottish Office developed a binary function. It administered its own departments wherever possible according to its own agenda, but more often than not it had to act first and foremost as a lobbyist for Scottish interests in British policy initiatives which came from other government departments that would have a major impact on its territorial domain. This was especially the case in economic matters, which were recognised by all as the most important area of government responsibility.

The Distribution of Industry Act 1945 and the Town and Country Planning Act 1947 were designed to ensure that there was a more equitable distribution of economic activity and to prevent industry gravitating to areas that already had more than their fair share of prosperity. In short, they were the two most important parliamentary acts to affect post-war reconstruction in Scotland, but their implementation was not devolved to the Scottish Office. Whitehall jealously guarded the purse strings of economic development.

The Distribution of Industry Act was planned at a British level, and replaced the special areas commissioners which had been established in the thirties to deal with the impact of the Depression. The Board of Trade was responsible for what were now renamed 'development areas'. The main Scottish development area retained the traditional boundary of the western central belt, but also incorporated Dundee and its environs and the area around Dingwall and Inverness in the Highlands, which was designated as the region's hot spot for industrial growth. The Board of Trade was authorised to build factories, purchase land (with compulsory powers if needed), make loans to industrial-estate companies, provide basic public services, reclaim derelict land, and – with the approval of the Treasury – give grants or loans to industrial or commercial projects. The board gave the bureaucrats the ability to coordinate planning with local authorities and to decide if planning permission would be given. Through the granting of licences, in effect the board had the power to stipulate where new factories would be built, and it also had the authority to convert Royal Ordnance works and munitions factories to peacetime production. Half of all new industrial building work in the United Kingdom in the first two years after the war was reserved for the development areas, and by 1955 some 62,000 Scots were employed in Board of Trade factories. In part, this was a result of successful lobbying by the Scottish Office and its political masters.

The Town and Country Planning Act was the second arm of the government's policy for the equitable distribution of resources. It was proposed that slum clearance in the inner cities would be accompanied by the creation of 'new towns' which, by means of planning, would act as magnets for new industrial growth. In Scotland, East Kilbride was the first such venture to emerge from this strategy in the late forties, although new town development would have to wait until the mid-sixties before it had much impact on Scottish society.

AUSTERITY

Apart from not having to worry about loved ones at the front, few noticed any significant changes once the war was over. Indeed, things continued pretty much as they had done. The government was omnipresent, rationing food, controlling supplies, and issuing edicts on what could and could not be done. There were still major shortages of all household items, and the black market continued to flourish. Conscription remained, and young Scots were sent to serve in the occupation of Germany, Palestine and other flashpoints under British government. There was an average of 85,000 Scots in the armed forces in the early fifties.

The extent to which little had changed was highlighted by the 1951 census, which showed that there was still a quarter of the population living in a house of two rooms or less and as much as a third of the population had to share a toilet. The war had needed a Herculean effort, and it is estimated that about a third of the wealth of the United Kingdom had been expended during the conflict. The task of reconstruction was enormous, and would have to be undertaken with diminished resources.

If that was not bad enough, the government had committed itself to an ambitious programme of social welfare and intervention in economic life to guarantee full employment. The omens for such ambitions were not promising at the close of war. The economic lifeline of Lend-Lease had come to an end, and the nation was saddled with £3 billion worth of debt. An American loan was predicated on the maintenance of sound fiscal policy, which would mean keeping sterling as a currency of international exchange, so there could be no printing of money to buy a way out of the problem. The international economy was in chaos, with most advanced economies in the world either devastated or subject to Soviet control. Furthermore, Britain, as a victor, inherited a number of costly overseas policing responsibilities. There was only one way out of this predicament, and that was to use what was available, earn what money could be made by exports, and regulate and control resources to effect an orderly return to normality. It would be a slow process.

Planning for after the war had been ambitious in its scope, and there were great expectations of what the state could do. One major difference between Scotland and the rest of the United Kingdom was that reconstruction in the latter was primarily concerned with rebuilding after war damage, whereas in the former it was about dealing with the social and economic legacy of the pre-war era. Scotland had escaped lightly from the war. It had not suffered extensive housing damage, nor had it experienced significant disruption to its economy; the problem of structural imbalance of its industries was a pre-war inheritance.

The incoming Labour government of 1945 made great play of the fact that it was going to nationalise the commanding heights of the economy. Coal was nationalised in 1947, railways and electricity in 1948. Although the iron and steel industry came under the control of the state in 1949, the incoming Conservative administration of 1951 promptly denationalised it, only for the Labour government to reverse the decision in 1967. All in all, by 1951 about a seventh of the working population (including local government) found itself employed by the state. Yet the reality of economic life in the late forties was that the state regulated all aspects of employment, owing to its control of materials and resources. An economic lifeline was thrown in 1947 with Marshall Aid. This American-sponsored funding for the reconstruction of Western Europe enabled the Scottish heavy industries to maintain maximum output as huge amounts of steel, engineering and shipping were required to rebuild the shattered society and economy of the Continent.

An examination of the index of production shows that output in the Scottish economy went up by a quarter between 1948 and 1954, and did so following the broadly established outline of the economy. By and large, the traditional sectors did well. Engineering, shipbuilding and electrical goods were the largest sector of the economy, employing almost 200,000 people, and increased output by almost 40 per cent. Textiles, employing around 120,000, was the next largest sector and increased output by a quarter. Metal manufacture (60,000 workers) increased by almost 10 per cent; chemicals (40,000 workers) rose by 20 per cent; vehicles, including locomotive and aircraft work (70,000 workers, of whom a third were employed in garages) increased by over 50 per cent. Only mining, employing 100,000, let the side down with a drop of 4 per cent in output.

Much of the demand was fuelled by export orders. Of the £15.5 million worth of textile machinery manufactured between 1948 and 1954, almost £10 million worth went overseas. Of the £50.5 million worth of industrial pumps and pumping plant, nearly £12 million worth was for

export. Likewise, of the £14 million worth of machine tools manufactured, more than a third was destined for overseas. In merchant shipbuilding between 1948 and 1954 a grand total of 3.46 million tons was laid
down for building, of which more than a third was for export. In terms of
tonnage, the departures with cargo from Scottish ports increased from
2.19 million tons in 1946 to 4.29 million in 1950, rising to 5.07 million
in 1954, but this was still lower than the 1938 figure of 7.1 million tons.

Although it is difficult to say with certainty, as separate figures were
not kept for Scotland, it would appear that almost 80 per cent of Scottish
exports were manufactured goods. Of that total, textiles were the most
important and accounted for almost a quarter of Scotland's export earnings
in 1948. In the same year, machinery accounted for 16 per cent, ships 8
per cent, iron and steel 8 per cent, road and railway vehicles 5 per cent,
and paper and cardboard 4 per cent. The export of coal made up 3 per cent
of the total. Whisky was another important commodity, and in 1948 it
accounted for some £16 million in export orders, which was 11 per cent of
the total. All in all, it is estimated that exports earned the economy some
£150 million in 1948. But this has to be balanced against the fact that the
value of imports was almost £190 million, leaving a deficit of £40 million.

More alarming still for the future of the Scottish economy was the
fact that its share of the British export value appeared to be in decline.
Although in 1948 its contributions to the value of British imports and
exports (9.4 and 9.5 per cent) were broadly in line with its share of the
population, the Scottish economy was showing alarming signs of veering
towards areas of low value. In manufacturing goods, Scotland was exporting nearly 10 per cent less than the British average per-capita value. It had
a lead in textiles, machinery and ships, but lagged significantly behind in
the export of commercial vehicles and electrical and domestic goods. The
'sunrise' industries of the thirties, which had been protected by government tariffs before the war and focused mainly on the domestic market,
came into their own after 1945 and were able to exploit the global export
market with little competition from the European mainland. As has been
pointed out earlier, this type of industry was at the cutting edge of the
consumer economy. Scotland, on the other hand, was making ends meet
by reliance on its traditional staples. Furthermore, when it is considered
that much of the export drive was fuelled by demand to restock and reset

the basic economic infrastructure of Western Europe, it can be seen that demand for capital investment goods would be of a short duration only. Once the economies of France, Italy and West Germany had laid down the basic infrastructure requirements to get things moving again, they would turn to their own domestic suppliers or to other firms which had been started on the European mainland. This was especially the case with machinery and textiles, which accounted for over 40 per cent of Scottish exports. By the mid-fifties, some 300,000 Scottish workers were dependent on overseas demand for Scotland's traditional industrial fare. In spite of the best efforts of the planners and the politicians, there seemed to be no escaping the pull of the heavy industries.

The stranglehold of the pre-war economy intensified after 1945. The service sector was slow to recover, and a range of occupations such as clothing, banking, food processing, building and retail employed fewer workers in 1947 than in 1939. Between 1948 and 1954 clothing increased output by 4 per cent; food, drink and tobacco by 11 per cent; wood manufacture by 3 per cent; and paper and printing by 8 per cent. The purchase of household goods, conditioned by shortages and rationing, likewise showed considerable levels of austerity within Scottish society. Although the value of sales went up for metal furniture, clothing, lace, jewellery and sports goods, it failed to match either increasing wages or inflation. Furthermore, sales of toys and games, pottery, brushes and brooms, and soap all declined. Sales by large retailers, including the co-operative societies, were sluggish. Between 1950 and 1954 there was a 28 per cent increase in the value of sales, with a 30 per cent increase in food and a 23 per cent increase in non-food. When inflation is factored into the equation, however, the figures come out at 10 per cent and 13 per cent respectively. The production of domestic food took a downturn. Milled wheat, processed oats, refined sugar, margarine, cooking fat and jam all declined in output. This was offset by greater food imports, which in 1948 came to about £63 million. The only activity to expand was export-earning whisky distilling, which doubled output between 1948 and 1954.

A cursory examination of the main structural differences between the Scottish economy and its British counterpart reveals that the imbalance had become even more firmly entrenched by the early fifties. Scotland had between a third and a quarter of all British workers engaged in boiler manufacture, marine engineering, shipbuilding and locomotive manufacture, and just under a fifth of these in iron and steel foundries and construction engineering. In textiles, it had nearly all the British workers in jute, three-quarters of linen workers, a third of those engaged in carpet manufacture, and a quarter of the rope workforce. It had nearly 40 per cent of the employees engaged in the linoleum and leather industry, a third of the explosive-manufacture employees, a fifth of wholesale bottling, and just under a fifth of cakes, biscuits and confectionery workers. The Scottish agricultural workforce made up about 15 per cent of the British total.

The most significant structural difference was in the areas of value-added production, such as chemicals and dyes, paint, pharmaceuticals, stationery, soap, cement, nylon, footwear, scientific instruments, electrical goods, machine tools, cars, aircraft, radios, telephones, and electric wires and cables, all of which were significantly under-represented in Scotland. If we add up employment for these sectors and compare the respective totals for the United Kingdom and Scotland, then the difference becomes apparent. These under-represented industries provided employment for 126,340 Scots compared to a total of 3,294,100 in the United Kingdom, which means that on a per-capita basis Scotland was employing about 60 per cent less of its workforce in these more lucrative industries. If we compare the heavy manufacturing sector and the traditional industries (excluding mining, which had near parity between Scotland and the United Kingdom), then the Scottish total is 305,510 compared to a British total of 1,365,500. Put another way, the Scottish per-capita representation in this sector was more than twice the UK average. Further evidence of the low-value nature of the Scottish economy is that, by taking away steel used in Scotland from steel made in Scotland, it would appear that about 40 per cent of the latter was destined for use overseas or in other parts of the United Kingdom.

Further problems were emerging by the early fifties. Productivity and output were beginning to lag behind the rest of the United Kingdom. Again, the structure of the economy was responsible for this. The consumer industries could make better use of new technology and mass-production techniques to increase productivity and output. This was not as easy in the traditional sector, where labour was still the most important component in the production process.

Government intervention was important in the regulation of the Scottish economy, and by 1952 there were 536 new factories built in the Scottish development areas at a cost of £22.4 million. This was broadly in line with a per-capita share of the British total. About 100 new enterprises were started annually in the period between 1945 and 1954, most of which were small-scale, employing between 100 and 200 people. Much effort went into attracting branch plants from England and America, and these made up about a quarter of these new enterprises, including factories for IBM, NCR, Burroughs and Honeywell. It should be pointed out, however, that major well-established businesses remained shy of Scotland. Only twenty-two branches of such businesses were established between 1946 and 1951, and, of the four which settled in Scotland in the following year, three were in the armaments industry. The importance of government intervention can be seen by the fact that 19,299 of the total 26,337 square feet of industrial building completed between 1945 and 1954, 19,299 were in the development areas.

By the early fifties average incomes in Scotland were about 10 per cent lower than in the United Kingdom, which did not bode well for the creation of a vibrant domestic economy which could attract new industry. History appeared to be quick off the mark in repeating itself. An income census for the Commissioners of Inland Revenue, published in 1951, showed that the per-capita income tax for Scotland was £130 and for England was £165. The wealth gap was becoming more apparent. A report in the *Scotsman* on 14 September 1952 highlighted the increasing rate of bankruptcy in Scotland. In 1947 there were 21 bankruptcies; in 1948, 36; in 1949, 55; in 1950, 71; in 1951, 102; and by 1952 the figure had risen to 127. A final piece of evidence which demonstrated that things were going back to the pre-war pattern was that emigration began to increase to its normal level. Between 1931 and 1951 the nation lost nearly a quarter of a million people, in spite of the emergence of immigration quotas and war. In 1951 the rate increased, and about 10,000 emigrated and a further 11,700 went south to England.

Yet, for all this, no one showed any great signs of alarm, even though the plans for the diversification of the economy were not being realised and the traditional sectors were actually increasing their importance. There is a twofold explanation for this state of affairs. First, the plans for diversification were driven by the experience of the inter-war years, in that collapsing demand in the traditional sector had led to high levels of unemployment. The primary motive in attracting new industry was not the need for new industry itself, but rather the need to maintain full levels of employment. With the traditional sector doing well as a result of post-war demand, there were plenty of jobs, confidence remained high, and unemployment remained low. Given that plans for diversification were driven by a belief that new jobs would have to be found, when these seemed not to be needed this took away the urgency of restructuring the economy. In any case, the traditional sectors soaked up labour more hungrily than the new, more productive and efficient, consumer industries. For politicians who kept a wary eye on the unemployment statistics there was no sense of alarm, for the time being at least. Furthermore, the number of young apprentices entering the traditional sector showed no sign of decline, indicating that many believed that the heavy industries had a future. Second, the cost of social-welfare provision was prohibitive. Government needed money, and taxes from full employment and, more importantly, export-related earnings were the best way to fund the developing Welfare State. Scotland's major contribution in both these areas was in the traditional heavy industries. A concerted effort at diversification in the immediate post-war era would have tampered with a vital source of income. Once again the maxim was, 'If it ain't broke, don't fix it.'

As was mentioned earlier, the rural community did well out of the war. The Agriculture Acts of 1947 and 1948 guaranteed farm prices and gave tenant farmers greater security of tenure. Incomes doubled, and the maintenance of rationing ensured that there would be a ready market for farm produce. Shortages after the war and a government desire to keep imports to a minimum meant that there was a drive to increase output by some 20 per cent. Yet, while the value of Scotland's agricultural output doubled between 1945 and 1954, most of this increase was due to inflation, which in the food sector was nearly 20 per cent from 1952 to 1954. A closer examination of the statistics shows that, although output was increasing, it was not increasing as fast as the value would seem to suggest. The main changes were in the keeping of livestock. The number of sheep was about half a million (7.5 per cent) smaller than in the pre-war period, the number of cattle increased by about a third of a million (25 per cent), the pig population more than doubled, while poultry added a million (15 per cent) to its total. Livestock was the most lucrative sector of the agricultural economy, but the figures for animals slaughtered (with the exception of pigs for bacon) showed only modest increases. Furthermore, the area under arable land between 1945 and 1954 contracted by 100,000 acres. Yet evidence of the farmers' prosperity is to be found in the use of tractors, sales of which went up from 23,000 in 1947 to 46,000 in 1954.

Housing was the main social problem inherited from the inter-war period. Pre-war building had failed to keep pace with demand, and overcrowding in Scotland was six times as great as in England and Wales. In 1951 half of all Scottish households did not have a fixed bath, one in sixteen had no toilet, and about the same number had neither a piped water supply nor a kitchen sink. Of the 1,378,000 Scottish homes, 76,900 consisted of one room, more than a third of a million were only two-roomed, while slightly less than a third of the total (422,000) were three-roomed. The Scottish Housing Advisory Committee in 1944 recommended that in future, to avoid overcrowding, not more than two persons per room be permitted, and this excluded the counting of the first room. This recommendation was the standard used by local authorities in planning their house-building programmes. Scotland emerged from the war with an additional 33,000 temporary houses or 'pre-fabs', and from 1945 to 1954, when licensing ceased, a total of 208,213 houses had been built by the public sector and 14,760 by the private sector.

The legacy of poor housing was such that there was a determination that new buildings would be of the highest standard, roomy and preferably with a garden. But, like everything else, house-building had to operate within the austerity rule as a result of shortages of materials. Initially the progress was painfully slow, and by the end of 1948 only 18,000 new homes had been completed. Thereafter the pace would quicken, but it would take until the mid-fifties before the target of completion of over 30,000 a year would be met. The numbers employed in the building industry remained fairly static, and even dipped between 1949 and 1953. The official index of production for 1948–53 showed that the industry's growth of 8 per cent in this period was less than half of the average for the economy as a whole. One consequence of the slow rate of construction was that standards were compromised. The initial desire to build houses with four rooms or more was first to go. The proportion of such houses among all those approved for local housing authorities dropped from 94 per cent in 1948 to 87 per cent in 1949, to 64 per cent in 1950, to 44 per cent in 1951, to 42 per cent in 1952. Greater use was made of non-traditional materials such as concrete, prefabricated slabs, aluminium, steel and timber, to take the place of stone and bricks.

Demand for the National Health Service was brisk in this period, and the Scots, with just over 10 per cent of the British population, accounted for 13 per cent of NHS expenditure. The nation's long history of bad health was a major contributing factor, but so was the severe winter of 1947. In 1950 the Scottish death rate was 13 per 1,000, compared to 11.6 per 1,000 for England and Wales. Although new drugs helped, tuberculosis remained a major problem, and the number of new cases reported in 1952 – 7,259 – was greater than the 4,700 recorded in 1939. This was a significant statistic, as the rate of infection with TB is largely affected by social conditions. Death from infectious diseases declined rapidly, as did bronchitis and pneumonia, although death from cancer remained steady. The Scottish appetite for fatty foods and an addiction to cigarettes meant that heart disease was the largest killer, accounting for almost a third of deaths in 1950.

The sick were cared for by an army of around 2,500 GPs, 2,000 hospital doctors and surgeons, and 20,000 nurses. There were 55,000 hospital beds, of which more than half were occupied by patients suffering from mental-health problems. There was a yearly average of over quarter of a million admissions to hospital in the early fifties, including the 500 or so patients who were taken by ambulance. Dental treatment cost the health service almost £1 million in 1953, and was administered to over half a million people. A further £211,000 was spent on dentures. In 1954 the National Health Service provided over 200,000 pairs of glasses at a cost of over a third of a million pounds. Nearly 10 million prescriptions were handed out in 1953. Undoubtedly there was a backlog of demand as many rushed forward to claim free medical attention; nevertheless, the figures do not paint a picture of a nation in the best of health. Further evidence of the state of Scottish physical well-being can be gleaned from the figures for National Insurance. There were around 100,000 claims for sickness benefit in 1951, and the weekly average of new claims rose from 13,900 in

1949 to 15,700 in 1954 at a total cost of £54.8 million. By this time, social services had an annual budget of almost £300 million, which was about a third of the total net income earned that year by the Scottish working population.

LANDSLIDE

In the general election of July 1945, the Labour Party won a landslide victory by securing 48 per cent of the UK popular vote, winning 393 seats and setting out to govern with a majority of 146. It was hailed as a momentous victory. There were a number of reasons for the result. Labour's stewardship of the home front had won the party much credibility, and, while many believed that the Conservatives were best able to win the war, they were not so sure of the Tories' ability to win the peace. Labour was a safe pair of hands. The result took the Conservative Party by surprise. It had failed to notice that opinion polls and by-election results during the war had shown a definite swing to the left. Even those who had noticed were taken aback. The Tories had blithely hoped that Winston Churchill's impressive wartime record would carry them to success and atone for the party's association with the mass unemployment and appeasement of the thirties. It did not, for the electorate was able to compartmentalise its respect for the war leader and its contempt for the 'guilty men' of his party. On the issue of the Welfare State, the Tories were not to be trusted. What was needed now was optimism and positive thinking; the Conservatives had for too long been associated with pessimism and negativity. Even while agreeing with the broad issue of greater state intervention, the party's old guard had a habit of voicing concerns which contrasted badly with Labour's unbridled enthusiasm. The military would have its say, however, and the announcement of the result of the election had to be delayed for twenty days while the votes of the armed forces were counted; it eventually showed that socialism and service for one's country went hand in hand. These factors which affected the outcome of the election in Britain worked to the same extent in Scotland.

North of the border, Labour won 49.4 per cent of the vote and notched up forty seats. It was an impressive result, although party headquarters in London was not slow to point out that the advance in Scotland was not as great as that south of the border. Even though it won a higher proportion of the total vote, because of the peculiarities of the first-past-the-post system Labour won only 54 per cent of Scottish seats, compared to the British total of 62 per cent. In part, the comment of the London headquarters was unfair. In the 1935 general election Labour had recovered to a greater extent in Scotland than south of the border, and in that respect its scope for further expansion had been limited. However, the Conservatives in Scotland had stood up remarkably well, winning with their National Liberal allies 41.1 per cent of the vote (compared with a UK tally of 39.6 per cent) and thirty seats, which meant that, with 40 per cent of the Scottish seats, the Tories did better than the British average of 31 per cent. Thus the main difference between the Scottish and the British election results was that the Scottish Conservatives did not collapse to the same extent as their southern counterparts.

The political battle lines north of the border were largely set by the wider British agenda. Housing was identified by both Labour and the Conservatives as the key area of policy, with the main difference between them being the Tories' stress on public and *private* ventures. The latter were missing from Labour's agenda. The Conservatives put less emphasis on the Welfare State, with the National Health Service being notably absent from a number of constituency manifestos. Pensions featured heavily in both parties' commitments, but by and large the manifestos were fairly timid affairs. Labour seemed to have lost its radical edge, and one effect of Thomas Johnston's wartime leadership was that consensus and centrism dominated party thinking. Certainly the Scottish input on education and health reform was not as advanced as that coming from south of the border. Nor did the party seem to address the big questions of social reconstruction which emanated from more radical elements in England and Wales. The most distinctive element was a lacklustre commitment to home rule, which was only skin-deep. The experience of the thirties had shaped Labour's evolution in the forties. Constituency organisation, local government and loyalty to the leadership were the party's hallmarks.

The divisions of the thirties which had led to nationalist and leftist secessions may have been responsible for the party's reluctance to engage with ideology. The pragmatism of Johnston had certainly delivered results during the war, and perhaps the magnitude of social problems led many to be sceptical about arcane and academic political debate when there was such a crying need for new houses and better health and education provision. The party appeared to be losing idealism. Constituency membership in Scotland was well below the UK average, and the explosion of membership which occurred in the south during the war passed the Scots by. Parliamentary candidates tended to be drawn from local-government councillors who had served their time and shown loyalty to the locality and the centre, and from trade-union officials. Given the run-down state of party organisation, canvassing and the humdrum business of electoral campaigning tended to rely on the trade unions, which were also vital for finance. In return, the unions could claim their pound of flesh by demanding a healthy union representation within the ranks of the Scottish Parliamentary Labour Party. All in all, it made for a rather dull political representation, as most Scottish Labour MPs were middle-aged men with limited outlook and vision.

Certainly there were few of the characters which had distinguished the party in the inter-war period. The Red Clydesiders had all gone. James Maxton drifted into impotence during the war and died shortly afterwards, David Kirkwood ended up in the House of Lords, Thomas Johnston retired from politics to chair the Hydro-Electric Board, George Buchanan became the respectable Minister for Pensions, and James Barr left politics in 1945. Although these stalwarts had never been as radical as portrayed, the new generation of Labour MPs failed to make the same impact on the public consciousness. Furthermore, with the possible exception of Johnston, who quit anyway, Labour in Scotland failed to produce the same calibre of politicians as those who emerged south of the border during the war and who continued to have an impact afterwards. There were no Scottish equivalents of the likes of Hugh Dalton, Aneurin Bevan, Ernest Bevin, Herbert Morrison, Sir Stafford Cripps and Walter Citrine, all of whom were better known north of the border than local MPs. Interestingly enough, of the best-known Scottish representatives in the late forties and early fifties, Manny Shinwell, the Minister of Mines, Emyrs Hughes, the editor of *Forward,* and John Strachey, the MP for Dundee, were all incomers. Perhaps the best-known Scottish radical, Jennie Lee, sat for an English seat.

Joseph Westwood was appointed Secretary of State for Scotland in

Clement Attlee's first Labour administration, only to be sacked for inadequacy and replaced by Arthur Woodburn in 1947. His failure to stop nationalist discontent (see below) meant that Woodburn lasted only until 1950, when he was replaced by Hector MacNeil. It is not too difficult to see why neither of these post-war Secretaries had a distinguished career. There was no distinctive Scottish legislation which either could claim responsibility for, because in the immediate post-war environment all the great pieces of social and economic legislation were passed by the British departments of government and were simply extended to Scotland. So it was difficult for the Scottish Office to take credit for the introduction of family allowances, increased pensions, nationalisation, the creation of the National Health Service, and education reform. Furthermore, in the arena of economic policy, which was essential to ensure full employment and rising wages, credit went either to Hugh Dalton's Treasury or to Sir Stafford Cripps's Board of Trade. Even in the important area of housing, local government and the Scottish Special Housing Association were quick off the mark to take the credit for the construction of new homes but to point the finger of blame at the Scottish Office for shortages, red tape and restrictions. Rather than leading policy, the Scottish Secretaries resembled administrators more than politicians, and, in an era of shortages, licences, rationing and controls, bureaucrats and administrators were not held in good odour by the general public.

If the Labour Party in Scotland was subsumed by its government's activities to the point of being almost invisible, the Conservatives were to make great play of their distinctive Scottish dimension. Although, as was mentioned earlier, the Scottish Tories did not do as badly as their southern colleagues, they did not expect to suffer such a resounding defeat. Like most political parties, they refused to believe that unpopularity could be the root problem, and therefore turned their attention towards membership and organisation. By the end of 1954 there were perhaps around a quarter of a million paid-up members of the Conservative Party in Scotland, which represented about a fifth of the party's voters there. Not only did new members help with canvassing and finance, the party increased its production of specifically Scottish propaganda to contrast with Labour's reliance on London-issued material. The Tories also made greater efforts to capitalise on postal votes, which were more important in marginal seats.

And they specifically targeted the young and women, with promises to
end rationing and state control, which would free up the household
budget for mothers and allow the young to spend more liberally.

To sum up the respective campaigning machines of Labour and the
Tories, the latter were able to canvass more completely – often up to 100
per cent in target constituencies – and could spend more money than their
opponents. Although Labour kept on increasing its absolute vote in Scotland in the period from 1945 through the general elections of 1950 and
1951, its share declined marginally from 49.4 to 47.9 per cent. The
vagaries of the first-past-the-post system meant that the number of Labour
MPs declined from 40 to 35. The Tories, on the other hand, rose from 41.1
to 48.6 per cent of the vote and their number of seats jumped from 30 to
35. By 1951 the Conservatives had made up lost ground and there was
only a hair's breadth between the two parties.

One of the main difficulties in explaining electoral history is how to
marry up the statistical evidence of voting with the pronouncements of
the political parties. It may well be the case that the electorate voted for
particular parties because of what was promised, and an analysis of the
social structure may indicate if the material interests of certain sections of
society can account for the numerical shifts. It has to be borne in mind
that the shifts in the number of votes in this period were relatively small,
but the nature of the electoral system exaggerated the degree of political
change. Two key elements explain the creeping success of the Scottish
Conservative Party in this period. First, there was a general sense of frustration at the slowness of recovery and the impact of controls and regulation. Second, the centralising policies of the Labour administration
neglected a separate Scottish dimension. Whether or not it was a factor in
explaining its recovery in the early fifties, the Conservative Party made
great play of its Scottish identity in attacking the policy of nationalisation:

> But Union is not amalgamation. Scotland is a nation. Those who
> advocated and carried through the policy of Union recognised this,
> and made many most thoughtful and intentional provisions to
> secure her position. They sought to preserve, and did preserve, the
> national character and distinctive traditions of Scotland . . . It is

only since 1945, under the first Socialist majority, that we have seen
the policy of amalgamation superseding that of Union. This must
inevitably result from the fulfilment of the Socialist creed, which is
basically one of amalgamation and centralisation. To this policy we
are fundamentally opposed . . . The effect of Socialist policy has
been to transfer the management and control of the State owned
industries of Scotland to Whitehall. The Act of Union never contemplated this unnatural state of affairs. Those who drafted it did
not see this new despotism. The concentration of power at the centre, the denial of effective action to any authority except the central
one, these are symptoms of the disease of Socialism.

Scottish Control of Scottish Affairs: Unionist Policy (Glasgow, 1949)

The Tories used the saltire flag during their election campaigns, and
this chimed with a sense of frustrated nationhood which found expression
in the signing of the National Covenant and the furore over the use of the
numeral 'II' by Queen Elizabeth (see below). Winston Churchill made use
of the threat that centralisation posed to Scottish distinctiveness in a
speech in Edinburgh on 14 February 1950:

The principle of centralisation of government in Whitehall and
Westminster is emphasised in a manner not hitherto experienced or
contemplated in the Act of Union . . . If England became an
absolute Socialist state, owning all the means of production, distribution, and exchange, ruled only by politicians and their officials in
London offices, I personally cannot feel that Scotland would be
bound to accept such a dispensation.

Yet, it would be wrong to characterise the Conservative Party as being in
favour of self-government or greater devolution. While the Tories stated
that Labour was indifferent to Scottish needs, the best they themselves
would offer was a hint that there ought to be more Scottish control,
although this was never defined nor elaborated on. Rather, it was more a
case of making political capital out of the government's unpopularity on
Scottish issues.

The growth of centralised planning and control may have given rise to concerns about Scottish identity being swamped by an overpowerful bureaucracy. The issue of home rule, which had surfaced from time to time during the war, had never been resolved one way or the other, in public at least. As should be apparent from the previous pages, Labour's post-war policy was based around centralised British state planning, but the party had never come out and said that home rule was off the agenda. John Mac-Cormick, who had left the SNP in 1942, had gravitated to the Liberal Party because it seemed to be the most committed to home rule. Mac-Cormick was the Liberal candidate for the Paisley by-election of February 1948, and Conservative mischievousness conspired to let him have a free run against Labour. He stood as a 'National' candidate, and the Tories unofficially supported him from the sidelines, causing great concern among his Liberal colleagues, who did not want too close an identification with the Conservative Party. MacCormick did well, but not well enough, and Labour held the seat.

For ever the optimist, MacCormick believed that his respectable polling was down to support for home rule, rather than opposition to the government. An unofficial local plebiscite in Kirriemuir had come out in favour of home rule, reinforcing the impression that the issue was a popular one. It was in response to these events that in October 1949 Mac-Cormick started the Scottish Convention as a cross-party pressure group designed to demonstrate to the government that a parliament in Edinburgh had widespread popular support. A campaign was launched to collect signatures in favour of home rule, and by 1950 some 1.7 million had subscribed. Armed with this evidence, the case was made to the Secretary of State for Scotland, Hector MacNeil, who gruffly responded that if there was such support then the Convention should contest elections to secure a mandate. In this, Labour was supported by the Conservatives, although the latter did not make as much noise as the former. According to an editorial in the *Scotsman* on 9 August 1950:

> What evidence will be accepted as convincing proof that the majority of the people desire self-government . . . They [the Labour and Conservative parties] imply that the desire for self-government should be demonstrated by voters at an election. When an election takes place, however, they claim that larger issues are at stake,

which overshadow the minor domestic problems of Scotland and urge the electors to ignore the latter. Self-government is a complex matter, but electors could surely express a more reasoned opinion on it if it were presented in isolation in the form of a plebiscite than if it were submerged by other complex issues at an election. Voters nowadays express a general preference for one party; their decision is seldom based on support for one particular item in the programme.

Until popular support could be demonstrated at the ballot box, the government would not take the issue of home rule seriously. MacCormick's bluff had been called: the very point of the Convention was to show support for home rule without contesting elections. The credibility of the Convention had been tested and found wanting. Home rule was like love and peace: everyone agreed with it, but MacNeil was sure that in itself it was not powerful enough to override conventional party loyalties. He was right, and the flag of the nationalist cause passed back to the SNP, which was left as the surviving champion of the self-government cause. Labour and the trade unions were stung by the nationalist intervention at Paisley, and became increasingly convinced that home rule was a right-wing plot – an attitude in part bolstered by Conservative criticism of centralisation.

There were further nationalist episodes in the early fifties. On Christmas Day 1950, Glasgow University students, led by the future nationalist and QC Ian Hamilton, stole the Coronation Stone or Stone of Destiny from Westminster Abbey, on the grounds that it had been stolen from Scotland in the first place by Edward I. The theft sparked a nationwide hunt, but the stone was eventually returned in April 1951 at the historically symbolic Arbroath Abbey, where the Scots had made their declaration against English overlordship in 1320. Rumours still abound that it was not the real stone which was returned, and various towns and villages throughout Scotland have their share of individuals who claim to know where the real one is. The coronation of Queen Elizabeth II caused further resentment. The use of the numeral 'II' was thought to be an insult to Scottish history, on the grounds that Scotland had not had a queen named Elizabeth in the past. It was seen as English arrogance to assume that England's royal line subsumed that of the Scots. Middle-class protests included stitching ERI into handkerchiefs. More subversive was the blowing up of postboxes bearing the offending numeral. Royalist terrorism worked, and Scottish postboxes to this day are the property of simply ER. A further furore occurred when the Queen came north to accept the Scottish regalia (Crown jewels) in a ceremony at St Giles' Cathedral in Edinburgh. Her two-piece suit and handbag were not thought to be sufficiently decorous for the occasion – yet another insult to the Scottish past. Then in 1954 the report of the Royal Commission on Scottish Affairs, which was set up by Labour under Lord Balfour, made the unfortunate gaffe of referring to Scotland as a region, and not a nation, of Britain. And in 1958 the Presbyterian nation raised its voice in protest when the *Daily Express* reported the possibility of the introduction of bishops into the Church of Scotland.

While such incidents are not important in themselves, they do indicate that Scottish identity was sensitive and that Scots were not prepared to lie back and be steamrollered by English assumptions. The interest in constitutional niceties and in Scottish history and the respect for the ancient traditions and institutions reveal that there was more than a touch of middle-class touchiness to these issues. Certainly a poll in Glasgow in 1950 showed that the working class there believed that they had more in common with fellow workers in England than with their middle-class co-nationals. Unlike Labour, the Conservatives were more attuned to national sensitivity, and if this did not gain them any votes, it certainly did them no harm.

The distribution of income in Scotland perhaps affords a better clue to how material interests could be married up to political behaviour. In 1950 the Board of Inland Revenue published figures showing that, before tax, 51 per cent of the working population earned under £300, 41 per cent earned between £300 and £600, and 8 per cent earned over £600. Significantly, 35 per cent earned between £300 and £500, demonstrating that there was a large section of society which, in terms of income, occupied the middle ground, making its capture vital for electoral success. The party that could hold its own traditional support but also reach out to the middle-income fringes of the opposition therefore had the best chance of winning. Although earnings on their own are a fairly unreliable guide to political behaviour, certain other factors can be brought to explain the shift towards the Conservative Party.

As has already been noted, it was the consumer sector of the economy which remained resolutely depressed in the period 1945–52, as a result of shortages and government restrictions. The building and distributive trades employed more than a third of a million workers by 1950 and, compared to the engineering and manufacturing industries, they had experienced relatively slow growth and, more importantly, slower increases in wages, which increased by a fifth between 1947 and 1951. The Labour government's emphasis on heavy industry and the need to maximise output to capitalise on exports did not go down well with all sections of society. Shopkeepers, store workers, plumbers, carpenters and other tradesmen had to work and earn in an environment in which it was believed that government was suppressing demand in favour of the industries which had the backing of the big trade unions.

Government policy also affected Labour's traditional supporters. A common complaint in Glasgow was the 'wage freeze', which had been instituted in 1948 as a temporary measure, and which went down like a lead balloon, especially when MPs voted themselves a pay increase in 1950. Taxation was another contentious issue. Many in the working class may have paid lip-service to the principle that it was an effective means of redistribution, but complaints about its effect of eating away overtime and bonus payment were frequently reported. The idea of income tax as a means of wealth redistribution may have sounded fine in principle, but, as is often the case with such principles, when it was first put into practice it may have lost its appeal. Although there were income-tax cuts in 1950, charges were levied on petrol. Tax on consumer goods – particularly everyday items – was another source of contention, and the general-election campaign of 1951 heard the slogan 'Cheaper cigarettes under the Tories'.

The outbreak of the Korean War in 1950 and a programme of rearmament the following year meant that charges were levied on the health service in order to ease the growing financial burden on the Exchequer. Scottish Labour left it to the rest of the country to protest. Complaints were also made about the slowness of the housebuilding programme, and one factor which may have swayed some voters towards the Conservative Party was the Tories' promise to build 300,000 new homes in the United Kingdom per year, which was dismissed by Labour as fantasy. In Glasgow, which had the worst housing problem, the waiting list had grown from

86,00 in 1945 to 94,300 in 1950. A common complaint was the amount of time it was taking to build the New Jerusalem.

Furthermore, government policy rebounded in different directions to make the situation worse. While subsidies were given for housebuilding, the main way for local authorities to raise capital was through loans. In 1951 the total amount of local-authority income in Scotland was almost £178 million, of which £54 million was raised by loans. Government grants came to just under £47 million, and rates contributed £37 million – the lion's share – of the balance. This property tax had the effect of polarising residential class and political divisions in Scotland. The fact that rates were set by local councils meant that the government was powerless to intervene, even if Labour councils used them as a means to subsidise council housing. The hike in rates, together with tougher laws on sanitation and health, meant that many landowners ditched their property. By 1953, 3,569 houses had been offered free to Glasgow City Council on the grounds that repairs and rates meant that landlords were unlikely to get an economic rent that could compete with council housing. There was little sympathy for the landlords, given the history of appalling housing standards, but it would mean that local-authority housing would dominate in future: the private rental market would shrink to the point of nonexistence.

Of the two parties, the Conservatives were best able to stretch to the middle ground. While making noises about reducing taxes and freeing up enterprise, they were also able to present themselves as the champion of a state house-building programme. Labour, on the other hand, was seen as cautious, orthodox, dogmatic and too much associated with austerity, restriction and control. It is said that political parties do not win elections, only lose them. Governments are judged not by what they will do, but what they have done. There is no doubt that the policy of control and regulation was necessary to stabilise the economy. Having achieved this, Labour lost the 1951 general election to a party which promised better times. The austerity of the late forties and early fifties paved the way for the affluence of the next decade.

SEVEN

AFFLUENCE,
1954–1966

Returning to Glasgow after long exile,
Nothing seemed to me to have changed its style.
Buses and trams all labelled 'To Ibrox'
Swung past tight as they'd hold with folks.
Football match, I concluded, but just to make sure
I asked; and the man looked at me fell dour,
Then said, 'Where in God's name are *you* frae, sir?
It'll be a record gate, but the cause o' the stir
Is a debate on "la loi de l'effort converti"
Between Professor MacFadyen and a Spanish pairty.'
I gasped. The newsboys came running along,
'Special! Turkish Poet's Abstruse New Song.
Scottish Authors' Opinions' – and, holy snakes,
I saw the edition sell like hot cakes!

Hugh MacDiarmid, 'Glasgow, 1960', (Glasgow,1935)

Local authorities like private builders are free to build houses to as
good a standard of size and construction as they wish, and must not
go below prescribed minimum standards. In consequence the size
and soundness of council houses is satisfactory and compares well
with what is being done in many Western European countries; but

with some few exceptions their external appearance and their surroundings are depressing. We should like to see these points where
Scottish housing compares badly with what is done elsewhere in
Western Europe now given as much attention as internal construction. Some care in design and layout, and a relatively small expenditure on maintenance of the ground about the houses, could make
an altogether more pleasant and impressive environment. Local
authorities and private builders should also be more ready to try out
modern developments in design and building methods and to take
account of the increased standards of living – the influence of television, the growth in car ownership, the possibilities of central
heating and the like. There is a danger that we may be building
now for the conditions of ten or twenty years ago.

Inquiry into the Scottish Economy, 1960–1961, chaired by J. N. Toothill
(Edinburgh, 1961)

On several occasions during interviews on housing matters we were
told of pressures put on the rest of the family by young girls who
wanted their parents and brothers to adopt different standards. One
housewife reported that her two daughters of 16 and 17 years of
age, who worked in a City dress shop, had threatened to leave home
and emigrate to Canada if they were not allowed a bedroom of their
own. The family only possessed one bedroom and the father therefore had to take a nightshift job to allow the girls some privacy and
the undisputed use of the room at night. The family had not quar-
relled, and the parents thought that 'it was only right' that the girls
should make these demands 'now that they were growing up'. 'It
was only natural that they would want somewhere to keep their
clothes and keep them nice, working in a dress shop.' Young girls
are probably the most enthusiastic advocates of this kind of change
everywhere, but the social structure of Govan emphasizes the likelihood of their taking up this role. The Govan area is deficient in
women's jobs and what jobs there are not very feminine in character. The girls who want to go to work, therefore, tend to travel into
the City as shop assistants, clerks, typists, etc., or to the Hillington
Trading Estate, where most of the women's jobs are of a light and

congenial nature. Their menfolk meanwhile are engaged mainly in manual jobs and, though these jobs require a great deal of skill and experience, to the girls they still appear to be dirty and unpleasant.

Tom Brennan, *Reshaping a City* (Cambridge, 1959)

SPEND, SPEND, SPEND

Like so many other periods in Scottish history, the period from 1954 to 1966 presents the historian with a paradox. On the one hand, the economic indicators for these years paint a gloomy picture of declining rates of productivity and a poor comparative performance. But, on the other hand, the social indicators show that there were increasing prosperity, growing consumption and better standards of living. As ever, the key to understanding what was going on is to marry up public perceptions with statistical reality.

By 1954 the Conservative government had managed to lift the majority of the controls and regulations which had been imposed after the war by its Labour predecessor. Most importantly for the majority, the rationing of food came to an end, and there would be no more queues for horse meat. People were free to spend their money where they wanted and on what they wanted. With the brakes having been put on the consumer economy for more than fifteen years, naturally there was a widespread boom as people rushed to stock up on goods which had been in short supply. It is one of the most quoted phrases in British political history, but when Harold Macmillan claimed in 1959 that the electorate had 'never had it so good' there was a large element of truth in his statement, even though the Scots did not have it as good as the English and even though there were still pockets of deprivation.

As we shall see, the period from 1954 to 1966 did have its economic problems, and for a generation of later historians it was a time when the rot set in and Scotland spectacularly failed to maintain its position in a world of increasing international competitiveness. Yet, for all that, it was also a time of greater redistribution of wealth and of unparalleled rises in the standard of living for most Scots. The facts and figures speak for themselves and show a population becoming wealthier, better fed and housed, more educated, and better cared for. Furthermore, there was a great deal of optimism and rising expectations, even at a time normally characterised by economic failure.

Poor housing was the major blight on the social landscape, and a total of 382,530 new homes were completed during the reign of the Conservatives from 1952 to 1964. Put another way, the number of houses built in this period was equal to a quarter of the total that had existed in 1951. All in all, between a million and a million and a half Scots – over a fifth of the population – moved into a new home. There was a social revolution, in that most Scots, for the first time in history, had access to a fixed bath and an indoor toilet. Whatever we may think today about the housing standards set in the fifties and sixties, they represented a major improvement on what had existed before, and most council tenants were glad and grateful that the state had provided for this most elemental human need.

Average wages increased by over two-thirds between 1952 and 1964, and more Scots had more money. Whereas male employment showed a marginal decrease between 1949 and 1962, the number of working women increased by 77,000, a rise from 31.5 per cent of the working population to 34 per cent. Married women made up an increasing part of the female labour force, and by 1961 the proportion had risen from 23 per cent in 1951 to 39 per cent. Much of the work done by women was low-paid and part-time, yet it cannot be discounted, for it provided many families with extra, and much appreciated, income. For women conditioned to believe their role was in the home and that their labour was not of the same worth as a man's, the opportunity to earn 'pin money' to top up the family budget was most welcome. It would take a later generation to point out that they were being ripped off.

The work cycle for women began after leaving school, and would normally last until marriage or pregnancy. After looking after the children, it was then possible to resume work. The bald figures actually disguise the size of the female workforce, in that women were more likely to drop in and out of work, rather than remain in regular employment. Factory work declined, and retail, secretarial and administrative jobs increasingly formed the bulk of female employment. As has often been pointed out, work in this sector may have been a factor in promoting ideas of upward social mobility, in that it moved many women away from the traditional industrial arena of Scottish working life into one which was more genteel, prosperous and middle class.

Average earnings are a good index of increasing prosperity, in that married couples were counted as one unit of assessment and it is possible to gauge the rise in family income. By 1960 the total amount of earnings in Scotland had nearly doubled since 1950, having risen from £688 million to £1,257 million. Although inflation over this period of about 30 per cent accounts for much of the increase, in real terms there was still a gain of over a half. Furthermore, the wide disparities in earnings were beginning to close. Overall, there was a movement in favour of middle-income earners. In 1950 the incomes of the bottom third of the income-earning population made up less than a sixth of the total income, and by 1960 there had been little change. In 1950 the middle third earned about a fifth of the total, but by 1960 this had grown to over a third. Whereas the top third earned three-fifths of the total income in 1950, by 1960 this had dropped to about half. Over the decade, the number earning between £600 and £800 increased by six and a half times, those earning between £800 and £1000 went up by nearly ten times, between £1,000 and £1,500 grew by almost six times, and those earning more than £1,500 increased by more than five and a half times. In the top income bracket of over £20,000, the number increased tenfold. All in all, about 44 per cent of the population was now in an income bracket above that which accounted for 94 per cent of earners in 1950. By 1965, a survey of weekly household incomes in Scotland showed that, compared to the rest of the United Kingdom, the nation had a slightly lower proportion of the population in the lower and upper income brackets, but by far the majority was in the middle. It is easy to see why the period should be associated with rising levels of prosperity.

Other indicators can be used to show increasing spending power. Between 1950 and 1958 sales by large retailers had increased by over 50 per cent. The number of television-licence holders rose from 62,400 in 1952 to 1,253,100 in 1965, and car ownership increased from 23,426 in 1953 to 113,000 in 1965. Sales of household goods more than doubled in the same period, and the numbers employed in the retail sector of the economy jumped from 177,000 in 1953 to just over a quarter of a million in 1963. The consumer age had arrived in Scotland. More women were pampering themselves, and there was a 60 per cent rise in employment in hairdressing and manicure services. Between the late fifties and early sixties an annual amount of 30,000 tons of sweets and chocolates and a further 30,000 tons of jam and marmalade were manufactured largely for the benefit of the nation's sweet tooth, and the yearly production of biscuits averaged just under 100,000 tons. An average of 50,000 tons of canned soup, fruit, fish and vegetables, 5,000 tons of butter, 20,000 tons of cheese, 50,000 tons of condensed milk, over half a million eggs, and almost 2.5 million barrels of beer were consumed annually. According to statistics from slaughterhouses, meat showed the largest increase in food consumption between 1952 and 1963. Beef more than doubled, mutton, lamb and pork increased by a third, and bacon – the cheapest – fell by about a quarter.

By 1965 there were 53,386 retail outlets, which, at 9.2 per cent of the UK total, gave Scotland slightly less than its proportional share, but this was compensated for by the Scots spending slightly more, taking them up to the UK average. The biggest increase was in the sale of household goods, and there were nearly 5,000 outlets providing furniture and electrical and other consumer goods. The number of restaurants increased by almost a third between 1960 and 1965, to 2,589. A reflection of the increasing appeal of consumerism and the good life is that the number of pubs remained static in the same period, at just over 4,200. Off-licences, which allowed the drinker to relax at home, increased by almost two-thirds. Credit was more easily available, and the Scottish banks worked in conjunction with hire-purchase firms to facilitate easier borrowing. Savings also increased, with the amount placed in the trustee savings banks rising by nearly £100 million in the period from 1960 to 1965. Nearly 44,000 private homes were purchased in the same period, showing that almost one in three Scots families preferred to own their home rather than rent from the council.

The self-employed and small employers had taken a hammering during the war and the austerity years, and seemed to be on the point of extinction. Between 1931 and 1951 the number of employers in Scotland dropped from 121,000 to 73,000, and the self-employed declined from 116,000 to 75,000 in the same period. Undoubtedly, the impact of the Depression, wartime and post-war controls, and the nationalisation of mines, health, power and transport all contributed to the shrinkage. Yet by 1965 signs of recovery were evident, even if the figures were still some way off from those for 1931 and the self-employed continued to collapse. In terms of growth, the areas which showed most signs of promise were those related to the consumer economy. Employers in the construction industry increased by just over a fifth between 1951 and 1961. In the same period, the numbers of firms in the distribution trade grew by over a third, and in financial and professional services the number of businesses nearly doubled. Employers in manufacturing declined by over half.

Society showed the outwards signs of prosperity. According to the urban sociologist Tom Brennan:

> In matters of personal behaviour, improvements have been as dramatic as in standards of living. There is very much less heavy drinking; very rarely does one hear of methylated spirits drinking at all. The socio-pathological features like child neglect and cruelty, which used to be associated with working-class districts of Glasgow, are now restricted to a few areas. People are better dressed, houses are very much better furnished and decorated, and are in every way cleaner and healthier.
>
> *Reshaping a City* (Cambridge, 1959)

There was constant building going on, more and more shops were opening, adverts and commercials – both in the cinema and, from September 1955, on television – promoted a wider range of household goods, and people had to keep up with the Joneses in terms of having the latest utilities and products. Housewives were the main beneficiaries of this boom, as the impact of domestic technology eased the burden of cleaning and washing. Houses could no longer be stocked with just the basic requirements, but had to make a statement about personal taste and consumption. It was an era in which neighbours would come round to admire the latest domestic acquisition. This was also a time when new materials made an impact. Plastic was exciting, new and modern, and the more gaudy the better. Nylon and polyester liberated textiles from their usual drab colours. Fashion and design in household goods became more important than utility. Homes not only would require vacuum cleaners, washing machines, televisions, radios, radiograms or record players, and electric or gas cookers, but would have to be decorated with wallpaper and have the newest designs of sofas and chairs, tables, lamps and other decorations. Prints could be bought cheaply, and thousands of houses had pictures of Spanish ladies, flying geese, farmyard scenes and Scottish scenery splattered on their walls. Plastic flowers and mass-produced vases and ornaments added the finishing touches. Out went the solid teak and oak of granny's sideboard, and in came the flash of Formica. 'Artificial' then had none of the negative connotations that it has now. The worse insult that could be experienced was to be told that your house was old-fashioned. Style in clothing also became important. The traditional 'good suit' for church weddings and funerals was augmented with other leisure clothes. The growth in the retail and service sector meant that, outside the workplace, fewer men in Scotland were to be seen in the traditional overalls. Clothes for the weekend – particularly, but not exclusively, for the young – became another necessity.

Workers were doing well in this period, and an examination of the average weekly family income of 442 shillings (including family allowance) in 1965 demonstrates that manual labourers were relatively well off. Hourly earnings in manufacturing industry rose by nearly 50 per cent in the period from 1960 to 1966, and out of thirty-two types of employment, fifteen paid more than 400 shillings a week. Workers in heavy industry, in spite of whatever difficulties they may have had in terms of competitiveness and productivity, did well, with iron and steel workers, industrial-plant employees, workers in mechanical engineering, shipbuilders, marine-engine builders and metalworkers all earning over 400 shillings per week. At 3 per 1,000, unemployment was at a historically low rate (although double the average for the rest of the United Kingdom) and the long-term jobless had almost disappeared, as only a fifth of the total had been out of work for more than a year. Most of the unemployment numbers were made up from those who were switching from one job to another.

Not only were workers earning and spending more, they had better social provision, courtesy of the state. Spending on social services rocketed from £221.8 million in 1951 to £442.1 million in 1961, and by 1965/6 it had reached an astonishing £735.1 million – a figure more than twice

the size of the Scottish income-tax receipt. Although the number of hospital beds remained constant at about 63,000 between 1955 and 1965,
the number of hospital doctors increased by more than two and a half
times to 2,791 and the number of nurses went up by a fifth to 26,000 full-
timers and 9,000 part-timers. The number of GPs remained constant at
about 2,500 in the same period, which meant that there were some 2,000
patients per doctor. Health spending in Scotland between 1960 and 1965
increased from £95.5 million to £141.1 million. Public expenditure in
Scotland during the period between 1955 and 1965 showed a huge
increase right across the board. The amount paid out in benefits and assistance increased from £137.9 million to £236.4 million.

Education was another big consumer, and a number of trends tend to
point to increasing social mobility. The amount spent on universities
increased fivefold, rising from £5.5 million in 1955 to £27.5 million in
1965. The number of students increased from 15,000 to over 25,000 in
the same period, with the proportion of women remaining constant at
about a third. The budget for non-university education rose in the decade
after 1955 from £55.1 million to £143.5 million. The number of schools
declined marginally from 3,758 to 3,450 in the same period, although the
annual sum spent on new schools and upgrades rose from £8 million to
£28 million per annum by 1964. Evidence of an increasingly aspirant
society is to be found in the number of pupils staying on beyond the minimum age of fifteen, which rose from 17,000 in 1955 to over 30,000 in
1965.

Although in 1960 housing accounted for a lower share of national
income than education, by 1965 it had overtaken it and the amount of
spending rose from £78.4 million to £149.2 million, demonstrating what
Scottish society saw as its priorities. Sending a son or daughter to university was a goal for a minority of Scottish families; securing them a council
house, on the other hand, was beginning to be seen as a right.

Not surprisingly, the apparatus required to equip and operate an
increasingly aspirant and consumerist society began to eat into government expenditure in Scotland. The annual budget for roads increased from
£29.7 million to £45.4 million between 1960 and 1965. No money was
spent on airports in 1960, but five years later it was £4.5 million.
Libraries, museums and the arts increased their spending by a third

between 1960 and 1965, and, ominously for the criminal classes, the police and prison budget doubled.

HOUSING THE PEOPLE

During the fifties and sixties it was a weekly ritual for many families to go down to the local council offices and read the official posted notices to see if they had been successful in their application for a new council house. Housing was the dominant social issue, and played an important part in politics. Labour was punished in 1951 for its slow delivery of new houses. The Tories did well in the fifties, as completions rose to 30,000 a year, but their popularity waned as production slowed down in the early sixties, and Labour emerged as the champion of council-house building in the elections of 1964 and 1966.

It is difficult to recapture the excitement felt by tens of thousands of Scots who left their cramped dwellings behind and moved into new homes complete with indoor toilets, fixed baths, hot and cold water, and all the latest mod cons. An oral-history project conducted in the Glasgow estate of Castlemilk in the late eighties recounted the experience of one tenant, Rose McLean:

> I remember the day the card came through the door telling me I had a new house in Castlemilk. That was in April 1957. I was all excited – I was getting A NEW HOUSE! I ran out and phoned my mother – I just couldn't wait . . . We got the keys and my husband took the oldest girls to see the house. They didn't know where to go, but it was a nice day and they got there somehow. We had three children and a baby of 9 months so I couldn't go to see the house just then – I thought it was awful far away. In fact I didn't see the house until the night we moved in. When they came back and said the house was on the ground floor I thought I was getting a back and front door you know – but it was a corner house with a big garden in Ardmaleish Road. They talked about the white sink in the kitchen and the BATHROOM – we only had a toilet in the stair. They were all thrilled.
>
> Castlemilk's People's History Group, *The Big Flit: Castlemilk's First Tenants* (Glasgow, 1990)

Although spartan by today's standard of living, compared with the often cramped, damp and smelly dwelling places of the past the new houses, apartments and flats seemed like the epitome of luxury to a generation which had been reared in some of the worst housing conditions in Europe. While relics of sixties housing still survive in some places and tell us today that standards were not great at that time, it should be borne in mind that what preceded them was destroyed in a programme of slum clearance. Had the slums survived, we might not be so quick to judge the tower blocks and apartments of the post-war era. Furthermore, many of the faults which made Scottish council housing notorious would take time to emerge. When people entered their new homes, by and large, the property was new and in good working order, and they looked after it.

Housing issues were dominated by poor stock and overcrowding. The problem was not confined to the cities, but affected all parts of the nation. Housing was notoriously bad in the mining villages, and with nationalisation it behoved the state to ensure that its employees had new homes, through the agency of the local councils. Most rural dwellings were without indoor water and sanitation. Small towns had their areas of run-down and cramped dwellings. Housing policy was directed towards the creation of new, purpose-built, estates away from the centres of the cities and big towns.

The situation in Glasgow was different, in that the Clyde Valley Plan proposed that there would be a planned fall in the city's population of between a quarter and a third of a million. (It should be borne in mind that the nation's largest city had about a fifth of the total Scottish population.) Government policy to deal with the 'overspill' called for the creation of new towns (see below) and the granting of housing subsidies to other local authorities which were prepared to take in Glaswegian refugees. The objective of the Glasgow city authority was to retain as much of the population as possible by using the technique adopted by the other cities and big towns – creating estates outside the centre, but still within the city boundary. These suburban developments catered for between 5,000 and 9,000 families.

Through the fifties and sixties, new estates sprang up through Scotland. In Glasgow, for example, there were Pollock, Easterhouse and Castlemilk; Edinburgh had Wester Hailes; Dundee had Whitefield; and

Aberdeen had Kincorth. Most of the towns also had their own council estates, which emerged outside the town centre. Inverness, Falkirk, Stirling, Dumfries, Kilmarnock, Ayr, Perth and Alloa, among many other smaller places, each developed purpose-built new estates to accommodate council-house tenants.

The chronological development of such estates can be seen in the types of accommodation built. Like everything else, council-house building was subject to government spending, and this had an impact on what was put up. Initially, terraced and semi-detached houses led the way, but these were later augmented by flats in tenements of three or four storeys, which were cheaper to build and more cost-effective at housing people at a time when the political emphasis was on delivering the maximum number of units of accommodation. Finally, in the early sixties, the most economical form of housing made its appearance in the shape of tower blocks. Such developments were directly affected by government policy through the subsidy that was given to housing.

Initially it was believed that growth in the economy would ensure that council housing would be largely self-financing once the principal problem of overcrowding had been solved. Up to 1957, this problem was the main target of government policy, and between £39 and £46 per dwelling was paid for three- to five-apartment housing under a programme of basic needs. After this the subsidy was cut to £24, with special payments given for houses for incoming workers (which worked largely to the benefit of the new towns) for housing which was dependent on the Glasgow overspill, and for housing tied to industrial development. Many councils took advantage of the overspill subsidy to fund development for local residents, being aware that an increasing population would allow them access to greater resource allocation from central government. The big spur to build flats with six or more storeys was the fact that, in addition to the basic £24 subsidy, councils would receive two-thirds of the savings made through not erecting lower-rise buildings. A further incentive was added in 1962 when the subsidy increased to £40.

One striking feature of the new estates was how quickly they could replicate systems of hierarchy in which certain areas would be designated 'good' places and others would be 'bad'. In part, this was due to the system of housing allocation. In the early fifties many families who were on the waiting list had been there from the thirties. Although the criteria used for allocation were based on need, there were other factors which influenced the choice of tenants for new housing. Candidates were grouped into three categories: 'ordinary', 'intermediate' and 'rehousing', in descending order of tenant worthiness. Factors which were taken into consideration included ability to pay, house cleanliness, and respectability. In many areas until the sixties, tenants could be visited at home by a housing and sanitary officer to check whether a family could be relied upon to keep a council house in a good state of repair. Those classed as 'rehousing' were generally on a low income, or state benefits, or 'incomplete' families (meaning that there was no father) or anti-social neighbours. The derogatory word 'scheme' or 'schemey', used to denigrate the place where someone lives, comes from the term 'rehousing scheme', which referred to an estate where social undesirables were kept together.

Naturally, those who were selected for the first council houses tended to have been on the waiting list for longest, were more likely to be a mature family unit, given that overcrowding was an issue, and had the means to pay a rent which was usually substantially higher than the old one. The 'best' tenants therefore tended to receive the best houses. This lent itself to the creation of social hierarchies, with those occupying the houses, who had been in an estate the longest and paid more rent, feeling superior to those who occupied the tenement flats, who in turn felt themselves a cut above those who lived in the high-rise flats. In Pollock, for example, the south of the estate acquired a bad reputation on account of its flats being rented by the lower 'intermediate' type of tenant. The same phenomenon happened in Wester Hailes in Edinburgh as the development spread westward, with the lowest-income families being last to be settled, furthest away from the city. Those classed as 'rehousing' tended to be at the end of the queue, and although the official segregation policy had been abandoned in the post-war era, the fact that an area contained a high proportion of those from 'rehousing' areas was enough in itself to attach a significant social stigma to a place. Furthermore, this type of hierarchy tended to reinforce itself, in that families tended to cluster around the same type of housing and young people were allocated points towards housing allocation on the basis of having a connection with the community.

Contacts with councillors to ensure that family members were given a house in a good area often brought accusations of cronyism and favouritism. Also, one reason why the problem of shortage was never solved was that there was always an aspiration to move to a better area, or a better house, which meant that, once housed, many tenants did not disappear from the waiting list. Having a house with a garden was what most people ultimately aspired to, and an attitude quickly developed that viewed much accommodation, particularly in flats and tower blocks, as a stopgap until something better came along. There was also a high turnover of tenants who moved to similar types of housing either on account of difficult neighbours or on the chance that they might like another area better. Some were motivated simply by the desire for a change.

The new estates were a world away from what most tenants had known in the past. But, although planning may have been all the rage, many of them proved to be neither well planned nor coordinated with the wider community. The lack of local amenities was the most common complaint. In part this was owing to the simple fact that in a crowded inner city, and for that matter a larger town, there was a high population density, which attracted the providers of amenities. This meant that, although there may have been a large number of people per shop or pub or whatever amenity, the fact that everything was jammed so close together meant that shops and services were within easy reach. In the new estates the situation was the reverse: as the population was more thinly spread out, it followed that shops and other amenities would be equally thin on the ground. For most, this meant a longer walk than they were used to in order to get to the shops. Another feature which cut down on the range of amenities was the policy of local authorities themselves. Ever eager to extend their grip on the running of society, the local councils tended to own the shop buildings. These were then rented out to the highest bidder, and in order to encourage high bids the number of shops and services was kept low, to give the successful applicant a near monopoly of local trade. This cost of the bid was passed back to the consumer in the form of higher prices. Easterhouse, for example, had only one shop and one café for a population of some 40,000.

Local authorities also displayed much of the traditional Scottish obsession with enforcing notions of public morality. Pubs were not given permission to operate on council land, which meant that the tradition started of having to go into town for a drink – along with the irrefutably logical attitude that, having caught a bus and travelled some distance to secure a drink, one might as well make a night of it. In the fifties cinemas found it difficult to obtain licences, on the grounds that they provided only frivolous entertainment, and by the time that attitudes relaxed the television had replaced the picture house as the staple form of entertainment. Bingo halls were likewise denounced, on the grounds that bingo was a form of gambling.

Further difficulties with the estates included no coordination with the local bus company, so there was an initial period when public transport was hard to get. Complaints were also made about the cost of travelling to work, as most of the estates tended to be sited further away from the traditional areas of employment. Also, as the estates were often added to in a piecemeal fashion, the social-services infrastructure tended to lag behind public need, so there were shortages of accessible hospitals and schools. Again, putting children on buses to travel to school added to the family outgoings.

Perhaps the biggest difference was the degree of communal upheaval. Old neighbours were missed, and the new environment of the estate introduced a greater physical distance between new ones. There was much talk of the old days, but the habits of tenement life, such as chatting to neighbours in the close, or the 'open-door' policy whereby adults and children popped in and out without so much as a knock on the door, were never quite replicated. The degree of upheaval in moving to the estates was such that the social stability of the tenements was never fully replaced.

The sheer functionality of the estates could make them grim places to live in. The standardisation of housing – basically there were only eight types used – and the perfect symmetry of their design, meant that the estates had a degree of monotony which left them bereft of character. Paving, parks, playgrounds and other breaks in the landscape came only as an afterthought. Row after row of the same type of tenement flat could fool visitors into believing they were somewhere in Eastern Europe. Indeed, Scotland had the highest proportion of state-owned housing in the democratic West. With the pursuit of quantity over quality, because governments were obsessed with meeting housing targets, many corners were cut, and what should have been a sound public investment turned out to be an expensive lame duck. Finance, rather than aesthetics, dictated policy, although the architects revelled in the opportunity to design high-rise and modernistic tower blocks. According to the *Architect's Journal*, in 1958, when asked how residents would dry their washing in a high-rise flat Sir Basil Spence, the designer of the tower blocks which were built in the slum-cleared areas of the Gorbals and Hutchestown, claimed, 'On Tuesdays, when all the washing's out, it'll be like a great ship in full sail.' Planners had full confidence that the tower blocks would be good places to live. The same *Architect's Journal*, describing the 'Hanging Garden of the Gorbals', declared that:

> For far too long the Gorbals district of Glasgow has been synony-
> mous with all that is foul in tenement living. And, until now, Scot-
> tish rehousing schemes have not been noted for making any
> striking contribution towards solving the problems of high-density
> living. This design for a 20-storey block of maisonettes in the cen-
> tre of Gorbals, is an interesting attempt by Basil Spence to develop
> further Le Corbusier's giant maisonette blocks. The large private
> balcony has been abandoned in favour of an even larger gallery gar-
> den . . . a space for some tubs of flowers, and to hang out the wash-
> ing, to give the baby an airing and to provide a garden fence to
> gossip over.

Certainly the artists' impressions of these futuristic designs looked very impressive, and the initial response of the tenants was very favourable, as mentioned before. Yet the reality of the construction of Scottish housing meant that serious problems were stored up for the future. First, because keeping costs down was the main driving force in government policy, the Scottish Office offered incentives for standardisa-tion and bulk buying. The construction companies knocked the dwellings together as quickly as they could, in the knowledge that their political paymasters were interested more in completion rates than in the finished product. Second, design took little account of the Scottish weather, and the architects' obsession for the flat roof meant that they created reservoirs for the abundant supply of rain, meaning that dampness became a common problem. Concrete may look good in drier climates, but in Scotland, because of the weather, it soon became grey and mouldy. No other material reflects so well a miserable climate. Also, cladding began to fall off as rust took its toll on the pins that supported it. Third, the workmanship was shoddy, at both the prefabrication and the assembly stage. However, so the argument went, tenants were getting houses for free, and they were expected to be grateful. That the public had a right to expect decent standards from the public sector was an unknown concept at this time, and the same types of problem plagued schools, hospitals and municipal buildings. Plumbing, heating and water supplies regularly went wrong, but were simply patched up until the next time. There was a lack of insulation, with walls that were thin and let out the heat and inadequate soundproofing that let in the noise. As houses, tenements and tower blocks settled, cracks would appear in the walls and ceilings. The widespread use of electric heating was inefficient and expensive. Ventilation was another problem, and steel window frames rusted with the build-up of condensation. A common way to tell how cold it was outside was to note the build-up of ice on the inside of the windows. Fire prevention and escape were unknown concepts, and tower blocks and tenements had minimal safety provision. The old and mothers with prams were imprisoned when the lifts failed to work. Some lifts could not accommodate stretchers or, in more extreme cases, a coffin. Evidence of the cowboy standards of workmanship are to be found in the soaring cost of housing repairs. This was £6.4 million in 1951, when much of the budget was devoted to shoring up old property. By 1961 it had risen by almost £1 million, to £7.3 million, but by 1965 it had jumped to £11 million as the flaws in building work started to come home to roost.

Although expectations may not have been high, it is no surprise that housing failed to come off the political agenda – especially when the problems associated with the new housing became apparent over time. Nor did council housing prove to be self-funding, as was originally hoped. The Labour governments of 1964 and 1966 found it necessary to appease public demand for better housing, and by 1971 a further 300,000 homes were added to the public-sector stock. In total, 85 per cent of all housing constructed between 1945 and 1968 in Scotland was in the public sector, compared to 52 per cent in England and Wales. But, as before, much of this programme was again dictated by financial considerations, and the qualitative results did not always live up to public expectations, especially when the Labour governments of the sixties ran repeatedly into major economic problems which dictated drastic public-sector cutbacks. The Tory government of the early seventies fared no better. The initial optimism of the fifties gave way in the sixties to rising expectations and demands which governments struggled to meet. The Cullingworth Report of 1967 found that, after more than twenty years of government-sponsored house-building one in every three Scots still lived in substandard housing or in accommodation that was unfit for human habitation. The report declared:

> We have found ourselves forced to use strong and emotional lan-
> guage. Some may feel that this is inappropriate for an official com-
> mittee of inquiry; but we have no hesitation in expressing ourselves
> thus. The situation in the country generally, and in Glasgow partic-
> ularly, constitutes an indictment of government policy. We place
> the blame squarely on the shoulders of central government, for
> though the local authorities have by no means come through our
> examination unscathed, the problem, especially in Glasgow, is of
> such dimensions as to place it beyond any single authority, even
> though it be the biggest authority in the country. The central gov-
> ernment have failed to provide the necessary leadership and the
> resources to encourage, assist and (in places) to compel local author-
> ities to tackle the problem which it requires.
>
> *Scotland's Older Houses* (Edinburgh, 1967)

The dominance of the public sector in Scottish housing in the post-war era throws up some uncomfortable issues. First, the accommodation built was not a good investment. Much of the housing constructed in the fifties turned out to have a life expectancy of twenty years, and much was demolished before the total interest on the loans taken out to build it had been paid. Many tenements and tower blocks sank into unlettable properties for which local government was doubly stung by having to pay for the cost of demolition. Other housing estates likewise fell into disrepair as the lack of amenities and drab con-

ditions drove many away. Furthermore, even by the late fifties, population density in the estates was actually higher than in the inner cities
as family size grew, and many houses became overcrowded. A slower
but more sustainable rate of growth, which concentrated on quality
rather than quantity, would have been a sounder long-term investment
– evidence of this is to be found in the fact that all the better-quality
houses constructed by local authorities are still standing to this day –
but Scottish politicians and local councillors baulked at the electoral
consequences. Low rents had become so much a part of political culture
that senior Scottish politicians argued against raising council rents as a
way to lower public expenditure in the late sixties on the grounds that
it would fuel excessive wage demands and lead to inflation. The obsession with meeting targets meant that the nation inherited a housing
stock that was cheap, dilapidated and in need of constant renewal and
repair, and that proved to be unsustainable. At their peak, housing subsidies accounted for 7 per cent of GDP, and they reached 12 per cent of
identifiable government expenditure by the late sixties. And it was not
only central government that bore the financial cost. Local government
paid for its share by loans, and the total amount of such debt rose from
£784 million in 1960 to £1,166 million in 1965. The interest repay-
ments on loans accounted for a sixth of local-government budgets, and
more was spent on borrowing than on housing. It was a substantial
investment, but one that was to pay limited returns.

A second issue relates to the wisdom of public subsidy. The average
Scottish household budget was not much less than that for England, yet
the Scots spent only an average of 8 per cent of their weekly outgoings on
rent, thanks to council policy. The private owner paid 25 per cent.
Whereas many in lower management, tradesmen, shopkeepers and other
self-employed workers in England would have bought their own house,
this did not happen in Scotland, and this section of society stood resolutely
in favour of council housing. If truth be told, many more Scots could have
bought their own homes, but they preferred to be subsidised by the state.
Although it can be shown that incomes were lower in Scotland, the differential was too small to account for the lower rate of home ownership compared with England. At the end of the day, council housing was a cultural
preference rather than an economic necessity for many Scots.

Furthermore, the system did not adequately address the real social issues of inequality in housing. As has been mentioned earlier, the better-off got the pick of the crop, while it was the poorer who got bundled into the substandard units. Housing operated on a step-up principle, in that people who moved to better housing left the not so good to others. For example, a family moved from a tenement to a house, leaving their old apartment for a family to move into from a tower block, which in turn let another family start on the council-housing ladder. The problem was that the step-up principle stopped when tenants secured a good home. They stayed put. Had moderate-income Scots bought their own homes, this would have freed good-quality housing stock for the less well-off.

If local-authority housing has been an investment disaster, private housing has not, and the nation has missed out on an area which has witnessed unprecedented levels of growth. The tendency to save rather than invest in private housing has meant that the nation has been poorer in the long run. Also, whereas private housing has increased in value and has not fallen into disrepair, the fact that Scotland was weak in this area meant that it took longer for the overall quality of housing to rise after the public-sector lifeline was cut in the late seventies. Scottish banks and building societies must also take their share of the blame, for they did little to promote lending. Indeed, they often used such invasive application procedures that many customers felt that the banks' managers saw themselves as doing a favour rather than providing a service. In fact, until the mid-seventies, the Scottish building societies were net exporters of capital. In housing, there never was a mixed economy, for the private sector faced major discrimination. Rates were used as a means to deter the private owner and as a way to increase still further the public subsidy for low rents. By the mid sixties private house owners paid 60 per cent of all domestic local rates, even though this group accounted for only 30 per cent of households. In 1965 Scotland's home owners were stung to the tune of £73 million – the equivalent of about £40 per household, which about matched the level of government subsidy per council house built.

Finally, the wholesale reliance on council housing may say a lot about the mentality of Scottish society. It is not indicative of a democratic ethos, in that most of the estates were planned, designed and built without any consultation with the people who were expected to live there. Indeed, the whole process is quite emblematic of the benevolent authoritarianism which characterised much of the state's dealings with the people in this period. The 'experts' knew what was best, and the public was expected to accept it with gratitude. Furthermore, the willingness to settle for a council house may indicate a lack of aspiration within Scottish society, or it may be that those who might have bought their own home emigrated (see Chapter 8). Government and politicians did little to encourage people to set their sights higher, and it may be said that the obsession with council housing was part of a wider lack of ambition which infected the Scottish nation. It also restrained mobility, in that people were reluctant to move to another area in search of work because it would mean giving up a good house and subjecting one's future to the lottery of council housing in another local authority. Secure housing may have also been another factor in promoting Scotland's high level of strike activity (see Chapter 8).

All in all, the record of housing in the period from the mid-fifties to the mid-seventies is not one of the nation's finest achievements. It shows that many of Scotland's better-off were lacking in ambition and happy to take a subsidy from the state. It demonstrates a failure to provide uniformly good housing standards, with shoddy building work (so the private sector cannot be lauded here), planning with a lack of foresight, meddlesome and authoritarian local government, and weak-willed action by politicians. And perhaps worst of all is that mismanagement during that period laid the foundations for the 'sink' estates of the eighties and nineties.

The new towns fared better than the estates. They were originally intended to accommodate the displaced population from Glasgow's housing redevelopment. By the early sixties, however, the idea of the new towns was explicitly linked with the new policy of economic growth, and it was believed that the settlements would be able to attract inward investment. The initial phase of development centred on East Kilbride (1947) to the south of Glasgow and on Glenrothes (1948) in Fife. The latter was designed to accommodate miners displaced from the exhausted Lanarkshire coalfields, who were expected to transfer to Fife. The project suffered a major setback in that the new super-colliery at Rothes turned out to be a lame duck, but the town itself maintained its validity through the idea that it could be turned into a growth centre. New settlements were also established at Cumbernauld (1956), Livingston (1962) and

Irvine (1966), and it was hoped that the five towns would eventually accommodate a total population of 372,000, though in reality the figure turned out to be 250,000. A further new town was designated at Stonehouse in 1972, but was scrapped in 1976.

The developments had a number of advantages. First, they were especially favoured in terms of government grants and incentives. Second, the new towns were run by development corporations, which meant that they were unencumbered by the need to accommodate the existing political-, economic- and social-interest groups which had to put in their twopenn'orth when it came to redevelopment elsewhere. Consequently the new towns developed with a wider range of social amenities than was the case with the housing estates. Third, the new towns were especially favoured with important transport links and sound social-infrastructure investment such as schools and hospitals. Although the developments were entirely dependent on council housing, the standard was not as bad as in some places and the towns were spared the worst of the tower blocks.

Compared to other parts of Scotland, the new towns performed better in terms of increasing new employment, largely by attracting incoming manufacturing firms, and by 1973 they accounted for 15 per cent of all the new jobs which had been created since 1968. By and large, the new factories tended to use production-line techniques and to be engaged in light mechanical and electrical engineering and instrument manufacture. Such units were also large employers of unskilled female labour. On the whole, the new towns failed to attract high-value research-and-development work, and were always subject to a high rate of business turnover since many of the factories were branch plants which would be first to face closure in any economic downturn. Like the estates, it took time for a new sense of community to develop, but, with more amenities than the city folk had left behind, this was at least possible.

THE BEGINNINGS OF THE STRANGE DEATH OF THE VICTORIAN ECONOMY

Hindsight is a problem for the historian, because it can distort the reality of the past as it was experienced by those who lived through it. So, alongside the tales of doom and gloom, it is necessary to emphasise the absolute improvements in the standard of living experienced by the majority of the population, because most people assess their situation not in relation to abstract economic criteria, nor to that of others in different societies, but on the basis of their own expectations, which are of an altogether subjective nature. In spite of inflation and rising taxation, most Scots believed that they were better off and that they were living in an era of unparalleled prosperity. If, for all that, the economy was experiencing fundamental problems, then for the majority it was up to government to fix it, and, after all, the government had done a good job so far.

The underlying problems can be defined as follows: first, there was a gap between per-capita national earnings in Scotland and those in the rest of the United Kingdom; second, wages and incomes were falling behind those in the rest of the UK, and productivity levels and competitiveness were poor, and, third, industrial relations were worsening. Finally, state intervention was increasingly being used as the principal mechanism to resolve these difficulties. What compounded these problems was that, while Scotland's performance was poor when measured against the rest of the United Kingdom, that was a period where overall British economic performance was deemed to compare badly with that of other nations. For example, using a wide range of criteria, the economy of the United Kingdom failed to keep pace with the economies of West Germany, France, Japan and the United States – all of which makes the Scottish performance even more dismal. Yet it should always be borne in mind that, while a Scot visiting West Germany or the south-east of England could not have failed to notice that both areas were much more wealthy than home, the fact remains that most Scots did not visit these places and did not know at first hand the explosion of wealth that was happening elsewhere.

The most common measure used by economists to assess the performance of an economy is its gross domestic product (GDP), which can be crudely described as what a particular nation earns, excluding income from foreign investments. Wages, salaries and the income of the self-employed are added to profits and the surplus from trade and public enterprise to work out a grand total. While it is difficult to measure this precisely, most economic historians are in agreement that from 1954 to 1965 Scotland's per capita GDP declined from 90.6 per cent to 88.4 per cent of the GDP of the United Kingdom overall, although it reached its lowest point in 1961 at 86.1 per cent. It is clear that this was a major underperformance in the economy. To put the problem another way, for the period from 1960 to 1961 the average Briton was worth £890, but the figure for the average Scot was £772. In other words, Scotland was underperforming against the UK as a whole by some 13 per cent. This figure becomes worse if Scotland and Northern Ireland are factored out of the British figure and Scotland is compared to England and Wales alone: then the difference becomes 22 per cent. In terms of growth of GDP, Scotland again underperformed relative to the rest of the UK in 1955–65, achieving only 10 per cent compared to 18 per cent.

A number of reasons can be cited for this poor performance. First, employment did not grow as fast in Scotland as in the rest of the United Kingdom, remaining virtually static at two and a third million between 1955 and 1965, whereas in the UK as a whole employment increased by over 7 per cent. Given that wages and salaries were the largest component of GDP, it is not surprising to find that Scotland was lagging behind. Second, not only was employment not growing, average weekly earnings were not growing as fast, and the Scottish figure was some 8 per cent lower than the British average by 1964.

By the early sixties, economic forecasters were beginning to realise that the boldly optimistic plans for economic diversification were failing to come to fruition. The traditional industries had thrived in an era after the war where competition from the ravaged economies of Europe and the Far East had been temporarily suspended. Coal, steel, shipbuilding and heavy engineering made up a larger proportion of the economy in 1958 than they had in the thirties, but by the late fifties they were experiencing serious problems. In 1947 it was confidently predicted that there would continue to be great demand for coal as the staple of energy production, but on nationalisation later that year it was found that half of the existing Scottish collieries, which were small in comparison to other British counterparts, were almost exhausted of reserves and many were in a poor state of repair. The planners had not reckoned on the growing importance of oil as an alternative energy source, nor had they adequately addressed the problems of exhaustion which faced the mines in Lanarkshire, which supplied most of heavy industry. The shortages of 1947, during one of the coldest winters on record, turned the steel industry towards oil as a more reliable source of energy, and in so doing denuded the coal industry of one of its key customers. Furthermore, although Scotland was slower than the rest of the United Kingdom in developing its electricity and gas industries, by the early sixties these two forms of energy had emerged as principal challengers to King Coal as a source of domestic fuel. The proportion of industrial energy needs met by coal declined from 32.5 per cent in 1955 to 15.5 per cent in 1966. A massive investment programme of £200 million in 1958 failed to produce cost-effective coal, and a brand-new colliery at Rothes in Fife failed to hit a seam. The decline of steam locomotives was another factor in limiting demand, as trains increasingly used diesel.

The Scottish mines survived by public subsidy and by government intervention which tied the expanding electricity programme to the use of coal; by 1966 the electricity industry was taking about 30 per cent of the total coal consumed. Production slumped by over 1.5 million tons between 1955 and 1965. Productivity levels were maintained only by a programme of drastic pit closures, and, whereas there were 166 collieries in 1958, after a decade this statistic had dropped to 47. In the same period consumption dropped by a quarter and was only half the amount predicted by the planners. Attempts to improve productivity by increased use of technology failed, as the number of workers on the surface was nearly double those underground. Absenteeism was a further problem, with the proportion absent at any one time rising from 12 per cent in 1958 to 16 per cent in 1965. Overall, the number employed in the industry declined from 84,700 in 1958 to 48,000 in 1965.

The extent of the coal industry's problems can be illustrated by highlighting the cost to the taxpayer in this period. Between 1955 and 1965 the National Coal Board was in deficit to the tune of £136 million in Scotland, while the UK total deficit was £146 million. To put this Scottish figure into some kind of context, it was more than the amount paid out in family allowances in Scotland. To be fair, most governments offered some type of subsidy to the coal and energy industries, yet what is striking about the Scottish case is the extent of this. Had it not been for the policy of tying the electricity industry to the supply of coal so that by the early seventies it was taking about 40 per cent of total production, the Scottish coal industry would have probably died out in the late fifties.

Steel was another sector which faced an uncertain future. Planning again came into the equation. Steel had been heavily reliant on the shipbuilding industry, and the official prognosis was that that sector of the economy was not expected to expand. The heavy plate steel which the industry produced mainly for ships was believed to have a limited future, and demand was expected to shift to lighter steel associated with the growth of the consumer industries. Furthermore, it was believed that the steel industry in Scotland needed more integration to provide better economies of scale, as much production was highly localised and small-scale. It was with this objective in mind that in 1961 the Secretary of State for Scotland, John Maclay, put pressure on the director of Colvilles, Sir Andrew McCance, to build a new steel-strip mill at Ravenscraig, near Motherwell, with a government loan of £50 million.

McCance was sceptical about the whole project, believing the planners' estimate of the future demand for steel in Scotland to be extravagant. It was thought that a new mill making light steel would act as a magnet for new consumer industry; however, as McCance pointed out, if that did not happen the new mill would be forced to sell most of its steel outside Scotland, where transport costs would put it at a competitive disadvantage. Work on the project was started in 1962, and in spite of the government's inducements to Rootes to build a car factory (later bought by Chrysler) at Linwood, outside Paisley, and to the British Motor Corporation (later British Leyland) to build a heavy-vehicle factory at Bathgate, near Livingston, demand for Ravenscraig steel was insufficient. The decision to build two mills simultaneously (the other one was sited at Llanwern in Wales) meant that there was competition for the southern market. Also, the mills being sited inland meant that access to the sea was not possible, further increasing transport costs. By 1967, when the Labour government nationalised the steel industry, the once profitable Colvilles was already reeling under bankruptcy caused by the Ravenscraig debt.

Shipbuilding perhaps best highlights the key weakness of the Scottish economy in this period. As was mentioned in the previous chapter, wartime planners believed that shipbuilding was a dying industry. Immediate post-war demand was high and the industry was buoyant, but there was still a reluctance to accept that the omens for the industry were anything but poor. It was believed that, once wartime damage had been replaced, the world's fleet would remain much as it had been. However, a number of factors would change all that. First, as the global economy picked up and consumerism hit the western world, the demand for ships continued to increase. Second, the use of oil as the main source of energy in the western economy meant that there would be an almost insatiable demand for the massive beasts of burden needed to carry it. On both counts, the shipbuilding industry failed to adapt to meet change. Although Scottish shipbuilding output remained fairly constant in the period from 1955 to 1965 at between 400,000 and 500,000 gross tons per annum, Scotland's position as one of the world's key centres of the industry declined rapidly. In 1950 the Clyde launched a third of the world's shipping tonnage; by 1960 this had declined to 5 per cent, and by 1970 it was less than 2 per cent. Far from going into decline, the construction of shipping in the world increased by about a third in the fifties, doubled in the sixties, and increased by another third up to 1976, after which it dropped back to the level of the late sixties by the end of the decade. Overall, from 1945 to 1975 the world's output of shipping increased tenfold. This was clearly not an industry in decline. The planners had got it wrong.

The Scottish shipbuilding industry during this period was constrained by a number of features. There was a major shortage of steel plates, which local suppliers struggled to meet, being dependent on imported scrap and coking coal that was in short supply. As was mentioned above, the government's obsession with producing light steel did the shipbuilding industry no favours. Also, in an industry which in the past had been renowned for its technological innovation and expertise, Scottish shipbuilders were painfully slow in adapting to the new circumstances of the post-war era. Indeed, their types of construction, the methods used, and the management and labour approaches had changed little since the thirties. New techniques of prefabrication, the use of welding instead of riveting, and the reorganisation of yards to accommodate large vessels such as oil tankers never happened. There was a failure of vision as the yards stuck to tried and tested methods. The development of prefabrication elsewhere in the world rendered much of the skill of the labour force redundant, but the fact that there were fifteen separate trade unions which jealously guarded lines of demarcation meant that new techniques of production would be impossible to implement on the Clyde. The Scottish builders were small-scale, and there was simply not enough space in the cluttered yards, nor any deep-water sites, to meet the growing demand for tankers and bulk carriers. Elsewhere in the world, government intervention was used to help with modernisation, capitalisation and expansion through the use of tax relief, low-interest loans and easy credit facilities, as well as direct subsidies. By the mid-sixties yards were facing competition from well-structured, heavily capitalised and efficient shipbuilders in Germany, the United States, Japan and Scandinavia.

The reputation of Scottish yards also suffered as they operated a costs-plus-profits pricing regime which meant that a customer never knew what the final price would be. This system had the further disadvantage that there was no incentive for early completion or even completion on time, and orders often piled up, causing delays. The rest of the world moved to a system of fixed prices, and even managed to deliver early. Short-sightedness dominated the management view. There were no efforts to raise capital for a process of modernisation, as in the short-term this would mean lost orders due to reorganisation. There was a reluctance to hire experts in marketing or management, so as not to compromise family control. Instead, the tendency was to exploit the position of advantage which the Scottish shipbuilders had inherited from a war-ravaged world economy and milk it for all it was worth. When international competition arrived, in the early and mid-sixties, its ferocity took the shipyards by surprise. A process of modernisation and reorganisation was begun too late. By 1963 William Denny of Dumbarton had gone into liquidation and Harland & Wolff had closed down its Govan yard. Others soon followed the path to closure and bankruptcy, and by 1965 the Fairfields yard was facing a major crisis which forced the government to issue a loan of £1 million to solve the immediate financial crisis.

In the meantime, the Geddes Committee was appointed to examine the industry and recommend proposals for its future. The committee's conclusions were scathing, and both management and the unions were blasted. The industry suffered from endemic short-sightedness; it had poor management and bad relations with workers; it paid insufficient attention to customers, and too often had unreliable suppliers. Furthermore, it did not use its resources well, and design, planning and marketing would have to be improved if the industry were not to collapse. The government stepped in. Yards would be grouped together to create economies of scale, the Shipbuilding Industry Board would provide greater coordination and cohesion, and there would be grants and loans for the purpose of modernisation.

The late sixties witnessed a series of mergers. Scotts and Lithgows on the Clyde amalgamated in 1967; Fairfields, John Brown's, Charles Connell's, Yarrow's and Stephen's came together to form Upper Clyde Shipbuilders in 1968; and on the east coast Henry Robb and the Caledon Shipbuilding Co. merged to form the imaginatively named Robb Caledon. However, the grants and loans which were available for modernisation and investment were used instead to meet contract losses. Rising inflation, increasing wage demands and overly optimistic tendering for contracts meant that most ships were built at a whopping loss, including the *QE2*. Between 1967 and 1972 the industry swallowed £160 million of government funds for a workforce of no more than 50,000, which, crudely put, meant that public funds paid for more than half the wage bill of the shipping industry during these years. The tales of management incompetence were legendary: when Upper Clyde Shipbuilders went into liquidation in 1971 (see Chapter 9), the financial inspectors could find no audited and approved accounts after August 1968. The industry limped from crisis to crisis in the late sixties and early seventies until, not surprisingly, government patience with lame ducks ran out.

In the cacophony of post-war industrial decline, the voices of textiles and engineering tended not to be heard as loudly as those of coal, steel and shipbuilding, even though, with 266,000 workers, textiles and engineering employed 20,000 more than the combined total for coal, steel and shipbuilding in 1955. Between 1955 and 1965 the number employed in textiles dropped by 18 per cent, from 120,000 to 98,000. Output was sluggish, with little change over the period. Engineering, the other vital component of the traditional sector, also had its problems, but did not fare as badly as coal, steel and shipbuilding. Sales of engineering and electrical goods rose by 47 per cent from £236 million in 1958 to £348 million in 1965. The proportion of export sales remained constant at 30 per cent. The workforce rose from 146,000 to 177,000. On the whole, it would appear that this sector of the economy was in reasonable health – compared to its traditional bedfellows at least. Sales of non-electrical machinery, such as contractors' plant, agricultural machinery, refrigeration, compressors, and industrial pumps and valves, rose by a quarter between 1960 and 1965, while industrial-plant sales rose by slightly more than that. The fledgling electrical sector did best of all with sales up by almost 40 per cent, although these represented only 1.2 per cent of the value for engineering overall. Over all, engineering had a good performance, but the fact remains that it was the traditional areas which shored it up.

All in all, it was apparent that the Scottish economy was failing to modernise. The traditional sectors – or what might be termed 'contracting' sectors, agriculture, mining, metals, shipbuilding, textiles, transport and distribution – were shedding labour at an alarming rate, and between 1954 and 1967 had lost 188,000 jobs. To offset this there was the new or 'expanding' sector of the economy – food and drink, electrical engineering, construction, insurance and banking, the professions and public administration – which had created 162,000 new jobs in the same period, a shortfall of 26,000. Given that the contracting sector was a larger part of the economy and the expanding sector was smaller, the objective was to match the rate of expansion to the rate of contraction to ensure that there was minimum disruption.

As can be seen from the above, it is clear that the area which was expanding was heavily reliant on government intervention. Construction, which was heavily dependent on the public purse, and government service accounted for almost a third of new jobs in the expanding sector. Furthermore, government intervention was responsible for shoring up the ailing steel, coal and shipbuilding industries, at enormous expense. In 1960 the percentage of the workforce employed in manufacturing was 31 per cent in Scotland, compared with 35 per cent in the United Kingdom as a whole.

It was in response to these problems that a committee of inquiry into the Scottish Economy was established under the chairmanship of J. N. Toothill in 1960. It identified the following problems, in order of importance. First, Scottish unemployment between 1948 and 1960 had been twice the British average, at 3.1 per cent. Although this was not necessarily severe, the possibility that the traditional industries might become vulnerable held the prospect that the jobless total could increase. Second, and following on from the first problem, the rate of growth in both pro-

duction and the labour force was too slow. Third, it was believed that population increase would mean a greater demand for jobs in the future, and
this demand had to be met. Fourth, although there had been some successes, diversification had not gone far enough and there was still a defi-
ciency in science-based industry and in the production of consumer goods.
The report recommended that the way to solve these difficulties was to
promote faster economic growth, rather than shore up the old industries.
If growth could be achieved it would drain away labour from the older
industries, leading to a more balanced and vibrant economy.

The report embodied a different approach from the planning models
of the war. Whereas it had been believed that there was too much concentration in the western central belt of industry and that new types of industry had to be brought in, the report switched focus to the more ambiguous
concept of growth points, believing it not too important where they were
established, as long as there were such points. Rather than focusing on
remedial action, the report recommended that the best way to deal with
unemployment was not to focus on areas with a concentration of the jobless, but to promote growth where it had the best prospects. This policy,
it was believed, would be more sustainable in the long run than palliatives
for unemployment. Much of this thinking was clearly influenced by the
spectacular rate of growth achieved in West Germany. The report also
drew attention to the importance of transport and infrastructure, believing that they offered good incentives for inward investment. Put bluntly,
the attitude was that it was better to focus on spreading wealth, rather
than on containing poverty. A list was compiled of the industries which
had demonstrated most growth in the UK economy, and their performance was compared with that in Scotland. In the category which had
grown by more than 50 per cent in terms of numbers employed, UK
employment had increased by 323,000, while in Scotland the increase was
only 16,000. For those industries which had seen employment increase by
between 30 and 50 per cent the UK increase was 155,000, while that of
Scotland was 12,000. The increases for 20 to 30 per cent growth were
240,00 for the UK and 12,000 for Scotland. Had Scottish growth in these
sectors kept pace with the UK rate it would have meant an additional
53,500 jobs. Furthermore, comparison of Scottish and UK figures for
industries which were contracting shows that those which shrunk by

10 per cent shed 101,000 jobs in the United Kingdom, but 21,000 in Scotland. Industries which declined between 10 and 20 per cent lost 122,000 UK jobs and 16,000 Scottish jobs, and those that contracted by more than 20 per cent lost 307,000 UK jobs and 26,000 Scottish jobs. Had Scotland's industries contracted in proportion to those in the UK overall, it would have lost 10,000 fewer jobs. Had Scotland kept pace with UK trends, the fewer lost jobs and more new jobs would have provided an additional 3 per cent growth to the labour force. Growth to create new employment was heralded as the way forward.

INTERVENTION

Yet, as we have seen, policy in the sixties did not abandon the traditional industries, and, in spite of the emphasis on growth, decline figured as much in the minds of politicians. As was stated earlier, the trick was to stimulate the pace of growth so that it overtook or at least kept up with that of decline. As was the case with coal, steel and shipbuilding, government spent huge sums in staving off decline at the expense of growth. In part, the reason for the mixed bag of economic fortune in this period is to be found in the simple, brutal fact that politicians cannot divorce policy from accountability to the electorate. The idea behind corporatism was that the trade unions, business leaders and politicians would work together to ensure that the economy was bringing benefits to all. A prosperous economy would mean well-paid workers, satisfied businessmen and a grateful electorate. But each of the three groups had its own agenda and its own interests, and more often than not corporatism produced not well-balanced plans, but compromises designed to pander to the aspirations of particular groups. The trade-union movement was strongest in the decaying industries, and naturally its key objective was to secure employment and provide high wages. More often than not the interests of trade unions and those of economic policy could not be married together, because the objective of the latter was to create growth in industries which had little union representation in Scotland. Similarly, the objective of the business community was to maintain profits, but, given the unprofitability of many industries, this could be done only with government support. The problem was that the business community in Scotland mainly represented the traditional sector, but government policy was to encourage the new, and the leaders of the traditional industries were loth to see subsidies and funding go to incomers. Government policy was about the future, but the electorate measured government success in the here and now. Rising unemployment and strikes were condemned as a failure not so much of management and unions, but of government responsibility. The quick fix became a hallmark of government intervention, which had to do more with party-political and electoral decisions than with economic policy.

At the end of the day, government, of whatever political complexion, carried the can. Try as it might, there was no use blaming irresponsible workers or inefficient managers for economic failure. It was the role of the government to fix things, and it was upon this criterion that governments were judged. In part, the politicians had only themselves to blame for this state of affairs, because each party actively encouraged the electorate to think that it could remedy all social and economic problems. When a government failed, the electorate took its revenge.

Politicians were also not averse to using economic policy for their own selfish purposes, which had little to do with investment for the future and everything to do with creating a congenial climate at election times. The 'stop–go' policy of the fifties was a classic case in point. Applied at a UK level, in the run-up to a general election taxes would be cut and public expenditure would be increased to create an environment of rising wages, increased spending power and full employment. This was the 'go' part of the policy. The electorate was led to believe that economic policy was paying dividends, and in gratitude it elected the government for another term. The effect of this policy, however, was to create a huge balance-of-payments deficit, increase inflation, and plunge the country into the red. Safely elected, therefore, the government would increase taxes and cut public expenditure to bring the books into balance. This was the 'stop' part of the policy.

The Tory governments from 1951 to 1964 shamelessly used this device for electoral advantage. If we examine the figures for Pay As You Earn (PAYE) – in other words, income tax from wages and salaries collected in Scotland – we see that the total remained fairly constant in the returns for the years 1954 to 1955, a general-election year. The amount

collected increased by no more than 6 per cent – although this was effectively a tax cut, because wages were increasing by more than that. After
the election was over, it rose by over 20 per cent in 1956 and a further 13
per cent in 1957. In 1958 it increased only marginally, and in the magic
year of 1959, when there was an election, it actually dropped, and this was
a more significant tax cut because of inflation. When the brakes were
applied in 1960, the PAYE returns increased by 17 per cent, and they continued to increase until 1963, when, in preparation for the election in
1964, tax was cut and the amount collected fell marginally. A major problem for the Conservative government was that it miscalculated and started
the boom rather early, which led to significant problems during the election. This could be described as a form of economic premature ejaculation,
and the 'go' period proved unsustainable. It was left to the incoming
Labour government to hike up tax to balance the books, and in 1964–5
the PAYE total increased by 20 per cent. Likewise, an examination of
expenditure on social services shows that peaks in spending coincided
with election years, which were then followed by slower rates of growth.

There are a number of points to make about this policy. First, it
lacked any degree of sustainability, and, whereas the successful economies
in the world had fast but steady growth, the British economy was subject
to these fluctuations. Second, political expediency was used to override
economic criteria, which helped to create a sort of boom-and-bust cycle
that did not help business confidence. Inflationary spirals, balance-of-payments crises and budget deficits would become routine events in the economic cycle. Third, it tied economic expectation very closely to the
political parties, and electoral success was determined not so much by
sound stewardship of the economy as by successful manipulation of the
economy (see below). While these were problems associated with the
entire British economy in the fifties and sixties, the effect in Scotland was
much greater because, as we have seen, government policy and intervention had much more of an impact there. Whatever the wisdom of state
intervention in economic policy may be, state intervention which stopped
and started was definitely not good.

While few would dispute that economic policy totally divorced from
politics is as undesirable as it is unachievable, the major problem in Scottish
political circles was the tendency to use state intervention for short-term

political objectives: in short, either to make the government more popular or to stop it becoming unpopular. While the Conservatives had displayed considerable flair in managing the British economy to maximum electoral effect in the elections between 1955 and 1964, their record in Scotland was not as good. Pit closures and the limited impact of Ravenscraig, Linwood and Bathgate were challenged by Labour as being evidence of an unambitious strategy for economic growth. Also, after the high point of house construction in the mid-fifties, the number completed began to fall, and Labour was able to present this too as a lack of ambition on the part of the Conservative government. Scotland's unemployment rate was twice that of England, and the absolute figure crossed the psychologically significant 100,000 mark in 1963, much to the Tory Party's discomfort.

While many Conservative voters may have been disgruntled with some of the party's policies on housing and rates, which saw the private home owner subsidising council housing through what was essentially a property tax, the major shift in political allegiance would appear to be that elements of the skilled working-class thought their prospects would be better with Labour. Whereas the early fifties were characterised by a sense of optimism and increasing prosperity, by the beginning of the sixties this feeling had run its course. There may have also been an element of being tired of the Tories, and a belief that a change was as good as a rest. Certainly the party's reports from the constituencies reveal that membership was declining and that the organisational structure was no longer in as good a shape as it had once been. Many of the Scottish skilled working class belonged to trade unions which negotiated wages at a UK level, and, as has been pointed out earlier, steel, ship and engineering workers were comparatively highly paid. The success of the unions at a UK level may have inclined their members' sympathies towards Labour. In any case the swing required to effect political change was small.

In the general election of 1959 the Tory vote in Scotland held up well at 47.2 per cent, which was slightly larger than Labour's 46.7 per cent. The main shift came in the number of MPs elected, with the Conservatives dropping from 36 seats to 31, while Labour increased its tally from 34 to 38. The vagaries of the first-past-the-post system worked to the advantage of Labour, and the party was able to gain Central Ayrshire, Lanark and the Glasgow seats of Craigton and Scotstoun – all constituencies with a significant industrial population, which appeared to be consolidating its support for Labour. The Tories captured the more middle-class Kelvingrove in Glasgow, only to lose it in 1964. The swing towards Labour continued in the 1964 and 1966 elections, with the party's share of the Scottish vote going up to 48.7 and 49.9 per cent, respectively, adding a further five and three seats to Labour's Scottish parliamentary total. The Conservatives declined quite significantly to first 40.6 and then 37.7 per cent of the vote, and lost first six then four seats. The Liberals had something of a comeback, winning one seat in 1959, four in 1964 and five in 1966, with their share of the vote rising from 4.1 to 6.8 per cent.

The reason for the limited Liberal comeback was that the party, under the local leadership of the energetic and charismatic John Bannerman, was able to carve out a niche for itself in the countryside. The Beeching rail cuts of the early sixties had an adverse effect on rural communities, and by 1965 the length of track in Scotland was cut by a fifth, which was about 1,500 miles. The number of trains fell by about half between 1960 and 1965, to just over 1,000. It was the small towns that bore the brunt of these cuts, and in the north and the borders, where the alternative transport of roads was not as efficient as it was in the central areas, the Liberals emerged to champion their cause. Also, the farming community had its own difficulties and fears about levels of subsidies and a declining workforce were picked up by the Liberals (see Chapter 8).

Yet it was Labour that emerged as the party of Scotland. Again, much of the reason for its success is to be explained at a British level, although specific Scottish factors were also important. Under the leadership of the young and dynamic Harold Wilson from 1963, the party was able to present itself as representing the future, whereas the Tories were saddled with the somewhat tweedy and old-fashioned Sir Alec Douglas-Home (pronounced 'Hume'). Within Scotland the Conservatives had an even more old-fashioned image than the party south of the border, with a large element of their MPs drawn from the landowning class. The general election of 1964 was the first to be conducted through the medium of television, and Labour was much more adept at exploiting this. Wilson was comfortable in front of the camera, whereas Douglas-Home's eyes wandered about shiftily in front of this newfangled machine. But it was the promise of the 'white heat of technology' which arguably did most to impress the Scots that the future lay with Labour. Intervention to modernise and improve the economy from a government that was committed to a hands-on approach was likely to attract much enthusiasm north of the border. The house-building programme was slowing down, and the public wanted it speeded up. The orders for industry were drying up, and people wanted more work and higher wages. Better schools, hospitals and social infrastructure were part of Labour policy, and these would provide work for the construction industry.

Labour appeared to be on track in Scotland, and the party's improved performance in 1964 was especially significant in that the overall Labour majority in the House of Commons was only four, but the Scottish party had returned an extra five MPs. This fact was not lost on the new Secretary of State for Scotland, Willie Ross, who skilfully played on the prospect that a failure of government policy in Scotland could lose Labour its majority. Even though the general election in 1966 returned a clear majority for Labour, Ross was still adept at promoting Scotland as vital to Labour's electoral future, on the grounds that the party was proportionately more successful north of the border. Labour's more interventionist strategy was soon evident. Investment in public housing increased by more than 60 per cent, while identifiable government expenditure in Scotland increased by 17 per cent between 1963 and 1966. Ross was energetic in putting forward the case for greater public expenditure in Scotland, and by the late sixties this was running at a fifth higher than the UK average.

The main thrust of policy in Scotland was that intervention would be used to bring about the transition from an economy overdependent on heavy industry to one which was transformed by the growth of new light industry. A series of measures was introduced to pave the way for this metamorphosis. The development areas were constantly extended, so that by the seventies the Edinburgh conurbation was the only part of Scotland not covered. In these areas the government offered incentives to investment by way of grants and tax allowances. In 1966 grants were made available for 40 per cent of investment in plant and machinery and 25 to 35 per cent of investment in buildings. This policy was designed to attract inward investment from companies overseas or in other parts of the United Kingdom – especially those industries associated with the production of consumer goods. In 1967 wage subsidies were introduced for manufacturing industry in the development areas, to help with competitiveness. The Scottish Office was reorganised with a new section, the Scottish Development Department, which was given the task of coordinating economic planning and infrastructure. In 1965 the Highlands and Islands Development Board was established to ferment growth in the north (see Chapter 8).

An ambitious project of investment in infrastructure, it was believed, would help in this period of transition. First, it would create employment in the construction industry, as workers would be needed to build houses, schools, hospitals, roads and government offices. This, it was hoped, would offset the seepage of workers from the declining traditional industries. Good houses, schools and hospitals would then help create an environment which would prove attractive to companies looking to invest in Scotland. The maintenance of full employment would create a buoyant market, which would act as a further incentive for industry to settle in Scotland: people with full wage packets make good customers. Also, an effective system of transport was considered essential for growth. In the mid-sixties work began on road bridges across the Forth, Tay and Clyde rivers which would open up areas to wider markets. An ambitious motorway system was created to link Glasgow and Edinburgh and to provide access to the markets of the south. The city of Glasgow got a new airport.

The net effect of the policy of growth was that, in terms of economic indicators, Scotland began to close the gap which had opened with the rest of the United Kingdom in the early sixties. Unemployment, although higher, did not maintain its traditional ratio of being twice the UK average. In terms of growth in productivity, not only was the decline reversed, but Scottish performance began to pull ahead of the UK average by 1969. The per-capita GDP of Scotland likewise told an impressive story, and by the end of the decade had climbed from 87 per cent of the UK average to 91 per cent. The gap in earnings had also diminished, with the Scots achieving parity by 1973.

Impressive though these figures are, however, they mask one crucial factor. Growth and prosperity were increasingly dependent on government intervention, which in the beginning had had the limited objective of setting the economy on the right tracks and leaving momentum to do the rest. This was not enough, and intervention ceased to be a means of guiding the economy and became more a means of propelling it.

EIGHT

GENERATIONS, 1966–1976

A nighean a' chùil bhuidhe, throm-bhuidh, òr-bhuidh,
fonn do bheòil-sa 's gaoir na h-Eòrpa,
a nighean gheal chasurlach aighearach bhòidheach,
cha bhiodh masladh ar latha-ne searbh 'nad phòig-sa.

An tugadh t'fhonn no't àilleachd ghlòrmhor
Bhuamsa gràinealachd mharbh nan dòigh seo,
A' bhrùid 's am meàirleach air ceann na h-Eòrpa
's do bhial-sa uaill-dhearg 's an t-seann òran?

An tugadh corp geal is clàr gréine
Bhuamsa cealgaireachd dhubh na bréine,
Nimh bhùirdeasach is puinnsean créide
Is dìblidheasach ar n-Alba éitigh?

(Girl of the yellow, heavy-yellow, gold-yellow hair,
the song of your mouth and Europe's shivering cry,
fair, heavy-haired, spirited, beautiful girl,
the disgrace of our day would not be bitter in your kiss.

Would your song and splendid beauty

Take from me the dead loathsomeness of these ways,
The brute and brigand at the head of Europe
And your mouth proud and red with the old song?

Would white body and forehead's sun
Take from me the foul black treachery,
Spite of the bourgeois and poison of their creed
And the feebleness of our dismal Scotland?)

Sorely Maclean, 'The Cry of Europe', from *Dàin do Eimhir*

(Edinburgh, 1944)

After fifteen months – as suddenly as they began – all operations in the island ceased ... Evacuation began within a week, and proceeded with smooth efficiency. The engineers and consultants left first by helicopters; then the office staff, on the *Skua* to Kirkwall, bearing files and charts and blueprints; then the labourers, gang after gang of them, on the cargo boats to Aberdeen and Leith, sharing the space with cattle and eggs and Hogsheads of whisky, the exports of Orkney. A month later a government ship called at the enlarged pier of Greenvoe and took away the heavy stuff – lorries, bulldozers, cement mixers, transformers, cranes, fire-engines. The huge radii of tunnels into Korsfea and the Knapp and Ernefea petered out, a black blasted star. The HQ complex itself, facing the west, remained a truncated battlement. (Every material of man grows at last mellow and beautiful, except concrete – as the years passed the site stared out of the heather like scabs of blindness. A concrete foundation is never sweetened by weeds and grass. It looks hot and hurt in sunlight; it resents the gentle or resounding kisses of the rain.) The watchmen abandoned the gates. The camp, a score of wooden huts of various sizes, was left to warp and wither. The three telephones in the office were dumb and deaf. In the canteen a dartboard fell from the wall. Dust sifted into piles of crockery in the cookhouse. The covers of a hymn book in the community hall began to curl. The rats and the birds and the spiders returned delicately and secretly. Grass sprouted through the floorboards ... In the spring another invasion took place, but this was only a small temporary holding operation ... NO ADMITTANCE notices appeared at four hundred-yard intervals ... The last labourer shouldered his pick and departed. The only people left were the dead in the kirkyard. The disturbed dust settled on a seedless island.

George Mackay Brown, *Greenvoe* (London, 1972)

It must be recognised and emphasised that there is a clear distinction between those who have homosexual propensities and those who indulge in homosexual acts. No sin or shame is involved in the former case. Indeed, amongst those who are homosexual by constitution are to be found men who render most valuable and unselfish service to the community and the Church, and men who make a distinctive contribution in the sphere of literature and the arts. As regards those who engage in immoral sexual practices, their behaviour in light of Christian teaching is sinful, and everything possible must be done to win them from wrong ways and redeem them from wrong desires. Like the sins of heterosexual immorality they must incur the condemnation of the Church ... the evil of prostitution cannot be abated except by uncompromising condemnation by all Christian people of the low standards in sexual relationships which are the root cause of this shameful traffic. Christians cannot regard prostitution as being a unique thing, but only as one very lamentable outcome of low standards of sex morality ... By the Christian standard, there is no absolute demarcation between the guilt of men and women who engage in prostitution and those who indulge in any kind of immoral sex relationship. It is therefore indubitable that what the Church must endeavour to combat is not only prostitution itself, but everything which denies the Christian concept of the sex impulse as a holy stewardship entrusted to men and women by God and the integrity of every man and woman as a child of God.

Church of Scotland, *Reports to the General Assembly, with the Legislative Acts* (Edinburgh, 1958)

YOUTH

Scotland was a consumer, rather than a producer, of global youth culture. The fashions and trends which affected British society arrived in Scotland and made their mark. Teddy boys appeared in the fifties, and were more likely to hang around street corners than in cafés. Gang culture never lost its grip on the youth of Scotland, with some groups, especially in Glasgow, claiming to have a heritage that stretched back to the thirties. The names of the gangs and their style of dress might have changed, but their modus operandi and mentality remained much the same. The correlation with deprivation also remained the same, with those gangs closest to the city centre being most associated with delinquency and crime. In more affluent areas and in the small towns and villages, youngsters were more inclined to hang together and look tough by chewing gum and smoking fags. More often than not, the main problem related to boredom, especially in the large new housing estates, where a lack of amenities meant that there was nothing to do. Indeed, youngsters often returned of a night to old habitats to hang around with friends.

Most young men were either apprentices or in low-paid menial work which contributed to a sense of frustration. They took their cue from the images of disaffected youth which appeared in the cinema and on television. An apprentice was expected to serve seven years' time before having the chance of earning a decent wage, and in the meantime he might be expected to carry out the bulk of the menial tasks, as well as being the butt of jokes. Work in heavy industry was very hierarchical, with every man accorded his place. The apprentice was at the bottom of the ladder, so the alternative social structure of the gang was a welcome relief. Those not fortunate enough to have an apprenticeship would be forced to take on some form of manual labour or else work in a shop or office. The same rigours of hierarchy applied, with the young being compelled to make tea and run errands, and given no responsibility and the bulk of undesirable tasks. In the working life of Scotland, the young were there to be exploited and to do the jobs that nobody wanted to do. Elders expected to be treated with respect, but were not forthcoming in giving it back. Much of what happened was simply unfair.

Things were no better at home. A strict family hierarchy brooked no nonsense. Young men and women handed over their wage packets or were compelled to pay for lodgings, being left with little for themselves. If father and son got on; all was well, if not, it would lead to serious altercations with threats of eviction, but the statutory 'not under my roof' was often enough to ensure obedience. The closeted atmosphere of the home was not made any better by the tendency for sons to follow fathers into the same line of work, often in the same place. Dependency was dragged out until the early twenties in many Scottish homes, and for both men and women marriage was the only escape. Meanwhile, sneaking out into an alternative peer-group social structure was a welcome relief.

The term 'generation gap' is widely used to convey a difference between the young and the old, but in the Scotland of the sixties and seventies that gap was as much psychological as anything else. Until it was dropped in the early sixties, most adult men had had experience of national service. Many had seen active service during the Second World War and in Korea. Others had had experience of the problems of Palestine, or had been part of the occupation of Germany. Most had grown up during the hungry times of the thirties, and knew first hand the reality of material deprivation. Their working environment was brutal, hard and uncompromisingly masculine. For example, social investigators found that there was a greater tendency for single men to do overtime than those who were married with large families to support. The reason married workers gave for this situation shocked and depressed their middle-class inquisitors. A working man was expected to give his family an allowance and keep the rest for himself, but overtime would mean that either he would keep the extra, which would trouble his conscience, or he would have to hand it over. At the end of the day, as he was unlikely to see any of the money, the response was, Why bother?

The culture of the Scottish workplace was strewn with sexist assumptions. Women were there to do the light work and to make cups of tea. The humour was brutal, hard and cynical, and attractiveness was regarded as the principal female merit. Ageism was successfully integrated into sexism. Women were either 'honnies', 'smashers', 'cuties' or 'dolly birds', who tended to be young, or 'boilers', 'battleaxes', 'boots', 'hags' or 'nags', who tended to be older. Whereas it was considered acceptable to whistle at and admire young women in short skirts and assail them with unwelcome 'compliments' in public, different attitudes prevailed at home. Many fathers monitored and enforced a dress code for wives and daughters to ensure that they would not go out looking like 'whores' or 'sluts'. Some even objected to make-up.

Machismo and sexism went hand in hand (an inappropriate metaphor). They were reinforced in the workplace, which reinforced them at home. Scottish men were caught in a spiralling vortex of manness that women had to put up with it. Yet not all women were passive, and a number of families were subject to matriarchal control in which 'Maw' wore the trousers. Where men proved unequal to the task of exerting authority in the home, women stepped into the breech, or breeches, and family discipline was usually the prerogative of the mother. The *Sunday Post*'s presentation of everyday life in its cartoon strip 'The Broons' was a fairly accurate depiction of the strong mother who exerted authority over all the family. Its comedy lay in Paw Broon being not only smaller than Maw Broon, but also subject to her will.

For those born after the Second World War, the world was very different from that known by their parents. There was more money, things always seemed to be improving, and technology was advancing at an incredible rate. Grinding poverty, long-term unemployment and the worst of the housing conditions were unknown to a generation that always wanted more. The normal aspiration for a car, a house with three rooms, and a full and increasing pay packet was taken for granted. How different the world seemed to an older generation which had witnessed much hardship! By the mid-sixties, Scotland's pensioner population reached over half a million. The novelist William McIlvanney reflected on the experience of the previous generation when he wrote in 1970:

> Basically now my reactions to that past were twofold: admiration, for people like my parents who had survived whole in conditions of astonishing injustice; and a sense of wanton wastage of the lives of so many others whom poverty, exploitation and social indifference had destroyed. I felt a need at least to understand that wastage, and if possible to see what had been or could be salvaged from it. My father's situation may illustrate what I mean. In a poem I have written about him I suggested that the General Strike of 1926 was for him what Midian was for Moses. He was a miner at the time and

the pain of that cataclysmic event never fully left him.

Karl Miller, ed., *Memoirs of a Modern Scotland* (London, 1970)

For many on both sides, however, the generation gap was unbridgeable. Obdurate attitudes across the divide prevented reconciliation, as one side whined about how hard life had been, while the other, in complacent expectation, took all that life was prepared to give. It was a common complaint that the young could not appreciate things and that the old could not understand the modern world. The older generation found the concept of credit or borrowing difficult, and believed that what you did not have you should not spend. For them, saving was the only means to acquire material possessions. The young, on the other hand, took to credit easily, and when they got themselves into trouble they could always rely on a generation which was used to saving and keeping something by for a rainy day. Social mobility was another bridge that many found hard to cross. A son or daughter who went to university was either a source of unmitigated pride or an awkward fact that had to be explained away. Often the mother held the former opinion, while the father held the latter. Working-class male culture in Scotland held that any man who did not work with his hands was a poof, a skiver, a snob, an upstart or any combination of the four. Some Scottish men were sensitive, but it was best to keep this trait hidden.

Youth culture certainly raised many hackles. Moral panic was a feature of the time. The young seemed increasingly discourteous, selfish and lacking in respect. Gang warfare was a source of concern, as were youth crime and increasing acts of violence. The numbers held in borstals (jails for the under-sixteens) increased by almost 50 per cent between 1960 and 1965, while crimes of violence went up by a third and the murder rate doubled during the sixties. An increasingly hysterical media blamed the young for this state of affairs. Though the increases looked bad, the statistical reality was that the average Scot had a 1 in 125,000 chance of being murdered in 1970.

As ever, much of youth crime was heavily localised, with the worse cases reserved for the sprawling housing estates of Glasgow. Most acts of violence tended to be directed towards other members of gangs and did not affect the general population. As gang members got older in the seventies, some branched out into racketeering, robbery and mainstream crime, with increasing use of razors and knives as symbols of power. The seventies was the era of the 'hardman', in which reputation counted for everything and the best way to establish one was to take on someone with a pedigree. It was a culture of violence that fed on itself. The fact that youngsters tended to hang around on street corners in most small towns and villages led many to conclude that they must be up to the same sort of mischief as was happening in the worst places. Looking and acting hard tended to compose the majority of their activities. Nevertheless, the nation's elders expressed concern that the youth of today had gone to rack and ruin. This impression was reinforced by widespread media coverage in the tabloids and, on occasion, on television. Glasgow became notorious. In the early seventies, for example, the TV programme *Nationwide* showed Glaswegian thugs boasting of their sword fights and nihilistic attitudes towards violence. However, some of the sheen was taken off their exploits by the need to subtitle their comments into English so that the audience south of the border – and, for that matter, in other parts of Scotland – could understand what was being said.

The increasing crime statistics seemed to back up tales of young people being out of control. Yet, for all the sense of moral panic, it has to be remembered that the figures were still quite low, and the impression of Scotland becoming a more violent society was one that was largely media-generated. However, it should also be pointed out that many of the acts of gang violence went unreported, as 'grassing' to the police went against gang ethics. In small-town Scotland, most of the fights tended to take place on disused ground far from prying eyes, with graveyards a particularly favoured venue.

Scotland experienced a toned-down version of the main waves of global youth culture. Mods, rockers, hippies and punks tended to be in short supply north of the border. The changing face of music and fashion made its impact, however, and Scotland's youth adopted beehives and mop-tops, wore miniskirts and tight suits, and listened to Elvis, the Beatles, the Stones and whoever else was internationally important in pop music at the time. Although a number of Scots contributed to this development in the sixties, such as Lulu, Donovan, Iain Anderson, Jack Bruce and Alex Harvey, they did so mostly as exiles, as the music scene at home was always a preparation for the big-city lights of London. Most of the big bands came north on tour, and the youth of Scotland turned out in droves to see them. Each of the cities had its venues: the Caird Hall in Dundee, the Usher Hall and the Playhouse in Edinburgh, the Capital Cinema in Aberdeen, and in Glasgow the Apollo Theatre and the Barrowlands. Up to the mid-sixties, before the advent of the big-stage production tour, smaller towns could also grab a piece of the action, and Jerry Lee Lewis, for example, shook, rattled and rolled the Doby Hall in the small Stirling-shire town of Larbert. In the seventies, the Scottish contribution to the music scene included the Average White Band from Grangemouth, Dun-fermline's Nazareth, Glasgow's Frankie Miller Band and Steelers Wheel, and, most famous of all, the Bay City Rollers from Fife, who unleashed a wave of tartan-clad teenage, female hysteria upon an unsuspecting world.

Money was a vital element in the development of youth identity and culture, which became progressively more expensive as time wore on. Buying the latest fashions and records was an essential part of being in with the in-crowd, and modes of dress were an immediate way of differen-tiating the young from the old, whether with miniskirts, hotpants, paral-lel trousers, platform shoes or bomber jackets. Privacy arrived in Scotland, and the bedroom became a citadel of teenage angst, adding a spatial dimension to the generation gap. Posters of pop stars appeared on bed-room walls, and a record player provided the necessary musical insulation from the world of adults. Cash was also needed for hanging out at the local café or dance hall, and having the necessary means to impress the opposite sex was all part of growing up in Scotland. In the mid-seventies the gen-eration gap could be smelled among men, as deodorant and aftershave made their appearance. Smelling nice, older men argued, was for women. Some men stuck resolutely to the principle of one bath a week.

Drink retained its strong attraction and, as pubs closed at ten o'clock, a tradition existed of pouring down as much booze as possible before time was called. The streets were then exposed to the phenomenon of 'rubber men' bouncing off the walls on their way home, possibly stopping off for a fish supper. Fights would inevitably ensue. Like much of Scottish indus-try, the pubs had changed little since the thirties. They remained bastions of a male-oriented culture, and the principal objective of entering one was to get drunk. Over time, innovations such as jukeboxes, televisions, nuts and crisps made an appearance. It took the 1975 Sex Discrimination Act to get many of them to install a female toilet.

The purchasing power of youth could be seen in cinemas, bingo halls and department stores across the length and breadth of the land being converted into nightclubs and discos to cater for the growing youth market, which was not content to spend a Saturday night getting drunk while watching a game of darts or dominoes. As traditional pubs did not cater for women, young men, directed by hormonal impulses, gravitated to venues in which there was the opportunity to 'pull' or 'score' – though they did tend to avail themselves of a little alcoholic fortification in the pubs beforehand, where booze was also cheaper.

Football retained its firm grip on the imagination of the male Scot, and a Saturday-afternoon ritual revolved around it. This would start with a visit to the pub for a few drinks; then came the purchase of a 'carry oot', followed by attendance at the match, where copious swearing at the referee and opposition helped to relieve stress. The stadiums were not subject to rigorous safety laws, and for the most part consisted of a 'stand' where punters would pack in like sardines, while the well-to-do were segregated in the small seating area. The stands were rough places in which the inebriated would often relieve themselves where they stood, or do it into an empty beer can to be hurled at the opposing supporters. The trick was to get the can to spin like a Catherine wheel and thus soak the maximum number of people. Traditional fare consisted of the Scotch pie and the cup of Bovril.

The sixties were cast as another golden era of Scottish football. The nation beat the world champions in 1967, and in the same year Celtic's 'Lisbon Lions' went on to win the European Cup, while Rangers won the UEFA Cup in 1971. Scotland exported its fair share of talented players, such as Denis Law, Billy Bremner, Tommy Graham, Kenny Dalgleish, Peter Lorimer and Joe Jordan, but also had its own domestic heroes, such as John Gregg, Colin Stein, Alex Ferguson, Jimmy Johnston, Billy McNeil, Tommy Gemmill and Joe Harper. Hooliganism attached itself to the Scottish game. The sectarian dimension of the old firm was commonplace, but the intensity of the chanting and the bigotry associated with it was fast becoming a national disgrace. In January 1971, 66 fans were killed and a further 145 were injured while leaving a Celtic–Rangers game at Ibrox when an exit stand collapsed. The national team acted as a focal point for a national effort at yobbery, and the Tartan Army was renowned for its hooligans, especially during the seventies when it marched south to face the auld enemy at Wembley. Inebriated tartan-clad yobs engaged in wilful acts of vandalism and even more wilful acts of stupidity, such as marching along the tracks of the London underground and diving head first into the fountains in Trafalgar Square. All this did little to enhance the image of the nation among fellow Britons. Such behaviour culminated in 1977, when fans invaded the Wembley pitch, tore up the turf, and removed the goal posts. It met its nemesis in Argentina in 1978 (see Chapter 9).

Television remained the staple means of entertainment, and played a big part in orienting Scottish sensibilities towards a British popular culture. It also brought a transition from a communal experience of leisure and recreation to one that increasingly centred on the individual family. Scots laughed at 'Carry On' films, Benny Hill and other comedy programmes, got caught up in the soaps such as *Coronation Street*, and tuned into dramas such as the *Sweeney* and *Sutherland's Law*. What Scottish programmes there were in the early sixties tended to reflect the 'White Heather' and Kailyard image of Scotland, *Dr Finlay's Casebook* being a good example. The advent of devolved broadcasting in the late sixties allowed more Scottish programmes to be screened, although the staple fare remained predominantly English.

Scottish comedy evolved in the music hall, especially in Glasgow, and the nation produced a generation or two of outstanding comics. Jimmy Logan, Chic Murray and Stanley Baxter all started in the music halls and were able, with varying degrees of success, to make the transition to the small screen. Glasgow excelled as the city of humour, and its black, sardonic and, at times, cruel way of seeing life was something that Scots readily identified with. A good case in point was Billy Connolly, who transferred to stand-up after a folk-music career. Connolly was a gifted observer of the changes that had taken place in Scottish society, and had an amazing ability to see the absurd in a lot of the ordinary. He brought into public the kinds of thing which most Scots – and the rest of the world too, for that matter – found funny. Sectarianism, bodily functions, love, sex, death and religion formed the subject matter of his humour. The Big Yin

split the nation in the early seventies: sell-out audiences laughed uproari-
ously, but dour, stern folk denounced him as 'dirty' and a disgrace to the
nation. Talk of 'jobbies', willies and nose-picking stretched the limits of
the moral guardians' liberalism.

Having a party with friends and family at the weekend was another
staple tradition, for which Connolly is probably the most authoritative
source. Dancing to the radiogram or record player replaced the more traditional forms of entertainment, such as singing and playing instruments.
Also, drink featured more prominently, as each guest was expected to
bring the ubiquitous 'carry oot', usually contained within a none too dis-
creet brown paper bag. The disintegration of the extended family can be
seen by the fact that parties tended more and more to concentrate upon
people of the same generation, usually young couples. Reciting songs or
stories, or playing fiddles and accordions, was for old farts. The era began
when visiting parents and the elderly was reserved for birthdays and
Christmas – and a hung-over visit on New Year's Day.

A two-week summer holiday became universal in the post-war era,
and Scots began to venture south to Blackpool, Morecambe and Scarbor-
ough, where the seaside town provided boarding houses for friends and
families to stay in. For most families in the sixties and early seventies, holidays were joint operations in which workmates, other family members or
neighbours would tend to go off together. For those who were a bit better
off and a bit more adventurous, packaged holidays to Spain were becoming increasingly common.

Family life began to change quite significantly in the sixties and seventies. Family size was becoming smaller – usually two or three children
– which was achieved initially through abstention, but then through the
revolutionary advent of the contraceptive pill. Women could now control
their fertility, which meant that, for most women, pregnancy and child-
rearing were confined to a limited number of years, and by their mid-thirties most could contemplate a life free from looking after young children.
Family planning had a mixed reception in Scottish society: it was available
in most areas, but could still encounter opposition from both Catholic and
Presbyterian moralists. The middle class were the first to make use of it,
followed by the skilled working class, and there was a close correlation
between the number of children in a family and levels of poverty. How-

ever, the causal relationship between the two is not clear. Do poor people have more children, or do people who have more children become poor? The available evidence tends to suggest the former.

The world of children changed dramatically in the post-war era. First, they were unlikely to have the same experience of death which had marred the lives of many youngsters in the inter-war period. Also, the progress of housebuilding, especially in the mid-sixties and early-seventies, meant there was a greater tendency for similar types of family to be housed together at the same time. That pregnancy was subject to greater control meant that the children within a family would tend to have a smaller range of ages than was the case in the past. Most brothers and sisters were usually separated by four years at most. The appearance of a younger sibling who broke the age-range boundary was usually referred to with knowing looks as an 'accident'. It became uncommon to have a brother or sister separated by a significant age gap, and most children grew up playing with others who had similar family structures and similar ages.

Children received greater attention, and were prime beneficiaries of the growth of a consumer society. Christmas day first became a public holiday in Scotland in the sixties, and provides clear evidence of the growth of consumerism: a spinning top and a tangerine would simply no longer do as a present, and birthdays also required a gift. Children were also seen as an index of a particular family's respectability and means. Clothes, toys, parties and other materialist manifestations were closely monitored by other children and their parents. It was tricky to get things right: provide too much and the child was spoilt; provide too little and the child was neglected. On television, children got their own programmes, and, in schools, more attention was devoted to child-centred learning. It should be pointed out, however, that the belt or strap was still used as a means to discipline the unruly, although the practice was on the decline, largely as a result of a new generation of teachers whose attitudes to life had been shaped by a more liberal climate at university.

Children who grew up in the sixties and seventies were probably the first generation since the Industrial Revolution to experience widespread relocation. Moving house has now become an individual family experience, but in the post-war period it was more of a communal activity, in which friends would often move with you. Otherwise, if the family went on its own, new friends would have to be made. In the estates around Scotland there was always an influx of new children with different experiences to share. In the overspill towns, young Glaswegians had to adapt to the new circumstances of small-town Scotland.

Another big change in family life was that people were marrying younger. The average marrying age for women fell between 1960 and 1970 from about 25 to 22, while that for men dropped from about 26 to 23. There was a rise in the number of still younger marriages, and in 1971 10 per cent of all women aged between 16 and 19 were married. The easier availability of housing and employment was a major contributor to this process.

In an age of increasing transport and job mobility, there was a greater tendency for families to move away from the traditional locality. Furthermore, it was a period in which population density in the big towns and cities was reduced considerably. This meant that there were increasing geographical barriers to the traditional extended family. In the old days, when families were packed in tenements, it was easy to keep in contact. Now, although some related families lived in the same town or city, they could find themselves in different estates. Much of this was a result of the lottery of housing allocation and the tendency to take whatever place was going. Changes in lifestyle also affected the extended family structure. By and large it was married women who were expected to maintain contact with both sets of parents. By 1970, over 60 per cent of women worked and, of that total, more than half were married. After a working day, there was little time for visits and contact. This situation was not helped by the fact that, although domestic technology had eased the burden of housework, women were hit by a double whammy in that not only should they go out to work to pay for life's little extras, they still had to contend with the traditional expectation that they were responsible for the washing, cleaning, cooking and looking after the children. The usual rationale given by men for this state of affairs was that, as they earned more, they should be looked after – and in any case, it was claimed, a man's job was harder than a woman's. There was a paradox in that, at a time when people were living longer, families saw less of one another than when life expectancy was shorter in the twenties and thirties. This was a further contribution to the generation gap, in the sense that the old had been used to extended families and had maintained regular contact with their parents when they were younger, only to see this form of living abandoned by their own offspring.

Another breakdown in the immediate family structure came with the increasing rate of divorce, which jumped from about 2,000 a year in the mid-sixties to 10,000 a year by the late seventies. This saw another confrontation between the generations, as the old argued that having made one's bed one should lie in it, but for a generation used to rising expectations and increasing aspirations this was not good enough. Divorce was becoming common enough to the young, but to grandparents who had lived through the thirties and the war, and whose watchword was 'till death do us part', the break-up of an immediate family was an alien and confusing experience.

Another traditional citadel of Scottish culture which failed to weather the storm of modernity in the late sixties and early seventies was the Church. For all the difficulties of the inter-war period, total church membership held up quite well. In the 1920s it was just under half the population, though it dipped after the Second World War to just over 40 per cent. The 1955 'Tell Scotland' campaign by the American evangelist Billy Graham injected life back into the Churches and membership recovered lost ground. Thereafter there was a steady decline, which only gathered pace by the mid-sixties, and the number who had some form of connection with a Church declined from over 40 per cent of the population in 1960 to just over 30 per cent in the mid-seventies. Not all Churches declined equally, however. It was the Church of Scotland which showed the most dramatic decrease, while faith in the Catholic Church held up remarkably well. There was a paradox in this too, while the Church of Scotland in the inter-war period was firmly wedded to the Conservative Party and renowned for its illiberalism, after the war it began to reflect the more leftist and socially aware attitudes of society in general. It moved with the people on issues of social welfare, housing, and decolonisation in Africa, and displayed more liberal attitudes towards issues like abortion, divorce and juvenile crime. While this was happening, however, it was the more aspirant and more middle-class members of the congregation – the very people who were most likely to share these more liberal attitudes – that were leading the initial exodus. Later the skilled working class would follow them.

Relocation did not help the Churches. In the creation of new estates and new towns, church provision was always falling behind, and, with a declining membership, securing the funds for a church-building programme was more difficult. Also, the creation of the Welfare State removed the Churches from some of their more immediate pastoral roles. For those in difficulty, the local social-work department was now the most likely first port of call. Though growing liberal attitudes were often shared by the Church, the population still associated organised religion with moral purity and feared that contact could mean intrusion into private lives. Yet the decline of membership did not necessarily mean that the Church was no longer an important social force. Ministers still played a part in local communities, and were often to be found on education and welfare boards. Non-denominational schools – which essentially meant schools that were non-Catholic – still conducted Presbyterian services at the end of term, and religious instruction remained part of the curriculum. And the quarter or more of the population that was still committed to a Church represented a substantial number.

Although the Catholic Church made few concessions to the forces of liberalism, it still had an extensive social network and maintained a greater presence in the lives of the community than was the case for the Presbyterians. Catholicism had a greater cultural dynamic, which made identification with the Church possible for a wider range of reasons than simply faith. There was a distinctive Catholic experience in Scotland which had been shaped by both thinking and unthinking sectarianism. An example of the latter was the professor of church history at Edinburgh University, J. S. Burleigh, who as late as 1960 wrote in his *A History of the Scottish Church* that Catholicism was an 'alien and foreign' intrusion into Scottish society. Sectarianism was still prevalent in many of the traditional industries and privately owned small businesses, where religious discrimination was used in employment practices. The religion of an applicant could be determined by the name of his or her school, as Catholics inevitably attended schools named after a saint. Such discriminatory practices eventually declined not through changing attitudes, but rather as a result of wider changes in the structure of the Scottish economy. Nationalisation militated against the ability to use discrimination in employment. The traditional industries were declining. Foreign companies became a more important source of employment, and religious bigotry made no sense to them. The expansion of jobs in local and central government was another important source of work on a non-sectarian basis.

When the youth of Scotland abandoned many of the trappings of mainstream tradition in the sixties and seventies, this had a greater impact on the Presbyterian Church, which had been part of that dominant tradition, than on the Catholic Church, which was not as closely associated with the mainstream.

Further avenues for increased social mobility for both Protestants and Catholics emerged as the universities experienced expansion in the mid-sixties as a result of the publication of the Robbins Report on higher education in 1963. The technological colleges of Glasgow and Edinburgh were upgraded to the University of Strathclyde and Heriot-Watt University respectively, while Dundee's college had the bonds to St Andrews cut and became a university in its own right. A new university was situated in Stirling, after much competition from Cumbernauld and Falkirk, to serve the centre of the country.

University expansion was favoured by both sides of the political divide. For Labour it would create a new class of technocrats and managers who would form an important plank of the corporatist state and would demonstrate to a new generation that socialist planning worked. For the Conservatives it would create a new group of upwardly mobile Scots who would see that their material interests were best served by the Tories. The numbers attending university increased to nearly one in ten of all young people by the mid-seventies, and, although not as radical as in some places of higher learning down south, student rebelliousness could catch the headlines. One example was when the Queen came to visit the University of Stirling in 1971 and students put on a general display of drunken rowdiness, much to the annoyance of the authorities and the local community. For months after the event, local bus drivers refused to stop at the university and shopkeepers and publicans would refuse to serve anyone with long hair.

Feminism and radical politics were more muted north of the border, and the waves of student protest which marked campus life around the western world in the sixties and early seventies were largely absent from Scotland. One reason for this may have been the tendency for most Scottish students to live at home, which cut down the time available for radical politics as they had to get home in time for their tea. Also, a sense of distance from the main centres of power may have been another factor. The Scottish radical student was more likely to travel to London than to protest at home, where there were little in the way of government buildings to act as an effective focus for demonstrations. One issue which was closer to hand was the bomb. It would have been even closer if scientists had not had second thoughts in the early fifties, as it was planned to test the first British atomic bomb in the Highlands. The plan was dropped before it was circulated to the politicians, as the region's rainfall would have complicated detection of the range of radioactive fallout. Scotland's uninhabited northern small islands were also used for chemical- and biological-warfare tests.

The Cold War had an impact on Scottish society largely on account of the nation's geography. As the nuclear deterrent increasingly evolved around the use of ballistic missiles fired from submarines, Scotland, sticking out into the Atlantic, became a vital strategic area for the monitoring of Soviet vessels en route to destinations in the middle of the ocean. The north-east coast bristled with radar and listening devices, and the RAF base at Leuchars in Fife was an important centre for operations against Soviet reconnaissance planes, as well as being a first line of air defence. The west coast got its fair share of listening posts, and missile ranges were established in the Western Isles. But most contentious of all was the basing of American submarines equipped with Polaris missiles at Holy Loch near the Clyde. The deal was hatched in 1960, after the failure of Britain's independent ballistic-missile programme. As part of the subsequent agreement for the purchase of Polaris submarines from the United States, the Americans were given a 'forward operating base' in the Clyde. The area became a focal point for the Campaign for Nuclear Disarmament (CND), and popular protests brought together several thousand pacifists, Christians, trade unionists, nationalists and environmentalists. The peace campaigns had more colour and idealism than was associated with conventional party politics, and blended traditional popular song with new words to give voice to their concerns:

The USA are gien' subs away,
Giein' subs away,

Giein' subs away-ay-ay-ay.
The USA are giein' subs away,
But we dinna want Polaris.

Ye can tell the Yanks tae drap them doon the stanks,
Drap them doon the stanks,
Drap them doon the st-a-a-anks ...

The siting of United States submarines in the early sixties drew objections on three fronts. Some objectors were against all weapons of mass destruction. Others objected to foreign weapons on Scottish or British soil. And a third group believed that these weapons, along with the base for British Polaris submarines at Faslane, would make central Scotland a probable first-strike target in any nuclear war. After military bases, important industrial complexes were believed to be next on the list for any nuclear strikes, and it perhaps should have alarmed Scotland's economists that the nation had only one likely secondary target: the petrochemical plant at Grangemouth.

CND demonstrations provided Scotland's radical youth with an alternative to the sedentary, conventional politics of the Labour Party, which struggled to elevate itself above the local-council level. As the activists saw it, the issue gave them something much more important, moral and meaningful to campaign for. Protest and direct action was an alternative form of politics that was chosen by younger generations throughout the campuses of America and Europe. It would be hard to imagine young people getting fired up and passionate in the local council, which was still the usual entry point into conventional political life.

From the mid-sixties until the present day, anti-nuclear activists have employed a variety of direct-action tactics, first, against Polaris, and in the nineties against its successor, Trident. A bedrock of support has been augmented from time to time by wider external developments. The deployment of Trident in the late eighties and the arrival of cruise missiles at Greenham Common in England added a feminist dimension to the campaign, which was reflected in Scotland. Demonstrations outside the docks were supplemented with people chaining themselves to gates, sit-downs in the roads and, most dangerous of all, boarding the submarines at sea. It is worth pointing out that the campaign against weapons of mass destruction now has the longest pedigree of any single issue in Scottish politics, and the siting of nuclear weapons in Scotland has provided a rallying point for probably the most socially diverse of all protest movements.

THE DEMOCRATIC INTELLECT?

The swinging sixties passed Scotland by, and the best guess is that sexual intercourse did not begin north of the border until sometime in the seventies. There was no flower power, few hippies, no love and peace, nor anything usually associated with western decadent youth culture. There was no storming of the left bank of the Clyde, no Highland love-in festival, no Timothy MacLeary to advocate the expansion of Caledonian consciousness. Nor was there much of the permissive society, even though a great many went looking for it. The closest most people got to it was on the telly.

Scotland's moral guardians put up a bold line of defence against any encroachments of vice and immorality. Even the world-famous Edinburgh Festival was not immune from the prying eyes of local councillors on the lookout for anything that might offend public decency and taste, even though it was well known that the bulk of the capital's citizens did not normally go to the Festival's events. Nudity was a particularly heinous crime, and in 1968, according to Arthur Marwick, who was working at the time in the history department at the university:

> Edinburgh councillors indulged in an orgy of asinine behaviour. First they complained loudly about a private performance at the Traverse Theatre in which a half-naked girl recounted her sexual experiences (by all informed accounts a thundering bore); they then complained even more bitterly when, on going along expressly to view the indecent performance, they were regaled instead with an equally boring but totally unsalacious programme which, with rare wit, the Traverse management had put on instead. It is not completely surprising if at times students seem to set out deliberately to bait local sentiment. Then the protests flood in, pressuring the university authorities (a liberal lot on the whole) towards an authoritarian stance.
>
> Karl Miller, ed. *Memoirs of a Modern Scotland* (London, 1970)

It was rumoured that there was at least 'one bare-naked lady' every evening in the Fringe performances, and councillors went out on moral patrol. Actors and actresses employed a number of devices to thwart the moralistic prying eyes of officialdom, such as flesh-coloured body stockings and dim lighting to simulate the effect of nakedness. This type of monitoring by local councillors could backfire, as happened in the early seventies when the provost of Falkirk made the front of the tabloid papers after a 'go-go' dancer had run the elected official's glasses through the inside of her bikini bottom. The story that he was checking to see if the venue was suitable for a licence sounded unconvincing. The depressing aspect of widespread moral puritanism was reflected in the fact that children would receive a beating for inadvertent nakedness, pregnant daughters were still being turned out on to the street, and the Scottish gay community was driven so far underground that no one knew about it.

Scotland's intellectual coterie were a miserable lot. Not for them the café ambience of Paris, or London's swinging Carnaby Street, but Milne's bar in Edinburgh, with its beer-stained floor, solid-nicotine atmosphere, and ten o'clock closing time. Whereas other societies in the world recognised their writers, poets and thinkers, Scottish society seemed to regard such people as a nuisance, believing that they should go and get a real job. It was a lonely occupation being an intellectual in Scotland, and more often than not a sense of frustration boiled over in attacks on the unthinking and philistine ethos which seemed to permeate the homeland. In his 1927 book *Caledonia*, George Malcolm Thomson had written that 'The Scots were incapable of considering their literary geniuses purely as writers. They must be either an excuse for a glass or a text for a sermon.' Very little had changed by the late sixties. The overwhelming impression of the nation was that it was a dreary place, lacking in sophistication and excitement. Although nationalism seemed to be on the up and up, the parochial and conservative nature of Scotland terrified many intellectuals, and Tom Nairn famously captured the resulting sense of frustration when he wrote in 1970:

> In a country spoiled by stale authoritarianism, the universal revolt of youth against authoritarianism should have a quite special sense and value.

It is to the extent – and only to the extent – that Scottish nationalism links itself to such new forces and ideas that it will avoid being the 'proper', suitable summing-up of the old problems. That is, the perpetuation of what we *are,* the tragic dénouement of our tragic half-history. It goes without saying that such a revolutionary nationalism can only exist by combating the past which conventional nationalism drools over, that what Gramsci called 'pessimism of the intelligence' is its life-blood. It can only exist as a cultural liberation from Scotland's myths. To acquiesce in the SNP's version of the future, in the year when a new generation cried *'Nous sommes tous des Juifs Allemands'* before the Palais Bourbon and ground the nationalism of the past to dust at the Saarbrücken bridge, is merely an uninteresting form of suicide. I will not admit that this is the best we can do, that a party incapable of even a symbolic firecracker in the path of the annual Royal Progress to Scotland has the right to *speak* for me as a nationalist ... I see that Scottish Nationalism now has the benediction of our annual General Assembly of crows. It must already be dreaming of the Inaugural Procession of the new regime to St Giles, where the All Mighty will smile on it too. As far as I am concerned, Scotland will be reborn the day the last minister is strangled with the last copy of the *Sunday Post.* I hope I'm not alone.

Karl Miller, ed., *Memoirs of a Modern Scotland* (London, 1970)

Yet the mid-sixties was a time when the nation was being rediscovered, and, although only a small-scale enterprise in the beginning, this would eventually pave the way for the cultural regeneration of Scotland in the late eighties and nineties. In the study of history and literature, academics and others made important reconnections with the past. A new generation of writers and poets helped to consolidate the achievements of the renaissance of the inter-war years and, perhaps more importantly, to bring those achievements to the attention of a wider audience. Ethnologists captured the dying songs, ballads and traditions of Scotland in the nick of time, and gave inspiration to a new generation prepared to take up the mantle of the music of the folk. Polemicists, commentators and theorists debated about the nature of Scottish society and its future. More importantly, they tried to relate it to what was going on elsewhere in the world. The stale crustiness of Scottish society's exterior hid an underground ferment of ideas.

The rise of nationalism had initiated much discussion on the question of the financial implications of independence, most of which was carried out by economists. It was a dry and arcane debate, based on statistical projections of what a future independent Scotland probably would and would not be able to afford. It was perhaps in reaction to the essential dullness of this issue that many commentators turned their attention to more fundamental questions of politics, culture and society. Scotland had a 'new left', which was sometimes described as 'neo-nationalist', and the state of the nation caused it considerable concern. Nationalism was a bit of a dirty word in leftist circles: unless associated with anti-colonialism, it was best avoided. Yet, for the new generation of the left, there were a number of issues in Scotland which they felt had to be addressed.

While Scotland was obviously not a colony, in that the nation had not been conquered and occupied, there were a number of features which hinted at aspects of a colonial experience, and writers such as Tom Nairn, Hamish Henderson, Alan Bold and Duncan Glen, taking up the mantle of Edwin Muir, began to question the peculiarities of capitalist development in Scotland. The Scottish people had suffered from this development, but Scotland also had an entrenched bourgeoisie that had prospered, so conventional theories of imperialism and nationalist anti-colonialism did not fit the Scottish model. An important influence on intellectual thought was Antonio Gramsci, a Sardinian theorist who related capitalist development to notions of cultural dominance. He provided a more intelligent theoretical base for the history of Scotland from the Union, rather than the conventional nationalist model in which class played no part and everything was the fault of the English. In their quest to reinterpret Scotland's past, Nairn, Henderson, Bold and Glen were joined by other commentators, though not of equal dogmatism, such as Neil Ascherson, J. P. Mackintosh and Neil MacCormick, who were able to point out that Scotland did not fit into bog-standard theories of national development. Scotland was different and peculiar, and, some might even have said, interesting.

The culture of the nation began to receive more attention from academia in the late sixties, although it is worth pointing out that the Scottish universities largely subsidised the scholarly study of English culture until the late eighties and mid-nineties, in that more academics specialised in the literature and history of south of the border than dealt with Scotland itself. Usually their subject matter was passed off as 'British', but it had a heavy southern bias. Scottish students were likely to be taught about Anglo-Saxon history and poetry, the Norman Conquest, the Wars of the Roses, Henry VIII and his six wives, and the triumph of the English parliament in the seventeenth century. Literature was more likely to begin with Chaucer rather than the makars, and the romantic poets such as Blake and Wordsworth, and novelists such as Dickens and Trollope, were more likely to be studied than their Scottish counterparts. In the late sixties, professors Archie Duncan and Geoffrey Barrow kept the saltire flying in the study of medieval history, and the latter's *Robert Bruce* proved to be a consistent best-seller. Gordon Donaldson led the way in the study of early modern Scotland, and Chris Smout, Rosiland Mitchison and William Ferguson pioneered the history of the modern era. Roy Campbell introduced the nation to modern economic history. Assisted by Grant Simpson, Ronald Cant and Don Withrington in the north, this small coterie laid the foundation for the future scholarly study of the nation's past. It was done at a time when Scottish history was regarded as being of only local interest, and the brightest students were encouraged to leave such parochialism behind and study 'real' history. Such achievements paved the way for future generations to educate the nation about its past and place the subject on the map of international scholarship. A number of populists also helped in this task. The authors John Prebble and Nigel Tranter satisfied a less academic appetite for the story of Scotland, and Gordon Menzies and Iain Grimble pioneered presentation of the subject on television.

Scottish literature began to make a comeback. Academics woke up to the artistic achievement of the inter-war renaissance, and in 1957 – somewhat late in the day – Hugh MacDiarmid was awarded an honorary doctorate from the University of Edinburgh for his achievements. Scottish literature began to appear on university curricula in the sixties, and scholars such as Kurt Wittig, David Craig and David Daiches were forerunners in promoting the idea of Scotland having a distinctive literary tradition. The late sixties was a period of considerable artistic outpouring by a new generation of Scottish writers and poets. Sydney Goodsir Smith, Norman MacCaig, Robert Gairoch and Edwin Morgan added to the Scottish poetic canon, while writers such as William McIlvanney and Carl Macdougall provided a more authentic Scottish voice in prose. In Gaelic, Iain Crichton Smith, Derick Thomson and Sorley Maclean demonstrated that the language was anything but dead. Yet, although writers such as Naomi Mitchison and Muriel Spark did hold a torch for Scottish women, culture remained firmly in the hands of men and the cultural projection of the nation was predominantly masculine until, in the eighties, a new generation arrived to address the issue of gender imbalance. Magazines like *Lines Review* provided a platform for up-and-coming talent, and would later be augmented by *Chapman* and *Cencrastus.* The School of Scottish Studies in Edinburgh, under the direction of Hamish Henderson, began collecting and preserving the richness of Scottish oral culture. Eduardo Paolozzi, Alan Davie and Ian Hamilton Finlay explored abstraction in painting and sculpture, and the philosopher George Elder Davie made an impassioned plea for the distinctiveness of the Scottish educational ethos in his *Democratic Intellect,* which railed against the process of Anglicisation which had overtaken the Scottish universities. A key point of Davie's argument was that the Scottish educational tradition was democratic, in the sense that it was influenced more by intellectual merit than by social class, and, although it has been challenged in recent years, this idea helped to reinforce notions that Scottish culture was more egalitarian than that of south of the border.

Scotland was not quite the intellectual and cultural desert that it often seemed. Scotland's intellects, artists and academics built a solid foundation from which greater cultural achievements would flow in the eighties and nineties.

THE COUNTRYSIDE

Change was as dramatic for rural Scotland as it was for urban society. The Second World War took a further toll on the great estates, which were still dotted around the Scottish countryside. After the war, increasing taxation and death duties hit the landed grandees hard. The 1947 Agriculture Act provided greater security of tenure for farmers, and the 1967 Act filled the remaining loopholes and gave tenants' heirs and successors the right to succeed to a farm. Furthermore, the onus was put on the landowner to show why a tenancy should not be continued. By the late sixties there were 55,000 farming units, although only 22,000 of these were worked full-time, the rest being small crofts.

The period from the late forties to the mid-sixties was a time of increasing prosperity for farmers, and many used their savings to buy their farms, so that by 1960 a third of all farms were owner-occupied. By 1991 the number had swollen to two-thirds. The social structure of the country-side underwent significant changes. The role of paternalistic grandees fur-ther declined, and many estates became owned by trusts; others were converted into limited companies. As a result, many of the social functions of the 'big house' ceased, as owners relocated elsewhere to live off their proceeds. The power of government had increased, and land could be com-pulsorily purchased for housing, forestry or industrial development. Any mines which had been part of an estate were nationalised, along with all the miners' houses. Legislation governing the state of rural housing meant that water, sewerage and electricity had to be provided, again increasing financial pressures.

Scotland contributed about 11 per cent of the United Kingdom's agricultural output, and the efficiency of the sector is illustrated by the fact that Scots farms tended to be slightly larger than their English and Welsh counterparts. Livestock from Scotland made up 16 per cent of the British total, and accounted for 40 per cent of Scottish agricultural pro-duction.

Government legislation following the war provided a guaranteed fixed price for a given quota of produce. Once the quota was filled, the price paid went progressively down, but this system was effective in guar-anteeing farmers a reliable income from their goods. Annual price subsi-dies in Scotland averaged between £20 million and £30 million in the sixties, and grants were also available for improvements and investments. In 1964, for example, such grants added a further £23.5 million to the bill, and by the end of the decade the total of grants and subsidies had reached £50 million a year and amounted to almost 20 per cent of the UK total.

Government intervention contributed substantially to the way in which agriculture developed in Scotland. First, it favoured the growth of larger farming units, which could take advantage of economies of scale. Second, it reinforced the regional trends towards specialisation that had been apparent before the war. Third, it helped to maximise output by increasing the rate of technological change, which brought a reduction in the amount of labour used. Arguably the introduction of new technology had greater repercussions in the countryside than in the towns, as the former work of nine people could now be done with one man and an adaptable tractor. Scottish farming increased its efficiency at an unprecedented rate and, in terms of value, post-war production rose tenfold. The widespread use of fertilisers increased yields, and the advent of new machinery, which could sow, plant, reap and process crops, meant that there was less need to rely on labour. Furthermore, as yields increased, the actual land area cultivated declined. The availability of grants for modernisation and investment promoted these trends, as did the policy of subsidies, which, although subject to a quota, meant that maximising production was the best way to make a good return.

As tenant farms became unoccupied, there was a trend for consolidation, thus maximising the output. Again, the advent of new machinery and fertilisers made it desirable to use them to the maximum extent, in order to get a good return from such investment. Farms which in the past might have had a more mixed form of activity would gravitate to those activities that yielded the best return. This particular development was most marked in the Lothians and the central belt, where the land was most suited to intensive crop farming. Likewise, economies of scale meant that dairy farming tended to go for bigger herds, so that maximum use could be made of the new milking technology and refrigerated transport. There was a switch in the breed of cow from the Ayrshire to the Friesian, which gave better milk yields. Better use of selective breeding was made to increase the weight of cattle for beef. Pigs and hens used to be dispersed throughout the country, but the development of more intensive methods of farming meant that egg production became a specialist activity in battery ranges, and large-scale pig farms gravitated to the north-east and south-east. Farming was one of the most productive sectors of the economy. Output per head employed was two to three times higher than in most of Western Europe, and only Denmark and Holland matched the achievements of the Scottish farmers. There is a certain irony in the fact that Scottish agriculture matched the productivity of Western European industry, while Scottish industry matched the productivity of Western European farming.

The 'industrialisation' of farming, with the widespread adoption of new technologies, meant that between 1950 and 1980 the agricultural workforce declined by 60 per cent, or some 53,000 workers. Eleven thousand part-time workers were also lost to the process of mechanisation. The Agricultural Wages Board intervened to guarantee a minimum rate of pay, and in 1962 the average annual wage was £520 – nearly 10 per cent higher than the average for industrial workers. Thereafter agricultural wages declined in relation to those of the rest of the population. Given that labour was an important cost input, high wages were a powerful incentive for the introduction of mechanisation and economies of scale, and the total wage bill declined by about a third between 1960 and 1970. A reduction in labour costs was also promoted by the decline in the prices of agricultural produce which began in the mid-sixties: it was only by maximising productivity that profits could be maintained.

There is evidence that life on a farm was now losing its attraction. The advent of full employment, together with increased availability of council housing, meant that it was easier to escape from the long hours, unremitting hard labour, loneliness and isolation that were some of the main drawbacks associated with life in the countryside. As the process of modernisation continued apace, farms became bigger, grain mills became larger, and much of the infrastructure of the rural community shrank as economies of scale were introduced, meaning that isolation probably grew. This was at a time when television presented an attractive world of modernity. Technological change had its impact on many traditional occupations. Tractors displaced the roles of the blacksmith and the ploughman; cheap fencing which required little maintenance removed the need for handymen to repair the drystone dykes; and bigger units of production meant that the farmer would use professional haulage firms, specialist agricultural suppliers, storage depots, and large-scale granaries. That many tenant farms became unoccupied may suggest that younger members of the family no longer wished to continue in their predecessors' tradition.

The advent of British entry to the European Economic Community (EEC) in 1973 held out the prospect of an even bigger challenge for the farming community. The system of target quotas which guaranteed fixed prices was changed to the formula of the Common Agricultural Policy (CAP), in which import controls and levies were used to keep out competition and any surplus production was bought up to ensure stable prices, leading to butter, grain and other 'mountains'. The CAP provided the most lucrative of the EEC subsidies, and, in order to take advantage of this, in 1971 the government promoted a drive to maximise output, in the knowledge that the more that was produced the greater would be the subsidy. The impact of the CAP tended to favour the dairy and arable farms of the Lothian area as milk and crops were better subsidised, while the north-east, which specialised in beef, and the south-west, which specialised in sheep did not do as well. (Under EEC regulations wool was classed as an industrial and not an agricultural product.) Also, CAP subsidies worked to the advantage of the big farms, increasing the trend for consolidation and further exacerbating the use of more intensive methods of production – especially following the economic slump of the mid-seventies, in which rising oil prices helped to increase costs to the farmers.

Arguably, the effect of the CAP has been to alienate farmers from the wider Scottish community. Intensive farming has not gone down well with the environmental lobby, which grew in strength throughout the seventies, and the policy of buying up surpluses to maintain price levels led to growing friction with consumers. Finally, the structure of subsidy has had the effect of favouring the farms of the south-east, which became very wealthy in the seventies, while those in the north-east did less well and the sheep farms of the borders stagnated. Indeed, the borders region experienced a fall in population in the sixties and seventies as the textile mills contracted and farming went into decline. It had a greater loss of people in this period than the Highlands. Along with the Dumfries and Galloway area, the borders had quite specific regional problems associated with declining industry, difficulties of transportation, and other problems associated with a rural environment, but, unlike the Highlands, it was an area that was neglected in terms of government regional policy.

The fishing industry of the north-east was another sector of the rural community which experienced dramatic change. The impact of new technology in the form of bigger trawlers meant that the number of fisher-men employed declined, and industrialisation likewise meant there was less reliance on labour in the processing of fish. The numbers employed full-time in the industry dropped by over 11 per cent from 9,460 in 1961 to 8,390 in 1971, with a similar fall in those who were employed on a seasonal or part-time basis. The industry was able to use government grants for a process of modernisation, and these increased from just over £400,000 to almost £1 million in the decade between 1960 and 1970. The grants were mainly used to convert from coal-powered boats to diesel, which had a greater range. The amount of fish landed during an extensive period of mod-ernisation in the first half of the sixties showed a steady rise from over half a million tons per annum to nearly three-quarters of a million tons.

The industry ran into problems by the early seventies, as non-EEC countries extended their territorial fishing waters, sparking the Cod War with Iceland, and the European Common Fisheries Policy had the effect of opening up EEC waters to ships of all member states. Again, under-invest-ment meant that Scottish ships were unable to compete against the highly industrialised ships from Spain and the Soviet Union, which had advan-tages of size and range. By international standards, half the Scottish fleet was made up of small boats. The invasion of factory ships led in the mid-seventies to the problem of overfishing and growing concerns about stock conservation. The thrust of government intervention tended to favour the extension of fishing in the West Highland coast, while the problems of the north-east received little attention.

EMIGRANTS AND IMMIGRANTS

Between 1951 and 1981, 753,000 Scots – about 15 per cent of the total population over this period – left the country for pastures new. Of that total, 45 per cent went south, while the rest went overseas. All in all, over 1.25 million Scots left their homeland in the period after 1914, giving the nation one of the highest rates of per-capita emigration in the western world. As was the case in the twenties and thirties, economic factors lay at the heart of the post-war Scottish diaspora. Emigration was seen as a fact of Scottish life, and almost a tradition. According to the report of the Toothill Inquiry:

It is easy to become alarmed about the steady annual loss by migration. It is a selective loss, almost certainly of the younger sections of the population. It is not however possible to stop migration by having a policy to discourage it – even if such a policy were desirable. No doubt whatever the conditions at home, many Scots will still migrate, as they have done even during the most prosperous periods. We believe therefore that the important thing to work for is a general improvement in the economy; whether or not this resulted in a substantial reduction in the outward movement it would be likely to increase the compensating movement in.

Inquiry into the Scottish Economy, 1960–1961 (Edinburgh, 1961)

Evidence gathered for the Toothill Inquiry showed that in the fifties about a quarter of those emigrating were under the age of fifteen years old, and that the numbers of males and females were almost equal. Forty-one per cent of emigrating females were described as housewives, which, taken together with the proportion who were children, indicates that perhaps between a quarter and a third of those who went abroad did so as a family. Of the adult women who emigrated, more than half were economically active, and of that proportion just over a quarter were described as working in the professional, managerial and clerical sector. Among adult males, this proportion was slightly smaller, at just under a quarter. Given that it was unusual for women to marry below their occupational status, and the tendency for males in that occupational sector not to have a working wife, it can be assumed that a significant number of single professional women were leaving the country for better employment opportunities elsewhere. The endemic sexism of Scottish society no doubt drove many women to seek more enlightened environments where a female doctor or lawyer would not be greeted with incredulity. The figures also show that a disproportionate number of the emigrants were skilled, and the report highlighted the worry that emigration was draining valuable experience away from Scottish society. Similar observations were later made for the sixties and seventies, and it was noted that the proportion of graduates which expected to find work outside Scotland was about half.

Migration to England and Wales can be closely related to the fortunes of the Scottish economy in comparison to those of its southern neighbour.

Scotland was losing a higher proportion of its economically active population, as more than half of all migrants were aged between twenty and forty-four. It was also giving up part of a future generation, in that about a fifth of those who went south were children. Evidence suggests that workers were 'pulled' south by the lure of higher wages and the possibility of promotion. Workers in the car, electrical and chemical industries, for example, could expect to be paid a fifth higher than in Scotland. Service workers were lured south in equal numbers to their manual counterparts, no doubt because the service-sector economy in England was better developed and had more avenues for advancement and higher pay.

When the figures for migrants coming to Scotland from England and Wales during the sixties are examined, further conclusions can be drawn about the relative attractiveness of Scottish society. Scottish migration south in this period outnumbered English and Welsh migration to Scotland by more than two to one. By tracking the movement of occupations between north and south it is possible to form some tentative conclusions about the structural weakness of the Scottish economy. Scotland exported three times as many skilled manual labourers as were imported. For semi-skilled manual workers, the ratio was that four left for every one that entered. Junior non-manual workers, such as clerks, shop workers and the like, gained one for every two and a half lost from Scotland. Interestingly, the further up the social ladder we climb, the lower the differential. Among professionals, the export rate was only a third higher than the import. Among managers of small firms two came in for every three that left, and among bigger firms the numbers were nearly equal. So, although Scots outnumbered the English and Welsh by more than two to one in overall cross-border migration, the social composition of the respective migrants was different. Almost 67 per cent of Scots moving south were either junior non-manual workers or manual labourers, whereas the proportion of such workers among those coming into Scotland was slightly more than half. Whereas only a fifth of Scots migrants were professionals and managers, the proportion among southern migrants coming north was a third. The proportions of middle-ranking white-collar workers were almost equal at 14 per cent of those heading south and 13 per cent of those heading north.

A number of conclusions can be drawn from this. First, given that more left than came in, it can safely be said that there were more opportunities for employment south of the border than north. Second, a higher proportion of professionals and managers tended to be drawn north, which may be explained by Scotland's higher preponderance of branch manufacturers, with firms based in the south preferring to use their own people rather than rely on natives. Also, public-sector posts in the civil service, local government and the universities were advertised on a UK-wide level, and that a lot of cross-border activity would be expected in this sector. Yet all this may also indicate that management skill was, or was perceived to be, weak north of the border.

Finally, it should be pointed out that not only was Scotland, in per-capita terms, one of the leading people-exporting nations, it was almost unique among the modern western economies in that it had no widespread non-European immigration. Whereas Commonwealth citizens arrived in England to take advantage of labour shortages, North Africans moved to France, and Turks poured into West Germany to take part in the European economic miracle, nobody wanted to come to Scotland. Asian migrants to Britain tended to get as far as the Midlands and north-west England, and the fact that so few ventured further north demonstrates that Scotland was not widely believed to be a land of opportunity. In 1966 only 2 out of every 1,000 Scots came from the New Commonwealth, whereas the figure for England and Wales was twelve times higher. If growing population is used as an indicator of social and economic success, then the following makes the point very clearly. Between 1921 and 1961 the population of England grew by 30 per cent, while that of Scotland grew by only 5 per cent.

As unemployment in the south grew in the seventies and opportunities dried up, almost twice as many Scots emigrated as migrated, but the growth of immigration controls abroad and a downturn in the world economy meant that the numbers leaving in this decade dropped by more than a third. Over time, there was a tendency for more single people to emigrate, and, increasingly as numbers declined, there was a heavy bias towards professionals and the highly skilled. In 1967, 37,300 Scots emigrated, but by 1972 the number had declined to 20,300. The annual figure remained in this region until the end of the decade. Evidence of the decline of family emigration can be seen in the figures for the under-sixteen age group, which dropped from 27 per cent in 1967 to 15 per cent

in 1978. Over the same period the proportion of housewives declined from
13 per cent to 11 per cent, although there was an increasing tendency for
married women to state their working occupation in documentation. The
proportion of emigrants who were professional or managerial increased
from 14 per cent to a third, while manual and clerical workers dropped
from 40 per cent to less than a third. As the economies of Australasia and
North America experienced problems associated with the world recession
following the Arab-Israeli war of 1973, in the mid-seventies the New
World became increasingly choosy about who its new citizens should be,
and opportunities for widespread emigration declined.

In total, 398,000 Scots emigrated overseas in the period between
1951 and 1981, and there are few families in Scotland today which cannot
boast of having relatives in North America, Australasia or some other part
of the world. By and large, emigrants tended to be better off and to have a
higher social status and more skills than the migrants who sought work
elsewhere in the United Kingdom. Although the period after the Second
World War witnessed an unprecedented growth in domestic incomes and
standards of living, it was not enough to hold back the traditional exodus
from Scotland. A number of reasons can be advanced to explain this. First,
the development of television, extensive print media (the Australian and
Canadian High Commissions published glossy colour brochures and pamphlets) and even the telephone meant that Scots were still better informed
than their forebears in the twenties about the quality of life which could
be experienced elsewhere. While things may have been getting better at
home, they were as nothing compared to the quality of life that could be
enjoyed abroad.

The fifties and sixties were associated with widespread optimism and
increasing aspirations, and, not surprisingly, part of this phenomenon was
a desire to move to societies which offered even greater opportunities.
Development in travel technology meant that journeys were quicker and
cheaper, and if things did not work out then it was possible to come back
home. Not only was travel cheaper, but increased incomes at home meant
that emigration was more affordable by many more people and did not
require such protracted saving as was needed to finance such a venture in
the inter-war period.

Government-assisted travel was also important as Canada, Australia and New Zealand sought to expand their populations through widespread immigration. All Europeans were targeted, but the British were preferred. The Australian experience of the Second World War had led many to believe that a large population was the best defence against any future Asian invasion, and in the sixties Australia opened a two-storey office in Edinburgh with the purpose of processing Scots applicants for a life down under. Scots made up between a quarter and a third of the British exodus to Australia in the sixties and seventies and an advanced guard of '£10 poms' paved the way for friends and families to follow suit. In the sixties Scots made up about a fifth of British emigrants going to Canada, which already had a significant Scottish community. Further opportunities for emigrants emerged from the regimes in Rhodesia (now Zimbabwe) and South Africa, which were looking for an influx of white Europeans to shore up their racist power structures. In 1965 the United States eased immigration restrictions and Scots once again began to make their way to the land of opportunity, accounting on average for between a quarter and a fifth of all British emigrants. The 1970 US census showed that there were 170,000 Scots living there, and by 1990 there were still over 100,000 Scots-born US citizens.

NORTHERNERS

In 1965 the Secretary of State for Scotland, Willie Ross, stated that the image of the persecuted Highlander had been ingrained on the conscience of the Lowlander. Pressure to recognise that the Highlands and Islands constituted a distinctive entity within Scottish society and that the area faced its own unique set of problems had been ongoing since the thirties. Depopulation and problems of infrastructure over a wide area and an extensive rural hinterland made the difficulties faced by the north of a quite different magnitude from those in the south. The Scottish Economic Committee had drawn attention to this in the thirties, the creation of the Hydro-Electric Board in the forties had been accompanied by an explicit acknowledgement of the board's wider communitarian role, and in the fifties the Taylor Commission added further weight to the argument that the area had to have its own agency to deal with its own particular problems. In addition to the official inquiries, considerable public sympathy for the state of the Highlands had been awoken by the publication of *The Highland Clearances* by the Canadian author John Prebble in 1963. Prebble brought the injustices of Highland history to a wider audience, and his harrowing descriptions of the brutal expulsion of the people in the name of modernisation and capitalism in the mid nineteenth century chimed with a growing interest in the Scottish past, as well as greater concern for the victims of the advance of global multinational corporations. Scotland, it was claimed, had its own indigenous society which had been destroyed by greed and avarice:

> At Culloden and during the military occupation of the Glens, the British government first defeated a tribal rising and then destroyed the society that made it possible. The exploitation of the country during the next hundred years was within the same pattern of colonial development – new economies introduced for the greater wealth of the few, and the unproductive obstacle of a native population removed or reduced. In the beginning the men who imposed the change were of the same blood, tongue and family as the people. They used the advantage given them by the old society to profit from the new, but in the end they were gone with their clans.
>
> The Lowlander inherited the hills, and the tartan as a shroud.
>
> John Prebble, *The Highland Clearances* (London, 1963)

The sense of historical struggle has been an important feature of Highland politics and society, and has influenced public debate. With planning all the rage, and state sponsorship of economic growth at the vanguard of Harold Wilson's government, the Highlands and Islands Development Board (HIDB) was launched in a blaze of publicity in 1965. There was much for the board to do. In the mid-sixties, per-capita income in the area was three-quarters of the Scottish average, which was itself a tenth below the British rate. Low income and poor social and economic opportunities, together with the perennial problem of land ownership, meant that the region had been haemorrhaging people at an unprecedented rate. The population dropped from 293,000 in 1931 to 286,000 in 1951, and was 278,000 on the eve of the creation of the HIDB. Although population loss was still greater in the borders, the sense of history worked to the Highlands' advantage, and much of the framing of the problem cast it as a long-term issue.

In the mid-sixties, the people of the Highlands and Islands were mainly engaged in smallholding agriculture, fishing, forestry, and various arts and crafts manufactures, often with individuals holding a variety of part-time jobs in various other occupations, such as estate work and building. The population tended to be older than in the rest of Scotland. Furthermore, there were variations in the rate of population loss, with the islands shedding more people than most of the mainland.

In assessing the prospects for Highland development in the late fifties and early sixties, academics and economists took a fairly negative view, arguing that the most important sector of the economy – crofting, fishing and forestry – would continue to decline and that propping it up would do no good in the long term. It was gloomily forecast that population loss would increase, and that the social and economic structure of the Highlands was decaying and dying. Tourism and forestry, it was concluded, did have scope for development, but not enough to maintain the population. Also, it was believed that investment in industrialisation would not be a solution, and that, instead of putting capital into the Highlands, efforts should be made to move labour out. Politicians, on the other hand, were much more upbeat, and took the reverse view.

By the time the HIDB came into existence, there had not been the grim decline which had been predicted, and overall the Highland economy seemed to be stable for most of the early sixties. Furthermore, in 1955 work had begun on building an experimental nuclear breeder-reactor power station at Dounreay in Caithness, and by 1966 the population of Caithness had doubled. The 1966 Labour government's *The Scottish Economy, 1965 to 1970: A Plan for Expansion* proposed that the Highlands labour catchment areas would receive investment. It was argued that, in the long term, forestry-based industry and tourism would become the economic salvation of the area, but that in the meantime 'a modest intermediate expansion of manufacturing employment will be necessary to ensure that the population structure of the region does not run down to an extent which would jeopardise the ultimate supply of labour on an adequate scale'.

Much of the endeavours of the HIDB went into small-scale projects and local industry, but, inevitably, most public attention tended to focus on the prestigious and large-scale investments. A pulp and paper mill at Corpach in Lochaber brought construction work from 1963, and the mill went into production in 1965. The building of an aluminium smelter at Invergordon began in 1969, and the plant was opened in 1972. Both of these operations were doomed to failure, for a number of reasons. First, although there was a tradition of aluminium smelting in the Highlands, the Invergordon site came on stream just before an escalation in fuel prices in the mid-seventies; together with higher transportation costs, this resulted in closure in the early eighties, with the loss of 900 jobs and a knock-on effect on the local community. The pulp mill closed in 1981 with the loss of 400 jobs, and was a victim more of short-sightedness than of trends in the global economy. Many of the forests near its location had not come to maturity, resulting in undercapacity, and its process of chemical pulping was superseded by mechanical pulping, rendering the mill obsolete and unable to compete with more efficient Scandinavian factories. It was clearly a casualty of the 'dash for growth'.

Although larger industrial investments were not successful, forms of economic activity which chimed with the social and economic structure of the Highlands and Islands did better.

Fishing received considerable investment, and the number of full-time fishermen in the region increased from 2,513 in 1966 to 2,959 in 1979. Although most of the boats were small, and the HIDB helped with the purchase of two-fifths of them, the industry did help provide a source of employment for the community. As it went into decline in the eighties, as a result of the European Common Fisheries Policy and overfishing, alternative forms of employment were found in fish farming, with salmon and shellfish being cultivated in the many inland sea lochs which were dotted along the north-west coast.

Small arts and crafts manufactures did well, and grew in conjunction with the tourist trade. High-quality products such as Caithness glass, luxury foods and Harris knitwear turned out to be the best types of product to counter the high transport costs associated with manufacture in the Highlands.

Tourism was the other significant growth area in the local economy. Although Highland scenery was world-renowned, it took time for the industry to establish itself. Until the mid-eighties, the area was beset with a number of problems. Transport costs and inadequate roads, together with poor facilities, meant that growth in the number of visitors was sluggish. The creation of a comprehensive tourist village in Aviemore with help from a government employment grant in the early sixties was a step in the right direction. The conservative hoteliers, shopkeepers and publicans had to be persuaded to show a more friendly face to visitors, to raise standards to levels acceptable to tourists, and to extend opening hours and lengthen opening seasons. Improvements in hotels, bed-and-breakfast accommodation and other services (many of them provided by English incomers) helped move the tourist trade towards the upper end of the market. By 1982, visitors to Scotland were spending more time in the Highlands, and the region attracted about a fifth of the nation's tourist expenditure. The development of visitor centres, skiing and self-catering accommodation, and a growing specialism in holidays with a nature and wildlife interest, helped to boost numbers. Luxury cruises around the Northern Isles allowed passengers to watch the wild- and sealife and stop off to purchase local goods.

By a focus on small-scale, high-quality goods and services, the economy of the Highlands has been put into better shape than it has been for many centuries. Evidence of the effect of this policy is that population ceased to decline in the seventies, and started to creep upwards. Another facet in the regeneration of the Highlands was the growth of incomers (from both Scotland and England) who were attracted by an alternative lifestyle far removed from the troubles of urban congestion. Indeed, incomers have been some of the most vociferous promoters of indigenous culture and the Gaelic language. Not only did this group bring in wealth, they also had skills and, perhaps more importantly, youth. The arrival of younger parents with small children helped to redress the age imbalance that had been a feature of Highland society. In terms of culture, greater efforts were made to shore up the survival of the Gaelic language. In 1968 the Gaelic Books Council was founded, and Sabhal Mòr Ostaig, the Gaelic College, was established on the Isle of Skye in 1973. The Western Isles Council instituted a bilingual policy in 1975, and there was a steady output of Gaelic television and radio throughout the seventies and eighties. For all that, however, the number of speakers decreased from 93,269 in 1951 to 58,552 in 2001.

The Highlands were the principal regional beneficiaries of Britain's entry into the European Economic Community, and the area was awarded 'Objective One' funding in the early eighties, even although it did not exactly meet the criteria (which helped to counter notions of the excessive bureaucracy of Brussels). In a way this was paradoxical, in that the region had displayed considerable opposition to entry into Europe in the mid-seventies. Objective One status recognised that the Highlands and Islands faced considerable problems with infrastructure and transport, and, in spite of the economy improving, such status was granted on the grounds that the area was a poor one in comparison to the rest of Western Europe. Successful lobbying was helped by the Conservative government of Margaret Thatcher being happy to support any cause which would screw money out of Europe. Certainly in terms of transport and dispersed population there was nothing to match the region within the United Kingdom, and, with the omnipresent voice of history to plead a special case, Objective One status was granted. European money was important in improving transport by building roads and bridges and in providing employment in construction. Also, grants were available for the upgrading of crofts, which in reality meant most people's homes. All of which led to an improvement in accommodation for a great many people.

The society of the north was affected by the discovery of oil in the late sixties and by further exploration and exploitation in the seventies. Almost a third of all manufacturing jobs in the Highlands and Islands in the seventies were oil-related, although the lion's share of the work was located in the north-east. By the end of the seventies, oil provided employment for some 9,000 workers in the Orkneys and Shetlands, although much of this was taken by incomers. The people of Orkney and Shetland are geographically the most peripheral of the Scots, and indeed much of their culture is oriented more towards Scandinavia than to Scotland. This cultural factor combined with the geographical distance to give the islanders a sense of being distinctive and apart. Indeed, just as the nationalist bandwagon began to role in the seventies, there was a similar movement in the Northern Isles which demanded greater autonomy and put the case that government from Edinburgh would be almost as remote as government from London, which itself, as some were wont to point out, was more remote than Oslo.

The people existed in settlements which were isolated, widely scattered, and subject to a hostile climate. Fishing, knitwear and crofting provided the mainstay of the Shetland economy, while work in Orkney was supplemented by whisky distilling and dairy manufacture. Oil had a bigger impact on Shetland, and the population of 17,300 in 1971 grew by over 5,000 during the seventies. The housing stock almost doubled, and incomes, which had been two-thirds of the Scottish average, began to creep ahead of that average. Schools and public services improved, and increasing wealth spilled over to the outlying islands of Unst, Yell, Fetlar, Whalsay and Out Skerries. Much of this transformation was due to the canny local council, which used compulsory-purchase powers to buy land for oil development. The objective of the council was to minimise disturbance to the population while at the same time maximising the financial return for the benefit of the local community. Deals were struck with the oil companies and central government, all of which worked to the benefit of the community, and oil provided more than 90 per cent of rate income in the eighties.

THE OLD

In 1974, women who were born in 1914 retired, while men the same age would have to wait until 1979. They had grown up during the Depression of the inter-war years, lived through the Second World War, survived the austerity of the immediate post-war years, and watched their grandchildren grow in the increasing affluence of the sixties and seventies. For most it had been a pretty hard life, but as they had drifted towards the age of retirement their world had largely been shaped by the optimism which had characterised the sixties, in that, having worked, believed they were entitled to, and had earned, a comfortable old age. However, it is difficult to avoid the conclusion that those who went through the toughest times in the twentieth century did not get the reward they deserved.

The 1981 census showed that 846,000 people in Scotland were over retirement age – 17 per cent of the population. The majority of the elderly were women, who outnumbered men by two to one among the 267,000 people in the category of 'over seventy-five'. It is difficult to calculate figures accurately, as many pensioners were reluctant to claim benefits and the true extent of old-age poverty in the eighties can never be known with precision, but perhaps three out of ten pensioners in Scotland were living on the poverty line. This is more than the number of people who were claiming poor relief on the eve of the Second World War. Many more were only marginally above the line.

There were a number of reasons for this state of affairs. First, the objectives of the Beveridge Report had not been fulfilled, mainly as a result of government cutbacks which linked pensions to the price index rather than the earnings index. As a result of this, the old-age pension in 1980 was about a third of the average manual wage, and it was to diminish even more as time wore on. Second, there had been a low take-up rate of private pension schemes, and even as late as 1980 only half of the workforce were covered by an addition to the state pension. Most of those who retired in 1980 had believed throughout their working life that the state pension would be adequate for their needs. Even those who may have read the writing on the wall found that it was too late to do anything about it, and in 1978 the average paid out by occupational pensions was just £10 per week, suggesting that many had signed up with schemes late in life and did not receive the amount that would have accrued during a full working life. However, even low supplementary pensions had the effect of disqualifying pensioners for additional state benefits, which is another factor in masking the full extent of old-age poverty. Third, couples were counted as one unit, and this masked the number of those dependent on a pensioner. Fourth, and most importantly, the state was mean. In Continental members of the European Community, average pensions were slightly more than half of average earnings, compared to a third in Britain, and it must also be remembered that earnings in the rest of the Community were generally higher. Ironically, the demands of the old were thwarted by the demands of the young, as mass unemployment returned in the eighties, adding considerable cost to the social-security budget. No one had predicted that pensioners would have to compete with single parents and the unemployed for a share of the benefits cake.

The elderly's financial problems were compounded by a number of social circumstances. Most of those who lived in poverty were to be found in council housing, and many of the problems described in Chapter 7 now came home to roost with a vengeance. The state housebuilding programme slowed down in the late seventies, before the issue of the elderly became a major problem. Most houses were constructed with families in mind, and there was a severe shortage of smaller apartments for elderly couples and single people. As a result, many were stuck in houses which were too large, with all the attendant problems of stairs, maintenance and heating. Keeping an overlarge house going with limited finance meant that most of the pension went on maintenance and food, with little left over. Heating was a major problem, because of poor insulation, and a house in Glasgow could cost a fifth more to heat than one in Bristol; for Aberdeen it could be a third more expensive. Cold spells were usually followed by increased admissions of the elderly to hospital. The old were often left behind when estates became run-down as 'good' families moved out and 'bad' families moved in. A lack of suitable accommodation elsewhere was a problem, but another factor was that, having invested time and money in a home, many did not want to leave it and happy memories behind. As time wore on, they could find themselves with new neighbours who had never worked or who were single parents, with an outlook on society and the world about as far removed as possible from their own.

The most exposed were single women. The death of a partner could be traumatic in itself, but the reduction in income, while the outlay on heating and maintenance remained the same, plunged many even further into poverty. Over 80 per cent of single pensioners were women, and they were the most vulnerable section in society. Gordon Brown, the MP for Dunfermline East, summed up the plight of one senior citizen in the early eighties:

'Eighty-two years old and hardly a stick of furniture to call my own. I can't afford to heat my house and eat as well.'

After five burglaries, a flooding and even a mugging, all in her eighty-third year, this is how Glasgow widow Margaret P—, sums up her life. But her biggest headache, she says, is having to live on £32.75 a week, after rent. Margaret simply cannot afford the food, gas, electricity, and other essentials that a pensioner needs.

Margaret's predicament typifies the new face of mass poverty in Scotland, and Britain, today. She is not starving, but she is not properly fed. She is not homeless, but her house is damp and barely tolerable. She may not die of hypothermia, but she has inadequate heating. She is not a prisoner in her own home, but does not have the resources to travel far. 'Luxuries' such as fresh meat, a colour television, or new clothes, cannot feature in her household budget.

'Introduction' in Gordon Brown and Robin Cook, eds., *Scotland, the Real Divide: Poverty and Deprivation in Scotland* (Edinburgh, (1983)

The elderly were not only victims of changing government attitudes to welfare in the eighties, the cultural tide had also moved against them. They were not valued as they had been in the past, as communitarian values broke down under a relentless rise of selfish individualism. For many of the old, who had been brought up to be self-reliant and disdainful of 'charity', who had given so much during the Second World War and had believed in ideas of service, duty and community, there was a terrible irony in being deserted when their need was greatest by the generation which had benefited most from their sacrifices. The idea that the decency of a particular society can be measured by the way it treats its old people is one that lost its resonance in late-twentieth-century Scotland.

NINE

DECAY,
1975–1987

The irresistible march of recent events places Scotland today at a turning point – not of our own choosing but where a choice must sooner or later be made. A resurgent nationalism which forces on the agenda the most significant constitutional decisions since the Act of Union is one aspect of what even the *Financial Times* has described as 'a revolt of rising expectations'. But the proliferation of industrial unrest and the less publicised mushrooming of community action also bears witness to the sheer enormity of the gap now growing between the people's condition of living and their legitimate aspirations.

Yet the great debate on Scotland's future ushered in by the Kilbrandon report and precipitated by North Sea oil and Britain's economic crisis has hardly been a debate at all. Dominated by electoral calculations, nationalist and anti-nationalist passions and crude bribery, it has engendered a barren, myopic, almost suffocating consensus which has tended to ignore Scotland's real problems – our unstable economy and unacceptable level of unemployment, chronic inequalities of wealth and power and inadequate social services ... The basic questions which face the Scotland of the nineteen-eighties remain unasked as well as unanswered: who shall exercise power and control the lives of our people? How can we harness our material

resources and social energies to meet the needs of five million people and more? What social structure can guarantee to people the
maximum control and self-management over the decisions which
affect their lives, allowing the planned co-ordination of the use and
distribution of resources, in a co-operative community of equals.

'Introduction', in Gordon Brown, ed., *The Red Paper on Scotland*

(London, 1975)

Nor can it be argued that political nationalism is one of the great
liberating causes of the human spirit. National self-assertion has
not done much for the cause of peace or the improvement of living
standards in this century; it is out of tune with man's struggling
attempt to gather himself into slightly larger groupings than before
for the better use of his limited resources. Nationalism is a poor
answer to the need felt by a great many people to have more control
over their own affairs, for one cannot be sure that a more narrow-
minded and centralised bureaucracy will not replace the one that
went before, however imperfect. Feeling of pride in one's land and
one's culture are both respectable and desirable, but they are perfectly compatible with membership of a somewhat wider political
family; to sacrifice the benefits accrued over 270 years in order to
gratify confused and ephemeral political ambitions would be tragic
and unforgivably foolish. Now it is up to the people of Scotland to
decide whether they really want to dismantle the United Kingdom
and bring about the end of Britain

Tam Dalyell, *Devolution: The End of Britain?* (London, 1977)

In the months preceding the Referendum of 1979 I remember in
particular three utterances by members of the Scots upper middle
class. A distinguished scientist solemnly assured me that 'we are a
very poor country and always have been'. The head of a well-known
girls' school declared 'We have never been good at governing ourselves and managing our own affairs.' An eminent philosopher of
advanced age asked me: 'What is going to happen to my pension?'
These statements I judged to be the quintessential voice of the
Scots bourgeoisie ... Now and again a picture comes into my mind,

a scene from the early 14th century. In a remote cave high up on a hillside at the north end of Loch Lomond Robert Bruce, recently made king of Scots at Scone but driven by the concerted hosts of his enemies into desperate flight, is explaining to his small band of followers how he proposes to recover Scotland from its conquerors and restore the kingdom to its pristine liberties. Like any good medieval king, he asks his friends to give him their comments and advice. The youthful James Douglas is eager to speak first. 'Sir, we are a very poor country and always have been.' Thomas Randolph, only a little older, shakes his head gravely. 'It is well known', he says, 'that we are not good at governing ourselves.' The king, a trifle dismayed by these remarks, turns to the experienced and comparatively senior Neil Campbell. 'What', asks Campbell, 'is going to happen to my pension?' After this, Robert Bruce is silent and thoughtful for a long time, before dictating a letter of abdication to the English king in which he admits that Edward I has been right all along.

G. W. S. Barrow, *The Extinction of Scotland*, inaugural lecture at the University of Edinburgh (1980)

THE NATIONALIST TIDE

In November 1967 Winnie Ewing won a stunning by-election victory for the SNP in the previously safe Labour constituency of Hamilton. It was a shock that took the political Establishment by surprise, but there were indications before this that the nationalists were on the march. During the fifties, a triumvirate of Arthur Donaldson, Robert McIntyre and Tom Gibson began the work of building the SNP into a modern political party. Although organisation and membership were small, they were coherent and disciplined and formed the nucleus from which the modern party developed.

The immediate post-war era was hostile to nationalism. Centralised planning and state intervention outbid the nationalist economic programme as the electorate focused primarily on employment, wages and welfare. Social scientists were confidently predicting that British society was on its way to becoming one of the most homogenous in the western world as religious and national distinctions declined. By the mid-sixties, things began to change. The assurance that the state would always provide was looking increasingly shaky as the Scottish economy spluttered behind that of the rest of the United Kingdom. As people moved to new towns and estates, traditional party loyalties could not be so readily grafted on to different areas. As aspirations and expectations became greater, the electorate increasingly came to judge politics and politicians on their ability to satisfy materialist demands. A new generation with different ideas, living in different places and doing different jobs from its forebears was not so easily brought within the pale of traditional party loyalties, especially in the mid-sixties, when the organisational apparatus of both the Conservative and the Labour parties had gone into decline. Professional politicians aided and abetted this process of consumer politics as they tried to outbid each other in presenting plans for prosperity. What they did not bank on, however, was the extent to which the electorate was prepared to shop around in an attempt to secure better promises. And if buying goods from a different political stall, albeit for only a short time, was one way of making the established parties take notice, so be it.

A new generation gravitated towards the SNP, its attitudes shaped by the radicalisation of western youth culture. The Labour government's decision not to scrap the American base in the Holy Loch and its tacit support for the war in Vietnam helped in this process. Whereas the Tories and Labour had clearly defined structural hierarchies through which prospective parliamentarians had to pass, younger members of the SNP were able to make a more immediate impact on the direction of the party. This greater openness to enthusiasm and dynamism was important in expanding membership, drafting simple sound-bite policies, and promoting propaganda. The adoption of a new symbol, a cross between the saltire and the thistle, demonstrated a more imaginative approach to campaigning. Armed with evidence to show that Scotland was not doing as well as the rest of the United Kingdom, activists took to the street. At the general election of 1966 the nationalists contested twenty-three seats, and, although the party's vote was only 5 per cent, the SNP's presence throughout the country was increased. In 1967, at a by-election in Pollock, Glasgow, the SNP won 28 per cent of the vote, which let the Tories win the seat from Labour. In the Glasgow local election in May 1967 the SNP won

60,000 votes. Even though it won no seats, this was clear evidence that the message was getting through.

With hindsight, cracks were emerging in the two-party mould, and dissatisfaction with the status quo triumphed at Hamilton. The nationalist candidate, Winnie Ewing, was of a different world from her opponents: young, passionate, articulate, attractive and female. The contrast with the 'grey men' of Scottish politics could not be starker. The nationalists had more campaigners on the ground, and ruthlessly exploited the electorate's grievances. Local ex-miners with health problems believed they had been shoddily treated, rising unemployment caused considerable concern (the figure for Scotland had again gone above the psychologically significant 100,000 mark), and economic turmoil had followed in the wake of the devaluation of sterling in 1967 – all these worked against the Labour government. Though the Prime Minister had claimed that devaluation would not 'affect the pound in your pocket', it seemed to be having more consequences than he had let on. In Hamilton, although the electorate may not have believed in the nationalist solution, the SNP appeared to be the party most prepared to listen. The election of a nationalist projected the community to the centre of British politics for a short time, as the media honed in on this spectacular upset. A SNP victory was an effective way to make government take notice. The following year the bandwagon continued, and the party notched up an impressive 30 per cent of the vote in the local elections and nationalist membership was rumoured to be more than 100,000.

The appearance of nationalism in the late sixties caused some, but not much, consternation in the British political parties. It was no great secret that problems with the economy were fuelling a sense of grievance and frustration that the SNP had been able to capitalise on (see below). Some degree of tokenism was required to appease the electorate and show that the main parties were taking the issue of Scotland seriously.

The Conservatives were the first off the mark. In 1968, at the party conference in Perth, the leader of the Opposition, Edward Heath, indicated his support for the principle of devolution and announced that a committee under Sir Alec Douglas-Home would make inquiries and suggestions. Though widely interpreted at the time as a commitment, the proposals were vague and insubstantial. Devolution was deeply unpopular with rank-and-file Scottish Tories, and the fact that the initiative came from the leadership did not give it much credibility with them. The 'Declaration of Perth' served only to confuse Scottish Tories, who had a long tradition of tooth-and-nail opposition to the creation of a Scottish parliament. It came on top of the decision to change the official name of the local party from the Scottish Unionist Party to the Scottish Conservative and Unionist Party, which may have helped to undermine the party's distinctive Scottish identity. For many of the rank and file, Unionism and support for devolution were irreconcilable.

In 1969 the Prime Minister, Harold Wilson, turned his attention to the rise of the SNP and appointed a Royal Commission on the Constitution, headed by Lord Crowther. The idea behind this was to give the appearance of doing something, which would avoid the need for real action for as long as the commission was deliberating. According to Wilson, the commission was designed to spend years taking minutes, but in public it gave the appearance that the government was taking the issue seriously. It was hoped that, by the time the commission reported, the SNP would have gone away.

In any case, the nationalists seemed to have hit their high-water mark by 1969, as by-election and local-council results failed to maintain the previous momentum. Although the SNP contested a record number of seats in the general election of 1970, and the sixty-five candidates secured 11 per cent of the vote, the party scored only one success, by winning the Western Isles. Hamilton returned to Labour. Political pundits concluded that the SNP was a spent force. At Westminster, the Conservatives were returned to power on a platform that advocated a reduction of public expenditure and a tougher stand against trade unions. Scotland moved in line with British electoral trends, in that the Conservatives' share of the vote went up (although only marginally compared to the rest of the United Kingdom – from 37.7 to 38 per cent), while Labour's share went down by the same proportion as in the rest of Britain (from 49.9 to 44.5 per cent). The Liberals lost two of their five Scottish seats, as did Labour (46 to 44), and the Tories gained three (20 to 23). With the composition of Scottish MPs more or less the same as in 1966, and the threat from the SNP in abeyance, it was time once more to turn to the fundamentals of politics: management of the economy.

For the historian of twentieth-century Scotland, the seventies are a difficult decade. Economics is intertwined with politics, and politics is entangled and suffused with economics. Not only that, the threads that wove the tapestry of politics and economics in Scotland were of the same hue and texture as those that formed the wider British fabric. Distinguishing them is difficult, and the period can best be described as a mess. There is no easy way to separate out the various strands for simple analysis.

Although the performance of the Scottish economy improved between 1965 and 1975, much of that was because of government intervention. Productivity rose to reach and momentarily surpass the UK average, and wages did the same. Yet it was very much a tale of two economies. The traditional sector declined, but this was offset by the growth in branch-plant manufacturing. Mainly because of Britain's perennial balance-of-payments problems – the country was spending more than it was earning – manufacturing was accorded most importance in the grander schemes of political economy at the time. Indeed, the size and health of the manufacturing sector were widely used as the key indicator of a nation's economic well-being.

In terms of total employment, manufacturing had been declining in most modern economies, but the rate of decline was a cause for worry in the United Kingdom and especially Scotland, as it was believed that this was the 'propulsive' sector of the economy that pushed up growth. Although not particularly out of line with the economies of Western Europe and North America, manufacturing's share of employment in the United Kingdom (34.8 per cent) and Scotland (32.4 per cent) was a good ten percentage points behind that in West Germany, which was cast as the example of the successful economy. However, it needs to be borne in mind that the proportion of the workforce employed in manufacturing is a crude economic barometer, in that older and more inefficient industries will employ more workers than those which are mechanised. The real growth area in the economy, north and south of the border during this time, was services, but it received little attention. Whatever their other differences, politicians, business leaders and trade unionists held to the dogma of the primacy of manufacturing.

By 1975, 59 per cent of Scottish manufacturing workers were employed by companies that were based outside Scotland. The obsession with attracting inward investment and consumer industry paid off, but it did so at a time when manufacturing was losing its value in the world economy. After Canada, Scotland had the highest per-capita US investment in the world. The big attractions of Scotland were low wages and a link into the European market. Much of the work was unskilled assembly work, often employing part-time female labour. Inward investment was not achieved without cost, however. Government incentives, in particular subsidies on wages under the 1964 Local Employment Act, increased from £15 million in 1964 to £193 million a year by 1973. Between 1966 and 1971, a grand total of £641 million had been spent on creating 105,000 jobs, which works out at over £6,000 per job – more than four and a half times the average annual wage at 1966 prices. Some of this money was spent keeping mining, steel and shipbuilding going, and the last of these soaked up about £90 million, which worked out at almost £15,000 per job. Nevertheless the number of jobs lost was 50,000 greater than the number of jobs created in this period as the traditional sector declined.

The biggest problem in the economy was a dearth of home-grown business. In part this can be explained by the prevailing attitude at the time, especially with regard to the economy, that 'big was beautiful'. Large multinationals were wooed because it was thought that they would bring most employment, by creating large-scale manufacturing units. This meant that, largely under the leadership of politicians, a dependency culture came into existence, in that the bulk of the population expected that jobs would be made for them by large companies, which were themselves pulled to Scotland by the lure of government money. Although no one could have predicted it, the Scottish economy exchanged one set of problems for another. Heavy dependence on the export market in the traditional industries was transferred over time to the new branch manufacturers. With fluctuations in the world economy – in particular the recession following the Arab–Israeli war of 1973, which quadrupled oil prices – branch-plant operations were inevitably the first to be closed down. In that respect they were more vulnerable than the traditional industries. A further paradox emerged in that, at a time when government pulled the main levers of the economy, much of the actual control of industry passed to company head offices in Detroit, Chicago and elsewhere, which meant that politicians had no real influence over whether or not these companies would up sticks and go.

The wider problems facing the British economy had the greatest impact on Scotland. Poor industrial relations and inflation were the two most significant British economic problems encountered north of the border. In the period from 1952 to 1980, the number of working days lost as a result of industrial disputes was 55 per cent higher than the UK average. The initial reason for this poor performance was to be found mainly in the traditional industrial sector as coal, steel, shipbuilding, engineering and dock workers had a higher tendency to strike – and in the period up to the mid-sixties this traditional sector made up a large part of the Scottish economy. However, many of these strikes were initiated at a British level, and it could be argued that the figures show not a greater tendency to strike in Scotland, but rather a greater predominance there of industries whose workers tended to strike.

If the figures for the period from the mid-sixties to the mid-seventies are examined, what emerges is that Scottish strike activity broadly follows British patterns, although the number of working days lost is still a good deal higher. Strike action tended to be precipitated by the threat of redundancies. Not surprisingly, in the sixties it was in the traditional sectors where most labour was being shed, and hence there was a greater fear of job losses there, and a greater tendency to strike in defence. Later, the same could also be said of branch-plant manufacture, which was probably more significant in this respect in the seventies, as by that time the traditional sector was not big enough in itself to account for the disparity between Scottish and UK working days lost on account of strikes. The fact that Scottish unemployment rates were consistently higher than the UK average may give some credence to the belief that fear of job losses was a factor in precipitating higher levels of industrial action. Another important feature was that the worst of the industrial-relations problems were located in the western central belt. If the number of workers involved in strike activity is calculated, as opposed to days lost through strikes, then the Scottish figure is 40 per cent above the UK average. Though bad, taken in conjunction with the number of days lost this shows that there was a tendency for a smaller number of workers to strike for longer or more often in Scotland. Certainly contemporary opinion held that a culture of strike-readiness was endemic in the Glasgow conurbation.

Inflation was the other twin evil of British economic performance in this period. 'Stagflation' was the term coined for inflation at a time when growth in the economy was stagnant – something that economists had believed to be impossible, until it happened. In spite of government intervention to impose wage restraint and a 'social contract' with the trade unions, it proved impossible to escape the inflationary spiral in the seventies. Exceptions were always being made for powerful unions, which had the effect of encouraging others to plead a special case. Rising prices led to a demand for higher wages; the increased cost of production when these were agreed to was then passed on in higher prices, leading once more to demands for higher wages. By 1972 inflation was running at 7.2 per cent per annum; by 1974 it was 16 per cent, and in the following year it reached 25 per cent. It was checked for a while, dropping back to 15 per cent in 1976 and to 8.4 per cent in 1978, only to rise again to 17.2 per cent in 1979. It was indicative of an economy in turmoil.

In spite of the Heath government's pledge to cut public investment and withdraw the state from active economic intervention, this policy did not get off the ground. The threatened closure and bankruptcy of Rolls-Royce and Upper Clyde Shipbuilders in 1971 meant a reversal of policy and a resort to nationalisation for the former. Public and political opinion was not yet ready to sanction a policy of letting lame ducks go to the wall. Public sympathy had already been roused by the shipyard workers, who staged a 'work-in', led by the charismatic shop steward Jimmy Reid. In many ways, the experience of UCS was emblematic of the wider failings in the Scottish economy. The management had been woeful in carrying out its responsibilities. It had failed to adapt to the wider international challenges facing the industry, was responsible for a chaotic system of industrial relations, and had an approach to business which could only be described as reckless. One thing that both management and workers agreed on, however, was that it was government that was responsible for their fate. Both camps looked for and expected government intervention to save them from closure. Eventually the government stumped up £35 million to keep the yards in business.

The policy of intervention and nationalisation was no longer being used according to economic criteria, but rather was used for political purposes as a means to save industries which were all but dead and shore them up at public expense. The principle was that political cost outweighed economic cost. Similar problems were experienced by the car industry in Scotland, where high transport and component costs meant that it had little chance of competing effectively against Midland manufacturers. Scotland's motor industry remained in splendid isolation, as the expectation that component manufacture would spring up in the surrounding area to feed the factories was not realised. Instead, parts had to be imported from the south and put together in the north, with the finished product being dispatched south to be sold. It did not take an economic genius to see that the industry was highly disadvantaged. Grants, subsidies, nationalisation of British Leyland in Bathgate, and the government sponsored buy-out by Chrysler of Rootes in Linwood kept things going, but with little prospect for long-term survival. Both Bathgate and Linwood barely managed to maintain output levels above 50 per cent of capacity.

The year 1973 was a bad one for strikes and industrial relations in the United Kingdom. One feature of this strike action was that it had a wide impact on the economy, and key workers had the ability to make other workers in other industries be laid off. In February a gas workers' strike laid off workers who found power to their factories cut. In May there was a one-day strike against the government's incomes policy. In November miners began an overtime ban, which cut coal production by 22 per cent in one week. In December, Aslef, one of the railway unions, began an overtime ban, and the resulting fuel shortages, which were made worse in the wake of the Arab–Israeli war, forced the government to institute the three-day working week. (For a peripheral economy on the edge of Europe, which was heavily dependent on exports and where transport costs were already burdensome, the rise in oil prices resulting from the Middle East conflict had a particularly deleterious impact.) In February 1974 the miners began a full-time strike, which was to bring the government down.

The period was also marked by a number of highly publicised closures, such as that of Plessey in Glasgow in 1971, though most jobs were lost as a result of cutbacks and streamlining. Scottish unemployment figures crept upward from 80,000 in 1970 to 130,000 in 1972. Although there was a sharp fall thereafter – back down to just over 80,000 in 1974 – the figures then climbed again just as steeply, peaking at over 160,000 in 1977, where they stabilised until the end of the decade, only to rise sharply again in the early eighties. The threat of unemployment was a constant fear that lurked in Scottish society through the seventies. Further economic pressure was brought to bear when interest rates rose to an unprecedented 13 per cent.

Added to the economic woes, there were political problems, all of which intensified the sense of crisis that dominated British society in the early seventies. When striking miners challenged the Prime Minister, Edward Heath, to hold an election, there were accusations that the trade unions were holding the country to ransom and that democracy was being circumvented. In any event, the Conservatives unexpectedly lost the election in February 1974 to Labour, but by an insufficient margin for a majority government to be formed. The new Prime Minister, Harold Wilson, did not have problems to seek. A growing economic crisis, problems with industrial relations, balance-of-payments difficulties, rising unemployment, together with dissension in his own party about Britain's membership of the European Economic Community, meant that his minority government was addled from the start. If that was not bad enough, the 'Troubles' in Northern Ireland were building up momentum, and the IRA began a bombing campaign on the mainland. The government limped along until October, when another general election was called. Labour was returned again, this time with a wafer-thin majority of three. It was against this background of mounting crises in British economic and political life that the SNP eventually made its electoral breakthrough. In many respects the rise of nationalism was the Scottish response to a British crisis.

A number of explanations can be mooted for the rise of the SNP in the mid-seventies, ranging from the discovery of oil to the emergence of third-party politics as a response to the failure of the two main parties to deal with the endemic problems of the British economy. Although seemingly checked in the general election of 1970, the SNP was nevertheless building up steam. The mounting chaos of the Heath government was certainly a factor in undermining the credibility of both Labour and the Conservatives in relation to managing the economy, and in England this led to an upsurge in support for the Liberal Party as an alternative to what was increasingly seen as the stale and fruitless machinations of the two main parties. Similarly, in Scotland the SNP came across as an alternative.

It is difficult to say with certainty what impact the discovery of oil in the North Sea had on the political fortunes of the nationalist movement.

Certainly its discovery was fortunate in that it came at a point just before the crisis in 1973 when OPEC cut back oil production, raising prices and triggering a downturn in the world economy. Oil could be presented as an economic saviour, after massive government intervention had failed to maintain the performance of the Scottish economy relative to that of the rest of the United Kingdom. Contemporary opinion held that the world's reserves were dwindling and that oil would become more valuable than gold. Scotland's black gold was a natural endowment which in and of itself, it was believed, would make the nation rich. This was a feature of the SNP's electoral campaign, and the slogans 'It's Scotland's Oil' and 'Rich Scots or Poor Britons?' were used to good effect. Nationalist strategy centred simply on the basic principle that a Scotland which was independent from the rest of the United Kingdom could divorce itself from what appeared to be the endemic problems of poor productivity, bad industrial relations and the rest of the package of what was known as 'the British Disease' and lie back and enjoy the spoils of oil revenues, which would provide a free telephone service, a superb health service, and the kind of affluence that was enjoyed by the oil-rich Arab states.

If nothing else, the emergence of oil into the debate on the fiscal relations between Scotland and England shattered the notion that the former was dependent on the latter for its economic well-being. Yet, for all that, Unionist economists did manage to fight a rearguard action, claiming that once Scotland had had to pay its share of the national debt there would be nothing left of the oil money. Some even argued that, if the territorial waters were marked out in a different way, it could be shown that the oil belonged to England.

As was stated earlier, it is difficult to say precisely what impact oil had on Scottish electoral behaviour. Undoubtedly some saw it as an effective means of escape from the woes of the British economy and were seduced by the prospect of selfishly keeping it to themselves. Others were undoubtedly appalled by this prospect. The historian and future nationalist Chris Harvie believed that there was still enough virtue and merit in the Union in 1977 to argue in his book *Scotland and Nationalsim* that 'Possibly the most promising option for Scottish politics is that the revenues from oil go to Britain, but that the Scottish legislature be allocated power and cash adequate for a total recasting of Scottish society.'

It should be borne in mind that a populist sense of British identity had been created and grafted on to Scottish society in the period from the Second World War. A crucial component in making this work was the belief that the British state was responsible for the welfare of all its citizens, and arguably this had conditioned a quasi-egalitarian outlook which would find it reprehensible to pursue independence out of naked self-interest. After all, the British state had provided Scotland with schools, hospitals and jobs, and, although there were difficulties, especially in the seventies, it was a tall order to ask people to turn their back on this. Some evidence for the existence of this attitude can be found in the fact that it was the young who tended to vote nationalist. At the end of the day, national identity has to do more with sentiment than with economics and, although the latter formed the mainstay of political debate, the former was never far away, often lurking just under the surface. The idea of Britain had a lot of emotional capital in Scotland during the seventies. The Scottish Tory Esmond Wright, writing in 1970, could barely keep this under the surface:

> The case for Scottish separatism is based on the belief that Scotland is a nation state and that the boundary lines of nation and state are identical. Some of their own leaders take pride in claiming that they want an independent Scotland to sit at the United Nations between Saudi Arabia and Senegal – assuming that either of these has any influence there whatsoever. They forget it was disruptive nationalism which destroyed the stability of central Europe and that the seeds of Hitlerism and irredentism were sown at the Peace Settlement of 1919. The repeated model they use for an Independent Scotland is Norway, forgetting the fact that Norway has none of our industrial problems because it has no industrial base, and no huge city like Glasgow to subsidize.
>
> 'In Defence of the United Kingdom', in N. MacCormick, ed., *The Scottish Debate* (Oxford, 1970)

Others went further and claimed that Scotland was not a nation – although this was a strategy more likely to inflame nationalism than to extinguish it. Unhelpful parallels were drawn with the troubles in Northern Ireland, with the more lurid claiming that nationalism would lead to a terrorist bombing campaign which could culminate in a sectarian blood-bath. The SNP was attacked by the left as an impediment to and a distrac-tion from the wider ambitions of socialism. On the right it was deemed a threat to tradition, and those in favour of the British armed forces and the monarchy rallied to the defence of the Union. One thing that nationalism could certainly claim credit for was that it injected life back into Scottish politics and considerably raised the talent of Scottish politicians. The sev-enties witnessed a crop of gifted new Labour politicians such as Donald Dewar, Gordon Brown, Robin Cook and John Smith, who had to cut their political teeth in defending the Welfare British State from the onslaught of nationalism. Likewise, Alec Buchanan Smith, George Younger, Mal-colm Rifkind and the combative Teddy Taylor emerged to revitalise the ranks of Scottish Tories.

Harold Wilson's hope that the Royal Commission on the Constitu-tion would fade into the horizon was forlorn, although he did have the sat-isfaction that it came back at a time when his opponent was in power. The Kilbrandon Commission (Lord Crowther had died before its work was completed) reported at the end of October 1973, the week before a by-election at Govan, bringing the issue back from the dead and, through its conclusion that devolution was not necessary, helping the nationalists to victory. Its report was also timely for the general election in February 1974. At that election the SNP notched up 22.5 per cent of the Scottish vote, winning seven seats. In the October election its support rose to 30.7 per cent of the vote, winning eleven seats. In terms of share of the vote, the SNP had overtaken the Tories (32.9 and 24.7 per cent) and was just under six percentage points behind Labour (36.6 and 36.3 per cent). In terms of seats, the nationalists did best in former Tory seats (nine out of eleven of those won), giving rise to the Labour accusation that the SNP was a party of 'tartan Tories'.

The real reason for nationalist success in these constituencies was that the SNP was able to harness the substantial anti-Conservative vote, partic-ularly in the council estates in medium-size towns. This was especially the case as Labour had been reluctant to build up its organisational presence in rural seats. The nationalists moved in and cleaned up. The Labour heartland proved a harder nut to crack, especially in the industrial west, and, although the party lost votes, these were not sufficient to deprive it of seats. Yet for many the signs looked ominous. Was the nationalist bandwagon unstoppable? It seemed so. Opinion polls showed no slowdown in support for the nationalists, and in January 1976 two Labour MPs, Jim Sillars and John Robertson, jumped ship to form the breakaway Scottish Labour Party. A flood of documents, debates and discussions considered the future of the nation, and for many the prospect of independence now seemed a reality.

HALTING THE TIDE

Conventional wisdom held that nationalism was being fuelled by disappointed expectations on issues of social and economic policy. This was no secret, and it had been part and parcel of Scottish Labour strategy in the sixties to ask for more money from central government on the basis that if none was forthcoming there would be an upsurge in support for the SNP. Greater intervention was the first line of defence against the rise of nationalism, and with this in mind the Scottish Development Agency (SDA) was set up in 1975 to manage Scottish economic development more actively than had been done in the past.

There was a fair amount of criticism of past government economic policy, and this was exacerbated by failures to exploit the potential of the new oilfields. Critics – led mainly by nationalists and economists – pointed out that the economy did not have the necessary expertise and skills to make best use of the new opportunities which were opening up with the discovery of the black gold. Left to their own devices, Scottish and British industry remained lacklustre in bidding for development work. Research, technology and manpower had to be brought in from outside, and it was argued that some degree of government intervention was needed to ensure that local business was able to join in the oil bonanza. In reality, such hopes were forlorn from the start, because the government – facing a massive balance-of-payments crisis and strapped for cash – was desperate to get the oil out as quickly as possible and was only too happy to leave it to the multinationals. The deals that the government struck were driven by the short-term need to get money flowing into the Exchequer sooner rather than later. It was said at the time, and has been repeated since, that the discovery of North Sea oil gave a greater boost to the economy of Texas than to that of Scotland.

The dash for oil revenues was not evidence of a coherent long-term strategy for economic development. More and more the penny was beginning to drop that economic intervention which was driven by political criteria was a bad investment and ultimately doomed. North Sea oil was the latest chapter in a story of economic failure. According to the economist David Simpson, writing in 1977:

> The policies which have been pursued under the objective of alleviating unemployment have not only been inimical to growth: they were almost exactly the opposite to those which would have been pursued under a policy objective of economic growth. I mean by this that the so-called 'regional policy' pursued by successive British governments has perpetuated the relative backwardness of the Scottish economy by perpetuating low productivity industries at the expense of directing labour and capital towards newer higher productivity industries. One only has to think of the huge sums poured into shipbuilding on the Upper Clyde, the aluminium smelter at Invergordon, the strip mill at Ravenscraig, Chrysler Linwood, regional employment primia, etc ... I would therefore argue that the single most important factor accounting for the poor performance of the Scottish economy in the past 25 years has been the absence of a coherent policy for economic growth.
>
> Donald Mackay, ed., *Scotland 1980: The Economics of Self-Government*
>
> (Edinburgh, 1977)

Much of the rationale behind the creation of the SDA was to counteract proposals from the nationalists that revenue from North Sea oil should be channelled into a special fund for the regeneration of the Scottish economy. Whereas it would be necessary to wait for oil to come onstream, the new agency could be put into operation more or less immediately. The SDA centralised a number of functions which were already undertaken by other government agencies, and it was hoped that streamlining would bring greater effectiveness. From the outset, it was clear that the agency would not bankroll lame ducks, but instead should focus on wealth creation. In short, it would concentrate on the new, rather than propping up the old. It had powers to provide loans for investment in industry at a competitive rate of interest, to disperse and dispose of publicly owned factories, and to engage in environmental reclamation. Part of its remit was that it should largely be self-funding. Although launched in a flurry of publicity, much of what was promised was hardly new but had been floating around the economic agenda since the 1960 Toothill Inquiry. In many ways the SDA arrived too late, because the year after it was created Britain went bust.

In October 1976 the Chancellor of the Exchequer, Denis Healey, announced that the nation would borrow £2,300 million from the International Monetary Fund, just as sterling went into free fall creating a massive balance-of-payments deficit. It was the largest loan ever granted in history. The post-war spending spree was over, and a condition of the loan was that Britain would put its economic house in order. Balancing the books would mean cutting public expenditure, raising taxes, and imposing wage restraints in order to curb the inflationary spiral. The result was mounting industrial disputes, which would culminate in the 'winter of discontent' in early 1979, when NHS and local-authority workers, lorry drivers and others all went on strike.

There was also mounting political turmoil. The government had had a bruising as a result of the referendum on EEC membership in June 1975, before which there was a Cabinet free-for-all, with ministers openly arguing against one another. The new Prime Minister, James Callaghan, who stepped in after the sudden resignation of Harold Wilson in early 1976, faced a challenge from the left of the party, which was unhappy at the pursuit of stringent economic policies. There were a number of abstentions in a vote on proposed cuts in public expenditure, resulting in defeat for the government. As if this was not bad enough, the government could keep going only with Liberal support after it lost its majority in November 1976. Discipline within the Parliamentary Labour Party was breaking down. Also, the troubles in Northern Ireland became worse. The Conservative Party had been reinvigorated by the election as leader of Margaret Thatcher, who promised to sort out the unions. It was against this background of economic and political turmoil that the debate on Scottish devolution took place. It should come as no surprise that a government reeling from crisis to crisis was not best placed to give it its utmost attention.

The Labour Party dusted off various proposals and ideas regarding devolution in 1976. Two things helped put the issue on the political agenda. First, in a worsening economic climate, the scope for the traditional method of appeasing Scottish grievances – namely investment to improve socio-economic conditions and demonstrate that the Union worked to the Scots' financial advantage – was severely curtailed. This was particularly problematic, given the assumption that socio-economic grievances were the driving force behind Scottish nationalism. If these grievances could not be addressed at source, then some other means had to be found to diffuse the nationalist threat. In the absence of money to throw at the problem, something had to be done to stop the SNP juggernaut. Second, therefore, a political response was necessary to stop the advance of the nationalist movement. Devolution emerged as a likely contender, in that it would cede an element of self-government to the Scots, but would stop short of independence. It was argued that the Scots wanted not separation, but rather a greater degree of political autonomy. The SNP, it was claimed, had exploited the wave of discontent at the lack of Scottish domestic political control, but if this could be appeased by a greater degree of self-government, then the nationalist vote would fizzle away. Devolution, it was hoped, would do the trick. The emergence of devolution on the political agenda was not driven by a belief in the virtue of reform of government for its own sake, but was rather the best option available, given the government's limited ability to appease the electorate with greater public spending. It was a pragmatic solution which was designed first and foremost to stop the rise of the SNP.

But would it? Not all were convinced that it would. The Conservative Party adopted its usual posture while in opposition: it prevaricated, hinting that the Scots could get something better than what was on offer from Labour, while at the same time, denouncing the scheme as a threat to the integrity of the Union. The Labour Party shuffled, hummed and hawed, seemed to be in support of it, stalled, and then – with a fair bit of influence from the London leadership – accepted devolution as policy in 1976.

Just as there were many within Labour who believed in the policy as a matter of principle, there were those who were likewise opposed to it. And the issue did not just divide the Labour Party: two opposition junior ministers, Alec Buchanan Smith and Malcolm Rifkind, resigned because of the Conservative Party's opposition to a Scottish assembly. Divisions were also just as bad in the SNP. Hardliners in the party believed that devolution was a ruse designed to stop the bandwagon on its way to independence, or at best to slow its progress. It was argued that devolution would divert attention away from the campaign for independence and sucker the electorate into accepting something second rate. It was claimed that it was best to keep things polarised between independence or nothing, as the absence of change would drive the electorate into the nationalist camp. Only the Liberals could claim to have a genuine long-standing commitment to devolution, and it was perhaps for this reason that the other parties ignored them.

Essentially, the debate was polarised between two different projections of what the eventual outcome of the devolution process would be, and these cut right across party lines. On the one hand it was claimed that devolution would lead to, depending on the choice of metaphor, the 'slippery slope' or the 'highway' to independence. This argument was put across most eloquently by the Labour MP for West Lothian, Tam Dalyell. Basically, any concession to nationalism would feed its appetite, which would never be sated until the power of constitutional change had been pushed to its limit, which would ultimately result in independence. Dalyell argued that attempting to solve the problem of electoral discontent by devolving more power to the Scots was a mistake. If the electorate came to believe that more political power was the best way to tackle social and economic discontent, voters would demand more and more until there was none left to give; only then would they come to realise that it did not hold the key to the answers they were seeking. At this stage, he claimed, the process of separation would be complete. It was best to keep the nationalist genie in the bottle. For this reason, and other, more practical ones, which will be discussed below, Dalyell and others in the Labour Party opposed the creation of a Scottish assembly.

On the other hand, many nationalists supported devolution for a similar reason, though they had to be cautious about it, given that the SNP was supposed to stand for independence and nothing less. Also, they did not want to give succour to devolutionists in other parties. Devolution, many nationalists believed, would provide a 'stepping stone' to independence. It would be easier to win the case for independence within a domestic Scottish political context that was to some extent sealed off from the wider British political arena than it would be under the present system. Furthermore, devolution would mean that independence would not be a 'leap in the dark': it would accustom the Scots to political decision-making. Also, as nationalists held that devolution was a flawed solution – a sort of halfway house – the increasing exposure of its flaws would help promote the case for independence. If, however, it worked, then there could be no reasonable argument against extending the devolved powers and gradually pushing them all the way. In short, an assembly would make an excellent springboard for an independent parliament.

Other arguments concerned the financial viability of an independent Scotland, attained with or without devolution as a constitutional intermediary. For nationalists, Scotland would be an oil-blessed and wealthy country, while Unionists claimed that it would end up like Ireland. The latter argument had to be revised when Irish per-capita GDP passed that of Britain in the eighties, and Albania then took the place of Ireland in this model.

The preoccupation of the Labour government with survival, the divisive nature of devolution, and the hasty construction of the proposals for it helped to undermine the progress of its bill through the House of Commons. The bill was subject to a barrage of criticism, mainly stemming from the so-called 'West Lothian Question', in which Tam Dalyell asked if, when a Scottish assembly came into being, it would be fair for him as a Scottish Westminster MP to voice opinions and vote on matters which affected the English localities, when no other Westminster MP would be able to have any say about Dalyell's own constituency of West Lothian, which would be under the jurisdiction of the Scottish Assembly. Devolution, the argument ran, was a constitutionally iniquitous system which favoured the Scots and the Welsh – whose nationalists were also to be appeased – at the expense of the English. The Parliamentary Labour Party's lack of discipline meant that the bill was ambushed from time to time. A failure to pass a 'guillotine' motion in February 1977 meant that all the bill's flaws and weakness could be exposed mercilessly in parliamentary debate. More crucially, in January 1978, there was passed the so-called Cunninghame amendment, named after the Scottish Labour MP George Cunninghame, who sat for a London seat. This stipulated that over 40 per cent of the total electorate had to vote 'yes' in a referendum for the act to come into effect. In short, the apathetic would be counted as voting 'no'.

If devolution's progress through the House of Commons was chaotic, it did not fare any better on the campaign trail. The 'no' camp was better organised, and had funding and support from the business community. Coherence was maintained by keeping to the relatively simple mantra that the assembly would lead to independence, and Scotland could not afford this. The 'yes' campaign had not the coherence, the organisation or the funding of the opposition. The SNP was lukewarm about the whole thing and failed to give it unqualified support for fear of being seen to sell out on the issue of independence. Labour had its devo-sceptics, who either failed to get involved or sniped from the sidelines. Both parties had to desist from the campaign in order to exchange political blows about government policy, which was not exactly a convincing demonstration of how the political nation could work together, and it was made clear that there could be no cross-party campaign. Only the Scottish Trades Union Congress remained steadfast in pursuing the issue. A further problem was that opinion polls seemed to show that a 'yes' vote was in the bag, and many assumed that the assembly would come into existence as a matter of course. This contributed to a lack of urgency which was not addressed until it was too late.

All the time, party politics continued unabated by the need for unity in the campaign for a Scottish assembly. The nationalists kept up the pressure by doing well in the May local elections in 1977, but thereafter things were further complicated by the advance of the SNP seeming to have drawn to a halt. In April 1978 Labour held on to the Glasgow Garscadden seat in a by-election, and polled almost twice the nationalist vote in regional council elections. In the following month Labour held on to Hamilton in a by-election, and in October the SNP lost its deposit at the by-election in Berwick and East Lothian. Labour was also buoyed up by evidence that the economy was starting to improve. Unemployment was levelling off, inflation was going down, and the government seemed to be having success in imposing pay restraint. Better news on the economic front coincided with opinion-poll evidence that support for devolution was beginning to falter, and, although still commanding most support, the 'yes' camp dropped from over 60 per cent to just over 40 per cent between 1976 and the end of 1978, with about 20 per cent of voters being undecided. If anything, this was a spur for the anti-devolutionists, who argued that, as the issue was coming under greater scrutiny and more flaws were being exposed, the electorate was increasingly developing cold feet.

The fact that the nationalist bandwagon stopped when the economy was beginning to stabilise was further evidence that the electorate's fling with the SNP was driven by socio-economic grievance, rather than the desire for constitutional change. This was also backed up by evidence from opinion polls, which consistently showed that a majority of nationalist voters did not believe in the party's flagship policy of independence. There was increasing confidence that the SNP vote was one of protest, not separation. All of which put further pressure on the nationalists, who initially had been mixed in support of devolution, but now increasingly came to see the vote for the assembly as a test of confidence. Failure to vote for a devolved assembly would not augur well for a vote for independence. No matter how the party tried to spin it, the public associated the nationalist movement with constitutional change, and the SNP's credibility was therefore increasingly tied in with delivering a positive vote for the assembly.

The crunch came on 1 March 1979. Of those who voted, 51.6 per cent voted 'yes' and 48.4 per cent voted 'no'. However, when the actual numbers were translated into proportions of the total electorate, which was necessary to see if the Cunninghame 40 per cent rule was satisfied, the result came out as 32.9 per cent of the electorate voted in favour, 30.8 per cent voted against, and 36.3 per cent did not vote. The proposals therefore went no further.

Why did the Scots fall at this most basic hurdle? Explanations are varied and colourful. One attempt to explain the defeat (though many would not and will not concede that it was a defeat) argued that the nation's psyche was reeling in the aftermath of the humiliation of the Scottish football team during the 1978 World Cup in Argentina. For many, the whole World Cup episode was emblematic of what was wrong with Scotland. Buoyed up under the leadership of Ally MacLeod, the Tartan Army marched off assuming that victory was certain, only to fall at the first hurdle and become painfully aware that they had deluded themselves into believing that they were a great football nation with a great football team. Given the huge chasm between belief and reality, many wondered how they could have been so stupid and how they could have got so carried away. Were there parallels with the idea of self-government and independence? Some commentators believe so. Others point at more immediate political circumstances. The referendum took place in the aftermath of the 'winter of discontent', which helped to discredit devolution since it was associated with an unpopular government. Furthermore, the Tories did not help by stating a fortnight before the referendum that the electorate should reject devolution on the grounds that the Conservatives would produce something better. Whatever the respective merits of these explanations, the plain truth of the matter is that devolution was a deeply divisive issue in Scottish society. Broadly speaking, a third wanted it, a third did not, and a third did not care. This hardly indicated the settled will of the Scottish people.

Paradoxically, the policy of devolution – which came into existence primarily to stop the SNP – ended up becoming most closely associated with the nationalist party. The referendum was a test of nationalist credibility, in that the party risked coming out of the whole fiasco with nothing. Though Labour now walked away from the issue, a substantial number of Scots had voted in favour of it, and the nationalists were left holding the baby: it was a policy which they were initially against, but one that they could not drop. The nationalists became the most passionate advocates of a Scottish assembly. But it was a no-win situation, and there was an increasing perception among the electorate that the party had backed a lame horse.

Furthermore, the parliamentary strategy of the nationalists confused voters, who could not make up their mind if the party was to the left or the right. The SNP had endeavoured to maintain a position of studied neutrality between the Tories and Labour, but, although supposedly non-partisan, this sent out mixed messages to the electorate. However, it was on Labour's handling of devolution that the SNP made its last stand during this parliament. After months of bickering and attempts to get the repeal order for the assembly removed – the devolution proposals were in the statute book and had required only approval in the referendum to become law – in May 1979 the nationalists voted with the Tories to bring the government down. According to the premier, Jim Callaghan, it was like turkeys voting for an early Christmas. But supporting a government that had abandoned devolution would have cost the SNP much credibility, and there was also a huge amount of bitterness among the rank and file at what they believed was Labour duplicity. At the general election of 1979, the SNP vote fell from 30.4 per cent to 17.3 per cent, which wiped out nine of the party's eleven seats. The nationalists were the biggest losers.

The collapse of the nationalist vote in 1979 does tend to confirm that much of the party's support in the seventies was soft and motivated by protest, rather than by belief in independence. Also, the SNP had failed to establish a clear constituency, as the party tended to attract voters from across the class and regional divides, and it was therefore difficult to hold together. And the SNP may also have been punished by the electorate for having brought down a Labour government. More than anything, it appears that it was the nationalists, not Labour, who were ultimately discredited by the devolution fiasco. Voting for the SNP had failed to deliver more power for Scotland and the separatist's bluff had been called. In Scotland, the Conservatives' vote went up from 24.7 to 31.4 per cent, which won them six extra seats and brought their tally to twenty-two MPs. Labour also increased its share of the vote from 36.3 to 41.6 per cent, and the party's existing forty-one MPs were augmented by another three. The Liberals stayed the same. South of the border, the Conservative Party fared better than its northern counterpart and, with a numerical neatness, won a forty-three-seat majority with 43 per cent of the vote.

THE IRON LADY

In popular Scottish mythology, the eighties match the thirties as the Devil's decade. Living memory has designated this era as the 'Thatcher Years', and the images of this period in Scotland are overwhelmingly dominated by dole queues, factory closures, political strife, and a bleakness

which was captured in much of the literature of the time. The contrast
with the popular perception of the eighties in much of the south – that it
was a time of extravagance, self-indulgence and affluence – could not be
greater. Long-term mass unemployment, poverty and an uncaring government were common to both the eighties and the inter-war era. But, unlike
the thirties, the eighties witnessed the decline of the Conservative Party in
Scotland, and this was indicative of a real political divide which opened up
between north and south of the border. Within a period of eight years, the
governing party of the United Kingdom would find that its vote in Scotland had shrunk to a quarter of the electorate and its number of MPs was
reduced to ten out of seventy-two. This was something that confused the
Prime Minister, Margaret Thatcher, who found it difficult to understand
why her ideological crusade had encountered such stiff opposition in this
northern backwater, which resisted the allure of the market and instead
clung desperately to old-fashioned collectivist and statist notions. After
all, as she pointed out, Scotland was the country where Adam Smith was
born, and it was he who had first extolled to the world the benefits of the
free market – although, as many have pointed out then and since, hers was
a very narrow interpretation of the work of one of Scotland's greatest moral
philosophers. The more that Thatcher promoted the free market under her
regime, the more the Scottish electorate was inclined to reject it.

The Conservative Party's decline in Scotland has many reasons. First,
it has to be said that in the early years of her government it was not what
Thatcher did, but rather what she did not do, that gave offence. Having
come to power on a ticket which proclaimed the virtues of the market
economy and a determination to push back the frontiers of the 'nanny
state', she did exactly what she said she would do: nothing. Government
intervention in the form of state aid to ailing sectors of the economy
ceased. It just so happened that the imposition of this policy coincided
with a major downturn in the global economy, and together these had a
devastating effect on Scottish society. With traditional industries clinging
on for grim life and vulnerable branch-plant factories liable to be closed
down by multinationals with little notice, there would inevitably be an
adverse effect on the Scottish economy. The Thatcherite response was to
take it on the chin. Those firms with competitive ability would survive by
becoming hardened to the market's knocks. The industries that collapsed

under international competitive blows would be left on the canvas, as there was no point in government picking them up only for them to get knocked down again. Unfortunately, Scotland's economic jaw line was brittle. The vulnerabilities of the Scottish economy were not new: rather it was the response of not shoring them up or providing any form of transitional aid that was novel. The crutches of state intervention were taken away. It was nasty and brutal medicine, and no amount of sermons could convince the patients that it was good for them.

There was an economic restructuring of a magnitude that had probably not been seen since the days of the Industrial Revolution. At a stroke, with little public expense and within a remarkably short period of time, the Scottish economy lost all its traditional problems which politicians had endeavoured to solve from before the Second World War. Unprofitable industries and businesses closed, the traditional sector more or less disappeared, services took the place of manufacturing, and the economy emerged in the latter part of the eighties as a lean, mean fighting machine which could match the Japanese in terms of per-capita exports. Between 1979 and 1988 the contribution of manufacturing to GDP declined by just under a quarter, while that of services increased by over a sixth. The number employed in manufacturing declined from 605,000 in 1979 to 412,000 in 1986, while investment dropped by two-fifths. The industries that had been propped up by the state – namely steel, coal, shipbuilding and car manufacture – all collapsed after a period of 'downsizing'. This fundamental restructuring of the economy was not, however, achieved without a significant social cost.

It is difficult to map out the precise shifts in the pattern of Scotland's occupational structure, other than to say that by 1987 it was fairly similar to England's. The difficulty stems from the habit of using broad occupational classifications, which can be quite meaningless and confusing. For example, a stockbroker and a fast-food worker are both classified as working in the service sector. The fact that employment in services was growing was often taken as evidence that the economy was thriving, as money was being spent and circulated. Indeed, the prevailing thought at the time was that services were associated with modernity, while industry was increasingly seen as the domain of the developing world. For all that, it cannot necessarily be said that the growth in services was evidence of a

vibrant economy if large sections of the labour force were being employed
in restaurants and low-skill work. Nor can it be said that the transformation of the Scottish economy was painless. Two recurrent themes dominated Scottish society throughout the best part of the eighties:
unemployment and low pay.

By 1983 unemployment had passed the 300,000 mark (14.6 per
cent), and this did not take into account the number of young people who
were hidden from the statistics on youth work schemes, nor those people
who had been transferred from unemployment to invalidity benefit.
Debate about 'fiddling the figures' was a regular political ritual. In 1985
unemployment peaked at 15.6 per cent, and thereafter it gradually
dropped to 8 per cent by the end of the decade. The belief that mass unemployment had been abolished at the end of the Second World War was laid
to rest, and it is important to remember that there were many still alive
who could remember the experience of the thirties, so there was a double
bitterness in that mass unemployment was being experienced by a society
for the second time in living memory. Men and women who had painful
memories of the hard times of the thirties had to watch their children and
grandchildren go through the same experience. For those who had
believed 'never again', this was the ultimate betrayal, and would generate
great bitterness. The vulnerability of the Scottish economy meant that the
rate of unemployment north of the border was usually between a quarter
and a third higher than in the United Kingdom overall. To add insult to
injury, this was the decade of the southern yuppies with 'loadsamoney',
and the disparities between north and south widened to the same extent as
during the inter-war years. All this did not help the government's popularity in Scotland.

There were, however, crucial differences between unemployment in
the eighties and in the thirties. First, in the eighties unemployment had
more of an adverse effect on the young. In April 1983 a third of men and
half of women out of work were under twenty-five years of age. Failure to
secure a job early on in life diminished the chances of securing one later, as
lack of experience and prejudice against the long-term unemployed
counted against candidates at interview. A hidden cost was borne by many
families in keeping out-of-work offspring in the family home. An associated feature was the development of a 'social security' culture among the

young in certain jobless black spots, where life increasingly revolved around and adapted to not being in work (see Chapter 10).

A second difference of unemployment in the eighties was that it was more random than the thirties. While certain areas did experience worse levels of redundancies, with the western central belt faring more badly than the east, and certain industries were more prone to be hit than others, a key feature of the time was the culture of maximising efficiency in the work-place. In effect, this meant shedding as much labour as possible. Although closures captured most public attention, most of those who were laid off were made redundant as part of a drive to maximise efficiency. The tradi-tional industries made up no more than 15 per cent of the total workforce, and by themselves do not account for the high rate of unemployment. There was a culture of 'slimming down' that was not only sanctioned but cele-brated by the government, and it was not unique to Scotland. In order to boost productivity and profits, shops, factories, offices and contractors, working to the new dogmas of time-and-motion management, stripped units down to the minimum labour requirements. This meant that no one was safe. Foremen, middle management, administrators and overseers were just as likely to fall victim to the axe of efficiency as those on the factory or shop floor. Furthermore, fear of the 'shake-out' was used as part of manage-ment strategy to encourage greater efficiency. Countless office workers and middle managers worked extra hours to ensure that their position was safe by outperforming colleagues. Competition was against not just other com-panies, but also fellow workers as a means to ensure job security. Those who could not maintain the pace set by the fastest would be first to go. The vocabulary of the workplace became infected with euphemisms like 'letting somebody go', 'downsizing', 'shake-outs' and 'streamlining'. With the power of the trade unions emphatically crushed following the defeat of the miners' strike of 1984–5, management became increasingly emboldened in raising demands on the workforce. Flexitime and multitasking replaced traditional lines of demarcation, and meant that more work could be done by fewer workers. The process of shedding 'excess weight' in the economy was universal, and could hit someone in Edinburgh just as much as in Dundee or Glasgow. The critical regional difference regarding unemploy-ment was that there were more opportunities to find a new job in the east. Just before the general election of 1987, a BBC Scotland poll found that 58 per cent of those interviewed believed unemployment was the top political priority.

It is difficult to calculate the exact effect of unemployment in the first half of the eighties, other than to say that it was fairly universal, and that *fear* of unemployment, rather than the experience of it, was something that the middle class and the working class shared. A critical factor in explaining the unpopularity of the Conservative government in Scotland was that even when the economy did improve, towards the end of the decade, the electorate was not prepared to forgive it for the instability and harrowing times of the early eighties. Sleepless nights cost votes.

A second factor is more difficult to pin down, but might be called popular political economy. Not only was the Thatcherite economic revolution not enjoyed in Scotland, it was not understood. A constant complaint made by trade unionist after trade unionist, as factory after factory closed, was that the nation would soon cease to make things, and that a nation that did not make things would not be able to pay its way in the world. The invisible economy of finance and services was not readily understood by a population which had been reared on the notion of a Scotland which paid its way by producing ships, engines and the like. For many, political economy could be understood only in terms of tangible things, and the idea that only things which could be handled could have any real monetary value was one that was widespread. De-industrialisation had a profound cultural impact which should not be underestimated. It had been a matter of faith for those who worked in shops, offices and banks that they were ultimately dependent on those who worked making things, as the latter had 'real' jobs. For them the service sector was an ancillary to manufacturing, and the idea that it could in fact lead the economy was not readily understood. Furthermore, Scotland in the eighties did not have many of the great drivers of the service sector that existed in the south-east of England. There was no great metropole of wealth. Glasgow was a metropole of poverty, and Edinburgh, though significant, did not have the same impact on its environs that London had on the south-east. The property boom did not affect Scotland to the same extent as it did England, as the private housing sector was so much smaller. An economy driven by services, tourism and investment was one that many found difficult to understand, and still more found it hard to believe that it would work.

There was considerable political furore about the extent of unemployment in Scotland and the way in which the figures were calculated, but
some facts seemed incontestable. In 1983 there were three-quarters of a
million Scots who were dependent on supplementary benefits for a living,
and it was reckoned that over a million people were living on or below the
officially defined poverty line. Some projections put the number of those
with low incomes and inadequate resources at over a million and a half.
De-industrialisation, streamlining and closure meant that many changed
jobs, usually from those that were reasonably paid to those that were not,
and low pay was just as significant a factor in causing poverty as unemployment. One of the reasons why Scotland had a good record in attracting inward investment was the prospect of low-paid workers. In 1981
Scotland had 13 per cent of all male and 60 per cent of all female full-time
workers who, even with overtime, earned less than 60 per cent of the average UK weekly earnings for men. The fact that overtime was included in
the calculation disguises the extent of low pay, in that those who worked
long hours could effectively remove themselves from this bracket, but
none the less their hourly rate precluded living on normal working hours.
In Grampian region for example, 15.5 per cent of male manual workers
were officially low paid, but if overtime is not taken into account then this
figure would rise to almost 30 per cent. In Scotland as a whole, the figure
for low-paid male workers would rise by 65 per cent if overtime were not
included, which effectively means that one in five Scottish male workers
was paid a rate of pay that put him in the bracket of low pay. These figures
do not include the substantial number of people who worked on a part-
time basis, who were mainly women, and if they are factored into the
equation, then one in three of the total workforce was in low pay. There is
no escaping the conclusion that, while poverty was bad in the eighties, it
would have been considerably worse if people had not been working extra
hours.

   Long hours, low pay and an unstable economy coincided with wider
changes in family life, and undoubtedly help to accelerate the existing
trend for divorce and separation. By the mid-eighties, over 100,000
households were single-parent and more than 20,000 families were headed
by an unmarried mother. Work was an economic necessity for most married women, and only one in twenty male workers conformed to the

widely held stereotypical notion of supporting a non-working wife. About a quarter of women with children under the age of five were working. Undoubtedly, but hard to prove empirically, long hours, low wages, and the omnipresent threat of unemployment did not help to increase stability in the family. In spite of the Sex Discrimination Act of 1975, there had been little advance for women in society, and the figures for low pay make this point eloquently. According to Esther Breitenbach:

> Women form over 40% of the work-force in Scotland. The main characteristics of their work is as follows: – it is low paid, low grade, semi-skilled, in the secondary part of the economy, and is frequently part-time. Women's average pay remains low in relation to men's, primarily because the sexual segregation in the work-force means that most women are in jobs that are not comparable to men's and which – because they are done by women – are accorded a lower value. Legislation such as the Equal Pay Act is completely unable to tackle this situation. In order for there to be an equitable distribution of earned incomes between men and women, there needs to be a equitable distribution of men and women throughout the labour force.
>
> *Radical Scotland*, October/November 1985

Although the changed economic and social circumstances of the eighties threw many received assumptions to the wind, there is little evidence that they changed the attitudes of men. Although at first glance there would appear to be a correlation between class and family breakdown, in that it was mainly among the unemployed and low-paid that most instances of child abuse and neglect, suicide, marital violence and domestic abuse were recorded, it may be that the middle-class were better at covering up their family 'problems'. Also, it is likely that incidences of domestic breakdown were increasing because women were no longer prepared to put up with abuse as their predecessors might have done in the past. As was mentioned in Chapter 8, the dispersal of the extended family, and the fact that most people tended to live next to other families that had similar social profiles, meant that many more women would now be inclined to rely on neighbours for support. This may have been important in breaking the conspiracy of silence surrounding domestic abuse, in that relatives had previously provided pressure to keep unworkable marriages going. In a society where women were becoming more influenced by friends of the same age, rather than relatives, there was arguably a greater sense of female solidarity. Again, the fact that more women than ever before were working, usually alongside other women, was important in contextualising issues of domestic abuse and providing support networks. Abused women could not be isolated to the same extent as in the past by keeping them at home and out of sight.

As ever, the brunt of the economic turmoil fell on the poor, the least educated and the unskilled. The trends that had been established towards greater redistribution of wealth and increased social mobility were reversed in the eighties, and the gap between rich and poor began to widen again. In total, after tax, in 1980–85 the top 10 per cent of earners took home more than the bottom 50 per cent, and the wealthiest 10 per cent owned four-fifths of the nation's wealth. Culturally, this was reflected in the work of the 7:84 Theatre Company, which took its name from the fact that 7 per cent of the population owned 84 per cent of Scotland's wealth.

As the economy steadied, further features emerged. It was the unskilled manual workers, rather than the white-collar workers, who were most likely to experience unemployment, particularly because it was more difficult for them to find work once made redundant. In the recession of 1987, when house prices collapsed in the south, there was not as great an impact in Scotland. All of which suggests that the first recession of the early eighties had been much deeper, longer lasting and slower to recover in Scotland.

Of course, not all Scotland experienced hardship in the eighties, and by the latter part of the decade there was enough statistical evidence to show that, in terms of per-capita prosperity, the nation was second only to the south-east of England in the United Kingdom. Scotland had its prosperous hot spots, and insurance and banking led Edinburgh to creep up into major affluence, while in the north-east there was a boom in oil-related industry. House prices soared in both areas. Even Glasgow and Dundee were making tentative steps towards economic recovery, fuelled by tourism, retailing and services. Over 100,000 Scots took advantage of the 'right to buy' and purchased their council house, creating a whole new generation of homeowners. Yet, for all that, Scotland's affluent class did not reward the Conservative Party, and economic recovery failed to revive the party's fortunes. If anything it made them worse.

By the mid-eighties there were at least a quarter of a million Scots who had come from manual working-class families and progressed into white-collar jobs, thanks largely to the Welfare State. Although the rate of social mobility was not as great in Scotland as in other parts of the United Kingdom, especially the south-east, there were nevertheless a significant number of people who had seen their social and economic circumstances improve. This was due mainly to education, which in Scotland was almost universally provided by the state. Not only did the state provide opportunities to elevate one's social status by means of educational qualifications, it often provided social climbers with the very jobs that marked the transition from working class to middle class. Teachers, social workers, local-government workers and civil servants were not only dependent on the state for their employment, they had also depended on the state to obtain the necessary qualifications in the first place. Social mobility through state employment was especially prevalent in Scotland as there was a disproportionate number employed in the state professions north of the border. This was perhaps the major cultural difference between north and south. In the latter, social mobility was more associated with enterprise and business. A debt of loyalty to the Welfare State was acknowledged by many middle-class Scots, and was an important factor in keeping Thatcherism at bay. Their identification with the state was reinforced by the Conservative government policy of cutting back expenditure on social services and local government. Furthermore, the constant haranguing of the public sector for 'bureaucracy, waste and inefficiency' did little to endear public-sector workers to the virtues of free enterprise.

Another factor which worked against the spread of Thatcherism north of the border was the fact that the social class which made for the most ardent Tory supporters – the independent skilled tradesmen and small business people who propped up party support in England – was not as well developed in Scotland. The affluent service-sector economy in which plumbers, electricians, builders, specialist retailers and the like all did well in the south was lacking in Scotland. Not only did Scotland lack the independent tradesmen and retailers, it was also missing out on many of the skilled factory workers in areas such as aircraft, cars, defence contracts and light engineering, all of which prospered during the Thatcher years. Although retailing grew to be a major part of the economy in the second half of the decade, the nation had nowhere near the levels of wealth that could sustain a thriving independent small-scale retail sector. Instead, there was a poor rate of business start-up, with politicians of all parties preferring to look towards inward investment as the major motor of the economy.

A further gulf emerged in the sense that, as the skilled and independent workers in the south turned to Thatcher, the British working class split along a national basis, with the Scots remaining loyal to Labour. Although the north of England held true to its Labour tradition, for reasons of simplification there was increasing talk of an English–Scottish divide, and this helped to undermine the sense of British solidarity, especially among the working class. There was a growing sense among many Scottish trade unionists and activists that the English working class had sold the pass. Political scientists have pointed out that class and Scottish national identity have become increasingly conflated from this period on. In assessing the legacy of Thatcherism in Scotland, it is very easy to concentrate on personalities and overlook the fact that local politics were being driven by a major social and economic transformation at a UK level. For the majority, that transformation was not to their liking.

DIVISIONS

The Thatcher government had its life made easy by the fact that most of the other political parties decided to implode. The eighties have been correctly portrayed as a decade of Labour impotence. Divisions within the party, impractical ideological concerns, and a divorce from political reality rendered Labour unelectable at a British level. Much of the party's bad image was media-driven, in that the tabloids were merciless in their attacks on the 'loony left'. Exaggerated stories about political correctness gone mad portrayed Labour's programme as one promoting a gay/lesbian, ethnic-minority, anti-nuclear paradise which would subsume 'traditional' British values. The SNP also clambered on the bandwagon of political self-destruction. By 1980, splinter groups on the right and left were mounting sustained attacks on the SNP leadership, which was already battered and bruised following the humiliation of the referendum defeat. Expulsions were the order of the day, and the party's process of maintaining some form of discipline overshadowed anything it had to say in the way of policy. Popular representations of the nationalists highlighted the party as moving to the left, though in actual fact it remained fairly centrist, as it always had been. Labour in Scotland, on the other hand, did not share in the convulsions that rocked the party south of the border. Trendy lefties made little impact, and Labour retained its traditional mould and avoided the 'loony left' label which became associated with many Labour councils south of the border. The Scottish party's organisational structure, its Byzantine internal politics, and its almost 'closed-shop' mentality meant that a leftist takeover was extremely difficult.

The principal problem with politics north of the border in the eighties was that Scotland became irrelevant. The Conservative electoral hegemony (based on votes in the south) meant that the Scottish Tory Party cared increasingly less about how its own electorate voted, safe in the knowledge that the Conservatives were sure to be returned to power in Westminster. This degree of arrogance did little to endear the party to the population, and further reinforced the notion that the Conservatives did not care about Scotland. Indeed, a salient part of Tory identity in Scotland during the eighties was a sense of being a persecuted minority, whose convictions were hardened by constant rejection at the polls. The fact that the Tories failed to command a measure of popular support from the electorate became increasingly problematic, especially after the election of 1987, which slashed the party's Scottish electoral representation.

Although it was not initially apparent that the Conservative Party was destined to govern indefinitely, Labour's defeat in the general elections of 1983 and 1987 posed awkward questions for the Labour Party in Scotland – especially as the party had done so well north of the border, but had been let down by a poor performance from southern colleagues. The problem for Labour was that Tory unpopularity in Scotland was not reflected in England, where, even with the realist Neil Kinnock at the helm, the party seemed unable to dent Tory support. The divergence between Scottish and English political behaviour was awkward for Labour, as a Unionist party, and it did not want to draw too much attention to this dichotomy, lest it be taken up as ammunition by the nationalists. Barely whispered at first, but repeated ever louder, the fear grew up that the Tories would indeed govern Scotland indefinitely, by virtue of their impregnable southern vote. Furthermore, as Labour increased its presence in Scotland, while the Tories collapsed, a key feature of its electoral strategy was to keep a watchful eye on the nationalists, who were more than ready and willing to capitalise on the gulf between Scottish and English electoral behaviour. Independence, the SNP argued, was the only sure-fire way to escape from Thatcher, as a Labour government was unlikely to be elected in future. Yet, with nationalists and Labour both denouncing one another, the Tories were able to carry on governing Scotland without much interruption. The big problem for Labour was that its official position admitted, albeit not very loudly, that there was nothing wrong with the Tories' concentration on governing the United Kingdom as a whole. As the UK party of government, the Conservatives had the right to rule by virtue of their overall British majority. To state otherwise would add fuel to the nationalist cause, which was already simmering because of seeming Labour impotence and growing dissatisfaction with social and economic conditions. Indeed, Labour was able to turn on the Tories by stating that their extremist policies would break the Union by driving the disaffected into the arms of the SNP.

A second political anomaly related to the form of government in Scotland. One thing became very apparent, very quickly: it did not take a large political following in Scotland for an effective administration to be imposed. While there is a tendency to believe that the advent of Thatcherism inaugurated an alien system of government in Scotland which went completely against the wishes of the people, the fact of the matter is that Thatcher was able to use the government system of her predecessors to impose her political will without need for modification. Thatcher did not change the system of government in Scotland: rather, she used it in ways which made apparent its inherently anti-democratic nature.

Throughout the post-war period, both Labour and Conservative governments had been accumulating power to the Scottish Office. This was not necessarily apparent, because by and large Scottish political opinion was broadly in tune with that of Britain as a whole. So a swing to Labour in Scotland would coincide with a Labour-controlled Scottish Office, and vice versa. What was different about the eighties was that politics were polarised. In the past, even when there was a swing to Labour in Scotland but the election of a Tory government, the two parties' policies were often not far enough apart to make much of a difference. Thatcherite policies, however, were viewed as extremist. One reason why home rule came back on to the political agenda in the late eighties was that the so-called 'democratic deficit', whereby the democratic aspirations of the Scots were not represented by the UK government, was made apparent and real by Conservative government policy. There was nothing constitutionally wrong in what was done: it was just that the limits of this arrangement had previously never been stretched as far, and most Scots now found them uncomfortable.

As the Tories were fond of pointing out, however, there was a majority of support in Scotland for parties that were in favour of the Union, and if people did not agree with UK-wide policies then they could go and vote for the SNP. It was an astute tactic to polarise the debate on the constitution between independence and the status quo, because the Tories were quite confident that, given a choice between the two, the majority would plump for the latter. Besides, they could embarrass their other Unionist rivals by forcing them to make the same point. Again, Labour did not wish to add grist to the SNP mill, and merely claimed that the Conservatives were endangering the Union by abusing their powers in Scotland in the face of opposition from the local majority.

In a world of politics that was polarised between left and right, with a nationalist movement licking its wounds and languishing on the sidelines, the centre tends to be forgotten in discussion of Scottish political development during the eighties. Nevertheless, it is possible to say that the eighties were the decade of the centre, in that the Liberals and Social Democrats (who combined to form the Liberal Democrat Alliance in 1988) had almost as impressive an electoral performance then as the SNP did in the seventies. At the general election of 1983, the Alliance increased the Liberal vote in Scotland from 9 per cent to 24.5 per cent – just four percentage points behind the Tories and ten percentage points behind Labour. The SNP continued its downward trend, dropping from 17.3 per cent to 11.8 per cent of the vote. Although the Alliance did not do as well in terms of seats, winning only eight, it was still a healthy showing.

Paradoxically, it was those most committed to proportional representation – the Liberal Democrats – who profited most from the first-past-
the-post system in the general election of 1987. Although their vote
dropped by almost a fifth, to 19 per cent, the Alliance was actually able to
increase its number of seats by one, to nine. The Alliance was helped by
the fact that anti-conservative voting was working in its favour. Before the
general election of 1987, there was much talk of using tactical voting to
make Scotland a 'Tory-Free Zone', but few were convinced that it would
work as well as it did:

> Tactical voting, needless to say, depends for its success on the elec-
> torate knowing who to vote for. In most of the Tory-held seats this
> is obvious and so the exercise is straightforward. In about half a
> dozen Tory seats in '83, Labour and the Alliance were fairly close in
> terms of votes received. If the present opinion polls can be trusted
> at all, then in most of these 'close' seats the Labour party must now
> be regarded as the main challenger than the Alliance ... if tactical
> voting takes place to any great extent at all, then it seems to be in
> little doubt that all Tory MPs are in some danger. The questions
> which remain are (1) how far can the Tories recover in the run-up to
> the election, and (2) to how great an extent can the Tactical Voting
> Campaign persuade the electorate in these seats to use their vote to
> the maximum effect. If the answers to these questions are (1) not
> much and (2) quite a lot, then we are on the brink of the biggest
> upheaval in Scottish politics this century, and potentially a consti-
> tutional crisis if Mrs Thatcher is returned to No 10 once more.
>
> *Radical Scotland*, May 1987

The electorate learned the principle of tactical voting fairly easily. Labour,
with 42.4 per cent of the Scottish vote (an increase of just under seven percentage points) was able to add a further nine MPs to its tally, taking the
total number to fifty. Even the SNP increased its tally by one MP, while its
vote rose to 14 per cent. The big losers were the Tories, who lost more than
half their MPs (a fall from twenty-one to ten) and whose vote fell from 28
to 24 per cent. Anti-Conservatism had been placed at the top of the Scottish political agenda in the general election of 1987, and the key factor in

determining the electoral outcome was the coalescing of the anti-Conservative vote in Tory and in marginal seats. Although Labour benefited the most from this, anti-Conservatism, as far as the electorate was concerned, was surmounting conventional party loyalty. While there was a change in the Tories' share of the total vote, its significance was magnified by tactical voting to deliver the key anti-Conservative results. A decrease of only a seventh in the party's vote proved enough to produce a loss of over half the Tories' seats.

One of the key features of Scottish politics in the late eighties and throughout the nineties was the dominance of Labour. Labour's grip on parliamentary constituencies and local councils became ever firmer, even though the party's share of the total vote was marginally declining. The explanation for this was the electoral system, which was of major significance in determining the party-political representation of Scotland for the rest of the century. Tactical voting when combined with the first-past-the-post system worked better for the Labour Party than for any other political organisation in Scotland. Labour was blessed with what is known as 'vote efficiency'. This term, coined by political scientists, describes how the first-past-the-post system works to any particular political party's advantage. In a first-past-the-post system, it is the winning of individual constituencies that matters, and if a party has enough voters in enough constituencies then it can really turn up trumps. As an example of how this works, consider that we have ten constituencies with ten voters in each, making a total electorate of 100. Party A wins 6 votes to party B's 4 votes in 8 constituencies. In the remaining two seats Party B wins 10 votes to party A's 0 votes. With only 48 per cent of the vote, Party A has won 80 per cent of the seats, whereas Party B, with a majority of 52 per cent of the vote, has won only 20 per cent of the seats. Although this is an extreme case, it does help to explain why Labour should have done so well in Scotland in the election of 1987 and those thereafter. Labour vote efficiency in Scotland was greater than Tory vote efficiency in England.

Yet, for all the talk of a Tory wipe-out north of the border and a constitutional crisis, the Conservatives carried on in government after the 1987 election. Labour's success in Scotland only helped to highlight the party's failure in England, and thanks to their English majority the Tories were set to rule Scotland once again. Hopes of a London Labour government remained forlorn. A new term entered the Scottish political vocabulary in 1987: Doomsday Scenario. In effect this characterised the situation in Scotland if the nation rejected Thatcherism at the polls once again but Labour experienced its third defeat in a row in England.

In Scotland the opposition was looking dangerously impotent. Before the election there had been rumblings about this, giving rise to much debate about how Scotland would cope with a third Conservative administration. The day after the general election of 1987, Doomsday had arrived.

RESURRECTION,
1987–2000

May I also say a few words about my personal belief in the relevance
of Christianity to public policy – to the things that are Caesar's?
The Old Testament lays down in Exodus the Ten Commandments
as given to Moses, the injunction in Leviticus to love our neighbours as ourselves and generally the importance of observing the
strict code of law. The New Testament is a record of the Incarna-
tion, the teachings of Christ and the establishment of the Kingdom
of God. Again we have the emphasis on loving our neighbour as
ourselves and to 'Do-as-you-would-be-done-by'.

I believe that by taking these key elements from the Old and
New Testaments, we gain a view of the Universe, a proper attitude
to work, and principles to shape economic and social life. We are
told that we must work and use our talents to create wealth. 'If a
man shall not work he shall not eat,' wrote St Paul to the Thessalo-
nians. Indeed, abundance rather than poverty has a legitimacy
which derives from the nature of Creation. Nevertheless, the Tenth
Commandment – thou shall not covet – recognises that making
money and owning things could become selfish activities. But it is
not the creation of wealth that is wrong but love of money for its
own sake ... What is certain, however, is that any set of social and
economic arrangements which is not founded on the acceptance of

individual responsibility will do nothing but harm. We are all responsible for our own actions. We can't blame society if we disobey the law. We simply can't delegate the exercise of mercy and generosity to others.

Margaret Thatcher, speech to the General Assembly of the Church of
Scotland, Edinburgh, 21 May 1988

It was time to put a brick through a window. Come on. Let us be honest and truthful about this, a brick through the window. But he couldnt be bothered doing it. He just couldn't be bothered. He would have to hide up a close after the event and it would be damp and draughty and if he got caught christ it would be so horrendously awful and pathetic: disaffected teacher puts brick through window, embarks on property rampage down the streets of Possil except everybody knows there's no property in Possil anyhow because they've no got fuck all, the rich having stolen it from them. So, the banks of the city and big bricks. At least it would be a bloody start. There was a pair of polis across the street who needless to report were observing him openly and frankly and not giving a fuck about who was noticing. But now they watched him watching them. And he stopped walking to call: You've no seen a bus by any chance! And he smiled a big smile, proffering the arse to the aggressors as usual.

James Kelman, *A Disaffection* (London, 1989)

There is a lot of truth in the belief that the Scottish people in general are more tolerant and accommodating than their English cousins. Even in India during 200 years of the Raj, the Scots were usually far more forbearing and far more considerate towards their Indian subjects. This characteristic of the Scots could be due to their mixed make-up of Scottish society or to their sympathies being with the other underdogs, considering that they themselves have been underdogs to the English for a long time. Whatever the reason, the Scots in general are more tolerant and more friendly towards strangers. Having said all that, it does not mean that all is well in Scotland. Yes, race relations are comparatively better in this

part of the United Kingdom than in many other parts. True the
ethnic minorities are, in general, happier here and doing well in
trade and commerce. But there is no room for self-congratulation or
complacency, because discrimination and racism, individual as well
as institutional, and a lack of opportunities do exist in present-day
Scotland. The new generations of Asians, Afro-Caribbeans and others labelled as ethnic minorities are already in revolt, and they are
not going to live with the present humbling and humiliating state
of affairs. They do not think of themselves as immigrants. They
have not seen any other society or any other country. They are the
new Scots. They want to be and deserve to be treated like any other
member of Scottish society.

> Bashir Maan, *The New Scots: The Story of Asians in Scotland*
>
> (Edinburgh, 1992)

THE CONSERVATIVE COLONY

The introduction of the community charge or poll tax has been depicted
as one of the defining moments of Margaret Thatcher's career as Prime
Minister. For many, it was a radical step too far, and the outbreak of civil
disturbances following its introduction in England in 1989 demonstrated
that that there were chinks in the Iron Lady's political armour. In Scotland, there is a belief that the poll tax was the policy that broke the unre-
formed Union's back and that, after its introduction, things could never be
the same.

The genesis of the community charge, to give the poll tax its proper
title, can be traced back to Conservative frustration with the electorate's
tendency to return high-spending Labour authorities in local elections.
For the Conservative hierarchy, this was deemed problematic on two
fronts. First, there was an ideological dimension, as it meant that there
were still bastions of organised Labour support in the country which,
through local government, were still able to wield considerable power and
were believed to be an impediment to the creation of a free-market society.
Furthermore, local government afforded some protection to trade unionists and the public sector. The destruction of these safe havens for the left
would consolidate the Conservative hegemony in British society. Second,

there were party-political considerations. Although central government had progressively cut the block grant to local authorities in an endeavour to curtail expenditure, and had introduced 'capping' (a limit on how much councils could spend), the shortfall between income and planned expenditure was often made good by pushing up rates, which fell most heavily on property owners, who were believed to be natural Tory voters. Some way to cut rates would be extremely popular with the Conservative grass roots. This was especially the case in Scotland, where revaluation on a four-yearly cycle pushed up rates north of the border at a faster rate than in England and Wales, where revaluation took place less frequently. Also, as homeowners made up a smaller proportion of the population in Scotland, it meant that they bore a disproportionate burden of the cost compared to in England.

It was in response to these concerns that the poll tax was formulated. The idea behind it was that, as everyone used local services, then everyone should be expected to pay. As most services were used fairly equally, then, so the argument went, it was only fair that everyone should pay the same. It was hoped that, when everyone paid the same charge, the electorate would become more discriminating in its choice of local government, in that a high-spending council would mean a universal rise in the poll tax in its area. Conversely, a council committed to low spending would mean a lower poll tax. It was believed that, as Labour authorities were committed to high spending and Tory authorities were committed to low spending, the latter would be more popular with poll tax payers. Subtle the idea was not. Part of the Tory plan for the introduction of the poll tax was the belief that voters would be guided by their pockets and turn against the Labour Party as the costs of local government bore directly down on them. While some may have been attracted by Labour promises for council activities, especially if the cost was going to be passed to the ratepayer, it would be a different thing, so Tory strategists believed, if all council electors were charged the same. The electorate, it was hoped, would punish spendthrift councils. To help this process along, central government cut funding allocations to local government, in the belief that Labour councils would have no alternative but to raise poll taxes and thus speed up disillusionment with high-spending councils. As so often happens with the best-laid plans, it backfired – and central government copped the blame for the whole thing.

In Scotland, the poll tax is often taken as the ultimate symbol of the Thatcherite imposition of unpopular policies on a reluctant nation that had rejected such measures at the ballot box. Insult was added to injury by the tax being introduced a year earlier in Scotland than in England and Wales. Put bluntly, the least Thatcherite part of the United Kingdom was being punished by the special imposition of the most Thatcherite policy to date. Many viewed it as a turning point. It was claimed that this was the real evidence that Thatcher really did not care about Scotland and regarded it as a guinea pig for her most extreme policies. Scotland, it was claimed, was treated as a Conservative colony. But this popular account overlooks one crucial detail: there was a fair degree of Scottish complicity in the introduction of the poll tax.

Local government had been a contentious issue for many years in Scottish politics, and had been the subject of a Royal Commission under Lord Wheatley which reported in 1969. Local authorities were deemed to be too small, there was duplication of effort, and, though an important arm of government, the local authorities did not have the ability to implement and contribute to the overall objectives of the planned economy. According to the Wheatley Report:

> The services that local government provides do not operate as well as they should. Staff are not always deployed to the best advantage. Plans – whether for relieving housing shortages, regenerating the centres of towns and cities, sorting out traffic chaos, or revitalising the economy of particular parts of the country – are often not fully realised. Friction tends to build up between neighbouring authorities because of an artificial conflict of interest, created by the structure of local government and nothing else. The ratepayer's – and the taxpayer's – money is frequently wasted on maintaining two or more separate organisations where one would do perfectly well. Some important services have outgrown the structure, and have had to be taken away from local authorities altogether.
>
> *Royal Commission on Local Government in Scotland, 1966–1969*
>
> (Edinburgh, 1969)

Economies of scale were a particular problem, especially for the social-work, education, fire, and police services.

The eventual outcome of the report was the creation of a two-tier structure of local government in 1975. Nine regional authorities took care of the big-budget services, such as police and education, while fifty-three district councils dealt with the administration of housing, cleaning and licensing. The regional authorities would have the ability to coordinate with central government and thus bypass the endless consultation which was needed with the various councils before plans could be implemented. It was expected that central government's regional policy would dovetail with regional local government.

Regionalisation produced a mixed bag of results. It created the largest local authority in Western Europe, Strathclyde Region, which had a popu-lation of over a million and encompassed a wide spectrum of Scottish soci-ety ranging from the deprived inner city to the West Highland village. In terms of population it dwarfed the other regions, whether the relatively small Central Region or the geographically huge Highland Region. Bor-ders, Dumfries and Galloway, Tayside, Grampian, and Fife were based on regional identity. The Edinburgh environs was packaged into Lothian Region, which contained the wealthiest part of the population. However, regionalisation came on-stream just when government intervention was being cut back for financial reasons, and the regional authorities – certainly by the eighties – found that policies of social and economic redistribution and equalisation within the community would have to be implemented increasingly from within their own resources. With the most poverty, Strathclyde had the biggest handicap, but the general consensus was that the regional governments were making a good fist of things. They cer-tainly did not have the same association with extremism that marred the image of large local authorities south of the border. Yet their power to redistribute services and provisions on the basis of need was regarded as an impediment to the imposition of Thatcherite free-market economics.

Rates had been the bane of the Tory Party in Scotland. The strong rep-resentation of Labour, particularly in the cities and the western central belt, meant that councils used rates as a means of subsidising cheap council rents. However, because of tax relief on mortgages, homeowners were subsidised to almost the same extent by central government. Yet, in keeping with the principle of creating a 'property-owning democracy' (the phrase was invented by the Scottish Tory Noel Skelton in the twenties), one form of subsidy was regarded as legitimate, while the other was not. As far as the Scottish Conservative grass roots were concerned, rates were a punitive property tax which targeted prudent people who put their capital into their home, while it rewarded the indigent who were happy to blow their money on frivolities. Against a backdrop of rising unemployment and in an atmosphere where the dole cheat, the state sponger, the single parent and the social-security scrounger were pilloried by the Tory leadership, there was a fair element of class prejudice in demands for rating reform.

The Tories may have been in a minority in Scotland, but they had a British majority at their back and were prepared to use it. There was, Scottish Conservatives argued, something corrupt about the whole rates system, in that Labour councils taxed Tory supporters highly in order to pay for policies that subsidised Labour voters. Furthermore, this situation was exacerbated by initial government policy in the early eighties as a result of the drive to cut back on public expenditure. Local government was deemed to be particularly capable of improvident spending, and central government progressively reduced the size of the block grant, which initially had constituted half of all local-government expenditure. The argument was that if local government wanted to spend lots of money on social services, then it should raise its own revenue, rather than rely on the taxpayer. When local government did raise its own revenue in response to the central-government cutbacks, it was largely at the expense of the middle-class ratepayers and those deemed to be natural supporters of the Conservative Party. So, in reality, it was central-government cutbacks which stimulated fresh interest in the rates issue.

Local-government reform made it on to the political agenda because it was popular with the Conservative Party rank and file, most of whom remained oblivious to the fact that it was central government cutbacks that were the prime cause of rising charges. The idea of a local income tax based on the ability to pay according to income, was dismissed because, although much fairer, it had little political advantage for either Labour or the Conservatives. It was thought that the poll tax would resolve all the issues at the heart of Tory grass-root disquiet, while at the same time dealing a mortal blow to Labour's local-government power base.

Scotland was not really a guinea pig for the poll tax: it was simply that local Tories wanted it implemented as soon as possible, and at the Scottish Conservative conference of May 1987 it was acclaimed as the next step forward. Indeed, many Tories thought it would be the saviour of the party in Scotland. Furthermore, what is often forgotten is that the original idea was hatched in Scotland, at the University of St Andrews, at that time a bastion for right-wing free-marketers. The Tory rank and file looked forward to a crusade against the rates and to the day when they would not shoulder the financial burden of Labour local government. There was no hostility from Conservative activists to the introduction of the poll tax, one year ahead of the rest of the United Kingdom in 1988. In fact there was quite the reverse, and many thought it would be a vote-winner.

In the run-up to its introduction, there had been a lot of noise from the opposition to the effect that the imposition of the tax a year earlier in Scotland by a government which had only minority support would trigger a constitutional crisis. The collapse of the Scottish Tory Party in the general election of June 1987 further confirmed this impression. Some even claimed that the early introduction of the tax was a violation of the 1707 Treaty of Union between Scotland and England. As was mentioned previously, the Conservatives knew that this ploy could only be played so far without the Labour Party ceding ground to the nationalist case, and there was probably an element of bravado in the hardliner Michael Forsyth's decision to go ahead with early introduction. Dennis Canavan, the Labour MP for Falkirk, promised that the fifty Scottish Labour MPs would make Scotland 'ungovernable' if the poll tax was introduced. But Tory policy was clearly poking Labour in the eye, as Labour, desperate to avoid being labelled as irresponsible, came out against non-legal activity and protest. The Parliamentary Labour Party was subsequently dubbed the 'feeble fifty' by nationalist opponents. Whether by accident or design, the poll tax convincingly demonstrated the authority of the Tory government and highlighted the weakness of the opposition, as the SNP and Labour embarked on a fairly bitter dispute about the legitimacy of a non-legal form of protest. So the tax divided the opposition, forced local government to charge the whole community for its services, and eased the financial burden, to some degree, on the middle-class ratepayer.

For all that, the policy backfired and the poll tax remained unpopular. First, continuous paring back of the central-government block grant meant that local raising of revenue for local government was going to increase no matter what form of revenue-generating device was used. Second, middle-class ratepayers who believed that they would be quids in found that they were not that much better off, while the rest of the community found that they were paying a lot more. The introduction of the tax was badly handled. All were liable to pay, and exemptions had to be applied for, including those for the disabled – which triggered the defection of the Labour MP Dick Douglas, who was unhappy with his party's feeble response and ended up in the ranks of the SNP in the early nineties. The poll tax was denounced for its inequity, in that it took no account of earnings or of ability to pay, and it was cited as hard evidence that Tory policy was about promoting the interests of the rich at the expense of the poor, as it was only the substantially well-off who benefited. Yet it would take rioting in London a year later before government would have a rethink and modify it.

The introduction of the poll tax highlighted the inflexible nature of British government in Scotland, and exposed inequities that had lain dormant since the end of the war. The corporatism of post-war Scotland, which had acted as a sort of surrogate form of democracy, was abolished, and the various interest groups and sectional interests that were previously able to impress their views upon government, now found themselves out in the cold. The attack on local government was also particularly significant because, as nationalised industries and state-sponsored economic intervention declined, services provided by the local authorities were in many ways (with the exception of the National Health Service) the last significant remnants of the corporatist Welfare State. The trade unions, local government, the Churches and the opposition parties were now all excluded from influencing the decision-making process. And, with three general-election successes behind them, it looked as if the Tories might be able to govern the United Kingdom indefinitely. Malcolm Rifkind, on his appointment as Secretary of State for Scotland in 1985, let it slip that he regarded the job as a bit like being a colonial governor-general, which was taken as further evidence that the Scots were being treated like second-class citizens. It was not the wisest thing to say, and increased the volume of complaints concerning the 'democratic deficit'.

Over time, what was formerly corporate Scotland would evolve to become civic Scotland. This transformation was brought about by several factors. First, the unions, local government, the Churches and the opposition parties could claim to represent significant sections of the community, and the imposition of Thatcherite policies exposed their impotence. They could not hold back unpopular policies no matter how much popular support they commanded in Scottish society. Clearly, if they wanted to maintain that support, it would be necessary to demonstrate that they were still capable of wielding some form of influence. As Thatcherism was firmly set against corporatism and the old cosy consensus, so long as the Tories were in power they were unlikely to achieve this. In the meantime, some form of action was necessary to demonstrate the relevance of this group in Scottish society.

Second, the 'old' Establishment was worried that the net effect of Thatcherism would be to drive Scotland into the arms of the nationalists. Opinion-poll evidence in 1988 seemed to show that the SNP was gaining support. In the same year a by-election victory in Govan for Jim Sillars, who had moved to the SNP in 1980, indicated that the nationalists were best poised to pick up protest votes, as the traditional parties seemed powerless in the face of the Conservative government. The SNP's 'Can pay, won't pay' campaign against the poll tax was more combative than the quiescence of the traditional parties, and the emergence of the Scottish Socialist Party activist Tommy Sheridan was also a threat to Labour in its traditional heartland. Consensus Scotland was increasingly squeezed by a polarised political system that was divided between an uncompromising take-it-or-leave-it Unionism and an independence-is–the-only-escape-from-Thatcherism nationalism.

Third, many were coming to the conclusion that there was something different about Scotland, and that a system of devolved government had merits in its own right. The political divergence between Scotland and England was self-evident from the electoral behaviour of the two nations, and this would have to be accommodated in an adaptation of the British political structure if the United Kingdom were to remain united. A salient aspect of growing support for a Scottish parliament was that this seemed the best way out of the Doomsday Scenario. The construction of the idea of civic Scotland was a polite way of saying that the Scots hated Thatcher.

There is a paradox in that the idea of civic society gained greater prominence among Scottish academics and commentators at a time when individualism was becoming more pronounced and large pockets of urban deprivation were appearing which were to all intents and purposes divorced from the rest of society. It is hard to square the former development with the latter.

Much effort was devoted to showing how the Scots were much more in favour of corporatism than the English, and that Scottish society had a social-democratic ethos. Unlike in the south, where the individual was championed, the notion of a civic community, it was claimed, was a powerful part of political culture in Scotland, and it was this which had caused Scottish and English politics to diverge. Yet, no matter how it is dressed up, the key element in motivating support for the creation of a devolved Scottish parliament was that it was seen as a way to deflect the policies emanating from south of the border without sundering the Union. In Edinburgh in July 1988 the Campaign for a Scottish Assembly launched the *Claim of Right for Scotland*, calling for an all-party constitutional convention to press the Conservative government for a rethink on the issue of devolution:

> Scotland, if it is to remain Scotland, can no longer live with such a constitution [i.e. the British constitution] and has nothing to hope from it. Scots have shown it more tolerance than it deserves. They must now show enterprise by starting the reform of their own government. They have the opportunity, in the process, to start the reform of the English constitution, to serve as the grit in the oyster which produces the pearl ... We are under no illusions about the seriousness of what we recommend. Contesting the authority of established government is not a light matter. We could not recommend it if we did not feel that the British government has so decayed that there is little hope of its being reformed within the framework of its traditional procedures. Setting up a Scottish Constitutional Convention and subsequently establishing a Scottish Assembly cannot by themselves achieve the essential reforms of British government, but they are essential if any remnant of distinctive Scottish government is to be saved

An important element in the idea of a constitutional convention was that it could be said to represent the democratic will of the people, in that its political-party, Church, local-government and trade-union support could be said to demonstrate that the organisation had majority backing on account of the large number of people that these organisations represented. It was hoped that this argument regarding the legitimacy of its popular support would help circumvent the traditional Westminster argument regarding the sovereignty of the British parliament: that only those with an electoral mandate could claim to speak on behalf of the people. It was with this in mind that the *Claim of Right* stipulated that sovereignty lay with the people of Scotland, and that a convention would legitimately represent them and would therefore have the right to present to the London government a demand for a parliament. Labour and the Liberal Democrats agreed to take part in the convention discussions, and in November 1990 the convention published its report, only to have it dismissed by the Conservatives. Two factors worked to the convention's advantage, however: the Conservatives were becoming more unpopular, and support for nationalism seemed to be growing.

The dismal Scottish Tory performance in the election of 1987 had brought unwelcome attention from the party south of the border, and in the same year at a speech in Glasgow the Chancellor, Nigel Lawson, lambasted the Scots for having a 'subsidy culture'. This was insensitive, but it was echoed by Margaret Thatcher in her memoirs:

> The pride of the Scottish Office – whose very structure added a layer of bureaucracy, standing in the way of the very reforms which were paying such dividends in England – was that public expenditure per head in Scotland was far higher than in England … If it [the Conservative Party] sometimes seems English to some Scots that is because the Union is dominated by England by reason of its greater population.
>
> *The Downing Street Years* (London, 1993)

For a government which preached the virtues of the market economy and denounced state dependency, the existence of a 20 per cent higher per-capita rate of identifiable public expenditure north of the border (which earned no political returns) was something that deserved closer attention. Commentators in the southern press increasingly denounced the Scots as 'subsidy junkies', and, at Westminster, Scottish Question Time, which previously was guaranteed to empty the chamber and fill the bars, now became a venue for the Tory backbenchers' popular pastime of 'Jock baiting'. All of which did little to help the Scottish Tories and their leadership.

One of the features of the Scottish Conservative Party was that it had missed out on the Thatcher ideological revolution that had swept through its southern counterpart. With the exception of the junior minister Michael Forsyth, the Scottish Tory leadership was predominantly drawn from the left of the party. George Younger, Malcolm Rifkind and Ian Lang, as Secretaries of State for Scotland, had vociferously defended the Scottish share of UK public expenditure and were well versed in the older Unionist notion that Scotland was distinctive and needed to be treated differently from the rest of the United Kingdom. But this idea found little favour as Thatcherism gathered increasing momentum. And, as the Scots were ungrateful, there was little incentive for sensitivity. The Scots could be kicked because, electorally, they did not matter.

The subsidy-junkie argument caused further problems in that it opened up an intellectual contradiction that ran through the heart of the Tory message in Scotland. On the one hand there was the message emanating from the south that the Scots got too much money and should be independent, entrepreneurial and stand on their own two feet without the English financially bailing them out. On the other hand, Scottish Tories actually used the argument that the Scots needed bailing out and therefore should not be swayed by the nationalist advocacy of independence as they could not afford it. It was better, claimed the defenders of the Union, to stay in Britain, because subsidies enabled Scotland to live beyond its means. Scottish Tories walked a tightrope on which they used the threat of nationalism as a way of keeping fellow-unionist opponents in check. After all, neither Labour or the Liberal Democrats were likely to dispute Conservative claims that the Union worked to the economic benefit of Scotland, for fear that it would bolster the SNP. For good measure, it was argued that if people did not like the present arrangement then they could always vote nationalist, as the Tories were banking on more defections to the SNP from Labour's ranks than from their own. Advocating independence from the state but dependence on the Union was a contradictory message, and difficult to sustain with any degree of conviction. Time and time again the Scots were pilloried for higher rates of public expenditure, yet at the same time were being told by the party in Scotland that these were essential because the nation could not stand on its own two feet. Even when the Thatcherite Michael Forsyth took over as Secretary of State for Scotland, he cheerfully boasted about how well the Scots were doing in terms of subsidies. These contradictions came home to roost in the Perth by-election of May 1995 (in one of the top ten wealthiest constituencies in the United Kingdom), when the Tories lost to the SNP. The Scots middle class did not like to be told that they were spongers.

The nationalists appeared to be developing a head of steam. Following the general election of 1987, there was an expectation that Labour's return of fifty Scottish MPs would make a difference to government policy. It did not. Before the Govan by-election held in the following year, when the SNP captured the seat, the nationalist candidate, Jim Sillars, wiped the floor with his Labour opponent in a TV debate. Labour's impotence in the face of the introduction of the poll tax was looking like a liability. In a number of by-elections and in the European Parliament election of 1989 the nationalist vote was creeping up. Opinion-poll evidence recorded growing support for independence, and in January 1992 the *Sun* newspaper came out in favour of the nationalist cause. This coincided with the announcement of the closure of the Ravenscraig steel plant, which was of greater political significance than economic. The plant had been stripped down, was efficient, and had done all that was asked of it, but this was not enough to save it. Its closure was portrayed as a betrayal of workers who had given their all, and as evidence that government policy was biased against Scotland.

With a new leader, Alex Salmond, the SNP was going on the intellectual offensive. A number of changes in strategy worked to the party's advantage. First, it adopted a policy of independence for Scotland with respect to Europe. At a time when the British government was gearing up to sign the Treaty of Maastricht, to bring about greater European integration, this had the advantage of ditching the party's isolationist tag. Given that Europe was an important market for Scotland, and that the power of the European Union was set to grow, the nationalist case was that Britain was becoming obsolete and it made sense for the Scots to deal direct with the EU. It was pointed out that other small European nations enjoyed success, and the spectacular economic performance of Ireland was cited as a case for Scottish emulation. A second change in nationalist direction was to challenge the assumption that Scotland was subsidised by England and instead paint a more positive picture of Scottish progress. This more upbeat message contrasted with the negativity of the Unionist parties' projections of the Scottish economy's ability to sustain independence. The nationalists questioned the current and ongoing degree of subsidy. In many ways this was a rather arcane debate, largely because it was based around projections, rather than reality. The necessary statistical evidence was not available to compute the fiscal relations between Scotland and England with any accuracy. This was because the only figures which were available for scrutiny were for *identifiable* expenditure, which could be classed simply as expenditure that the government chose to identify as relating to Scotland. This was believed to make up between two-thirds and three-quarters of total government expenditure on Scotland, which meant that large sums of money were missing from the equation. However, as one commentator, George Rosie, pointed out, the bulk of *non-identifiable* expenditure was reckoned to be in the form of tax and mortgage relief, defence and research contract work, of all of which Scotland received very little, so the actual expenditure on Scotland was probably less than was supposed.

In the general election of 1992, the Conservatives won again, even with Thatcher gone. The result was Doomsday with a vengeance. In Scotland the Tories marginally improved their position in terms of the share of the vote (from 24 to 25.6 per cent) and increased their tally of seats from ten to eleven. Labour's share of the vote went down (from 42.4 to 39 per cent), but the party retained fifty seats. The Liberal Democrats lost one seat (a fall from nine to eight) with a drop in the vote (from 19.3 to 13.1 per cent), while the nationalists received a greater share of the vote (an increase from 14 to 21.5 per cent), but their number of seats remained unchanged from 1987 at three. Although the nationalists failed to make an electoral breakthrough, it was by no means clear that the SNP had been stopped.

Labour had been improving in England. The new party leader, John Smith – a Scot – was credible, and a significant number of other Scots, such as Gordon Brown, Robin Cook, George Robertson and Donald Dewar, had enhanced the standing of the party. With Thatcher gone, and under the leadership of John Major, the Conservatives were looking vulnerable at a British level. Pundits had predicted a Labour victory, and, although the party's defeat was a shock, the idea that there would be for ever a succession of Tory governments in London was not as believable as it once was. By this time, however, the debate on home rule had developed an unstoppable momentum, and the Conservatives' refusal to countenance a referendum on the issue was an important factor in maintaining its impetus. The Scottish press, most of the other media and leading commentators were all in favour of a parliament in Edinburgh. The work of the convention had developed some basic principles that seemed to point the way forward and that had the consent of the Liberal Democrats and the Labour Party. Proportional representation, greater representation for women and, unlike in the previous proposals for a Scottish assembly, powers that would be reserved by Westminster – all these avoided the complex rigmarole of deciding what the parliament would actually do.

BRAVEHEART

The demand for constitutional reform was one aspect of wider changes which affected Scottish identity and culture in the late eighties and nineties. And no one can say for sure whether it was wider changes in culture and identity which fuelled the demand for home rule or whether it was politics which impacted on culture and identity. Probably it was a mixture of both. In essence, Scottish identity became more distinctive in terms of expressing itself as a 'national' entity, while at the same time, there was a discernible decline in what might be described as Britishness. At its crudest level, this can be shown by the fact that throughout the period, the number of people describing themselves as 'Scottish' and 'more Scottish than British' in opinion polls increased, while the number describing themselves as 'British' and 'More British than Scottish' decreased. What is more difficult to say with any degree of accuracy is what constituted both Britishness and Scottishness, as these terms

changed their meaning over time. It is also difficult to identify the forces
directing this change, and why these forces should have impacted in ways
that affected national identity, which in turn increasingly affected politics.
But it is necessary to explain what the different meanings of Scottishness
and Britishness were, and how they changed, in order to show how one
became more pronounced while the other declined in influence.

For many political commentators, the upsurge in home rule and
nationalism (which never really manifested itself to any great extent in
terms of electoral politics) was attributable to the *Braveheart* factor which
followed the worldwide success of Mel Gibson's epic 1995 film which
depicted the life of Sir William Wallace at the time of the Wars of Independence at the end of the thirteenth century. Wallace was portrayed as a
Scot who put patriotism above all else and who fought a campaign against
English colonisation before finally being betrayed, captured and executed.
Although the film can be interpreted as an allegoric depiction of the rights
of the individual pitted against the claims of the state – hence its popularity among the right wing in America – its message of Scottish freedom
from English domination was one that can be said to have ignited nationalist passions in Scotland. Certainly the SNP made the most of the film's
message, and campaigned outside cinemas with the message that Scots
should be Bravehearts and join the nationalist movement. Others complained that the film appealed to narrow and chauvinistic anti-English
sentiment and should be avoided. Yet, for all the debate about *Braveheart,*
there were many signs before this that Scottish national identity and culture were expressing themselves in ways that might be said to be distinctive from Scottish/British or British manifestations. At the same time,
British identity in Scotland started to decline, or rather repackaged itself
as Scottish.

The idea of civic nationalism was promoted by Scotland's political
and media commentators as a broad descriptive concept which gave a sort
of intellectual coherence to the nation's rejection of Thatcherite values.
The trade unions, Churches, opposition parties and local government –
basically those who had been frozen out of the governmental decision-
making loop by the Conservatives – took on the task of speaking for civic
society. Industrial closures, the anti-poll-tax campaign, protests against
Trident and nuclear weapons, as well as the demand for a Scottish parlia-

ment, meant that the late eighties and early nineties witnessed increased civic activity in the form of political campaigning which tended to bypass the political parties as protesters looked to their own resources to take their message to the public. This in turn meant that trade unions, Churches and other assorted activists were increasing their profile by means of political protest. The mobilisation of various sections of Scottish society against government policy helped provide credence to the concept of civic society in that this widespread movement was coming from the grass roots and not from politicians.

As a concept, civic nationalism distanced itself from notions of ethnic nationalism, in that all within the community were included regardless of background or ethnicity. The Scots, it was claimed, had different values of political culture from the English. They were more in favour of state inter-vention and the social institutions of the state, such as comprehensive edu-cation, the National Health Service and other organs of the Welfare State. Paradoxically, these were all residues of the British state which had been created in the forties, but by sleight of hand they were increasingly painted up in tartan and claimed as part of a Scottish political culture. The change in ownership was not as surprising as at first might appear. The demand for home rule was driven by organisations seeking to defend institutions all of which had their origins in values and beliefs created in Britain during and after the Second World War. That the rest of the British political nation had rejected these values that the Scots seemed desperate to cling on to meant that they had to be increasingly represented as Scottish. In this sense, it was not a perception that the Scots had changed that drove the changes of the eighties and nineties, but rather the fact that Thatcherism had robbed the Scots of an acceptable or credible vision of British identity. Corporatism was transmuted into civic nationalism.

British identity was further undermined by wider social and political changes. The monarchy, the military and Parliament had been the three most important symbols of Britishness for most of the twentieth century, and had helped to shore up British identity in Scotland. Apart from the furore about the Queen adopting the numeral II (see Chapter 6), the monarchy was popular in Scotland for most of the post-war era. The royal family had an annual summer residence in Balmoral, and were often to be seen decked in tartan. The fact that the Queen Mother was Scots was another important factor in shoring up monarchism in Scotland. But, as in the rest of Britain, a decline in deference affected reverence for the royals, and arguably this process was accelerated in the eighties and nineties by greater attention being paid to ideas of meritocracy and social mobility. That the 'yuppie' shattered the social homogeneity of Britain's moneyed classes was perhaps a factor in diminishing notions of deference based on class which had permeated British society and had arguably helped give it a degree of coherence in the past. The impact on Scotland was that in the media and in positions of public pre-eminence there was a tendency for more Scottish accents to be heard.

The decline of Britain as an independent military power was also significant in diminishing notions of Britishness. With the exception of the Falklands campaign in 1982, when support for the SNP dropped to its lowest level in a decade, there were no military adventures to rally the people to the Union flag. And, although their number was reduced, by the time of the first Gulf War in 1990 Scottish regiments were flying the saltire flag and the media north of the border would talk about Scottish jets taking part in bombing raids.

The dignity of Parliament also declined in this period. Apart from the unpopularity of Conservative governments, the recurrence of 'sleaze' and corruption helped to undermine public confidence in politicians and the British system of parliamentary government. As has been mentioned earlier, the fact that the Conservative Party used Parliament for what was seen as the imposition of unpopular policies on Scotland made the whole institution seem alien. Changes in the wider world helped to undermine traditional faith in the British political structures. The rise of the European Union was seen as offering one way to circumvent the powers of Parliament, and the SNP began its recovery in the late eighties with its slogan 'Independence in Europe'. It became a commonplace assertion – not backed up by any evidence other than the tendency to fly the European flag on municipal buildings – that the Scots were more pro-Europe than the English, who were obsessed about keeping warm beer and cricket safe from Johnny Foreigner. The evident power of the market and of the global economy further diminished belief in the ability of the British parliament to achieve practical benefits for the people. If government was powerless to stop such global pressures, did it matter if it was based in London or in

Edinburgh? Multinational corporations exercised more control of the economy than government as the nineties witnessed both increasing inward investment and also closures.

Just as ideas of Britishness were changing or declining, ideas of Scottishness were on the rise. The period from the mid-eighties witnessed a cultural renaissance on a par with that of the inter-war period. One point made by a number of commentators is that the upsurge in cultural activity may have been a result of the failed 1979 referendum on devolution, in the sense that politics was discredited as a vehicle for the expression of Scottish national identity. Literature and art allowed individuals the ability to express their sense of identity in all its complexity, free from political travails. Scottish literature made its mark on the world. A new generation of writers, such as Alasdair Gray, James Kelman, Irvine Welsh, Iain Banks, Tom Leonard, Janice Galloway, Liz Lochhead and a host of others, took part in a prolific outpouring of material which demonstrated a culture that was becoming more at ease with itself. While Kelman and Welsh portrayed the specific realities of a society plagued by inequalities, injustice and problems, others, such as Gray and Banks, wrote on themes that had more universal relevance. The need to wear one's Scottishness on one's sleeve was becoming increasingly redundant. Scottish literature was maturing. Not only was the quality of Scottish writing improving, the demand for it was growing. Student numbers in Scottish literature and history increased at universities throughout the nineties, and this was reflected in a greater scholarly output from academics. The university curriculum reflected wider cultural changes in society, and Scottish themes moved more to the centre in the humanities and social sciences. An attempt by the University of Edinburgh to 'freeze' the chair in Scottish history in the early nineties was met with public condemnation. In schools, greater attention focused on the place of Scottish culture and history in the syllabus. The designation of Glasgow as European City of Culture in 1990 gave a further boost to the role of artists in society and helped push the case that a distinctive culture had important economic spin-offs.

A number of wider developments helped in this process of Scottification. In popular culture, developments in new technology reduced what might be called the 'British' monopoly. It became not only more feasible, but cheaper than it had been to make Scottish TV and radio programmes.

Not only that, there was greater demand for them. One feature that has helped maintain a distinctive sense of Scottish identity is that the nation is relatively well insulated from English media encroachments. Only 10 per cent of newspapers read in Scotland are produced south of the border. Also, there is very little in the way of broadcasting overlap, in the sense that the Scottish TV and radio stations, although using a lot of material which is not produced at home, are able to provide a Scottish packaging. (In contrast, newspapers and media broadcasts in Wales mainly emanate from England.) A steadily increasing output of home-produced broadcast material reinforced the idea of a distinctive Scottish identity, and nowhere was this more apparent than in the field of TV comedy. *Naked Video*, *Rab C. Nesbit*, *Scotch and Wry* and *Chewin' the Fat* all demonstrated the vitality of Scottish humour which could work only because full use was made of the Scots vernacular or language. Scots got increasing coverage of their football and sports, and by the mid-nineties persistent demands were being made for the BBC in Scotland to broadcast its own news instead of that produced in London. The eighties and nineties witnessed an upsurge in the Scottish popular-music scene, with a fair number of bands achieving international success. Wet, Wet, Wet, Hue and Cry, Simple Minds, Big Country, Orange Juice, Deacon Blue, and Lloyd Cole and the Commotions all managed to raise the profile of Scottish popular music, and this upsurge was reinforced by the fact that one of the most successful groups internationally, The Proclaimers, had quite literally more of a Scottish voice than any previous band:

> I've been so sad
> Since you said my accent was bad
> He's worn a frown
> This Caledonian clown
>
> I'm just going to have to learn to hesitate
> To make sure my words
> On your Saxon ears don't grate
> But I wouldn't know a single word to say
> If I flattened all the vowels
> And threw the 'R' away

You say that if I want to get ahead
The language I use should be left for dead
It doesn't please your ears
And though you tell it like a leg-pull
I think you're still full of John Bull
You just refuse to hear

'Throw the "R" Away' (1987)

Gaelic culture also took part in this development, with Runrig performing songs in both Gaelic and English and achieving a degree of international success, especially in Germany and Canada.

Even the Conservative government could not hold back this cultural
onslaught. In an endeavour to appease Scottish national sentiment, while
not giving in to demands for political devolution, the Tories tried a number of symbolic gestures that would militate against the claims that the
Scots did not receive fair treatment from Westminster. In 1993 the Conservative government set out its Scottish policy in *Scotland and the Union:
A Partnership for Good.* The double meaning of the title – that the Union
would last for ever and that it worked for the good of Scotland – was set
out in the document's historical survey, which pointed out the benefits
that Scotland had obtained from the union with England. In many
respects this was a return to the old-fashioned Unionism in which Scotland was regarded as a partner with England, and a rejection of the ethos
of 'unitarism' which had characterised the Thatcher years and took no
account of national differences. Scotland was to be treated more sensi-
tively. Edinburgh, as one of Britain's capital cities, was chosen as the host
city for the European summit in 1992. Twenty-five thousand demonstrators turned out to greet the delegates with demands for Scottish home
rule. In 1996 the Secretary of State for Scotland, Michael Forsyth, presided
over the return of the Stone of Destiny, the Scottish coronation stone,
which had been captured by Edward I in the Wars of Independence in the
late thirteenth century. In many ways all this was too little, too late. If
anything, Tory affirmation of Scottish national identity seemed to
acknowledge the political legitimacy of national grievance.

According to much of the survey material assembled by social scientists following the referendum on a Scottish parliament in 1997 (see

below), discontent with the Thatcher and Major years was the biggest factor in determining support for devolution. The material also provides other intriguing insights into the development of Scottish national identity. One feature is that class identity and national identity became increasingly conflated. Although the objective classification of individuals places the middle class at about 40 per cent of the population, this figure drops substantially if the criterion used is self-definition. In other words what people believe themselves to be is more important than how their socio-economic status defines them in determining their politics. A large number of Scots – it is difficult to quantify exactly how many – still defined themselves as working class, even though they might work in well-paid office jobs and own their home. Much of Scottish discontent with the Conservatives was due to Tory policies being believed to be anti-working-class and over time this transmuted into a sense of their being anti-Scottish. Whereas the victims were originally seen to be the working class, they had now become the Scottish nation as a whole. One of the key barriers to political nationalism in the past had been the rigidity of class barriers, which were deemed more important than national ones. By the nineties this was no longer the case, and both the Liberal Democrats and Labour had to accommodate this shift in attitudes. Scottish national identity had been politicised by the experience of Conservative governments to the point that a renegotiation of the constitutional arrangement was thought necessary to appease it.

TRANSFORMATION

The historian who walks on the ground of the present does so with a degree of trepidation, as the terrain is one more properly crossed by social scientists. The dust from recent events has not had time to settle into discernible patterns, and the ramifications and consequences of such events have still to work their historical course. The closeness of the recent past can make objectivity difficult, and this is especially the case for the last decade of the twentieth century. In the future, historians will mark out that decade as the context for one of the most important transformations in modern Scottish history. In the period from the mid-eighties to the end of the century, the Scottish economy metamorphosed from being largely backward and industrial into one which was modern, high-tech and led by the service sector. Traditional industry remained only in isolated pockets. In terms of social and occupational status, economic profile and a variety of other socio-economic indicators, the nation moved into line with England and Wales.

Paradoxically, just as this happened, so there was a greater tendency for the nation to diverge politically from England, in the sense that the Conservative Party could not capitalise on increasing prosperity north of the border. By the mid-nineties, Scotland was on the European Union average for most socio-economic indicators, so political change was not driven by economic decline or social discontent to any great extent.

The economic recovery was fuelled by the development of electronics, banking and insurance, petrochemicals and tourism. Although often presented as involving cutting-edge technology, the Scottish electronics industry initially was more to do with assembly work rather than with research and design. Employing over 55,000 by the mid-nineties, the industry relied on a number of traditional Scottish economic features. Low wages and a dependence on exports and foreign investment capital demonstrated that the sector had a lot in common with previous manufacturing in Scotland. So, although often put forward as an example of the 'new' Scottish economy, it had more in common with much of Scotland's economic past than its proponents liked to admit. For all that, the industry increased the value of its output by more than four times during the eighties, and by the mid-nineties it was responsible for the manufacture of a third of Europe's personal computers and a quarter of the world's bank machines. The industry was vulnerable to swings in the world market and to branch-plant closure, like much of industry in the sixties and seventies. Also, many of the factories had limited spin-off benefits to indigenous companies in the area of supply and provision, as most of the assembly components were imported. Research and development – the high-quality section of the industry – was slower to establish itself, and it is only within recent years that indigenous enterprise has begun to break into the software and programming market.

Financial services were the big success story of the Scottish economy in the latter part of the twentieth century, and Edinburgh emerged as one of the most important capital markets in Western Europe. By the end of the century the sector employed more than a quarter of a million people and had assets of nearly £2 billion. With ten of the largest fifteen Scottish companies ranked by turnover, it has emerged as one of the key engines of the Scottish economy.

Hopes that North Sea oil would regenerate the economy remained forlorn, especially after 1986, when the price of crude oil fell dramatically. As was mentioned in Chapter 9, government desire to extract as much oil as quickly as possible meant that indigenous industry was unable to adapt to the new opportunities. The collapse in prices diminished incentives, and platform-construction yards in the north-east initiated widespread redundancies. By the end of the century, however, a number of specialists in exploration engineering and drilling had developed, and petrochemicals at Grangemouth had expanded as a result of the ability to tap into oil extraction.

Tourism expanded in the eighties and nineties, but, as in much of the previous economic history of the nation, was vulnerable to downturns – now initiated either by the swings in the global economy or by the threat of international terrorism. However, tourism was also assisted by the increasing international profile of the nation, which was boosted by a succession of Hollywood movies, such as *Rob Roy*, *Loch Ness* and *Braveheart*. The increasing global obsession with 'roots' and ethnicity in the New World has led to an upsurge in interest in the old country from descendants of Scots. In 1998 the US Senate passed Resolution 155, which decreed that 6 April would be commemorated as Tartan Day, to mark the contribution of Scoto-Americans to the development of the United States. The increasing kudos attached to Scots ethnicity can be demonstrated by the jump in the number of Americans describing themselves as Scoto-American: from about 4 million in 1990 to 15 million by 2000. Similar developments took place in Australia, New Zealand and Canada. There was a ready-made market for tourism to exploit.

Overall, the Scottish economy made mixed progress in the last decade of the twentieth century. On the positive side, there was the development of a more balanced economy which used specialisation and quality in order to compensate for market distance. Financial services, tourism which attracts the upper end of the market, and specialist electronics production are all indicative of high-quality and high-value economic activity. On the negative side, there is still an overreliance on low wages as the principal means to maintain market competitiveness. Also, there is still a strong reliance on the international trade cycle, so that the Scottish economy is vulnerable to the ebbs and flows of market conditions in a very pronounced manner.

One of the main difficulties of the Scottish economy in recent years has been the poor rate of business start-up and the high rate of business failure. The greater growth of indigenous businesses would have diminished to some extent the overreliance on external trade and helped to build up a greater domestic market for the products of other local business ventures. Scotland was still too reliant on external forces for much of its wealth creation. In part, this state of affairs was determined by two key factors. First, government policy for most of the eighties and nineties was designed to attract inward investment, much of it highly mobile and likely to flee if market opportunities diminished or appeared better elsewhere. Second, entrepreneurial culture in Scotland has been held back by an overwhelming reliance on the state to provide work initially – directly and latterly by attracting inward investment. While there have been a number of successful business leaders, such as Tom Farmer, Brian Souter, Ann Gloag and Tom Hunter, these have tended to be the exception rather than the rule. Perhaps conditioned by historical experience, Scots have tended to be canny with money, and the nation had a greater proclivity towards saving than spending until the nineties. The risk culture associated with business start-up was not one readily associated with achieving social mobility, and culturally there has been an emphasis on finding a safe and secure job.

One group which did demonstrate a greater degree of entrepreneurial flair was the immigrant community: the New Scots. By the mid-nineties, those of Asian origin numbered about 50,000, or about 1 per cent of the population – a very low figure in comparison to most Western societies. Most have their origins in Pakistan, and came to Scotland via expulsion from Africa in the early seventies, or via England. By using extended family networks, the community has expanded into a prominent role in the small-retail sector, and its work ethic has been reflected in its small shopkeepers keeping long opening hours and displaying greater staying power than most of their indigenous competitors. The other significant impact of the Asian community on Scotland has been in terms of cuisine, with curry now the official 'national' dish.

It was held as a commonplace truth that the Scots were less racist than other parts of the United Kingdom, but this view has been challenged in recent years. First, the absence of much tension can be explained by immigrants having been such a small part of the community, so that statistics relating to racism will inevitably be small. Also, a number of high-profile cases, such as the firebombing of a mosque in Edinburgh and the unsolved racist murder in 1998 of Surjit Chhokar, have revealed that the Scots' perception of themselves as a tolerant nation is misplaced. The recent arrival of asylum seekers in Glasgow has likewise highlighted racial intolerance, and the Scottish popular press has shown itself to be no better in promoting racial harmony than its southern counterparts.

The English have also been subject to native intolerance since the nineties. By far the largest group of immigrants, numbering more than 400,000 or about 8 per cent of the population, in the Highlands and the north-east they have been subject to campaigns from extreme nationalist groups such as Settler Watch and Scottish Watch.

By the end of the century, the number of homeowners in Scotland had increased from a third in 1945 to two-thirds, average incomes hovered near the UK average, and Lothian was the most prosperous part of Britain outside London. Property prices in Edinburgh started to spiral upward in the nineties. In terms of the occupational structure there was little to distinguish Scotland from the rest of the United Kingdom and, according to the 1991 census, 47 per cent of Scottish households were those of professional, managerial or skilled non-manual workers – in other words, what might be described as middle class or lower middle class.

The increasing prosperity was accompanied by a growing polarity between what might be termed as those who have and those who have not. For the majority, the nineties were a period of significant material advance. Rising wages, increased purchasing power and a powerful boom in consumerism meant that most Scots had never had it so good. Most families owned their home, had a car, and went on foreign holidays, and what was once the preserve of the minority in the sixties and seventies is now part of normal aspirations and expectations. The flip side of this development was the appearance of significant pockets of deprivation. The polarisation between the 'haves' and the 'have nots' can be illustrated by some figures from the 2001 *Scottish Household Survey*, which show that in Glasgow 46.7 per cent of households have an income under £10,000 per annum, while 16 per cent have over £20,000. In the more affluent Lothian, the contrast is not as sharp, but still significant nevertheless, as 28 per cent of households survive on less than £10,000 while more than a third have more than £20,000. Initially labelled the 'underclass', but now referred to as the more politically acceptable 'socially excluded', the low-income group did not experience the wider material improvements enjoyed by the majority. As had happened in the thirties, the excluded were (and are) mainly identified by locality: the so-called sink estates. By the end of the century there were some 400,000 Scots who were in receipt of income support, which effectively meant that they did not have the wherewithal to live without state assistance. As the world moved on, it left the traditional Scottish working class behind.

During the late eighties and the nineties, a silent revolution took place in the city and large-town centres. The traditional working man's pub disappeared except in the outskirts, where, paradoxically, an increasing number of its clientele were without work. The central pubs were replaced by wine and theme bars, most owned by large companies. These occupied buildings formerly owned by banks and businesses, and catered for a younger and more affluent customer. Dungarees and boiler suits were no longer to be seen. Some workers adapted to the new world, but others were left behind. Within a decade the world that most Scots had inhabited for the best part of the twentieth century vanished. This was reflected in the literature of the time, as the critic and poet Edwin Morgan pointed out in his discussion of James Kelman's novel *The Busconductor Hines* (1984) and Irvine Welsh's *Trainspotting* (1993):

A decade has passed between *The Busconductor Hines* and *Trainspotting* and they inhabit different spaces, different worlds. Here is the Busconductor telling his young son how to make mince and tatties. It begins like this:

Item: 1 pot. Item: ¾lb mince. Item: 2 onions, medium sized then a ½lb carrots, a tin of peas and also a no – not at all, dont use a frying pan to brown the mince; what you

do is fry it lightly in the same pot you're doing the actual
cooking in. Saves a utensil for the cleaning up carry on.
So: stick mince into pot with drop cooking oil, lard or
whatever the fuck – margarine maybe. Have onions
peeled and chopped. Break up mince with wooden spoon.
Put pot on at slow heat ...

And here is the hero of *Trainspotting* listing what you need to come
off heroin:

Ten tins ay Heinz tomato soup, eight tins ay mushroom
soup [all to be consumed cold], one large tub ay vanilla
ice cream [which will melt and be drunk] two boatils ay
Milk of Magnesia, one boatil ay paracetemol, one packet
ay Ristead mouth pastilles, one boatil ay multivits, five
litres ay mineral water, twelve lucozade isotonic drinks
and some magazines: soft porn, Viz, Scottish Football
Today, The Punter etc. The most important item has
already been procured from a visit tae the parental home;
ma Ma's bottle ay Valium, removed from her bathroom
cabinet.

Between mince and cold turkey there is quite a gap. Drugs are not
a problem in Kelman's world. In Welsh's world no one would waste
time making mince and potatoes.

Scottish Left Review, September 2002

The decline of the traditional industrial and patriarchal society has
thrown up severe problems in its wake. There was no transition phase, and
the economic and social transformation of Scotland has perhaps been as
fast as that of the former Soviet nations. While many commentators have
promoted the notion of a Scottish affinity with the idea of civil society, the
response to the resulting problems has provided little real evidence to support the existence of such an affinity on the ground.

The dispossessed communities which are scattered throughout Scotland have a number of features in common. First, many have had a long-
standing reputation for being in a 'bad' area, in some cases established
before the Second World War. This stigma has intensified in the last
decade, as the polarisation of those with possessions and those without has

gathered pace. In the sixties and seventies a 'bad' area would have had the majority of men in work and would have had its pockets of people who were to all intents and purposes deemed respectable. As the majority became more prosperous, however, there was a tendency for those in employment to move away, leaving the unemployed behind. Needless to say, not everyone who lives in a deprived area is unemployed, but there has been a growing perception outside the community that that is the case. Coming from an 'undesirable' area has meant facing discrimination, especially in terms of employment. A second feature is the development of what might be called a 'social security' economy. Poor areas have poor prospects for local employment, and a lack of money has meant that the private business sector there usually consists of no more than a community shop and a pub or two. All other amenities and facilities are provided by the state.

A third feature is that the social and economic circumstances have a profound effect on culture and identity. Such areas are not only geographically excluded, they are also culturally isolated from the mainstream of society. By the end of the century, poverty in Scotland had become largely generationally determined. If you were born poor, the chances are that you will continue to remain poor. Low self-esteem, a constant awareness of relative deprivation, and isolation lead to a culture of low expectations and low generational aspirations. To live in deprived areas is to have the odds stacked against you. Countless reports have stated the obvious: that to grow up in areas of poverty will limit life chances. Youth crime in such areas is largely determined by the fact that the socially excluded have little sense of wider social obligation and a deep mistrust of the state. The benefits system, social workers and the police are the main representatives of mainstream society in such communities, and it is hardly surprising that there is little wider sense of belonging to civil society.

Perhaps it is the culture of low expectations which does the greatest damage. To grow up in an environment where there is little first-hand contact with what the rest of society takes for granted must have an impact. Little has been written about the role of gender in such communities, but a number of observations can be made. Poverty is not conducive to traditional family life, and in many places men have become redundant in the sense that, deprived of the traditional role of work, they play no real part in such communities. Normality in many of these communities is maintained by women, who have been left with the brunt of bringing up children and of maintaining as normal social relations as possible. What men do in areas ravaged by unemployment remains a bit of a mystery, even though, for the nation as a whole, unemployment among men, at 9.1 per cent in 2000, is almost a third higher than that among women and there are marginally more women classed as economically active than men. Likewise, the attendant problems of youth crime, drugs and alcoholism have a greater uptake among men, and the resultant social misery is left to female partners and mothers to deal with.

Heroin made its impact on Scottish society in the late eighties, and by the end of the century there were at least 60,000 registered addicts, although the actual number of users is likely to be a lot higher. The drug was not confined to the run-down urban estates of the big cities, but also ravaged many of the fishing towns of the north-east, and few places have remained immune. It is also extending its tentacles into the more affluent parts of society. With drug addiction comes crime. As recent surveys have shown, petty criminals are more likely to offend against their own community than to take their behaviour elsewhere, so areas which have a high incidence of drug problems also tend to suffer much of the crime which is attendant upon these. Some estimates have put the cost of drug addiction in terms of policing, crime, rehabilitation, unemployment and the like at about £2 billion – about 3 per cent of national income.

Low expectations have given rise to the phenomenon of becoming pregnant in order to secure council accommodation, on the basis that this will not be achieved by any other means. One in five Scottish children lives in a 'workless' house, and it is estimated that about one in three children is officially living in poverty. And, in spite of the attempts to stimulate better performance by publishing league tables, schools in deprived areas have poor results because of low expectations and little parental involvement.

Problems of poverty have been compounded by a number of factors. First, following in the wake of de-industrialisation, there were few local opportunities for employment. Most work was situated elsewhere, and what was in the vicinity was usually low paid, part-time and unskilled. Such jobs tended to be taken disproportionately by women. A problem with low-pay work is that it has the tendency to cancel out the benefits system, so that in reality there is little financial incentive to go and seek employment. Bureaucracy further complicates matters, in that those who do find work will have to have their benefits reassessed and recalculated, and this cumbersome operation is so prone to mistakes that taking work can incur a significant financial risk.

The second factor compounding the problems faced by run-down areas is that the type of work that is available beyond their boundaries is usually linked to the service economy, where 'aesthetic' values have a great deal of currency. Statistically, the middle-aged, the overweight and the not pretty have difficulty getting work in an industry where there is a premium on recruiting employees who must look good because they will be serving customers. Bad speaking voices and strong accents are another employment liability associated with the growth of the aesthetic economy, and the fact that most of the big towns and cities can rely on a pool of part-time labour drawn from an increasing number of students has further diminished employment opportunities for the dispossessed. As survey after survey has shown, poverty is strongly associated with bad diet and poor health, which further militate against the production of shiny, happy people.

Some have benefited from the development of the socially excluded: those who make up what might be called the poverty industry. During the eighties and nineties, a growing army of social workers, voluntary agencies, special-initiative workers and others were drafted in to deal with those who were increasingly living beyond the pale of society. Paradoxically, the growth of poverty and unemployment among segments of the former working class has created a welter of employment opportunities for the middle class. One problem associated with the poverty industry is that most of its workers are themselves geographically removed from the problem, and, in spite of the large amounts which are spent on tackling social problems, very little of the money actually finds its way directly into the communities which need it most. Another difficulty associated with many of the initiatives is that they are dependent on short-term funding, which means that there is little in the way of sustainable development as one project is scrapped and replaced with a different one. And some of the issues with which these initiatives concern themselves merely sidestep the main one. Campaigns to promote a healthy lifestyle, in which local communities are exhorted to take more exercise, eat fresh fruit and vegetables and cut down on booze and fags, do not really address the main problem, which is that an unhealthy lifestyle tends to go hand in hand with poverty, which is itself an outcome of unemployment. They do, however, give politicians the satisfaction of knowing that they are trying to help. The poor would probably prefer the money spent on such campaigns to go directly into their pockets.

PARLIAMENT

Much of the impetus for the cross-party Scottish Constitutional Convention came from the failure of normal party politics in Scotland. The forum, led by Canon Keynon Wright, provided an opportunity for political debate that was not constrained by party loyalties, and was facilitated by the Scottish Trades Union Congress, the Convention of Scottish Local Authorities and the Churches. At the end of the day, however, it would still take a Westminster parliament to enact the mechanism for the creation of a Scottish parliament, and this outcome was sealed when the Labour Party avowed its commitment to the convention's proposals.

The Conservative Party started to implode after the 1992 general election. A disastrous entry into the European Exchange Rate Mechanism piled on economic pressure, forcing up interest rates and devaluing sterling as a currency. High-profile sleaze allegations hit the party, and the leadership of John Major was called into question as he struggled to maintain a grip on Cabinet discipline. Following Labour's landslide electoral victory in May 1997, Donald Dewar, the Secretary of State for Scotland, quickly drafted the Scotland Act, which set out the legislative process for devolution. It was decided that the process would have to be endorsed by a referendum in Scotland as a means to confer popular legitimacy on a Scottish parliament. Some eyebrows were raised at this tactic, believing that Labour's electoral mandate was on its own enough to implement the proposals. In the past, the decision to seek popular endorsement could have led to accusations of duplicity, but the timing of the referendum for September 1997 helped to focus minds.

As in 1979, two camps were created: one for the 'yes' and one for the 'no' argument. The 'yes' campaign was much better prepared, and, unlike in 1979, the nationalists and Labour, together with the Liberal Democrats, were prepared to work in harmony. The SNP drafted in Sean Connery to lend his support, and Labour could draw on the commitment of leading Scots in the Cabinet. The nationalist leader, Alex Salmond, was able to convince his party that support for devolution would not be a sell-out of the commitment to independence, but rather would provide an ideal stepping stone. For a brief time there was an unusual sense of harmony in Scottish politics. The 'no' campaign could only achieve half-hearted support from the Conservative Party, which had had all its Scottish MPs wiped out in the 1997 election. The Tories were still reeling from the shock, and did not want too close an identification with a campaign which was likely to be rejected by the electorate. Also, it was thought that proportional representation in the new parliament would provide the most likely way back into Scottish political life for the Conservative Party. Even the Tories' business allies kept quiet, with many of the larger companies stating that they were comfortable with devolution. The 'yes' campaign managed to sidestep awkward issues on the grounds that many of them had been discussed extensively before. Questions about whether devolution would lead to a demand for still greater Scottish autonomy and ultimately independence, what would happen if there was a disagreement between Edinburgh and Westminster, and other such issues – all of which had been debated extensively in the past – failed to ignite, and potential divisions in the 'yes' camp failed to materialise.

The campaign, in early September, was cut short by the aftermath of the death of Diana, Princess of Wales, which meant that the whole process was condensed into 100 hours. On a turnout of 60.4 per cent, 74.3 per cent of the Scottish electorate then voted in favour of a Scottish parliament and 63.5 per cent voted in favour of the tax-raising powers which would enable the parliament to vary the rate of income tax by 3 per cent compared to the rest of the United Kingdom. For most this was the evidence needed to show that devolution was the 'settled will of the Scottish people'.

The Scottish Parliament has 129 members, and a major difference from Westminster is that it is in part elected by proportional representation. There are seventy-three constituency seats, which are determined by

the first-past-the-post system, and a further fifty-six regional seats are allocated by a second vote and are used to achieve proportionality. In the first
election, in April 1999, the Labour Party became the largest group (with
fifty-six seats), but, as was expected, this was not enough for Labour to
form a government on its own, and it had to rely on the Liberal Democrats
(seventeen seats) to form a coalition. The SNP, as the second largest party
(with thirty-five seats), became the official opposition. With 15.5 per cent
of the total vote, the Conservatives obtained eighteen seats, all of them as
a result of the regional vote to ensure proportionality. Another effect of
proportional representation was that Tommy Sheridan of the Scottish
Socialist Party, Robin Harper of the Greens and the deselected Labour candidate Dennis Canavan were all returned.

The campaign for the first election took place in the aftermath of
the Kosovo crisis, during which the nationalist leader, Alex Salmond,
described military intervention as 'an unpardonable folly'. The SNP
may have lost votes to an increased sense of patriotism, as British soldiers were used in peacekeeping duties. Also, the nationalists were
committed to raising income tax by a penny in the pound, and, in spite
of opinion-poll evidence which stated that the Scots did not mind paying extra for better public services, the reality is that most voted with
their pockets.

The young parliament did not have problems to seek. The architect
of devolution and the first First Minister, Donald Dewar, died suddenly
within the first year. His successor, Henry McLeish, resigned within a year
following a scandal involving expenses. With Jack McConnell at the
helm, some stability was established thereafter.

One of the key difficulties facing Scotland's new batch of politicians
and civil servants was inexperience. In its first financial year, the parliament had an underspend of £400 million, which was almost as much as
could have been generated by using the differential tax-raising powers. In
many respects, devolution was a way for 'New Labour' to maintain its
commitment to the previous government's spending limits: it could argue
that, with a new parliament of their own, the Scots should not expect to
receive increased public spending from Westminster. The fact that there
had been high expectations in Scotland that a Labour government would
reverse Tory spending cuts was thus neatly deflected by the existence of a

Scottish legislature which had overall responsibility for most of the key spending departments.

The style of government has changed, in that coalition will henceforth be the norm given that the proportional voting system means that no party is likely to obtain an overall majority. The parliament is also less confrontational than Westminster, and many of the key decisions are taken by committees. One effect of this is that its proceedings are less interesting to watch, and many former Westminster MPs found it difficult to adapt to life in Edinburgh without the rough and tumble of the British parliamentary debates. The parliament displayed a short-lived radical streak by abolishing tuition fees for students, providing free personal care for the elderly, and repealing Clause 28 of the Local Government Act, which banned the promotion of homosexuality in local government. For all that, the Scots, like most other people, quickly became disillusioned with politics and politicians, and at the second election in 2003 nearly half the electorate did not bother to vote.

There are a number of reasons for this state of affairs. First, as in most modern western societies, politics has been shaped by a commitment to policies which acknowledge the central role of the global market in economic affairs. In this respect, compared with governments in the past, the room for manoeuvre is very limited, and that the Scots have embarked on a path of having their own government at a time when governments worldwide have been acknowledging that their powers are limited is, if nothing else, ironic. Second, too much of the demand for a parliament in Edinburgh was, at the end of the day, constructed around notions of what the Scots did not want, rather than what they did want. Corporatism evolved into civic nationalism, only for this to evaporate once the parliament was created. For all the talk of Scotland being more radical than England and of the nation being predisposed towards left-of-centre redistributive policies, these characteristics have not really manifested themselves in any meaningful way. There is little to differentiate between the policies pursued at Holyrood and those pursued at Westminster.

A third factor, and one that is not confined to Scotland, has been the growing disaffection with conventional party politics. Of those who did vote in 2003, many found the Greens, the Socialists and the independents more attractive than the mainstream parties. In a sense, this could mark the beginning of a new development in politics, with the conventional political parties having become so distant from the electorate that voters have turned to a wider and more diverse grouping to represent their interests – the so-called Rainbow Parliament. The fact that the ideological differences between the mainstream parties have narrowed to such an extent that presentation and spin have become more important than policies and ideas has not found much favour with the voter. Even the question of independence has lost much of its *raison d'être* in a world dominated by global economics and multinational conglomerations. Whether the election of 2003 was a blip or a portent of things to come is something for future historians to decide.

CONCLUSION

I'll ha'e nae hauf-way hoose, but aye whaur
Extremes meet – It's the only way I ken
To dodge the curst conceit o' bein' richt
That damns the vast majority o' men ...
  Hugh MacDiarmid, *A Drunk Man Looks at the Thistle* (Edinburgh, 1926)

Historians are by nature cautious creatures. Not for them the grand sweeping judgements or generalisations that condense a mass of detail into clearly defined patterns. The artist or the social scientist is better equipped than the narrow empiricist historian when it comes to reducing complexity to manageable and intelligible forms. That said, the history of Scotland since 1914 does suggest a number of generalisations which seem fairly incontestable.

In one sense, it was an age of extremes. For example, if we take the issue of the role of the state, what we find is that the history of Scotland in the twentieth century has bounced from one extreme to the other and back again. The oscillation between these extremes has meant that much of the periodisation of Scottish society has been determined by one form of economic policy cleaning up the mess of the previous one. Between 1918 and 1939 Scotland was left to its own devices to deal with a global economy that was extremely precarious. State policy in the form of low interest

rates, agricultural subsidies and, after 1931, tariff protection worked to
the benefit of the south, but had no effect on Scottish society. In short, the
nation had an overdose of the free market. Consequently, after 1945, when
government intervention became state policy, there was much for it to do
in terms of clearing up the effects of a previous economic system that did
not work. Perhaps as a result of the legacy of the inter-war period, the
post-war era was characterised by an overdose of state intervention. By the
late seventies Scotland was so dependent on state intervention in social
and economic policy that this could not be turned off without serious
problems of dislocation. These came about after 1979, when the economic
pendulum swung violently in the other direction. There was a wholesale
collapse of what had constituted the traditional social and economic base
of the nation. Scotland was completely transformed – indeed, the change
was of such a magnitude that the nation of 1950 had more in common
with that of 1850 than with the Scotland of 2000. Such swings left their
scars on Scottish political life. Perhaps something in between these two
extremes of economic policy would have been more conducive to less
social disruption and greater long-term prosperity.

   Another point worth emphasising is the contrast between the success
of individual Scots and the collective failure of Scottish society. No matter
how its record is dressed up, the nation did not satisfy the aspirations of a
significant element of the population, which sought to satisfy its ambitions by leaving. Although difficult to quantify with any degree of accuracy, it is probably true to say that more Scots found success outside
Scotland than in it. Furthermore, any casual glance at the world of politics, business, arts, academia, media or sport shows a fair sprinkling of
Scots who have made it to the top. There is certainly an impression that
Scots punch above their weight when it comes to getting on in the world.
This stands in direct contrast to Scottish society, which in terms of its performance relative to the rest of the United Kingdom has historically
underachieved – be it in terms of wages, health, housing, prosperity or the
economy. In comparison to other modern Western European societies,
Scotland's record is even more dismal. Overall, it is hard to avoid the conclusion that a nation that can produce so many individual success stories,
but cannot channel this success back into society in general, is one that has
let its people down. This is in spite of the fact that educationally and sci-

entifically the nation has been a high achiever. Scotland has furnished the world with doctors, engineers, scientists, inventors, business leaders, politicians, artists and sports people, but has left it for others to use their talents. Part of the problem has been that ambitious Scots have had the opportunity to fry bigger fish in the rest of the United Kingdom or overseas. Historically, success and Scots go hand in hand, but success and Scotland do not. Over the twentieth century a better balance between individual success outside and collective success at home would have been healthier for Scottish society.

One feature of the nation since 1914 is that it has largely been directionless. Although Scotland has possessed a leadership class, its achievements have been poor. As was mentioned above, part of the problem is that the best leaders could be siphoned off to elsewhere. Business leadership lost its nerve in the inter-war era, and in the post-war era it was too ready to avail itself of the services of the state. Politicians have either ducked off to play on the bigger British stage or have followed the lead set by their London masters. (While this might be construed as a nationalist interpretation, it has to be remembered that perhaps the two most able Scottish politicians in the last century, Thomas Johnston and Willie Ross, were able to give firm political leadership in Scotland without endangering the Union.) Similar criticisms could be made about Scotland's cultural leaders, who have regularly pooh-poohed writers and artists who have gone on to attain international recognition. And, for all the talk about civic Scotland, the cities of Glasgow and Edinburgh have hardly demonstrated much in the way of a community of shared interests. The same can be said about the countryside and the fishing towns, which to all intents and purposes have been abandoned as the nation's cultural, social and economic agendas have been hijacked by urban Scotland. The conduct of Scottish local government in the last century has displayed parochialism of world-class quality. Those who have led Scottish society since 1914 have not acquitted themselves with honours.

Finally, there is the issue of what is Scotland. Historically speaking, as a nation it has had a poor definition of itself. It has oscillated between a 'here's tae us' triumphalism and a chronic lack of self-confidence – the so-called 'Scottish cringe'. Too often the achievements of successful Scots outside Scotland have been used to mask the failings of Scottish society, and too often the debate about culture, identity and leadership has been squeezed into political camps for or against the Union. For a nation which has prided itself on its hard-headed pragmatism, Scotland has been too prone to idealisation and myth-making. The myths of Scottish education and of the democratic ethos have had little substance in fact. If this book has achieved anything, it will be to have shown that the history of Scotland in the twentieth century leaves much room for improvement in the twenty-first.

BIBLIOGRAPHY AND GUIDE TO FURTHER READING

GENERAL STUDIES

There is a comprehensive and growing literature on the history of Scotland in the twentieth century. For those interested in placing the period in context, the following GENERAL HISTORIES OF SCOTLAND are to be recommended: M. Lynch, *Scotland: A New History* (London, 1991); R. A. Houston & W. W. J. Knox, eds., *The New Penguin History of Scotland: From Earliest Times to the Present Day* (London, 2001); T. M. Devine, *Scottish Nation, 1700–2000* (London, 2001); A. Cooke, I. Donnachie, A. MacSween & C. A. Whatley, eds., *Modern Scottish History: 1707 to the Present* (East Linton, 5 vols., 1998); W. W. Knox, *Industrial Nation: Work, Culture and Society in Scotland 1800 to the Present* (Edinburgh, 1999); T. C. Smout, *A Century of the Scottish People, 1830–1950* (London, 1984); D. McCrone, *Understanding Scotland: The Sociology of a Stateless Nation* (London, 1992); and Chris Harvie, *Scotland: A Short History* (Oxford, 2002).

The history of Scotland is bound up with that of the rest of the United Kingdom, and the following will help to place twentieth-century Scottish history in its BRITISH CONTEXT: Peter Clark, *Hope and Glory: Britain 1900–1990* (London, 1996); Kenneth O. Morgan, *The People's Peace: British History 1945–1990* (Oxford, 1992); P. J. Cain & A. G. Hopkins, *British Imperialism: Crisis and Deconstruction, 1914–1990* (London, 1993); D. Reynolds, *Britannia Overruled: British Policy and World Power in the Twentieth Century* (London, 1991); and R. Floud & D. McCloskey, eds., *The Economic History of Britain since 1700* (Cambridge, 1994).

For work dealing more specifically with the period 1914 TO 2000 IN SCOTLAND, see T. M. Devine & R. J. Finlay, eds., *Scotland in the Twentieth Century* (Edinburgh, 1996); Chris Harvie, *No Gods and Precious Few Heroes: Twentieth Century Scotland* (Edinburgh, 1998); and A. Dickson & J. H. Treble, eds., *People and Society in Scotland, vol. 3: 1914–1990* (Edinburgh, 1992). The following JOURNALS are a good place to start for articles: *Scottish Historical Review*, *Scottish Social and Economic History*, *Scottish Labour History* and *Scottish Affairs*.

STATISTICAL INFORMATION

A underutilised source is to be found in *Parliamentary Debates* (Hansard), where official responses to MPs' questions provide much in the way of raw statistical information. Census returns provide much useful information on Scottish society, but are subject to bouts of reclassification – especially in occupational status – which make it difficult to track changes over time. B. R. Mitchell, *British Historical Statistics* (Cambridge, 1988); David Butler & Gareth Butler, *British Political Facts* (London, 1994); A. H. Halsey, ed., *British Social Trends since 1900* (London, 1988); and F. W. S. Craig, *British Electoral Facts, 1885–1975* (London, 1976), are standard reference works for statistical information. Economic statistics for the inter-war period can be found in the annual Board of Trade surveys, *Clydesdale Bank Annual Economic Survey,* various reports from the Scottish Economic Committee and the Scottish National Development Council, and annual reports from the Board of Education and the Board of Agriculture. The *Glasgow Herald Trade Review* and the issues of the *Census of Production* for 1907, 1924, 1935 and 1948 are useful in charting the decline of the Scottish economy in the inter-war period, and the annual League of Nations *World Economic Survey* helps to put these figures into an international context. The post-war period is covered by the *Digest of Scottish Statistics* (London, 1954–71), and some of the early editions contain material relating to the inter-war period. After 1971, the same type of information is to be found in the *Scottish Abstract of Statistics* and the *Scottish Economic Bulletin*. Information relating to the rural economy is to be found in *A Century of*

Agricultural Statistics (London, 1968) and *Scottish Rural Profile* (London, 1991).

SOCIETY

For BRITISH SOCIAL HISTORY, see John Stevenson, *British Society, 1914–45* (London, 1984), and Arthur Marwick, *British Society since 1945* (London, 1982). For SCOTLAND, a good starting point is T. C. Smout's 'Scotland', in F. M. L. Thomson, ed., *The Cambridge Social History of Britain* (Cambridge, 1990), and his *Century of the Scottish People, 1830–1950* (London, 1984).

On HOUSING see R. Rodger, ed., *Scottish Housing in the Twentieth Century* (Leicester, 1988); S. Damer, *From Moorepark to 'Wine Alley': The Rise and Fall of a Glasgow Housing Scheme* (Edinburgh, 1998); D. Niven, *Scottish Housing* (London, 1979); Sidney Jacobs, *The Right to a Decent Home* (London, 1976); T. Begg, *The History of the Scottish Special Housing Association* (Edinburgh, 1978); and Miles Glendinning, ed., *Rebuilding Scotland: The Post-War Vision, 1945–1975* (East Linton, 1997). Contemporary accounts are to be found in *Report of the Royal Commission on the Housing of the Industrial Population of Scotland, Rural and Urban* (Edinburgh, 1917); Scottish Housing Advisory Committee, *Planning Our New Homes* (Edinburgh, 1944); and *Scotland's Older Houses: Report of the Sub-Committee on Unfit Housing {chairman J. B. Cullingworth}* (Edinburgh, 1967).

URBAN LIFE is charted in G. Gordon, ed., *Perspectives of the Scottish City* (Aberdeen, 1986); I. Maver, *Glasgow* (Edinburgh, 2000); M. Keating, *The City that Refused to Die* (Aberdeen, 1988); M. Keating & R. Boyle, *Remaking Urban Scotland* (Edinburgh, 1986); and W. H. Fraser & C. Lee, eds., *Aberdeen: A New History, 1800–2000* (East Linton, 2000).

RURAL SOCIETY is less well served, with Richard Anthony's *Herds and Hinds: Farm Labour in Scotland, 1900–1939* (East Linton, 1996) the only modern treatment. J. Littlejohn, *Westrigg: The Sociology of a Cheviot Parish* (London, 1964), provides useful insights into small-town Scotland in the sixties. A. Fenton, *Country Life in Scotland* (Edinburgh, 1987); G. Sprott, *Farming* (Edinburgh, 1995); and the journals *Review of Scottish Culture* and *Scottish Studies* help fill the gaps in what is known of rural life in Scotland.

POVERTY is one of the most extensively written-on subjects in modern Scottish history, and I. Levitt, *Poverty and Welfare in Scotland 1990–1948* (Edinburgh, 1988); N. MacDougall, ed., *Voices from the Hunger Marches* (Edinburgh, 1999); and Gordon Brown & Robin Cook, eds., *Scotland, the Real Divide: Poverty and Deprivation in Scotland* (Edinburgh, 1983), illustrate the extent of poor social conditions in Scotland in the twentieth century.

INFANT MORTALITY is an emotive subject, but is still treated too much from the perspective of statistical analysis, rather than examining its broader cultural and social impact. See R. A. Cage, 'Infant Mortality Rates and Housing: Twentieth Century Glasgow', *Scottish Social and Economic History*, 14 (1994), and D. Kebbie, 'Investigating Infant Mortality in Early Twentieth Century Scotland: Aberdeen and Dundee Compared', *Scottish Social and Economic History*, 17, 1 (1997). More detailed information is to be found in the various reports from the chief health inspectors for local-government health boards in the twenties and thirties.

SCHOOLS and EDUCATION are covered in D. Withrington, *Going to School* (Edinburgh, 1997); R. D. Anderson, *Scottish Education since the Reformation* (Dundee, 1997); G. E. Davie, *The Democratic Intellect* (Edinburgh, 1961) and *The Crisis of the Democratic Intellect* (Edinburgh, 1980); and W. Humes & H. M. Paterson, eds., *Scottish Culture and Scottish Education, 1800–1980* (Edinburgh, 1983), but the most modern and up-to-date treatment is to be found in Lindsay Paterson, *Scottish Education in the 20th Century* (Edinburgh, 2003). Contemporary accounts offer useful insights into the thinking behind much of educational policy in the post-war period, and in particular James Scotland, *The History of Scottish Education* (London, 2 vols., 1969), demonstrates much of the power of the myths about Scottish education, as well as its elitist approach. G. S. Osborne, *Scottish and English Schools: A Comparative Study of the Past Fifty Years* (Pittsburgh, 1966), contains much useful statistical material. Janetta Howie, *Penny Buff: A Clydeside School in the Thirties* (London, 1975), provides insight into what it was like to be a teacher, and annual reports by HM Inspectors of Schools provide much information on what were believed to be the strengths and failings of the system.

Studies of CLASS have tended to focus disproportionately on the workers, and the role of the Scottish middle class still awaits a serious treatment. A. A. MacLaren, ed., *Social Class in Scotland: Past and Present* (Edinburgh, [1976]), and T. Dickson, ed., *Capital and Class in Scotland* (Edinburgh, 1983), both have useful chapters on the twentieth century. The relationship between social class and national identity is explored in D. McCrone, S. Kendrick & P. Straw, eds., *The Making of Scotland: Nation, Culture and Social Change* (Edinburgh, 1989). Studies of the Scottish working class include J. D. Young, *The Rousing of the Scottish Working Class* (London, 1979), and N. MacDougall, *Studies in Scottish Labour History* (Edinburgh, 1978), and those who want a flavour of the radicals' polemics should read T. Johnston, *A History of the Working Classes in Scotland* (London, 1944).

The socio-political phenomenon of the RED CLYDE has spawned a publishing boom in its own right. In particular, see I. Maclean, *The Legend of Red Clydeside* (Edinburgh, 1983); J. J. Smyth, *Labour in Glasgow, 1896–1936* (Edinburgh, 2000); A. McKinlay & R. J. Morris, eds., *The ILP on Clydeside: From Foundation to Disintegration* (Manchester, 1991); W. Kenefick & A. McIvor, eds., *Roots of Red Clydeside* (Edinburgh, 1996); R. Duncan & A. McIvor, eds., *Militant Workers: Labour and Class Conflict on the Clyde, 1900–1950* (Edinburgh, 1992); J. Melling, *Rent Strikes: The Peoples' Struggle for Housing in the West of Scotland, 1890–1916* (Edinburgh, 1983); J. Hinton, *The First Shop Stewards' Movement* (London, 1973); and – for those who wish to confine themselves to a bibliographical and historical overview – T. Brotherstone, 'Does Red Clydeside Matter Any More?', in Duncan and McIvor, *Militant Workers* (*v.s.*). Some autobiographical accounts of the period are to be found in H. McShane (with Joan Smith), *No Mean Fighter* (London, 1978); D. Kirkwood, *My Life of Revolt* (London, 1929); and W. Gallacher, *Revolt on the Clyde* (London, 1936).

For studies of CLASS RELATIONS BEYOND GLASGOW see J. Holford, *Reshaping Labour: Organisation, Work and Politics – Edinburgh in the Great War and After* (London, 1988); J. McG. Davies, 'Social and Labour Relation at Pullars of Perth, 1882–1924', *Scottish Social and Economic History*, 13 (1993); C. Whatley et al., *The Lives and Times of Dundee* (London, 1993); W. Walker, *Juteopolis: Dundee and its Textile Workers, 1885–1923* (Edinburgh, 1979); C. M. M. MacDonald, *The Radical Thread: Political Change in Scotland. Paisley Politics, 1885–1924* (East Linton, 2000); and W. H. Fraser & C. Lee, eds., *Aberdeen: A New History.* Ian MacDougall, ed., *Voices*

from Home and Work: Personal Recollections of Working Life and Labour Strug-
gles in the Twentieth Century by Scots Men and Women (Edinburgh, 2000) is a
treasure trove of oral history gathered from throughout the country.

On the UPPER ECHELONS of Scottish society see T. M. Devine, ed.,
Scottish Elites (Edinburgh, 1994); R. Johnston, *Clydeside Capital* (East Lin-
ton, 2001); and J. Scott & M. Hughes, *The Anatomy of Scottish Capital*
(London, 1980).

RELATIONS BETWEEN THE SEXES are beginning to receive their due
historical attention: in particular, see A. M. Hughes, 'The Politics of the
Kitchen and the Dissenting Domestics: The ILP, Labour Women and the
Female "Citizens" of Inter-War Clydeside', *Scottish Labour History,* 34
(1999); E. Gordon & E. Breitenbach, eds., *The World is Ill Divided* (Edinburgh, 1990) and *Out of Bounds* (Edinburgh, 1992); J. D. Young, *Women
and Popular Struggles* (Edinburgh, 1985); E. King, *The Hidden History of
Glasgow Women* (Edinburgh, 1993); E. Breitenbach, *Women Workers in Scotland* (Edinburgh, 1982); and R. Mitchison, 'The Hidden Labour Force', in
R. Saville, ed., *The Economic Development of Modern Scotland* (Edinburgh,
1983). Recent studies of Scottish society are more sensitive to gender, and
much useful material is to be found in *Scottish Government Yearbook, Radical Scotland, Scottish Affairs* and the Equal Opportunities Commission's
Equality Issues in Scotland.

The experience of CHILDHOOD is another neglected area, and the
historian has to rely mainly on autobiography: see in particular Molly
Weir, *Shoes Were for Sunday* (London, 1970), and R. Glasser, *Growing Up in
the Gorbals* (London, 1987). Lynn Abrams, *The Orphan Country: Children of
Scotland's Broken Homes from 1845 to the Present Day* (Edinburgh, 1998), and
Brian Ashley, *A Stone on the Mantelpiece: A Centenary Social History of the
RSSPCC* (Edinburgh, 1985), examine issues in child welfare. Robbie and
Nora Kydd have edited an interesting anthology, *Growing Up in Scotland*
(Edinburgh, 1998), which provides fascinating recollections of Scottish
childhood. Three useful collections of personal testaments are B. Kay, ed.,
Odyssey: Voices from Scotland's Past (Edinburgh, 2 vols., [1980–81]); C. Bell,
ed., *Scotland's Century* (London, 2000); and T. M. Devine & P. Logue, eds.,
Being Scottish (Edinburgh, 2002).

For the HEALTH of the nation, see C. Nottingham, ed., *The NHS in
Scotland* (London, 2000); D. Hamilton, *The Healers: A History of Medicine in*

Scotland (Edinburgh, 1982); G. McLachlan, ed., *Improving the Common Wealth: Scottish Health Services* (Edinburgh, 1987); and R. Johnston & A. McIvor, *A Lethal Work: A History of the Asbestos Tragedy in Scotland* (East Linton, 2001). Useful contemporary material is to be found in J. Boyd Orr, *Food, Health and Income* (London, 1936); *Annual Report of the Department of Health for Scotland*; *Report of the Unemployment Assistance Board in Scotland*; and *Report of the Committee on Scottish Health Services* (London, 1936).

RELIGION, especially sectarianism, has attracted much attention. See B. Murray, *The Old Firm, Sectarianism, Sport and Society* (Edinburgh, 1985); T. Gallagher, *Glasgow: The Uneasy* (Manchester, 1987) and *Edinburgh Divided: John Cormack and No Popery in the 1930s Edinburgh* (Edinburgh, 1987); S. J. Brown, 'Outside the Covenant: The Scottish Presbyterian Churches and Irish Immigration, 1922–38', *Innes Review, 42* (1991); and S. Bruce, *No Pope of Rome: Militant Protestantism in Modern Scotland* (Edinburgh, 1985). For the social history of religious adherence, see Callum Brown, *Religion and Society in Scotland since 1707* (Edinburgh, 1997). The PRESBYTERIAN CHURCH(ES) are covered in T. Gallagher & G. Walker, eds., *Battle Hymns and Sermons: Popular Protestantism in Modern Scotland* (Edinburgh, 1987); S. J. Brown, 'The Social Vision of Scottish Presbyterianism and the Union of, 1929', *Scottish Church History Society, 24* (1990), and 'A Vision for God: The Scottish Presbyterian Churches and the General Strike of 1926', *Journal of Ecclesiastical History, 42* (1991); R. D. Kernohan, *Scotland's Life and Work* (Edinburgh, 1979); and John Highet, *The Scottish Churches* (London, 1960). Important biographies are A. Muir, *John White* (London, 1960), and Clive Rawlins, *William Barclay* (London, 1984). THE CATHOLIC COMMUNITY is studied in T. M. Devine, ed., *Irish Immigrants and Scottish Society in the Nineteenth and Twentieth Centuries* (Edinburgh, 1991) and *St Mary's Hamilton: A Social History, 1846–1996* (Edinburgh, 1997), and in R. Boyle & P. Lynch, eds., *Out of the Ghetto: The Catholic Community in Modern Scotland* (Edinburgh, 1998). On the links between SCOTLAND AND ULSTER, see G. Walker, *Intimate Strangers: Political and Cultural Interaction between Scotland and Ulster in Modern Times* (Edinburgh, 1995), and I. S. Wood, ed., *Scotland and Ulster* (London, 1994).

On IMMIGRATION to Scotland, see Terri Copli, *The Italian Factor*

(Edinburgh, 1991); D. Stockdale, 'Dundee and European Migrants', in Chris Whatley, *The Remaking of Juteopolis, Dundee, c. 1891–1991* (Dundee, 1992); and Bashir Maan, *The New Scots: The Story of Asians in Scotland* (Edinburgh, 1992).

Given the tremendous outflow of people from Scotland in the twentieth century, it might be expected that EMIGRATION would have been studied more than it has. Unfortunately, and in spite of the abundance of primary material, it has received little attention. For an introduction, see T. M. Devine, ed., *Scottish Emigration and Scottish Society* (Edinburgh, 1992), and M. Harper, *Emigration from Scotland between the Wars* (Manchester, 1998). On the post-war period, *Inquiry into the Scottish Economy, 1960–1961: Report of a Committee Appointed by the Scottish Council (Development and Industry) under the Chairmanship of J. N. Toothill* (Edinburgh, 1961) has useful information. The Highlands were an area that suffered extensively from out-migration: see E. A. Cameron, *Land for the People? The British Government and the Scottish Highlands, c. 1880–1925* (Edinburgh, 1996); L. Leneman, *Fit for Heroes? Land Settlement in Scotland after World War One* (Aberdeen, 1989); F. F. Darling, *West Highland Survey* (Oxford, 1957); and D. Thomson & I. Grimble, *The Future of the Highlands* (London, 1968).

THE ECONOMY

Perhaps more so than other topics, the economic history of Scotland is closely tied to that of Britain, especially with regard to issues such as government policy, and the student of the Scottish economy needs to keep one eye on wider developments in the United Kingdom. For GENERAL UK HISTORIES see M. W. Kirby, *The Decline of British Economic Power since 1870* (London, 1981); C. H. Lee, *The British Economy: A Macroeconomic Perspective* (London, 1986); P. Deane & W. A. Cole, *British Economic Growth, 1688–1959* (London, 1969); and S. Pollard, *The Development of the British Economy 1914–1967* (London, 1972). On the inter-war British economy see B. W. E. Alford, *Depression and Recovery? British Economic Growth 1918–1939* (London, 1972); H. W. Richardson, *Economic Recovery in Britain, 1932–39* (London, 1967); D. H. Aldcroft, *The Inter-War Economy* (London, 1973) and *The British Economy: The Years of Turmoil, 1920–1951*

(London, 1986); S. Pollard, *The Gold Standard and Unemployment Policies Between the Wars* (London, 1970); and A. S. Milward, *The Economic Effect of the Two World Wars on Britain* (London, 1970). For the post-war period see Alec Cairncross, *Years of Recovery: British Economic Policy 1945–51* (London, 1985); James Cronin, *The Politics of State Expansion* (London, 1991); B. W. E. Alford, *British Economic Performance, 1945–1975* (London, 1988); Sean Glynn & Alan Booth, *The Road to Full Employment* (London, 1987); Wilfred Beckerman, ed., *Slow Growth in Britain: Causes and Consequences* (Oxford, 1979); and J. F. Wright, *Britain in the Age of Economic Management* (London, 1979).

There are a number of recommended GENERAL ECONOMIC HISTORIES OF MODERN SCOTLAND: R. H. Campbell, *Scotland since 1707: The Rise of an Industrial Society* (Edinburgh, 1985) and *The Rise and Fall of Scottish Industry 1707–1939* (Edinburgh, 1980); Bruce Lenman, *An Economic History of Modern Scotland* (London, 1977); and A. Slaven, *The Development of the West of Scotland, 1750–1960* (London, 1975), are good starting points. A more recent treatment which focuses more specifically on the financial relationship between Scotland and the rest of the United Kingdom is to be found in C. H. Lee, *Scotland and the United Kingdom in the Twentieth Century* (Manchester, 1995). On the post-war period, R. Saville, ed., *The Economic History of Modern Scotland, 1950–1980* (Edinburgh, 1983), is indispensable. A good article highlighting many of the uncovered aspects of Scottish economic history in the twentieth century is G. C. Peden's 'An Agenda for the Economic History of Twentieth Century Scotland', *Scottish Social and Economic History,* 13 (1993).

Much useful information can be gleaned from CONTEMPORARY ACCOUNTS. See in particular W. R. Scott & J. Cunnison, *The Industries of the Clyde Valley during the War* (Oxford, 1924); G. M. Thomson, *Scotland: That Distressed Area* (Edinburgh, 1932); J. A. Bowie, *The Future of Scotland* (Edinburgh, 1939); J. A. A. Porteous, *Scotland and the South* (Stirling, 1947); J. Gollan, *Scottish Prospect* (Glasgow, 1948); A. Cairncross, ed., *The Scottish Economy* (Cambridge, 1953); G. MacCrone, *Scotland's Economic Progress, 1951–60* (London, 1965), *Regional Policy in Britain* (London, 1969) and *Scotland's Future: The Economics of Nationalism* (Oxford, 1969); T. L. Johnston, N. K. Buxton & D. Mair, *Structure and Growth of the Scottish Economy* (London, 1971); D. Mackay, ed., *Scotland, 1980: The Economics of Self-Government* (Edinburgh, 1977); J. Butt & G. Gordon, eds., *Strathclyde: Changing Horizons* (Edinburgh, 1985); C. Lythe & M. Majumdar, *The Renaissance of the Scottish Economy* (London, 1982); and N. K. Buxton, *Scotland in a Rapidly Changing World* (Edinburgh, 1986).

On specific sectors of the economy, the STEEL INDUSTRY is covered by Peter Payne in *Colvilles* (Oxford, 1980), *Growth and Contraction: Scottish Industry c. 1860–1990* (Dundee, 1992) and 'The End of Steelmaking in Scotland', *Scottish Social and Economic History*, 15 (1995). SHIPBUILDING is examined in J. R. Hume & M. S. Moss, *Beardmore: The History of a Scottish Industrial Giant* (London, 1979); H. Peebles, *Warship Building on the Clyde: Naval Orders and the Prosperity of the Clyde Shipbuilding Industry* (Edinburgh, 1987); P. L. Robertson, 'Shipping and Shipbuilding: The Case of William Denny and Brothers', *Business History*, 16 (1974); A. Slaven, 'A Shipyard in Depression: John Browns of Clydebank', *Business History*, 19 (1977); and J. Foster & C. Woolfson, *The Politics of the UCS Work-in* (London, 1986). For the TEXTILE INDUSTRY see J. Butt & K. Ponting, eds., *Scottish Textile History* (Aberdeen, 1987), and W. S. Howe, *The Dundee Textiles Industry: Decline and Diversification* (Aberdeen, 1982). CAR MANUFACTURE is dealt with in S. McKinstry, 'The Albion Motor Car Company: Growth and Specialisation', *Scottish Social and Economic History*, 11 (1991), and D. Sims & M. Wood, *Car Manufacturing at Linwood: The Regional Policy Issues* (Paisley, 1984). MINING in Scotland is examined in B. Supple, *The History of the British Coal Industry, vol. 4: 1913–46* (Oxford, 1987), and W. Ashworth, *The History of the British Coal Industry, vol. 5: 1946–82* (Oxford, 1986). The fraught nature of industrial relations in mining can be charted in R. Church & Q. Outram, *Strikes and Solidarity: Coalfield Conflict in Britain 1889–1966* (Cambridge, 1998). The OIL INDUSTRY is explored in Chris Harvie, *Fool's Gold* (London, 1994). For BANKING see S. G. Checkland, *Scottish Banking* (Glasgow, 1975), and R. Saville, *Bank of Scotland: A History, 1695–1995* (Edinburgh, 1996).

WORKERS AND TRADE UNIONS are covered in A. Tuckett, *The Scottish Trade Union Congress, 1897–1977* (Edinburgh, 1986); Keith Aitken, *Bairns o' Adam* (Edinburgh, 1997); James Kinloch & John Butt, *History of the Scottish Co-operative Wholesale Society Limited* (Glasgow, 1981); J. Hinton, *The First Shop Stewards' Movement* (London, 1973); and I. MacDougall, ed., *Essays in Scottish Labour History* (Edinburgh, 1979). A lot has been written on the MINERS: see R. Page Arnot, *A History of Scottish Miners* (London, 1955); A. B. Campbell, *The Scottish Miners, vol. 2* (London, 2000); I. MacDougall, ed., *Militant Miners* (Ilkley, 1981); and the autobiography of Abe Moffat, *My Life with the Miners* (London, 1965). William Kenefick, *Rebellious and Contrary: The Glasgow Dockers, 1853–1932* (East Linton, 2000) charts the development of trade unionism on THE CLYDE WATERFRONT.

Official and semi-official inquiries into THE STATE OF THE SCOTTISH ECONOMY are W. R Scott, *An Industrial Survey of the South-West Central Scotland* (London, 1930); *Reports of Investigations into the Industrial Conditions in Certain Depressed Areas of … IV. – Scotland, etc. {by … Sir Arthur Rose}* (London, 1934); Scottish Economic Committee, *Scotland's Industrial Future: The Case for Planned Development* (London, 1939); M. P. Fogarty, *Prospects of the Industrial Areas of Great Britain* (London, 1945); *Industry and Employment in Scotland 1946* (London, 1946); P. Abercrombie et al., *The Clyde Valley Regional Plan, 1946* (Edinburgh, 1949); *Report of the Committee on Scottish Financial and Trade Statistics {chairman Lord Catto}* (Edinburgh, 1952); *Review of Highland Policy 1959* (London, 1959); *Inquiry into the Scottish Economy, 1960–1961: Report of a Committee Appointed by the Scottish Council (Development and Industry) under the Chairmanship of J. N. Toothill* (Edinburgh, 1961); *The Scottish Economy, 1965 to 1970: A Plan for Expansion* (Edinburgh, 1966); and *Oceanspan: A Maritime-Based Development Strategy for a European Scotland, 1970–2000* (Edinburgh, 1970).

POLITICS

The best, and most comprehensive, study of Scottish politics in this period is to be found in I. G. C. Hutchison, *Scottish Politics in the Twentieth Century* (Basingstoke, 2001), and the latter chapters of the same author's *A Political History of Scotland: Parties, Elections and Issues, 1832–1924* (London, 1986) are indispensable for the politics of the post-First World War period. General overviews are provided by M. Fry, *Patronage and Principle: A Political History of Modern Scotland* (Aberdeen, 1987), and R. J. Finlay, *A Partnership for Good: Scottish Politics and the Union since 1880* (Edinburgh, 1997).

The ROLE OF GOVERNMENT and its development in Scotland can be charted in J. S. Gibson, *The Thistle and the Crown: A History of the Scottish Office* (Edinburgh, 1988); G. S. Pottinger, *The Secretaries of State for Scotland 1926–76* (Edinburgh, 1979); and I. Levitt, *The Scottish Office: Depression and Reconstruction 1919–59* (Edinburgh, 1996). Two important articles deal with the EVOLUTION OF GOVERNMENT in Scotland: J. Mitchell, 'The Gilmour Report on Scottish Central Administration', *Juridical Review* (1989), and R. H. Campbell, 'The Committee of Ex-Secretaries of State for Scotland and Industrial Policy, 1941–45', *Scottish Industrial History*, 2 (1979).

LOCAL GOVERNMENT is studied in C. de B. Murray, *How Scotland is Governed* (Edinburgh, 1938), and more recently in Arthur Midwinter, *The Politics of Local Spending* (Edinburgh, 1984). Municipal politics are discussed in W. L. Miller, 'Politics in the Scottish City, 1832–1982', in G. Gordon, ed., *Perspectives on the Scottish City* (Aberdeen, 1985).

HOW THE SCOTTISH POLITICAL SYSTEM WORKS and how it interacts with Westminster are covered by L. Paterson, *The Autonomy of Modern Scotland* (Edinburgh, 1994); J. Kellas, *The Scottish Political System* (Cambridge, 1993); and A. Midwinter, M. Keating & J. Mitchell, *Politics and Public Policy in Scotland* (London, 1991). A contemporary overview of POLITICS AND SOCIETY is to be found in Alice Brown, David McCrone & Lindsay Paterson, *Politics and Society in Scotland* (London, 2000).

The LABOUR PARTY is covered in I. Donnachie, C. Harvie & I. Wood, eds., *Forward! Labour Politics in Scotland, 1888–1988* (Edinburgh, 1989); R. J. Morris & A. MacKinlay, eds., *The ILP on Clydeside: From Foundation to Disintegration* (Manchester, 1991); J. Holford, *Reshaping Labour: Organisation, Work and Politics – Edinburgh in the Great War and After* (London, 1988); W. W. Knox & A. MacKinlay, 'The Re-making of Scottish Labour in the 1930s', *Twentieth Century British History*, 6 (1994); and Chris Harvie, 'Labour in Scotland during the Second World War', *Historical Journal*, 26 (1983). W. W. Knox, *Scottish Labour Leaders, 1918–39* (Edinburgh, 1984), is a comprehensive guide to the key figures in the Labour movement between the wars. Labour and the home-rule issue is discussed in M. Keating & D. Bleiman, *Labour and Scottish Nationalism* (London, 1979), and D. Howell, *A Lost Left: Three Studies in Socialism and Nationalism* (Manchester, 1986). Useful biographies include G. Brown, *Maxton*

(Edinburgh, 1986); W. W. Knox, *James Maxton* (Manchester, 1987); G. Walker, *Thomas Johnston* (Manchester, 1988); and I. S. Wood, *John Wheatley* (Manchester, 1990).

The CONSERVATIVE PARTY in Scotland has had less coverage, in spite of its good performance during the course of the twentieth century. Gerald Warner, *The Scottish Tory Party* (London, 1988), treats its subject sympathetically, if a bit too uncritically. James Mitchell, *Conservatives and the Union: A Study of Conservative Party Attitudes to Scotland* (Edinburgh, 1990), charts the evolution of the Tory Party's policy towards Scotland. C. M. M. MacDonald, ed., *Unionist Scotland* (Edinburgh, 1998), has a wide range of essays covering various aspects of the Scottish Conservative Party. Useful articles which deal with more specific areas of the history of the party are D. W. Urwin, 'The Development of the Conservative Party Organisation in Scotland', *Scottish Historical Review,* 44 (1965); S. Ball, 'The Politics of Appeasement: The Fall of the Duchess of Atholl and the Kinross and West Perth By-Election', *Scottish Historical Review,* 69 (1990); and D. Seawright & J. Curtice, 'The Decline of the Scottish Conservative and Unionist Party, 1950–1992: Religion, Ideology or Economics?', *Contemporary Record,* 9 (1995).

NATIONALISM AND THE SNP are covered in R. J. Finlay, *Independent and Free: Scottish Politics and the Origins of the Scottish National Party, 1918–1945* (Edinburgh, 1994); J. Brand, *The National Movement in Scotland* (London, 1978); H. J. Hanham, *Scottish Nationalism* (London, 1969); and J. Mitchell, *Strategies for Self-Government: The Campaign for a Scottish Parliament* (Edinburgh, 1996). Studies which take a wider perspective on the national question are Chris Harvie, *Scotland and Nationalism: Scottish Society and Politics, 1707–1994* (London, 2nd edn, 1994); T. Nairn, *The Break-up of Britain* (London, 1981); and K. Webb, *The Growth of Scottish Nationalism* (Glasgow, 1978).

The LIBERALS have received only cursory treatment, and there is no in-depth study of the party in Scotland during the twentieth century. Some aspects of the party's decline in the first half of the century are covered in S. Ball, 'Asquith's Decline and the General Election of 1918', *Scottish Historical Review,* 61 (1982), and W. Walker, 'Dundee's Disenchantment with Churchill', *Scottish Historical Review,* 49 (1970). J. Fowler, ed., *Bannerman: The Memoirs of Lord Bannerman of Kildonan*

(Aberdeen, 1972), has useful information on the role of the post-war Scottish Liberal leader.

CONTEMPORARY POLITICS are brought up to date with A. Marr, *The Battle for Scotland* (London, 1992); A. Kemp, *The Hollow Drum: Scotland since the War* (Edinburgh, 1993); and R. Levy, *Scottish Nationalism at the Crossroads* (Edinburgh, 1990). L. Bennie, J. Brand & J. Mitchell, *How Scotland Votes* (Manchester, 1997), covers the 1992 general election, and A. Brown, D. McCrone, L. Paterson & P. Surridge, *The Scottish Electorate* (London, 1999), covers the 1997 general election. The 1997 referendum on the Scottish Parliament is studied in D. Denver, J. Mitchell, C. Pattie & H. Bochel, *Scotland Decides: The Devolution Issue and the Scottish Referendum* (London, 2000).

CULTURE

The idea of 'INFERIORISM' in Scottish culture is explored in C. Beveridge & R. Turnbull, *The Eclipse of Scottish Culture* (London, 1989). LITERATURE is studied in R. Crawford, *Devolving English Literature* (Oxford, 1992); C. Craig, ed., *The History of Scottish Literature, vol. 4: The Twentieth Century* (Aberdeen, 1987); R. Watson, *History of Scottish Literature* (London, 1985); I. Murray & R. Tait, *Ten Modern Scottish Novels* (Aberdeen, 1985); M. Burgess, ed., *The Other Voice: Scottish Women's Writing since 1808* (Edinburgh, 1987); C. Whyte, *Modern Scottish Poetry* (Edinburgh, 2003); and D. Gifford, S. Dunnigan & A. MacGillivray, eds., *Scottish Literature* (Edinburgh, 2002).

Studies of SCOTTISH IDENTITY include Neil Acherson, *Stone Voices* (London, 2001); C. Craig, *Out of History* (Edinburgh, 1989); A. Calder, *Revolving Cultures: Notes from the Scottish Republic* (Edinburgh, 2000); D. McCrone, S. Kendrick & P. Straw, *The Making of Scotland: Nation, Culture and Social Change* (Edinburgh, 1989); J. Hearn, *Claiming Scotland: National Identity and Liberal Culture* (Edinburgh, 2000); and C. Harvie, *Cultural Weapons* (Edinburgh, 1992).

ART and BUILDING are covered in D. Macmillan, *Scottish Art, 1460–1990* (Edinburgh, 1990); J. Morrison, *Painting the Nation: Identity and Nationalism in Scottish Painting, 1800–1914* (Edinburgh, 2003); and M. Glendinning, R. Macinnes & A. MacKenchnie, *A History of Scottish*

Architecture (Edinburgh, 1996). D. Hutchison, *The Modern Scottish Theatre* (Glasgow, 1977), and J. Purser, *Music in Scotland* (Edinburgh, 1990), examine the PERFORMING ARTS, while E. J. Cowan, ed., *The People's Past* (Edinburgh, 1990), charts the rise of the folk-music scene. CINEMA and TELEVISION are covered in M. Thomson, *Silver Screen in the Silver City: A History of Cinemas in Aberdeen, 1896–1987* (Aberdeen, 1988); C. MacArthur, *Scotch Reels* (London, 1982); D. Bruce, *Scotland the Movie* (Edinburgh, 1996); and W. H. MacDowell, *BBC Broadcasting in Scotland, 1923–1983* (Edinburgh, 1992). The development of the EDINBURGH FESTIVAL is covered in G. Bruce, *Festival in the North* (London, 1977).

INDEX